GLASSBLOWING

An Introduction to Artistic and Scientific Flameworking

Third Edition

By Edward Carberry

700 South First Street, Marshall, MN 56258

Third Printing, November, 2005

Note: Books may be ordered directly from the publisher or through most bookstores or glassblowing suppliers.

M G L S Inc.
700 South First Street
Marshall, Minnesota 56258
(507) 532-4311

Library of Congress Catalog Card Number 2001117300

ISBN 1-888833-08-4 Black and White Spiral Bound
ISBN 1-888833-04-1 Black and White Cloth Bound
ISBN 1-888833-09-2 Color Spiral Bound
ISBN 1-888833-10-6 Color Cloth Bound

Printed in the United States of America

Table of Contents

Preface

The wide acceptance and enthusiasm shown for the first two editions of my book for beginning glassblowers has been extremely gratifying. This third edition represents a complete revision, including a whole new chapter on repair of scientific glassware, one new appendix, a number of new exercises and projects, and all new digital photographs. In total, there are over 550 figures, and over 440 of these are in digital quality color (in the color editions). This number of figures represents a more than a *five fold increase* over those appearing in the second edition. Difficult procedures and techniques have been clarified, technical information has been updated, and many new references have been included. The greatly expanded and updated appendix listing suppliers now includes web and e-mail information. This feature will be of value use to those just getting started.

The third edition has 358 pages, representing a sixty percent increase over the second edition. Both versions are available in spiral or cloth binding, and both are printed on special, high quality paper.

It remains my sincere desire that more and more individuals will try glassblowing and in doing so find it to be as exciting and fulfilling as I have. If this book, even in some small way, helps students of all ages to learn and appreciate this art, then my work and this book will indeed have been worthwhile.

Marshall, Minnesota
February, 2003

Edward Carberry, Ph.D.
Professor of Chemistry
Southwest State University

Introduction

Many people never come to appreciate the fact that glass is indeed one of the most exceptional materials that we have available. It touches each one of us in a multitude of ways in almost every facet of our lives. Without it, modern science would be nonexistent, technology would be primitive, and our daily lives perhaps unbearable. Take a look at the room you are in, or your home, or your place of work. Mentally remove everything containing any glass. All of a sudden, so many things we come to depend on would no longer exist.

But in addition to the many necessary roles that glass plays, it also serves each of us in countless ways to make our lives more enjoyable more comfortable and more beautiful. Go to any museum or art gallery and you will find that glass is the medium for some of the greatest art treasures in the world. Glass, by its very nature, is an unusual, an exciting, a brilliant, and a mysterious material. Its appearance and properties can be varied more than perhaps any other substance. It can be fashioned into intricate scientific glassware or into graceful and delicate forms. Yet, despite its importance in our world, it is unfortunate that most people will never experience the joy of working with glass or ever take the time to contemplate its importance in their lives.

Over the years, all types of glassblowing have remained somewhat closed arts. Only a small number of people have had the opportunity to learn to work and shape glass. Not long ago, many glassblowers wanted to see it stay closed. Nonetheless, we now find ourselves in an exciting new age of openness in the field. Secrets are being shared so that many may learn and enjoy. The number of glassworkers who feel that teaching too many people will flood the market and make their work less valuable is decreasing each and every year. Quite honestly, this has never proven to be the case in other similar areas of art. There are many photographers, painters, potters, jewelers, and wood workers, yet we all realize that there will always be a market and an appreciation for good work in any of these areas. The skilled artist will always be in demand.

Of course, very few individuals will decide to select artistic or scientific glassblowing as their lifework. But this does not imply that ordinary people like you and I should not be able to learn and participate in this art. Many students take up pottery just so they may experience the joy of creating and the pleasure of working with the medium. There is no better way to learn to appreciate the factors that make up both good pottery and good art. Very few pottery students continue in pottery, and fewer yet become professional potters. Thus I feel that these same observations would apply to those who choose to learn glassworking. You may never become a professional glassblower, and some may never light a torch again after learning the skill. But everyone who studies glassblowing will certainly gain a better understanding and a deeper appreciation of glass in the world they live in.

I firmly believe that if given the opportunity, anyone who is interested, willing to spend the necessary time, and at least somewhat coordinated (or at least persistent) can learn the basics of glassworking. This book was written for these people, not for the established glassblower. It was based and developed, to a large part, on the experiences gained from a course in glassblowing, taught over a twenty-five year period of time at Southwest State University in Marshall, Minnesota.

A word of caution should be expressed about the way the book is written. Don't be deceived by the step-by-step "cookbook" approach that is used in the exercises and projects. All forms of glassblowing are indeed real arts. No matter how clearly the steps are spelled out or how detailed the procedures may be, there is that "certain something" that cannot be taught, explained, drawn, or photographed. This is the overall feel for the glass, the feel for the tools, and the wisdom of knowing the proper instant of when to do what. Subtleties such as color of the heated glass, the feel of the glass and the sound of the flame are some of the important clues. The accomplished glassblower is familiar with all of their meanings. It is this understanding, along with experience and passion for glass, that is the glassblower's "art".

Every one using this book must realize that the exercises and even the projects in this book are not meant to be ends in themselves. Thus, for example, the project describing the construction of a flower is meant to illustrate the techniques of shaping with tools, making joints, and drawing out glass. If, in addition, a beautiful flower results, all the better. Therefore, even the students who do not like the looks of the decorative hand pumps should try the exercise anyway, as they will benefit from it. Once the basic skills are practiced and learned, students are urged to develop other more imaginative products. But first learn the basics! It has often been said, "learn to walk before trying to run". The exercises and projects are designed to illustrate and utilize the fundamental techniques described in each chapter. They are only meant to teach you to walk! You will have many opportunities to "run" later, but first learn the basics!

There is no doubt that the best way to learn glassblowing is to enroll in a formal class or at least a brief workshop. This book was originally written specifically for this application in a classroom setting. However, it is entirely possible for an individual to learn the basics of glassblowing on their own with the aid of this book. Nonetheless, having said this, it is fair to say that there is no substitute for an effective teacher. A single demonstration or constructive criticism by an instructor can save the student many hours of work and a multitude of frustrations. If a picture is worth a thousand words, then it seems that a well done demonstration may well be worth a whole chapter! Thus, whenever possible, take advantage of formal instruction. On the other hand, don't be discouraged from trying to learn on your own. I have learned 90% of what is in this book that very way–by trial and error and error and error.

As is true with so many things in life, persistence is most important. Things are not likely to go well the first time, or the second time or maybe even the tenth time. I always like to tell my students that the first one hundred attempts are always the hardest. Many laugh and simply don't believe me, but it turns out to be very true. I went though many, many cases of glass while I was first learning. Practice, practice, practice–this is the key. And the second key is "never stop learning". Every day I glassblow, I learn something new, and this is the way it should be. Learning and growth are signs of life.

Now, with all this in mind, good luck, keep at it, and above all else, have fun! I am confident that each serious student can and will create some awesome glass products!

Glassblowing Course Information

As indicated, this text was designed for a one quarter or a one semester course of general glassblowing (glassworking). Ideally, the course should be divided into two sections: One for those primarily interested in scientific glassblowing, and another for those interested in artistic (or general) glassblowing. At Southwest State University, our two credit courses involve approximately four hours of actual class and laboratory work. Usually the first hour, highly structured and well planned, is devoted to lecture and demonstrations. The second hour is devoted to close supervision of each student as he or she works through the assigned laboratory exercises. The third and fourth hours are normally scheduled on other days and provide for more individual practice by the student. It turns out that most students work more than four hours each week as they strive to become even more proficient. Completed practice pieces are usually handed in for evaluation by the instructor. At the next lab, comments are made to the students concerning their work. Using this method, an experienced instructor can handle a surprisingly large number of students. There is no doubt that smaller classes are better, but if sufficient equipment and suitable laboratory space are available, at least fifteen students can be accommodated in one section. The glass laboratory at Southwest State has eighteen student stations–a large teaching glass lab by any standards.

In a typical one term course (quarter or semester), all students should cover the material in the first three chapters. In addition, artistic students should be able to complete nearly all of the exercises in Chapter 4. The units on lace techniques in Chapter 5 and the glassblowing techniques in Chapter 6 should be reserved for only the better students and only in longer semester classes. These techniques can be very frustrating until mastered.

The number of laboratory projects completed will also depend on the ability of the student and the nature of the course. It is reasonable to expect that one project would be completed about every two weeks of class. Also, students are urged to use their imagination to develop other projects whenever possible. Some students may wish to spend less time on the rod working and move into the glassblowing chapter. But, as indicated, this is recommended only for the better students. Alternately, the material in Chapters 5 and 6 could be incorporated into a second term of glassblowing. Obviously, a semester course will be able to include more material than would a one quarter course.

A typical one quarter course for scientific glassblowing students might include the first three chapters plus most of the laboratory projects in Chapter 7. Obviously, Project Scientific Five, which involves the design and construction of some complex piece of scientific glassware, could conceivably take up most of the time in one term, especially if all of the parts described in the write-up are required. This might be suitable for a second term of scientific glassblowing, but not as much emphasis should be placed on this project in an ordinary beginning class. In fact, instructors are urged to encourage projects which are not overly difficult. Projects should be carefully chosen so as to fit the specific ability of each student. There should be a very high probability that the student will, indeed, be able to complete the project successfully.

Readers will note that there are many areas of scientific glassblowing which are not covered in this book. This certainly is the case. This book was never intended to be a reference book for accomplished glassblowers. Students and workers alike are urged to consult the many other excellent recognized books for techniques not included in this introductory text. Nonetheless, it should be noted that the material presented in this book should be more than enough to satisfy even the best students in any one term course of beginning glassblowing.

It may be that both teachers and students will find a number of errors in this third edition, or they may know or develop easier methods to accomplish the same ends. The author would really be deeply grateful to receive any such information, as well as any constructive criticisms. The author is still learning too!

Additional details on setting up formal glassblowing classes are given in Appendix H, "Notes to Instructors". I wish you success.

Acknowledgements

This book would not have been possible without the help of a very great number of people. Many professional glassblowers, academic colleagues, students, and friends have helped in so many ways. It would honestly be difficult to thank each one individually; therefore, I wish to do so collectively. Belated but sincere thanks go to my first glassblowing teacher (and glassblower friend), Joe Wheeler who headed the chemistry glass shop at the University of Wisconsin back during my days as a graduate student in chemistry.

Special thanks go to my son, Daniel, and my wife, Linda, for their fantastic jobs of proofreading, a skill at which I am not very proficient. Daniel was also photographer exceptionale for nearly all of the great digital photos. Special Kudos go to Linda for her constant encouragement, patience, and understanding. I am not an easy person to get along with while I am writing a book of this magnitude.

But I also want to acknowledge and to extend thanks to the large number of students who learned this art along with me at Southwest State University. In fact, I dedicate this book to all of my students in all of my courses over the past thirty five years of teaching. This amounts to a lot of students! I have never stopped learning, and my students continue to inspire me, even as I grow older (and older). I have been blessed in so many ways, but to be able to participate in things one loves (in these cases chemistry and glassblowing) and to be paid for it besides, is almost too good to be true. As I tell my friends, colleagues and students, "it has been a very great trip"!

The illustrations and line art used throughout the book are reproduced with the generous permission of the following companies: ChemGlass, Ace Glass, Bethlehem Apparatus, Corning Glass, Kimble Kontes Glass, Wilt Industries, Pistorius Machine Company, Carlisle Machine Works and Wale Apparatus. I am extremely grateful to each.

Edward Carberry, Ph.D.

Chapter 1
THE NATURE OF GLASS

Glass is an extremely unusual and truly remarkable substance, but because we come in contact with it each day, we may fail to understand this point. Daily, we have come to depend on it for thousands of applications. It is essential to the homemaker and consumer. It provides an unique medium for expression to the artist, and it is a versatile and durable material to the scientist, engineer, and architect. Man has been amazed by this substance for over three thousand years, and yet most agree that it is still a material of the future. Perhaps after you learn more about it and work with it in the lab, you will come to realize that glass is indeed extraordinary in every sense of the word!

BRIEF HISTORY

The history of glass goes back to the first volcanoes, nature's way of making this remarkable substance. Today one can see this natural glass in samples of obsidian, a dark and hard glassy type of volcanic rock (Figure 1.1). Early man recognized its unusual properties and used pieces of obsidian for tools, weapons and jewelry.

No one is really certain as to when man actually discovered how to make glass himself. Many believe that the discovery may date back to over four thousand years ago. Pliny, a Roman naturalist and writer who lived about two thousand years ago, gives an account of the discovery of glass, around 1200 BC, by the Phoenicians in his book of natural history.[1]

Figure 1.1 *The rounded edges of obsidian rock are characteristic of all glasses.*

He states: "In Syria there is a region known as Phoenice... In this district rises the river Belus, which, after a course of five miles, empties itself into the sea... The tide of this river is sluggish, and the water unwholesome to drink, but held sacred for the observance of certain religious ceremonials. Full of slimy deposits, and very deep, it is only at the reflux of the tide that the river discloses its sands... The story is, that a ship, laden with nitre, being moored upon this spot, the merchants, while preparing their repast upon the sea-shore, finding no stones at hand for supporting their cauldrons, employed for the purpose some lumps of nitre which they had taken from the vessel. Upon its being subjected to the action of the fire, in combination with the sand of the seashore, they beheld transparent streams flowing forth of a liquid hitherto unknown. This, it is said, was the origin of glass." Although the account is interesting, very few people believe it to be accurate. In fact, a number of glass artifacts have been discovered which actually predate this period.

The ancient Assyrians and Egyptians not only made glass beads and glazes, but left some tablets indicating various kinds of glasses and even directions for making them. Thus, although no one is really certain as to the actual date that man first discovered how to make glass, it is generally recognized that it occurred somewhere between 3000 and 4500 years ago.

The very first glass items were solid objects such as beads and pendants (Figure 1.2). Hollow forms were later made (starting around 1400 BC) by dipping a core of clay into molten glass. The core was then laboriously removed, leaving a hollow vessel (Figures 1.3 and 1.4). The first "blown glass" was probably made around the time of Pliny (about 50 AD) and served to provide the ancient alchemists with glass vessels with which to begin the study of science.

A rapid expansion in the use and manufacture of glass occurred during the last part of the Roman Empire. Glass technology soon spread to Constantinople and the Byzantine Empire where the first stained glass windows appeared. Later, Venice became the center of the glass industry. Extensive mosaics and fine mirrors were produced until the 19th century when technology began declining there. By that time it had spread all over Europe.

Figure 1.2 *Egyptian necklace, probably before 1500 BC. (With permission from the Corning Museum of Glass, Corning, NY.)*

Glass was first made in America in 1608 in Jamestown, Virginia. The early products included glass beads (for trading with the Indians), window glass, bottles, and tableware. The industry soon spread to New Jersey, Pennsylvania, and eventually to New York where the Corning Glass Company[2] was started in 1868. Some of Corning's early products included glass bulbs for Edison's new electric lights and colored lenses for railroad lanterns. Eventually the company formulated the now famous Pyrex® brand glass which is resistant not only to large changes in temperature, but also to chemical reactions and weathering. Developments in glass technology came about so rapidly during the first part of the 20th century that many have called this period of time the Glass Age.

Figure 1.3 *Core-formed vase, probably Syria 4th-3rd century BC. (With permission from the Corning Museum of Glass, Corning, NY.)*

Figure 1.4 *Another core-formed vase, Probably Syria 4th-3rd century BC. (With permission from the Corning Museum of Glass, Corning, NY.)*

COMPOSITION AND PROPERTIES OF GLASS

Certainly, the original discovery of how to make glass was an important one, even though it was probably accidental. But more important was the understanding of exactly what ingredients were needed and in what proportions, as only certain combinations give glassy materials.

It is important to realize that glass is not just a single substance nor a single combination of substances. There are thousands of different materials which may exist in the glassy state. Some glasses are pure substances (that is, a single element or compound), but most are mixtures of many different compounds.

What then is the definition of a glass? Webster says that a glass is "a hard, brittle substance, usually transparent or translucent, made by fusing silicates with soda or potash, lime and sometimes, various metallic oxides."[3] A chemist might describe a glass as a substance without any regular internal structure, or perhaps as a "super-cooled" liquid, that is, one which has not yet crystallized but still has sufficient rigidity so as to appear solid. Glasses have no definite melting point, but instead soften over a wide temperature range. The physical and chemical properties can vary greatly depending on the substances which make up the glass and their relative proportions. An excellent article on the nature of glasses has appeared in Scientific American.[4]

Most common useful glasses contain silica (silicon dioxide or sand) which is the most outstanding glass-forming oxide. In fact, a glass called fused quartz can be made from pure silica. The fused quartz glass has many desirable properties, including great mechanical strength, a very low coefficient of expansion, and its inertness to most chemicals. Unfortunately, very high temperatures are necessary to fuse the silica in the making of the glass, and therefore it is very expensive and difficult to manufacture. Thus, other oxides are added as fluxes to lower the viscosity and likewise the softening temperature. This is much the same as the melting point depression phenomenon observed when an impurity is added to any pure substance.

The most commonly used flux is soda, usually added in the form of sodium carbonate. This lowers the viscosity as desired and makes what is called a soft glass. Unfortunately, it also makes the glass more soluble, less resistant to chemicals and weathering, more brittle, easier to scratch, and increases its coefficient of expansion, thus making it more difficult to anneal. The quality of the resulting glass can be improved if small amounts of lime (calcium oxide) and/or alumina (aluminum oxide) are also added. These increase its chemical resistance and make the surface harder. Likewise, other oxides can be added to improve the quality even more. If boron oxide is substituted for most of the soda, a very hard glass having a low coefficient of expansion and great chemical resistance is obtained. This borosilicate glass is known most commonly as Pyrex®. If lead oxide is substituted for most of the soda, the result is still a soft glass, but one with the ability to bend light strongly, making cut edges appear to sparkle. This is the basis of crystal glass. Other oxides can be added to make glasses with unusual properties for specific applications. For example, the substitution of neodymium oxide and praseodymium oxide for the lime produces a glass called didymium which transmits all colors except the bright yellow light that is emitted from hot glass. This material makes excellent eyewear for glassblowers.

Thus, slightly different formulations may give glasses with quite different properties. It is easy to see that the number of different glasses is almost unlimited. The Corning Glass Company alone has well over fifty thousand formulas for different glasses. Obviously some of these formulations are much more important than others. A few of the more important types of glass and their properties and technical information are summarized in the tables shown is Figures 1.5 - 1.10.[5] You may not wish to study this data in much detail right now, but later on you will find these tables and this information more meaningful and useful.

Figure 1.5 INFORMATION ON BOROSILICATE GLASS

Other Common Names	Pyrex®, or No. 7740 or No. 774 (Corning trade names) Kimax®; or KG-33 (Kimble trade names) Duran® Schott Glaswerke trade name) Simax® Kavalier Glassworks trade name)[6]
Chemical Nature	Very little soda and potash and no lime; substantial amounts of boron oxide, B_2O_3 (about 12%)
Physical Properties	Low coefficient of expansion ($33 \times 10^{-7}/^oC$) and high resistance to most chemicals
Softening Temperatures	821°C or 1510°F (at 1 atmosphere) 670°C or 1238°F (under vacuum)
Working Temperatures	1252°C or 2286°F (range where seals are made)
Annealing Temperatures	560°C or 1040°F (anneals in about 15 minutes; must cool slowly)
Strain Temperatures	510°C or 950°F (anneals in about 16 hours; can cool quickly)
Applications	Scientific glassware, kitchenware, industrial plumbing

Figure 1.6	**INFORMATION ON SOFT GLASS**
Other Common Names	Lime glass, G-8, No. 0080 (both Corning code numbers)
Chemical Nature	Soda, potash and/or lime added as fluxes
Physical Properties	More soluble, less resistant to weathering & chemical action, very high coefficient of expansion (93.5 x $10^{-7}/^{o}C$., 3 times that of borosilicate glass), but difficult to anneal
Softening Temperatures	696°C or 1285°F (at 1 atmosphere) 585°C or 1085°F (under vacuum)
Working Temps	1006°C or 1843°F
Annealing Temperatures	510°C or 950°F (must cool very slowly)
Strain Temps	473°C or 883°F
Applications	Bottles, common household glassware, window panes, light bulbs

Figure 1.7	**INFORMATION ON LEAD GLASS**
Other Common Names	Potash soda lead glass, flint glass, S/F glass, G-1, No. 0010 (both Corning code numbers). Technically this is also a *soft glass*
Chemical Nature	Lead oxide (PbO) used as a flux in place of much of the soda
Physical Properties	This soft glass bends light more strongly than most other glasses, adaptable for glass to metal seals, high coefficient of expansion (93.5 x $10^{-7}/^{o}C$). A high oxidizing flame is needed in working to prevent blackening due to reduced elemental lead
Softening Temperatures	626°C or 1159°F
Working Temps	983°C or 1801°F
Annealing Temperatures	432°C or 810°F (cool slowly)
Strain Temps	392°C or 738°F
Applications	*Crystal* glass, neon signs, other metal to glass seals

Figure 1.8 INFORMATION ON FUSED QUARTZ GLASS

Other Common Names	Fused silica, vitreous silica, quartz, Corning No. 7940, Spectrosil (GmbH)
Chemical Nature	Nearly pure (>99.8%) silica (SiO_2)
Physical Properties	Good mechanical strength, low coefficient of expansion, chemically inert even when hot, very high softening point, transparent to ultraviolet light
Softening Temperatures	1650°C or 3002°F
Working Temps	1082°C or 1980°F
Annealing Temps	987°C or 1809°F
Strain Temps	Special chemical resistant scientific glassware, very precise optical flats
Applications	Fused silica, vitreous silica, quartz, Corning No. 7940, Spectrosil (GmbH)

Figure 1.9 INFORMATION ON VYCOR GLASS

Other Common Names	Corning No. 7913
Chemical Nature	Borosilicate glass which has been placed in acid to dissolve out all of the sodium and boron oxide. It is then refired. The result is 96% silica.
Physical Properties	Low coefficient of expansion ($8 \times 10^{-7}/^{o}C$), correspondingly high resistance to heat shock, extremely high softening point and great chemical resistance, can be used up to 900°C for long periods of time
Softening Temperatures	1500°C or 2732°F
Annealing Temperatures	910°C or 1670°F
Strain Temperatures	820°C or 1508°F
Applications	Laboratory glassware for high temperature work

Figure 1.10	INFORMATION ON ALUMINOSILICATE GLASS
Other Common Names	Corning No. 1720
Chemical Nature	Approximately 60% silica with alumina and lime as fluxes.
Physical Properties	Good electrical and chemical properties, resistance to high temperatures, moderate coefficient of expansion ($42 \times 10^{-7}/^{o}C$), can be worked by normal glassblowing techniques
Softening Temperatures	915°C or 1679°F (at 1 atmosphere)
Working Temperatures	1202°C or 2196°F (range where seals are made)
Annealing Temperatures	712°C or 1314°F (anneals in about 15 minutes; must cool slowly)
Strain Temperatures	667°C or 1233°F (anneals in about 16 hours; can cool quickly)
Applications	Thermometers, combustion tubes, electronic vacuum tubes

PURCHASE AND STORAGE OF GLASS

Tubing and rod made by United States manufacturers are generally sold in four foot lengths. Tubing is normally standard wall in thickness (about 1 mm), but it may be purchased in medium-heavy wall (ranging from 1.2 to 4.5 mm, depending on the diameter of the tubing) and heavy wall (ranging from 2.0 to 9.5 mm). In addition, capillary tubing, having very thick walls and a very small inside diameter, is available for special scientific applications.

Both tubing and rod are available in a wide range of diameters which are always referred to in terms of outside measurements. For standard wall tubing and most common sizes of rod, these diameters are always given in millimeters. For some reason, the diameters of medium-heavy wall tubing, heavy wall tubing, and large sized rod are given in inches. Each major United States glass manufacturer, Corning and Kimble (Kimble is a division of Kimble Kontes), lists borosilicate standard glass wall

Figure 1.11 *Horizontal glass storage case at Southwest State University in Marshall, MN.*

tubing available in sizes which range from 2 mm to 178 mm and rod from 2 mm to 38 mm. Schott Glaserke, West German makers of Duran® borosilicate, produce tubing in 220 different diameters, ranging from 3 mm to 315 mm. Glass is usually sold by the pound. Most catalogs indicate the number of feet per pound for each size as well as the number of pounds per case. A case of glass may be anywhere from 5 to 35 pounds, depending on the size and the manufacturer. Most commonly these come in cases of 25 or 30 pounds. The price per pound is generally independent of size, except for the very small diameters (less than 5 mm) and the very large diameters (more than 40 mm), which are considerably more expensive.

Figure 1.12 *Vertical glass storage case in author's home lab. This cabinet has doors to keep dust out.*

Tubing and rod stock should be stored separately and rotated so that the oldest is always used first. Ideally, glass stock should be limited to a five year supply because glass does "age", becoming more difficult to work and more likely to shatter upon heating as it becomes older. This may be quite noticeable in glass which has been stored under unfavorable conditions for 10 years or more. Aging is due to a change in composition of the glass. The fluxes on the surface of the glass, over time, react with moisture, carbon dioxide and other reactive substances in the air. Soft glasses with large amounts of sodium, calcium and lead oxides are likely to deteriorate the most. Old glass should always be cleaned thoroughly and washed with a 1-2% solution of hydrofluoric acid (see page 287) before using. This will remove the aged surface layers, but fresh glass stock is always best.

Horizontal storage (with doors) of the glass is always preferred (see Figure 1.11), but in smaller labs, vertical storage is often most expedient (see Figure 1.12). In either case, effort must be made to keep dust from entering the tubes and settling on the surfaces.

COLORED GLASS AND COLORING GLASS

Color can add a great deal to the attractiveness of many glass products. Unfortunately, the number of colored glasses which are totally compatible with the normal colorless types of borosilicate is rather limited. Over the years, numerous products have come and gone, the most notable being the dark blue cobalt glass referred to many times in this book. A number of years ago, several manufacturers even made some types of colored tubing, including amber and uranium yellow. Unfortunately, at this time no United States manufacturer makes colored borosilicate tubing. Some glassworkers, however, may still be able get hold of some of these older stock items.

At present there are two brands of borosilicate compatible colored rod which are widely used: North Star® and Colrex®. Both come in a large variety of colors. Each type of colored rod, however, is rather unique. North Star® is best described as a reheat or heat activated colored borosilicate rod. The colors of these rods are not fully apparent until annealed. The colors produced are usually rather transparent in normal oxidizing flames.

The second product, Colrex®, tends to be more opaque, but is distinctly different from the North Star® glass. It is constructed having a highly pigmented interior surrounded by a thin, clear glass cladding. This clear sheath is added to act as a thermal buffer, preventing color loss due to decomposition of the pigments by the intense heat of the flame, since most pigments are prone to decompose at high temperatures. The sheathing also allows the glass to be used for food and medical applications. It is fair to say, however, that there is somewhat of an art to using this colored rod effectively. The more intense colors present the greatest challenge, as these pigments don't always survive being heated to the temperatures normally required for most flameworking. The variety of colors offered by both brands gives the glassblower a great opportunity to make novelty and artistic products that will really catch the eye.

An alternative to using colored glass is to paint or stain glass products. These so-called glass stains are applied with a brush after the item has been annealed. Needless to say, these are not as permanent as is colored glass; in fact, some colors may fade with age, and most can be removed with organic solvents. Nonetheless, they offer the glassblower an opportunity to add a wide variety of colors with great ease. Normally, these can be purchased at craft or hobby stores.

It is also possible to etch glass items, giving them a rather beautiful milky white appearance. Etching glass creams are also usually available at craft and hobby stores, but be aware that these were designed for use on soft glass. The instructions may call for a 5-10 minute treatment, but in reality, it may take up to 24 hours to act on borosilicate glass which is much harder and much more chemically resistant. Be sure to use extreme caution in using these products, as most contain hydrofluoric acid or similar compounds.

You may also wish to experiment with gold or silver coatings on your finished glass items. These finishes are attained by painting annealed products with specially prepared emulsions of these metals. The items are then annealed a second time, allowing the solvent to bake off, leaving a thin surface of shiny metal. The trick to using these is to apply a very thin and very uniform coating of the substance the first time around. It is difficult to correct mistakes! These coatings can usually be purchased at ceramic shops or at larger craft stores. It should be pointed out that a more complicated process of coating the inside surfaces of blown glass with silver has been used by both artistic and scientific glassblowers for nearly 150 years. A good description of this method was published by J. Merritt.[7]

TYPES OF GLASSBLOWING

There are really two different types of glassblowing: offhand (freehand or hot glass) and lampworking (flameworking). The offhand technique is the older method. Here, the artist starts with molten glass which may have been made from scratch from the basic ingredients, or else as the result of remelting broken glass pieces. The molten glass is gathered on the end of an iron blowpipe, shaped with marvers and wooden boards, and finally blown (Figure 1.13). In a large shop, the blowing is usually reserved for a master glassblower called the gaffer. Beautiful pieces of glassware can be created in this way by skilled artisans. Unfortunately, a great deal of instruction is needed, and a great amount of time and expense is necessary to set up such a glass shop. In practice, one must plan to spend a large part of a day both in preparing to work and in the actual working, as the great ovens are not easily turned on and off. Also it is usual for several people to work at once since much of the work requires

Figure 1.13 *Offhand glassblower, 18th Century engraving by C. Grignion. (With permission from The Corning Museum of Glass, Corning, NY).*

some help from an assistant. Anyone who has the opportunity to try some offhand glassblowing is strongly encouraged to do so.

In contrast to offhand glassblowing, lampworking does not require a great expenditure to get started, and anyone can learn the basic operations with a minimal amount of instruction. Furthermore, one can work alone when he or she wishes, for as long as desired. In these respects, lampworking is the ideal kind of glassblowing for most persons interested in glass. In lampworking, one uses a torch to convert rod and tubing into either artistic or scientific glassware. The extent of a person's art is limited only by their imagination and skill, and the skill often comes easily with practice.

Until very recently, many glassblowers have kept their art a well guarded secret. Courses in glassblowing were very rarely taught anywhere. Books on the subject were scarce and detailed instructions were often totally lacking. There were really only two ways to learn glassblowing--either as an apprentice under a master glassblower (indeed a very difficult position to find) or on your own by trial and error. The profession was a very closed one. Interestingly, predictions still indicate that there will be a shortage of glassblowers in the coming years, especially in the scientific field.

Recently, however, a small but increasing number of universities and community colleges have begun to reverse the trend by offering courses in glassblowing. Many times, however, these are directed only to a limited group of people, namely chemistry majors. The reason for this is that chemists normally require glassblowing services more than any other professionals. Some courses, however, are more open and may be taken by anyone who is interested. Many now believe that glassworking should be a course much like ceramics or photography which can offer something to people who are "merely interested" and not dedicated to making it a lifelong profession.

The remainder of this book is directed chiefly to these people, although hopefully a few will be excited enough to pursue glassblowing professionally. The detailed step-by-step descriptions should enable a person to learn on their own, although at least some formal instruction is strongly recommended.

At this point, before getting into the actual glassblowing exercises, it may be wise to restate two rather important ideas from the introduction. These concern the nature of glassblowing as well as the nature of this book. You can skip over them if you wish, but the message in each is important.

Don't be misled by the "cookbook" approach used in this text. Glassblowing is very much an art. No matter how clearly the steps are spelled out or how detailed the procedures may be, there is that certain something that cannot be taught, explained, drawn, or photographed. This is the overall feel for the glass, the feel for the tools, and the wisdom of knowing the proper instant of when to do what. Subtleties such as color of the heated glass and the sound of the flame are important clues. The accomplished glassblower is familiar with all of their meanings, and this is his art.

Furthermore, it should be realized that the exercises and even the projects in this book are not meant to be ends in themselves. Thus, for example, the project describing the construction of a flower is meant to illustrate the techniques of shaping with tools, making joints, and drawing out glass. If, in addition, a beautiful flower results, all the better. Therefore, even the students who do not like the looks of the decorative hand pumps should try the project anyway, as they will probably benefit from it. Once the basic skills are practiced and learned, students are urged to develop other more imaginative products. But first learn the basics! The exercises and projects in this book are all designed to illustrate and utilize the fundamental techniques described in each chapter.

Now, with all this in mind, good luck, and have fun!

ENDNOTES

1 *The Natural History of Pliny*, translated by J. Bostock and H. T. Riley, H. G. Bohm, London, 1857, p. 379.

2 *Everyone interested in the history of glass is strongly encouraged to make a point to visit the Corning Museum of Glass in Corning, New York. Every aspect of glass and its history is expertly displayed.* Plan to spend more than one day. See "Corning Museum of Glass" on page 337 for contact information.

3 *Webster's New Universal Unabridged Dictionary*, Third Edition, 1996.

4 R. H. Charles, "The Nature of Glasses," *Scientific American*, Sept., 1967, pp. 69-84.

5 *Specifications Handbook*, Corning Glass Works, p 15.

6 Simax®,a new borosilicate line produced by Kavalier Glassworks of the Czech Republic, is specially designed to resist high strains in products demanding high chemical and thermal endurance. Composition: 80.4% SiO_2, 13.0% B_2O_3, 2.4% Al_2O_3, 2.4% Na_2O and K_2O. For additional information, visit http://www.optikavod.cz/ques/simax/simax-kavalier-e.htm.

7 J. Merritt, "Silvering", *Proceedings of the 42nd Symposium on the Art of Scientific Glassblowing, American Scientific Glassblowers Society*, 1997, pp. 75-76.

Chapter 2
TOOLS OF THE GLASSBLOWER

Only a few special items are necessary for the beginning glassblower, and by and large, the same are used for both artistic and scientific work. Nonetheless, a wide range of tools and equipment are available for special applications. In this chapter, we will take a brief look at the basic glass laboratory and a number of the tools and items that can be used. The information should be helpful if you are interested in setting up your own glassblowing lab. Many of the tools described will be discussed again more thoroughly in subsequent chapters which call for their particular use.

THE GLASSBLOWING LABORATORY

The glass laboratory may simply be an area set aside on a table in your basement, or it may be a large room designed and built specifically for this use (Figure 2.1). As an absolute minimum, one should have a sturdy table with a three foot square piece of fire resistant board. The area chosen should be well lighted both from above and slightly in front of the worker. Usually almost any area that would be suitable for a gas kitchen stove would be safe enough for glassblowing, but there must be sufficient ventilation, as the high temperatures of the flame can produce a number of nitrogen oxide gases, some of which are rather toxic.[1,2]

Figure 2.1 *View of the author's home glass laboratory.*

A small wooden box is ideal for storing tools. Space adjacent to the workbench is needed for the necessary gas and oxygen tanks. A large metal pail or wastebasket should be handy for disposing of hot glass and other glass pieces. No paper should ever be discarded in this container. Also, select a comfortable chair of appropriate height.

In a large glass laboratory, each person should be allotted a minimum space of 36 inches wide and 30 inches deep on a bench approximately 37 inches in height (Figure 2.2). The gas and oxygen valves should be convenient, as should be storage areas for the various tools.

Ideally the glass rod and tubing stock should be stored horizontally in a dust-free cabinet. Vertical storage, however, is often necessary due to space limitations and is satisfactory if the tops of the tubing are covered to keep dust from settling on the inside surfaces.

Natural gas should be used if it is available. Otherwise a propane tank and regulator are needed. Propane burns with a hotter flame than does natural gas and can produce more soot. The propane regulator decreases the gas pressure (less than one pound pressure is needed) and keeps the pressure steady. Regulators may cost anywhere from $45 to over $120 depending on their quality (Figure 2.3). The less expensive ones are usually fine for glassblowing. The same regulator used on an acetylene tank can be used on propane tanks. When not in use, these tanks should be stored outside as a safety measure. Small 20 pound tanks can be rented from some dealers but most now require purchase of the tank (approximately $35). A 20 pound tank full of propane costs only about $5 and will last a long time for normal glassblowing operations.

The oxygen tank may present more of a problem. Oxygen is required for working with borosilicate glass, and this book assumes the use of such rod and tubing. (If soft glass is used, an air compressor is needed

Figure 2.2 *Various tools and torches commonly found on the flameworker's lab bench.*

Figure 2.3 *Gas regulator*

instead, since an air-gas mixture is then used).An oxygen tank may already be available if someone in the family does welding.If not, it will need to be leased or rented from a welder's supply company. Often the tanks are leased for a ten year period of time and the charge may be about $200. Over the long run, this is much cheaper than the usual monthly charge (demurrage) of about two or three dollars. It may be wise to rent a tank for several months to first see if you are really interested in pursuing glassblowing at home. Oxygen tanks come in a variety of sizes, but the most common sizes are the 120 and 244 cubic foot tanks. A 244 cubic foot tank will usually supply enough oxygen for about 40-60 hours of normal glasswork. Such a tank-full costs in the neighborhood of $30; the 120 cubic foot tank-full would run close to $22. Regardless of tank size, an oxygen regulator is needed. This regulator may look similar to that used for propane, but it is constructed differently and has different threads. Oxygen tanks must always be securely fastened with straps or chained to a wall or to the glass working bench.

Special heavy duty rubber hose is available for glassblowing, but any plastic hose suitable for use with gases (especially Tygon®) is sufficient for use in a glass laboratory. All hoses should be concealed as much as possible on the workbench so as to minimize the possibility of their contact with any hot pieces of glass. Tygon type tubing is especially sensitive to heat. A hot piece of glass, if placed on such tubing, will melt right through the tubing and could cause a fire. Thus always keep the hoses as short as possible and as protected as possible. This might include running such hoses under the bench top, passing these through drilled holes.

GLASSWORKING TORCHES

A number of different types of torches or burners are available from several different manufacturers. These range all the way from the humble Bunsen burner to the most elaborate bench and ribbon burners. Each has its own application and its own place in the glass laboratory. Some burners are strictly gas-air while others are gas-oxygen; some may be used either way if the tips are changed.

Probably the most universally used torch (and quite fortunately also the most versatile and inexpensive) is the hand torch (e.g. National 3-A, Figure 2.4). These torches certainly may be held in the hand, especially for use in scientific glassworking, but most often are placed on a stand, leaving both hands free for manipulation of the glass. The stands can be as simple as a fire brick, or they may be specially constructed for such torches. These torches can be purchased from a number of suppliers for about $75. A quality stand may cost nearly as much.

Figure 2.4 *National Hand Torch*

Various types and sizes of tips are available for such hand torches. For most borosilicate use, the OX type are used. These range from OX-1 (smallest) to OX-5 (largest). In addition, one can purchase N type tips (for use with air for soft glass or in soldering or brazing metals), AO type tips (for acetylene and oxygen), and AG type tips (for acetylene and air). Some artistic glassworkers use an AG-2 tip with oxygen and natural gas and report obtaining a much hotter flame, but most who work with borosilicate glasses stick to the OX series. Although there are certainly exceptions, the smaller size tips are used more for scientific glassworking, whereas the larger sizes are used more for artistic and novelty work. Many artistic workers can easily get by with only an OX-5 tip.Some torches come with an unremovable tip (e.g. Bethlehem Sharp Flame). Such torches are suitable for most work but lack the flexibility of torches with removable tips. Other hand torches are shown in Figures 2.8 - 2.9.

Workers who do a significant amount of

Figure 2.5 *Carlisle CC Rank & Pinion Bench Torch*

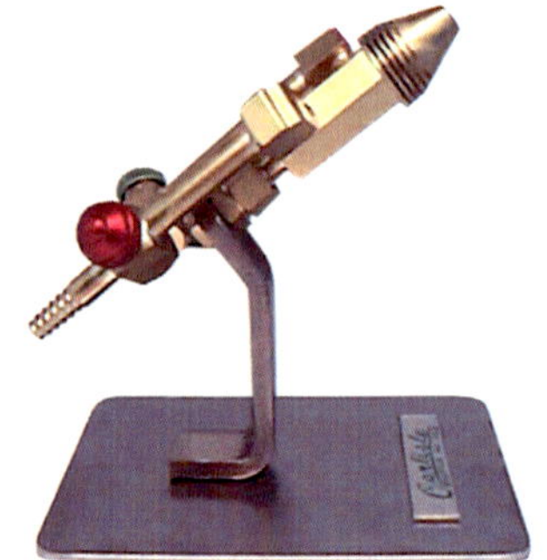

Figure 2.6 *Carlisle Mini Bench Torch.*

glassworking may want to consider a larger burner capable of producing a wider variety of flame sizes and temperatures. Such burners are normally called bench burners and are available from a number of manufacturers. Unfortunately, they are rather expensive. The most popular burners appear to be the Carlisle bench burner (Figure 2.5) and the Carlisle Mini-burner (Figure 2.6). Prices of such torches range up to $800 or more. These burners can produce two concentric fires which may be operated independently. Thus, there are two sets of oxygen and gas needle valves. The central fire can be varied from a sharp needle point to a powerful jet, or both fires can be used to reach very high temperatures for working tubing or rod of very large diameters or small to medium quartz glass.

Some workers like to use a crossfire torch or opposing fire (Figure 2.7). These are combinations of at least two torch tips which heat the work on both sides simultaneously. In some, the number of burner tips may be changed and can be focused on a common point or spread out to make a wider working area. These torches are used most often for soft glasswork and thus normally utilize a mixture of gas and air (not oxygen).

Figure 2.7 *Carlisle 253-N crossfire torch.*

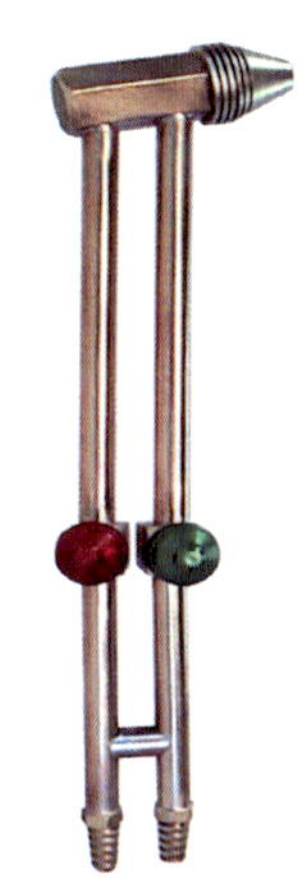

Figure 2.8 *Carlisle Mini CC hand torch.*

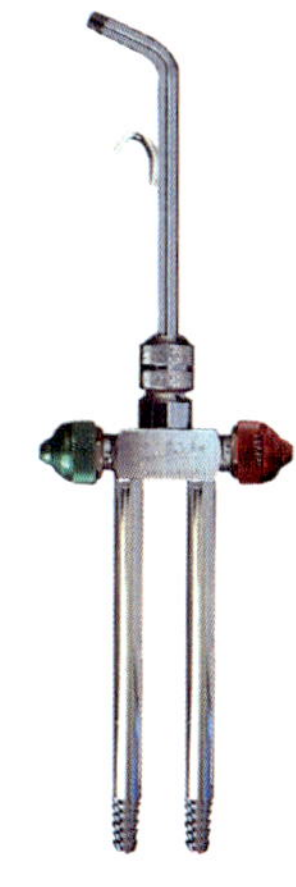

Figure 2.9 *Carlisle Universal hand torch.*

Figure 2.10 *Fisher (Meker) burner.*

Bending tubing can be done in a number of ways. Often small diameter tubing can be bent satisfactorily using a wing tip attachment on a Bunsen or Fisher (Meker) burner (Figure 2.10). Although these use an air-gas mixture and therefore do not obtain extremely high temperatures, they can be used to bend tubing up to 10 mm in diameter.

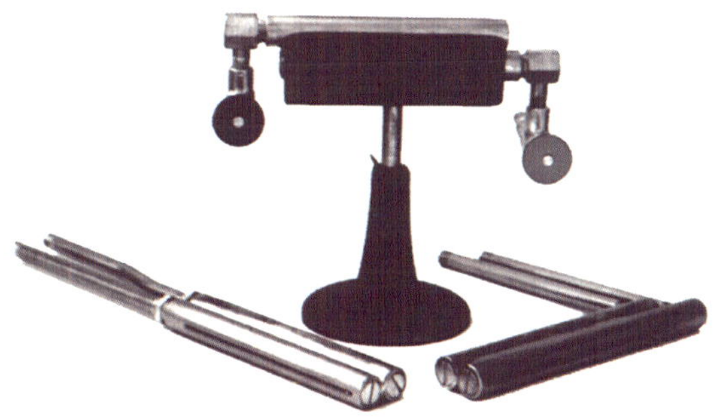

Figure 2.11 (Left) *Carlisle SMT ribbon burner showing all three burner tips.*

Figure 2.12 (Right) *Bethlehem ribbon burner.*

Special ribbon burners (Figures 2.11 and 2.12) are used for heating large sections of tubing or rod as is necessary when making large bends or coils. These may be purchased in a range of burner lengths, with 4 inch being the most common.

GLASSBLOWING EYEWEAR

Special eye glasses must be worn by all who work with borosilicate glass (Figure 2.13). These serve three main purposes. First of all, all glass, even borosilcate, contains small amounts of sodium. When any substance containing sodium is heated, an intense yellow flame (flare) is produced. Although this by itself is not dangerous, this yellow light obscures most of the glass, making it very difficult to see what is going on in the flame and to see the actual changes in temperature which the glass undergoes. Secondly, heated glass emits significant amounts of infrared (IR) light, and this type of light is very damaging to the eyes. Glassblowing eyewear filters out most of this harmful radiation. Thirdly, the eyewear protects the eyes from broken glass in much the same way as any laboratory safety glasses would.

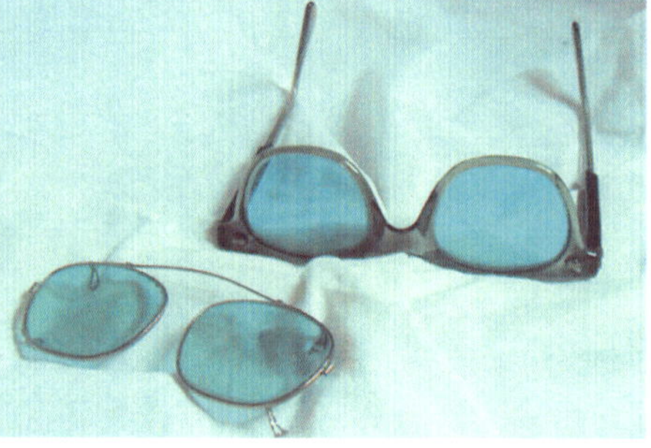

Figure 2.13 *Clip-on and regular glasses.*

Earlier it was believed that didymium glasses (glass which contain a special formulation of both neodymium oxide and praseodymium oxide) were the only satisfactory glasses to use, but it is now known that didymium does not provide as much protection as once thought. These have been shown to allow the transmission of over 70% of the damaging infrared light.[3] It is now thought that didymium glasses should be used only if you are doing occasional glassblowing or if soft glass is being worked. Soft glass products less infrared because lower temperatures are used to work the glass. In the past, some lenses were also made of G-20 glass which, like didymium, reduces the yellow flare, but does an even better job of absorbing infrared light.

New glass formulations are now available which accomplish greater filtering of the infrared region, as well as reducing the sodium flare color. For those who do extensive work with borosilicate glass, eyewear with AGW-186, the newer AGW-203 or Phillips 202 lenses are now recommended. For those working with colored borosilicate, eyewear with AGW-200 #4, AGW-286 #4, AGW-203 are recommended.

When quartz or Vycor® glass items are heated, very bright light, extremely intense in the infrared region, is emitted. In these cases, AGW-286 #8 is recommended. In addition you could use welder's goggles incorporating Filterweld, Noviweld-didymium, or filters of shade six or greater should be used. For extreme protection from infrared radiation, spectacles many workers use Schott KG-3 glass.

A thorough study of the optical hazards in glassblowing has been reported by Myers[4] and Tassin[5]. A later review was published by Oriowo, Chou and Cullen[6] and absorption spectra of the newer AGW eyewear is available online[3].

Most glassblowing eyewear is fitted with non-corrected lenses although special corrective lenses can be made for those requiring them. Clip-on lenses are also available and can be worn over regular eyeglasses.

SMALL TOOLS & GLASSWORKING ITEMS

Many different tools and small pieces of equipment will be helpful to the glassblower. Some of the more important items are described in the sections which follow.

ASBESTOS PRODUCTS

Asbestos items have traditionally found extensive use by the glassblower in a wide range of important applications. Recent realization of the hazards of using asbestos products have forced the rapid development of substitutes which retain the majority of the desirable properties of asbestos. A number of such products are now available and are described below. In some situations where individuals have to continue using transite (an asbestos based board) for bench tops, the surface can be sealed by painting it with several coats of waterglass[7] (sodium silicate solution) or by spraying it with polyurethane varnish. Hot pieces of glass may stick to the surface for a while, but after the surface has aged for several days or been used for a while, a durable finish results in some protection from harmful asbestos dust. However, the glassworker should make every effort to avoid all asbestos. If any asbestos is found in your lab, consult an expert. Never attempt to remove asbestos items or asbestos coated items yourself.

ASBESTOS SUBSTITUTES

A large variety of materials which can be used in place of asbestos are now available from glassblowing supply companies. In many cases, these products out-perform and out-wear their asbestos counterparts. In some applications, woven glass can be used as an substitute, but there are also many new and unique materials available such as Nor-Fab®, Ceramfab®, Zetex®, Nomex®, Kevlar®, Heatex® (fiberglass) and PBI (polybenzimidazole). Carbon and graphite fibers also find wide use. Each has its advantages and disadvantages, but most have excellent heat resistance, high tensile strength, and exceptional chemical resistance. Specific uses include bench top boards, gloves, and tape. Some of these are discussed in more detail in the appropriate sections below.

BLOWPIPE AND SWIVEL

These are absolute necessities for scientific work, but the artistic craftsman will also find them useful when working with tubing. Usually the blowpipe consists of a length of lightweight latex tubing fitted on one end with a plastic mouthpiece and on the other end with a brass or stainless steel swivel (Figure 2.14). The swivel prevents the blowpipe hose from becoming twisted as the glass is rotated during the glassworking operations. The swivels come in several sizes, most commonly 3/16", 1/4", 5/16" and 3/8". These may be straight, or bent at a 90° angle. It is a good idea to have at least two sets of blowpipe and hoses with different sized metal inserts.

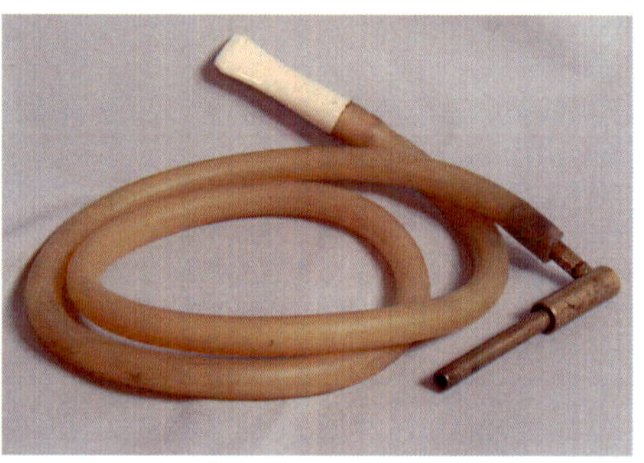

Figure 2.14 *Swivel and blowpipe assembly*

CORKS, RUBBER STOPPERS, AND RUBBER POLICEMEN

Corks are used to close the open ends of glass tubing. An assortment of sizes ranging from size 000 (smallest size) to at least size 2 is convenient for most small diameter tubing work. One-holed rubber stoppers are useful in preparing the second end of the tubing for the swivel of the blowpipe. A wide range of sizes should be available. Rubber policemen are commercially available, but can also be easily made. These are really nothing more than pieces of rubber tubing with one end closed off, providing still another way to close open ends of the glass tubing or apparatus that is being worked on. Homemade varieties can be made from tubing by pinching it closed with a clamp or small cork.

FILES

These can be used to score glass tubing or rod whenever a glass knife is not available. Flat machinist's files are best because they can be easily sharpened by grinding. Small triangular files are preferred by some workers, but these cannot be sharpened. The handle end of any file is also a handy tool for making patterns on hot glass in a variety of artistic projects.

FLARING TOOLS (REAMING TOOLS)

These are usually made from flat brass in the shape of a triangle and fitted with a handle. They may range in shape from very narrow (sharp) to very wide (blunt). Some consist of two blades at 90° angles to one another (Figure 2.15). These tools are used to expand glass tubing into funnel type shapes. Like any glassworking tool, they should never be used directly in the flame.

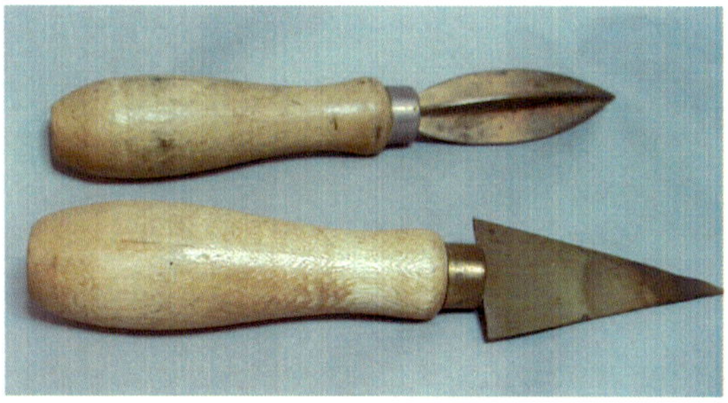

Figure 2.15 *Typical brass flaring tools.*

FLASK HOLDERS (FINGERS)

These holders, sometimes called "holding fingers", are specially designed tools for holding flasks or bulbs while constructing or repairing the neck (Figure 2.16). The insulated handle usually slides back and forth for size adjustment.

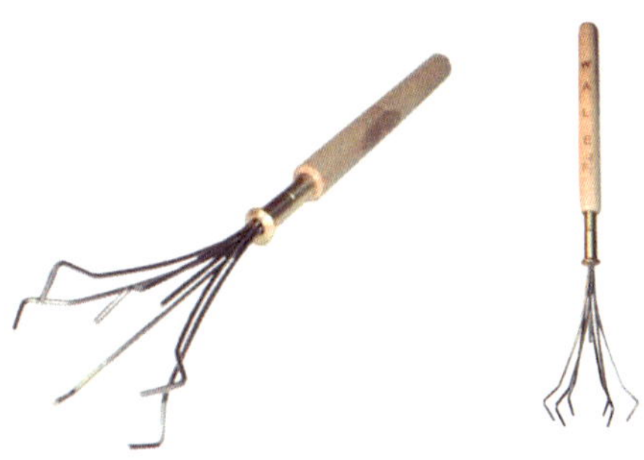

Figure 2.16 *Flask holder or holding fingers (Wale Apparatus).*

FORCEPS

Forceps are extremely useful to the glassworker, especially in many artistic procedures. A larger pair of biological specimen forceps (10 inch) are often quite suitable, but special glassblowing forceps fitted with heat resistant vulcanite handles may be better for some applications although they are also much more expensive (Figure 2.17). Neither type should ever be placed directly into the flame. Sometimes glass workers attach metal plates to the ends of the forceps making them into useful shaping tools (see section on Shaping Tools on page 38).

Figure 2.17 *Two types of forceps.*

GLASS KNIVES

These "knives" utilize a tungsten carbide, Carbaloy®, Kennametal®, or similar alloy cutting edge for making scratches on glass (Figure

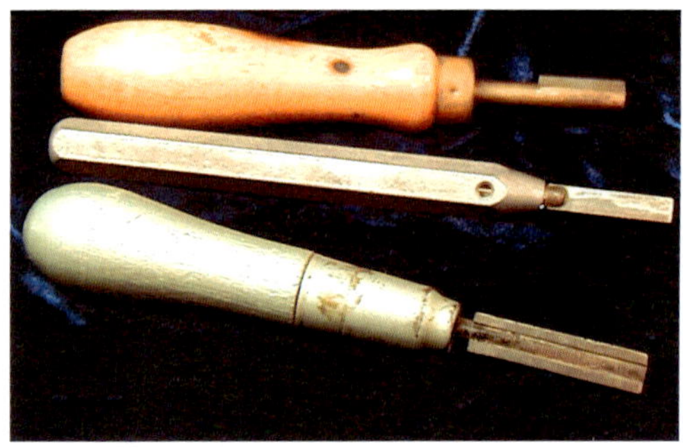

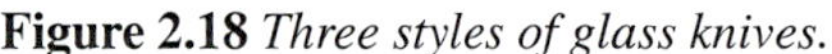

Figure 2.18 *Three styles of glass knives.*

Figure 2.19 *Samples of graphite plates to be used on the glassblowing bench top.*

2.18). Usually the resulting scratch mark is considerably finer than that made by a file, and this normally leads to much cleaner cuts. The cutting edges can be carefully sharpened when necessary on special grinding wheels.

GRAPHITE PLATES

A graphite (carbon) plate is extremely important in flameworking. A small graphite plate (at least 4" by 6") should be kept on the work table close to the torch at all times (Figure 2.19). These are especially useful in making end marias and for shaping procedures which involve pressing tools onto the hot glass. The work bench surface should never be used as a substitute for a graphite plate in such shaping procedures.

GRAPHITE RODS

Often graphite rods of various diameters are used in place of brass shaping tools, especially in the case of flaring small diameter tubing (Figure 2.20). Caution should be exercised since these conduct heat very rapidly. Once again, like all tools, they should never be used directly in the flame. The tips of these rods can be tapered nicely by using a regular pencil sharpener. Points can be made on a very small rod if the rod is carefully centered in the smallest hole of the sharpener and held there firmly while being sharpened.

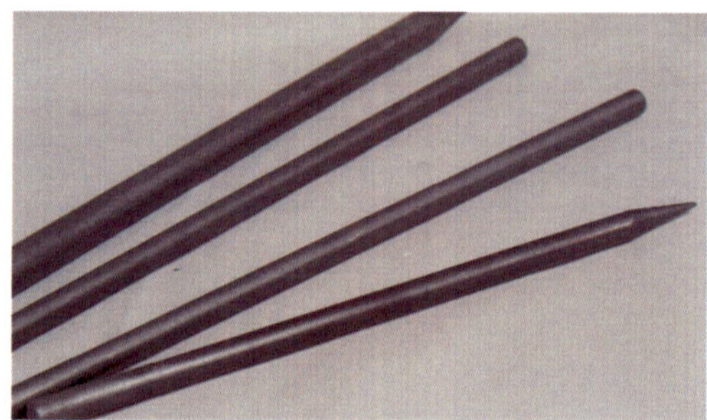

Figure 2.20 *Graphite rods for shaping*

GRAPHITE HEX

Larger diameter, six-sided graphite rods which are tapered and attached to a handle are very useful in reaming and flaring larger diameter tubing (Figure 2.21). A graphite hex are is especially useful for scientific work on the glass lathe.

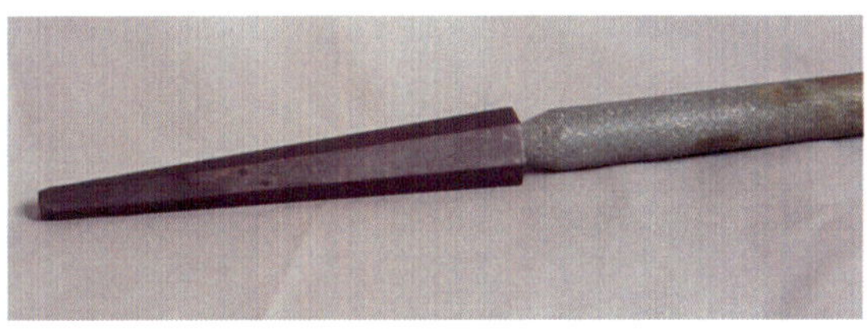

Figure 2.21 *Graphite hex for flaring tubing.*

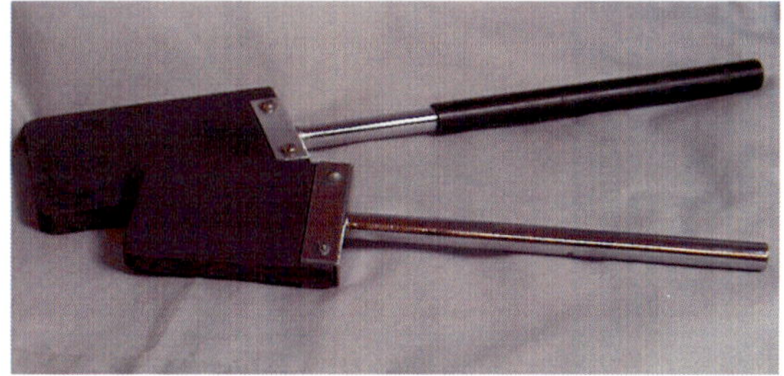

Figure 2.22 *Graphite paddles or marvers.*

GRAPHITE PADDLE (MARVER)

These are graphite plates fitted with handles and are used for various shaping operations (Figure 2.22). Most glassworkers will want to have one of these handy. Sizes vary, but a 2" by 3" paddle is usually an ideal size for most applications.

HEAT RESISTANT GLOVES AND MITTENS

. Obviously, these are important for working with hot items or for handling items just out of the annealing oven (Figure 2.23). But they can also serve as excellent cooling chambers. Small items of glass which would be awkward to immerse in vermiculite can be placed between the gloves to cool slowly, before annealing in the oven. These are now available in many materials including Kevlar® Heatex® (fiberglass) and PBI (polybenzimidazole).

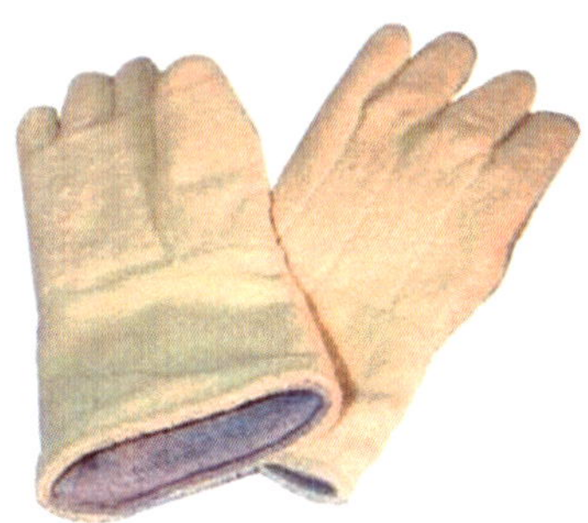

Figure 2.23 *Kevlar heat resistant gloves (Wale Apparatus).*

HEAT RESISTANT TAPE

Tape is a real necessity for scientific glassblowing. It is available in a variety of widths and thicknesses and can be used for supporting inner tubes, for closing small open ends in tubing, and for lining and protecting standard taper joints or multistoppers (Figure 2.24). Many glassworkers choose the new woven glass type tapes, while others use tape or paper-like materials made from Nor-Fab®, Ceramfab®, or other similar substitutes.

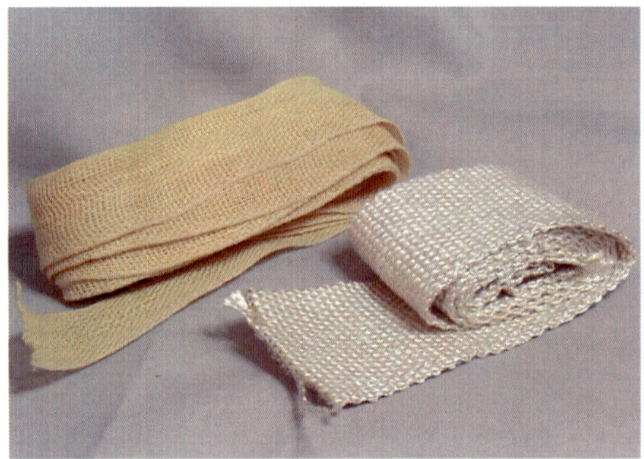

Figure 2.24 *Two examples of heat resistant tape.*

Figure 2.25 *Electric hot plate*

HOT PLATE

An electric hot plate is extremely useful in the construction of many items of artistic glassware (Figure 2.25). Parts made previously (such as birds for tree branches or bird baths or musical instruments for various angels) can be kept hot so that when ready to incorporate the item in your work, they do not need to be reheated. The likelihood of their cracking is greatly reduced in this way. A discount store heater will serve the purpose as will a common covered frypan.

LIGHTERS (FOR TORCHES)

Although beginners may use matches to light their torches, most glass workers use a flint or pietzieo lighter for this purpose. This is highly recommended, as it is easier to keep the bench top free from contaminants. For safety reasons, propane lighters are not recommended.

MARKING TOOLS

There are many operations which are aided by using some sort of marking tool. Special glass marking pencils and wax pencils are two common varieties. Normal markers have ink which is burned up when heated.

METAL RULER

A good fire resistant ruler, usually made of either aluminum or stainless steel, is a valuable tool in any glass

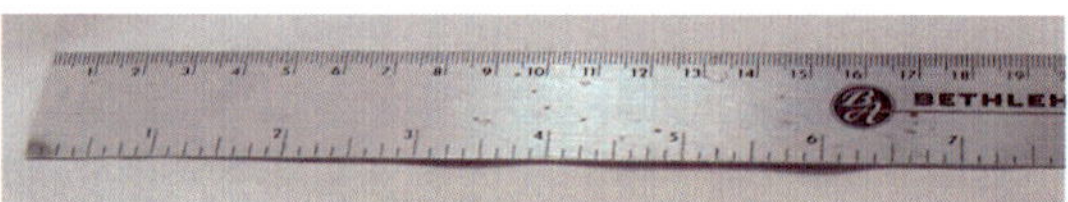

Figure 2.26 *Stainless steel laboratory ruler.*

lab. The markings are usually etched into the surface for permanence and for greater ease in reading (Figure 2.26).

PLIERS (NEEDLE NOSE)

Every glass lab should have a pair of good quality needle nose pliers. These are useful in a wide number of applications. The author has found it very useful to grind a circular grove in the needle nose, to hold round glass pieces (Figure 2.27). Speciality "cold glass rod cutting" pliers and "cut-running" pliers are also available, but one can usually get along without these.

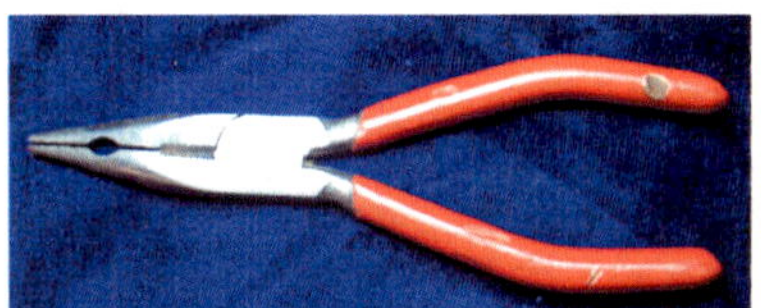

Figure 2.27 *Modified needle nose pliers.*

POLAROID PLASTIC FILM

A convenient and inexpensive polariscope (see page 41) can be fashioned out of two pieces of polaroid film, held at ninety degree angles to one another (Figure 2.28). The glass piece to be inspected is inserted between the film sheets and then held up to a bright, diffuse light (in back of the plastic sheets). This is a simple "tool" that every glassblower should have handy.

Figure 2.28 *Simple polariscope fashioned by superimposing two pieces of polaroid film.*

PLUROSTOPPERS (MULTISTOPPERS)

A plurostopper (multistopper) is a set of concentric stoppers (Figure 2.29) which can be made to fit almost any larger size diameter glass tubing (normally from at least 22 mm to 70 mm). These are used as plugs or vents for use with a swivel and blowpipe and are made of either black rubber, neoprene or silicone. The black rubber is usable up to 158°F, the neoprene up to 212°F, and the silicone (most versatile of all) up to 450°F. The outside of each is usually wrapped with a layer of fire resistant tape to insulate the stopper from the hot glass. These sets of stoppers are relatively expensive (around $100) and should always be kept together as a set when not in use.

Figure 2.29 *Sets of multistoppers for use with large diameter tubing.*

ROLLERS

A set of free-turning adjustable rollers are invaluable for supporting rotating glass tubing while heating to make flares (Figure 2.30). In some situations, with a set of high quality rollers, an experienced glassworker can rotate the tubing so rapidly that flares come out without the use of other tools.

Figure 2.30 *Two examples of adjustable rollers. Usually a pair of these is used. (Left: Wale Apparatus; right Lab Supply & Equipment Company).*

SHAPING TOOLS

Many different tools can be used to shape hot glass. In fact any non-flammable item can potentially be used as a tool. Just remember that all tools, including shaping tools, are used outside the flame. Never put any tool directly in the flame! Some tools (Figure 2.31) are used to keep glass shapes (on a handle) flat. Others are used to impart patterns on hot glass. Many of these are fastened at the end of pliers or forceps (Figures 2.32 and 2.33).

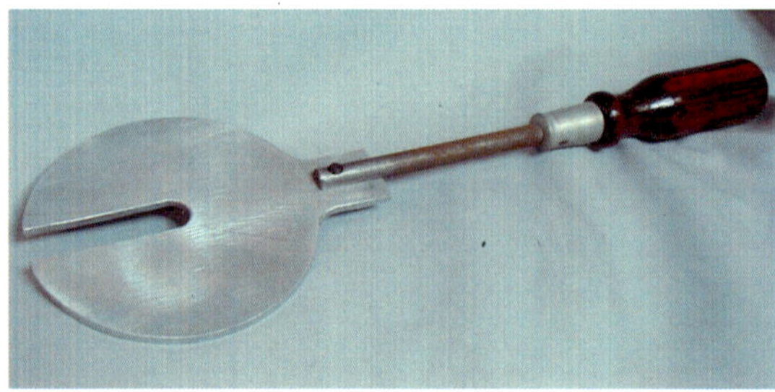

Figure 2.31 *Shaping tool made from attaching slotted aluminum plates on handle.*

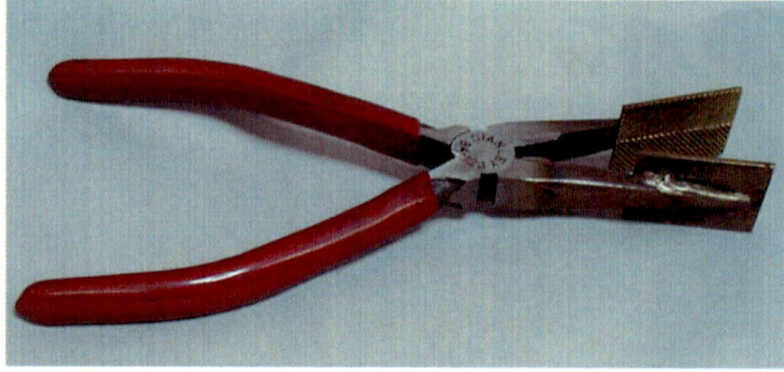

Figure 2.32 *Shaping tool made from attaching brass plates at the end of pliers.*

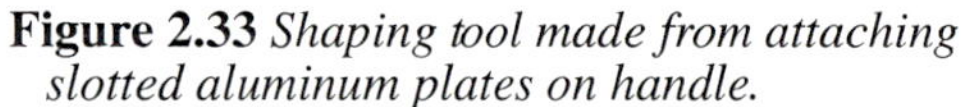

Figure 2.33 *Shaping tool made from attaching slotted aluminum plates on handle.*

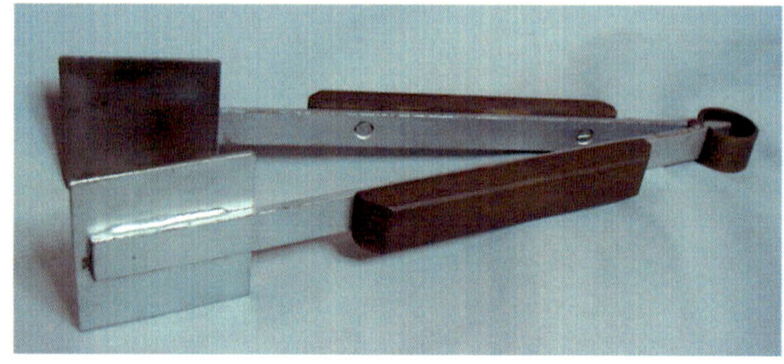

SPANDLE

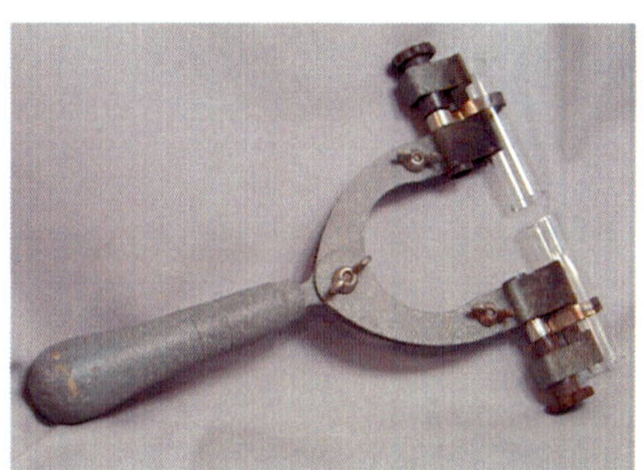

Figure 2.34 *Spandle for holding glass pieces.*

A spandle is a helpful tool which may greatly simplify many scientific glassblowing operations such as making straight butt seals or "T" joints (Figure 2.34). It consists of a handle with two tubing vises which can bc adjusted to any angle and will hold a wide range of tubing diameters. Usually this tool enables one to produce acceptable results with a minimum of practice; however, these are rarely used by experienced glassblowers.

SUPPORTS

Such supports consist of two parallel pieces of heat resistant material which have a number of notches suitable for keeping hot pieces of glass off the bench top while they cool (Figure 2.35.

Figure 2.35 *Glass support for the bench, made of heat resistant material*

TUBING (HOSES)

Blowpipe hoses are usually made from 5/32 OD latex tubing. The best tubing to use to connect your torches to the tanks or utilities is a special color coded twin tubing which may be coated with protective NorFab overbraid. Tygon® tubing is also suitable, but extreme care must be used to insure that hot glass never comes in contact with it!

TUBING CUTTER (WHEEL TYPE)

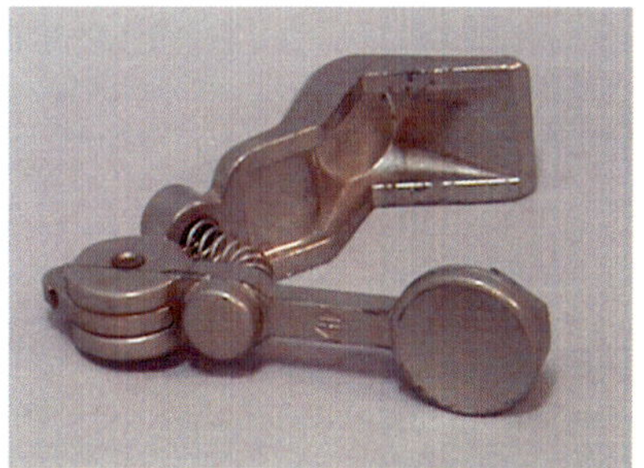

Figure 2.36 *Wheel tubing cutter fo*ı *larger diameter glass.*

This is a spring loaded cutter with a replaceable cutting wheel (Figure 2.36). It is used to impart a straight scratch on larger diameter tubing. When using these, one should be careful not to exert too much pressure, as the glass could crush, causing serious injury.

TUNGSTEN NEEDLE (PICK)

This tool is composed of a piece of tungsten wire held firmly in an adjustable handle. It can be used for making holes in hot glass, repairing cracks, or flaring very small tubes.

VERNIER CALIPER

These are calibrated sliding instruments which are used to measure either the inside or the outside diameter of glass tubing or the outside diameter of rod (Figure 2.37). Normally these are calibrated in both millimeters and inches. A six inch caliper is the most common size used. Some versions may utilize a dial or digital readout, but these are usually rather expensive.

Figure 2.37 *Stainless steel vernier caliper*

WIRE GAUZE (WIRE SCREEN)

A small piece of sturdy wire screening is very useful when used like sandpaper to remove jagged edges and any irregularities from the ends of glass tubing or to remove the thin portion of blown out glass during the construction of many types of scientific seals (Figure 2.38). Stainless steel is best, but an iron screen will work just as well. Use caution with the sharp edges!

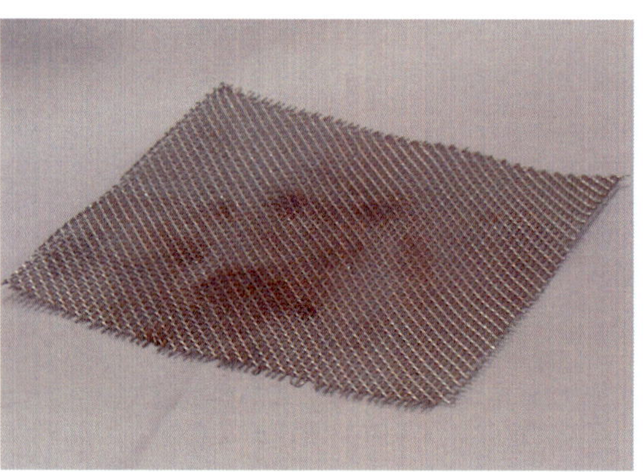

Figure 2.38 *Sample of wire gauze, used to remove excess thin glass pieces.*

SPECIAL LARGER EQUIPMENT

ANNEALING OVEN

Whenever hot glass is cooled too rapidly or whenever joints are made between different pieces of glass, internal stresses become incorporated in the glass. Under certain conditions such as reheating or physical handling of the glass, the stresses may become "relieved" by the process of cracking along the stress lines. Obviously, this is not the most desirable way to relieve the internal stresses.

Figure 2.39 *Wilt 125 annealing oven.*

Instead, one can anneal the glass, allowing the stresses to dissipate slowly by letting the glass molecules realign to more favorable positions over a longer period of time. Items should usually be flame annealed (see page 89) to some degree after their completion or even after completion of various steps in the construction of complex items. The general rule of thumb is that ideally, an item should be flame annealed for about the same amount of time that was spent in its construction. If the article will also be oven annealed, the amount of flame annealing can usually be cut in half, or in some cases, even eliminated. Thus, the annealing oven is a very important and well used piece of equipment in any glass laboratory. Items are usually annealed at the end of the working day so that they will be ready for removal from the oven the next morning.

Annealing ovens come in a wide range of sizes, from relatively small bench models to extremely large models which may occupy most of a good sized room. Wilt Industries (and others) make units suitable for the smaller glass lab (Figure 2.39 and 2.46). All annealing ovens have some type of temperature controller. In some of the smaller ovens, temperature programming is done manually, but the larger, more expensive ovens, include timing devices which heat up the oven slowly to the annealing temperature, hold the glass at the annealing point for a predetermined period of time, and then automatically shut off to allow the glass to cool slowly over a long period of time. Large industrial units may contain blowers to circulate the air in order to insure even heating of all portions in the oven.

Those working in smaller labs may be able to build a simple oven.[9]

POLARISCOPE

A polariscope is very useful because it allows glassworkers to see the stresses within the glass, allowing them to assess the durability of their work. Basically, these instruments are rather simple, consisting of a strong, diffuse source of light covered by a sheet of Polaroid plastic (Polaroid absorbs all light except that in a single plane). A second piece of Polaroid is then held (or supported) so that its plane is at right angles to that of the first. This is easily determined by looking through both pieces of Polaroid while rotating one until a minimum of light is transmitted. The item to be inspected is then held between the two pieces of Polaroid. Stresses show up as dark and light striped patterns within the glass. This is due to the fact that stressed glass will "rotate" the transmitted light slightly so that it is no longer at right angles to the second piece of Polaroid. This is why some areas are lighter and some darker. After correct annealing procedures, all stress patterns should be eliminated.Excellent, low cost instruments can be obtained commercially from Wale Apparatus (Figures 2.40 -2.41).

Figure 2.40 *Wale 6" Square Polariscope.*

Figure 2.41 *Wale 10 x 19" Polariscope.*

It is also possible to construct a useful polariscope made by affixing a large piece of Polaroid plastic film over a diffuse plastic window with a rear source of light (Figure 2.42). The item to be examined is then held in front of the lighted Polaroid window, and a second piece is then held between the item and the eye of the viewer. The second piece of Polaroid needs to be properly rotated so as to minimize light transmission, as this will indicate that the "lines" are perpendicular to one another. This sort of instrument is especially useful in a classroom setting where a number of hand held Polaroid sheets can be used at the same time.

It should be pointed out that two hand held pieces of Polaroid film can also serve as an excellent, very low cost "instant polariscope" for the beginning glassworker (see page 37).

Figure 2.42 *Homemade polariscope used in the glass lab at Southwest State University where the author*

GLASS LATHE

This piece of equipment is most important to the scientific glassblower. A glass lathe looks some what like a woodworking or metalworking lathe except that it has two coordinated moving chucks instead of one. Likewise, it is fitted to handle special precision tools and glassblowing torches. Commercial glass lathes are available from a number of manufacturers in a wide range of sizes, models, and prices (Figures 2.43 - 2.45).

Figure 2.43 *Bethlehem Model 100 glass lathe in the author's home lab.*

Figure 2.44 *Litton Bench Model glass lathe (courtesy of Wale Apparatus).*

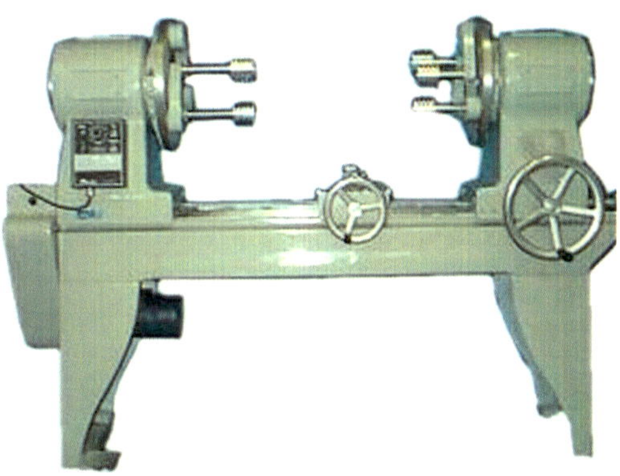

Figure 2.45 *Example of Litton Floor Model glass lathes (courtesy of Wale Apparatus).*

It has long been the assumption that one should not attempt work on a glass lathe until becoming a totally proficient hand operator. Now, however, many feel that if beginning scientific glassblowers are able to use a lathe, and are relieved of the difficult job of maintaining coordinated rotation, they will be much more successful in learning to make good seals. With a lathe, many students can produce surprisingly good seals and rather advanced glass products very early in their training. Glass lathes are usually sound investments for scientific laboratories which are unable to have the services of a fully trained glassblower. The lathe usually allows interested persons with some ability in glassblowing to produce attractive, high quality products.

It possible for individuals unable to afford these somewhat expensive pieces of equipment to construct homemade versions that may serve their purposes. Some plans are shared on the world wide web.

HOT-WIRE CUTTING APPRATUS

Large diameter tubing can often be satisfactorily cut using the hot-wire technique (see page 52). A special apparatus incorporating an electrically heated wire and cold running water can be purchased commercially, but much simpler and equally effective units can easily be constructed (Figure 2.46). A nichrome wire, held on a noncombustible support is powered by a variable transformer.

Figure 2.46 *Homemade hot glass cutting apparatus for cutting large glass.*

GLASS CUTTING SAW

If one needs to cut large diameter tubing or make a cut near a standard taper joint, the operation can best be done by using a mechanically driven, water-cooled cutting wheel. Cutting saws are especially useful in scientific repair work. These machines range from in size from small four or six inch bench-top models (Figure 2.47), to large, heavy-duty floor models. The cutting wheels may contain imbedded industrial grade diamonds or may be made of an abrasive such as rubber-bonded silicon carbide, specially designed for borosilicate and quartz cutting. The diamond blades are initially much more expensive, but will last much longer and usually prove to be safer. Water-cooled silicon carbide wheels become quite soft, are easily distorted, and can break during improper usage. Not only is this dangerous, but the wheels are also rather expensive. In the long run, diamond blades are the best investment.

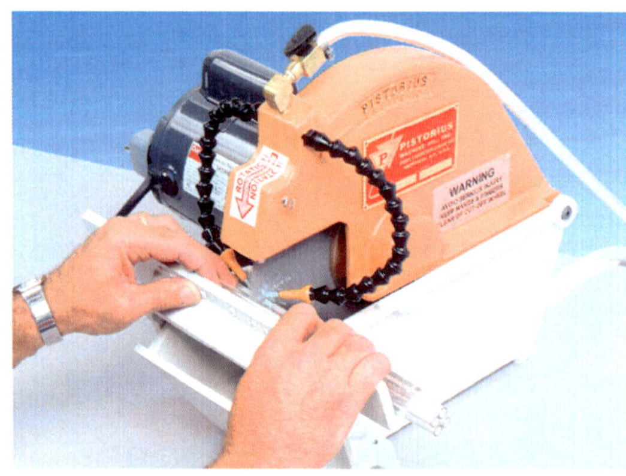

Figure 2.47 *Pistorius Model GC12B Glass Saw.*

MISCELLANEOUS TOOLS FOR THE GLASS LAB

Professional glass laboratories may find use for a wide variety of additional special equipment. These include glass grinding wheels, vacuum pumps, small welders, drill presses, and bench grinders. Although these are rarely used in the labs of beginners, some of these items are shown and described in Figures 2.47-2.49.

Figure 2.47

Wilt Model L-177-18 Lapping Machine used to produce a fine surface finish. a variety of grits and felt/diamond resin smoothing pads can be used.

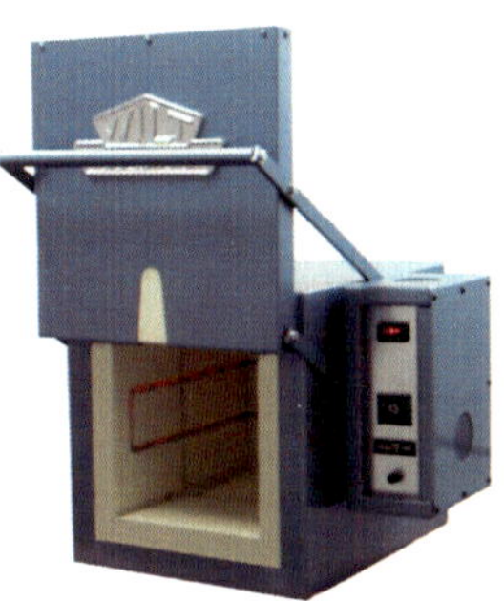

Figure 2.48

Wilt Model 120B Electric Holding Oven is used to keep glass uniformly hot during long procedures. It can also be used as an annealing oven in small glass

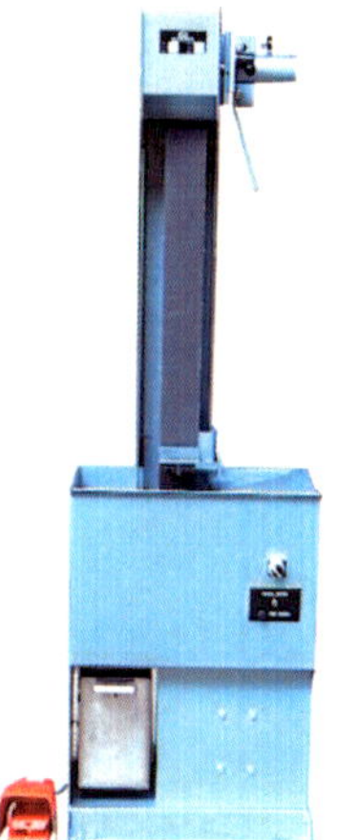

Figure 2.49

Wilt Model 4106 Wet Belt Sander is used in production labs for grinding larger pieces of glass. A wide range of belts of different grits. Diamond belts can also be used. Smaller versions of this sander are available.

The tools and equipment illustrated in this chapter were reproduced with the permission of the following companies:

Bethlehem Apparatus
Wilt Industries
Pistorius Machine Company
Carlisle Machine Works
Wale Apparatus

ENDNOTES

1. F.M. Van Damme, "The Forming of Highly Toxic Fumes in the Air While Working with Glass," *Fusion*, Aug., 1979, pp19-22.
2. F. Van Damme, "Ventilating a Scientific Glassblowing Lab", *Proceedings of the 25th Symposium on the Art of Scientific Glassblowing, American Scientific Glassblowers Society*, 1980, pp. 81-90.
3. Personal communication and webpage information: http://www.auralens.com/gwlensinfo.html#agw186. 4. webpage:
4. G. E. Myers, "Optical Hazards in Glassblowing", *Fusion*, August, 1976, pp. 9-19.
5. J. Tassin, "Effectiveness of Eye Glass to Remove Damaging Radiation from Gas Flames", *Proceedings of the 26th Symposium on the Art of Scientific Glassblowing, American Scientific Glassblowers Society*, 1981, pp. 36-43.
6. O. Oriowo, R. Chou, and A. Cullen, *Fusion*, August, 1997, pp. 36-47.
7. D. Blessing, "Safety and Hazards", *Fusion, May*, 1982, pp. 16-17.
8. D. G. Maul, "Construction of an Annealing Oven," *Proceedings of the 37th Symposium on the Art of Scientific Glassblowing, American Scientific Glassblowers Society*, 1992, pp. 52-57.

Chapter 3
BASIC GLASSWORKING OPERATIONS

OPERATION OF THE HAND TORCH

Most artistic and scientific glassworking can be done using a simple hand torch such as that manufactured by National and distributed by nearly all glassblowing supply houses. For this reason, the exercises described in this book will assume the use of such a torch and will likewise always assume the use of clean and relatively new borosilicate rod and tubing.

LABORATORY EXERCISE ONE

USING THE HAND TORCH

1. The hand torch should always be positioned so that the gas valve (red) is on your right and the oxygen valve (green) is on your left (Figure 3.1). After making certain that the oxygen regulator is turned on at the tank, turn on both gas and oxygen bench valves. Bench valves are usually on when the handle is pointed straight out. The off position is usually either to the right or to the left. This is a good time to check to see if the proper size tip is on the torch. A #5 tip is best for most rod working, while a #3 tip is usually suitable for most small diameter scientific tubing work.If using propane, a #4 tip is best for general work.

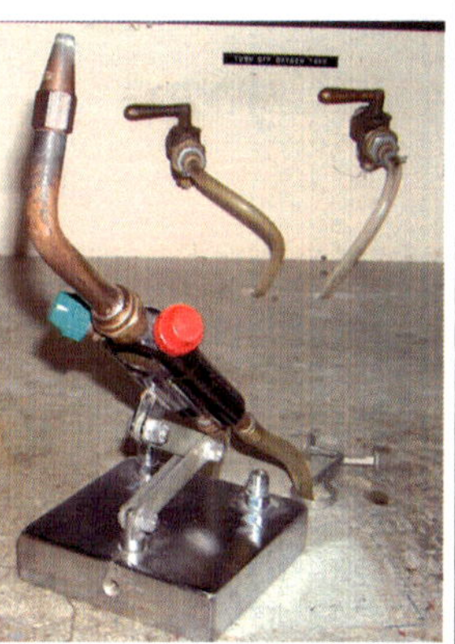

Figure 3.1 *Hand torch with tubing set under bench to shut-off valves.*

2. If your torch has not been used for some time, it may be wise to open both valves on the torch for about 2 seconds each to remove any air from the lines. Then carefully close them both again.

Hand torches have very delicate needle valves and should never be over tightened!

3. To light the torch, turn the gas on at the torch and ignite with a match or spark lighter. If a match is used, bring it down so the flame touches the tip of the burner. Now adjust the gas so that the yellow flame is about 6-8 inches long. Too much gas flow will actually blow out the flame. This will happen when the flame ceases burning at the tip of the burner. Now open the oxygen valve slightly (at the torch), and slowly increase the amount of oxygen until the proper flame is obtained.

4. Beginners should pay a great deal of attention to flame sizes, cone sizes, and the sound of the flame. Experience will make all of these meaningful. A good all-around flame is obtained by starting out with about an 8 inch gas flame and adding enough oxygen so that the inner blue cone is about 3/8 to 1/2 inch high. The flame should make a quiet whooshing sound. The hottest part of the flame is always located just slightly above the inside blue cone. The beginner should spend some time experimenting with the gas and oxygen levels and observing their effect on the flame size. Start out with a 6 inch yellow flame, adding enough oxygen until a half inch blue cone is formed. Note the size, shape, and sound of the flame. Then turn off the oxygen again. Now repeat the process, starting out with a 10-12 inch yellow flame. This time once the half inch cone is formed and noted, add more gas followed by more oxygen, again maintaining a half inch blue cone. Once again, note the size, shape, and sound. Mentally compare the three different flames you have studied.

5. To turn the burner off, always turn off the oxygen first at the torch, and then turn off the gas. Never over tighten the valves!

6. When you are done working for the day, be sure to turn off the gas and oxygen valves on the lab bench, and if you are the last person in the laboratory, be sure to turn off the oxygen tank valve.

Understanding your particular torch, being aware of the meaning of the various colors of heated glass, and knowing how to adjust the flame to get the desired results are all acutely important in the process of glassblowing. Knowledgeable practice of these is the "art" which is glassblowing. Practice is the only teacher. An excellent technical discussion of flames appeared in a publication of the American Scientific Glassblowers Society.[1]

CUTTING GLASS ROD AND TUBING

Since glass rod and tubing is normally purchased in four foot lengths, one of the first operations that faces any glassworker is that of cutting the rod or tubing to the proper length. Cutting may not be the proper term to use since one does not usually cut glass in the same sense that one would cut metal or wood.

Cutting or "breaking" a piece of glass requires two conditions to occur simultaneously, namely a flaw of some sort and a tension or a strain. Although there are many different possible ways to bring these about and thus to accomplish cutting, the two most common methods are scratching followed by breaking between the hands, and flame cutting. These and several other techniques are described below.

SURVEY OF SCRATCH AND BREAK METHODS

Glass, when free of any imperfections, is amazingly strong. Such glass can withstand tensile loads of more than two million pounds per square inch.[2] This is more than ten times as much stress as many metal alloys can tolerate! However, even the smallest scratch or crack drastically weakens the glass. As soon as rod or tubing is exposed to such a stress, the cracks literally grow and spread. Furthermore, it has long been known that wetting the scratched surface reduces the strength of the glass even more.[3] It is only recently that the reasons for this have been understood.[4] Thus, we take advantage of these facts in our cutting methods. A scratch is imparted where the cut is desired. It is then usually wetted (saliva is fine), and sufficient tensile stress (stretching force) is exerted, resulting in fracture of the glass. Beginners soon discover that the amount of stress needed to cause such fractures is surprisingly small.

This method is well suited for most normal cutting. Rod up to 11 mm and tubing up to 20 mm in diameter can usually be easily cut by this method. Nonetheless, the beginner should start with small diameter rod (4 mm) and gradually work up to a larger diameter rod and tubing.

Glass can be scratched in a number of different ways. Triangular files or flat files are probably the most common tools, but a glass knife is best and can produce cleaner cuts when used properly.

Cutting Rod With A Triangular File

The rod or tubing to be cut is placed on the bench top and held firmly while imparting a scratch at the desired position with a triangular file. The glass should never be sawed. A single, strong scratch in one direction made perpendicular to the length of the rod should be sufficient

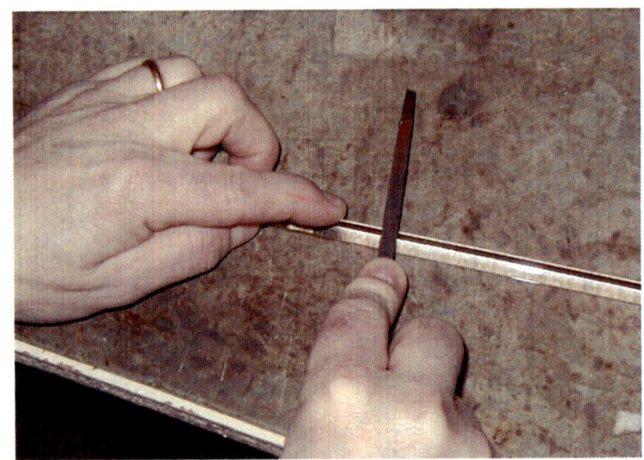

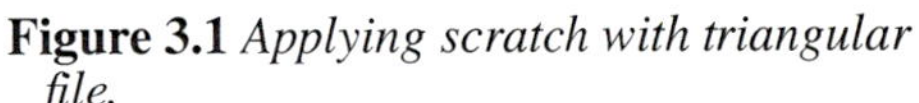

Figure 3.1 *Applying scratch with triangular file.*

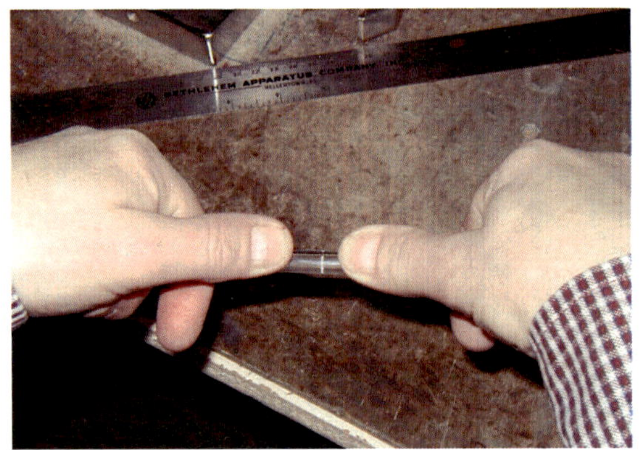

Figure 3.2 *Position of hands for breaking tubing & tubing. scratch is on side away from person!*

(Figure 3.1). The scratch is then wetted slightly, and the rod is broken by an action that is both bending and pulling at the same time (Figure 3.2). If the glass does not break immediately, stop! When done properly, the glass will break easily without much pressure. If too much pressure is required, the scratch should be deepened, but be sure to make the second scratch in exactly the same place at the same angle. Should some difficulty still be encountered or if you are hesitant to try, the following method may be used. Scratch the glass as described previously. Then place firmly against your stomach with the scratch facing outward. Then pull the ends apart (Figure 3.3). Don't worry about bending the glass as this will happen naturally. You should find that the glass breaks rather easily now.

Cutting With A Glass Knife

This procedure is very similar to that described above for file cuts. The only real difference is in the manner of imparting the scratch. The scratch can be made on the bench in exactly the same way as done with the file, but a better method is to hold the glass in your hands while scratching it. Place your thumb directly above where the cut is to be made and press one edge of the glass knife under the rod or tubing, exerting a very slight upward pressure with your index finger (Figure 3.4). A knife does not require the force that a file does. In fact, it seems that if you press too hard with a knife, it will not scratch as well. If you find that you are unable to make a good scratch with your knife, it may be that it is in need of sharpening. The stress is imparted in the same way as previously described. The fracture should be accomplished easily, and a cleaner cut should result. If a jagged edge results, you may be bending the rod or tubing too much. If this is the case, concentrate more on pulling the glass apart.

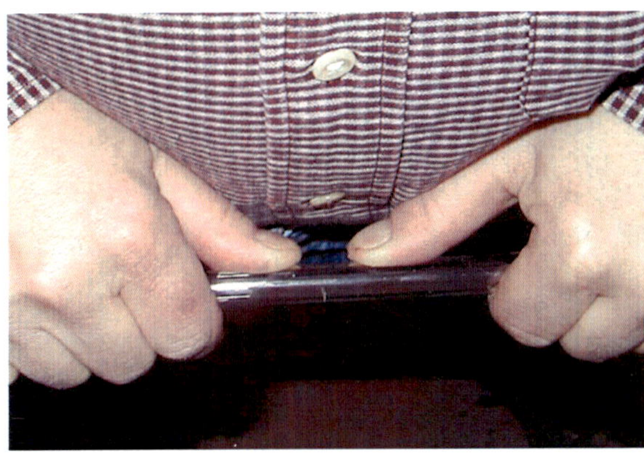

Figure 3.3 *Alternate method for breaking larger diameter tubing and rod.*

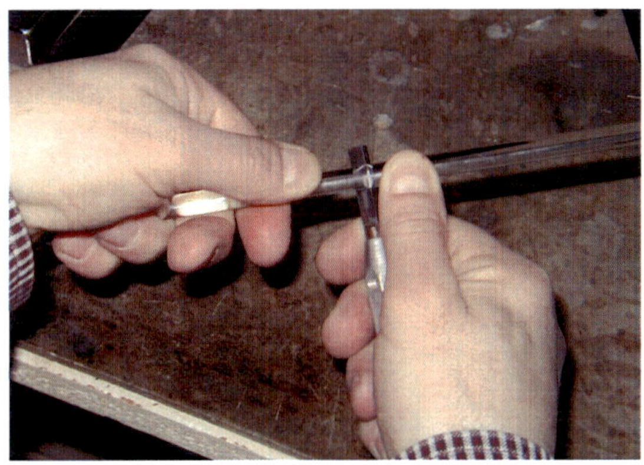

Figure 3.4 *Applying scratch on the bottom of the glass piece with a special glass knife.*

Figure 3.5 *Using a cutting edge to remove short ends from tubing or rod.*

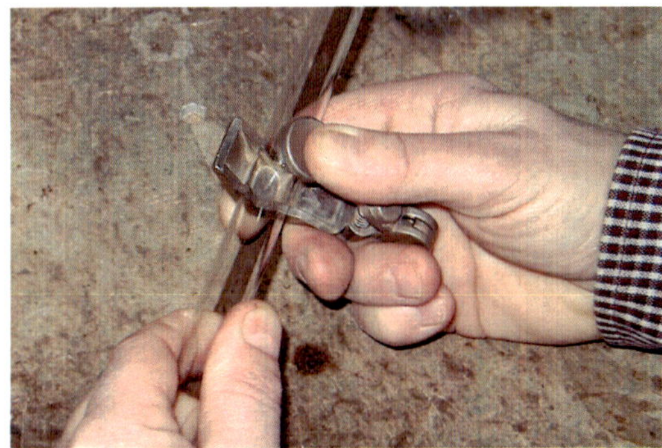

Figure 3.6 *Applying scratch with a wheel-type cutter (for large diameter tubing).*

Cutting Very Short Pieces Or Removing Short Ends

If it is impossible to get a good grip on the ends of the glass because they are too short or perhaps too hot, the following method should be used. Scratch the glass using either file or knife as described above. Then place the scratch directly above a slotted cutting edge as shown in Figure 3.5, and then strike the end of the glass with the blunt end of your file or knife with a glancing blow. The tubing or rod should break with ease

Cutting With A Wheel-Type Tubing Cutter

Scratches can be imparted on large diameter tubing above 20 mm with a cutting wheel (Figure 3.6). The advantage of using such a wheel is that the scratch tends to be much straighter, but considerable pressure is sometimes required, and the small cutting wheels simply do not last very long. Special caution should be taken to avoid using so much pressure that the tubing is crushed. Such incidents can cause serious injury to the worker. If you find it difficult to make a good scratch, the cutting wheel should be replaced. Once the scratch is imparted, the break is made in the usual manner.

Cutting With A Small Hot Rod

Very large diameter tubing or tubing that cannot be manipulated (such as in assembled pieces or in chemical apparatus) can be cut in a different manner. After being scratched with a file, knife, or a cutting wheel, the tubing is cracked by applying the tip of a small piece of white hot rod (4 to 6 mm) to one end of the scratch (Figure 3.7). The thermal stress imparted by the hot rod should cause the crack to extend completely around the tubing in the place desired. A slight tap usually cleaves the glass at the fracture. It is common, however, that these cuts may not be as uniform as desired.

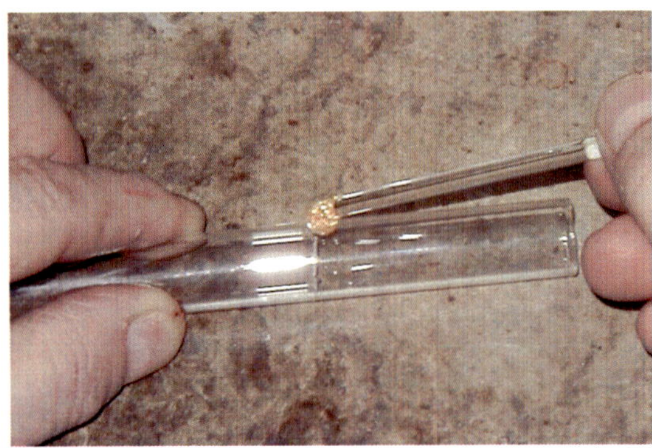

Figure 3.7 *Cutting large diameter tubing using a scratch and a hot rod.*

Cutting By Heating A Scratch

This method is very similar to the hot rod technique described above. A deep scratch is made about one-third of the way around the tubing. One end of the scratch is then repeatedly moved into and out of the upper portion of a very small, hot flame. Once again, the thermal stress should cause the crack to extend completely around the tubing.

For this operation, a small tight "hissy" flame should be used. This flame is directed near (slightly above) but not on the far side of the scratch. If done correctly, the cut will occur quickly, within a second.[x] This method can produce very clean cuts.

Cutting With A Hot-Wire

Large diameter glass tubing can sometimes be satisfactorily cut using a heated wire. Several different methods exist. In one case, the scratch is made in the usual manner, but around the entire piece of tubing.

This can be accomplished with a cutting wheel or by guiding the file or knife with one or two layers of masking tape wrapped around the glass at the point to be cut. The scratch is then placed in direct contact with a heated wire. The tubing should then crack along the scratch, but it may be necessary to rotate the tube, bringing all of the glass in contact with the wire. One type of apparatus suitable for making such cuts is shown in Figure 2.43 on page 44.

Another method involves wrapping a wire around the tube (no scratch is required), applying the heat to the wire and then allowing cold water to come in contact with the tube after the current has been shut off!

CUTTING WITH A MECHANICAL SAW

For large diameter tubing or for situations where it is critical to get an absolutely uniform cut on the first attempt, as in the repair of scientific glassware, a water cooled diamond or Carborundum cutting saw can be used to advantage (Figure 3.8). The glass piece is fed into the saw at a very slow and constant rate. Every effort must be made to hold the glass piece sturdily as any lateral motion will cause pressure on the cutting blade and may result in breakage of the glass or the blade. Carborundum blades soften considerably from the water and can break easier than expected. Both parts of the piece being cut should be held firmly, as quite often one part breaks off prematurely and may fly into the blade. When cutting large diameter tubing, it may be wise to make a surface cut all the way around the tubing before cutting through on any one side. This will usually prevent pieces of glass from breaking off during the cutting process.

Quite often, glass pieces that have been sawed will leave a gray line when they are sealed to another piece of glass. This can be reduced somewhat by fire polishing the sawed edge before making a seal to it.

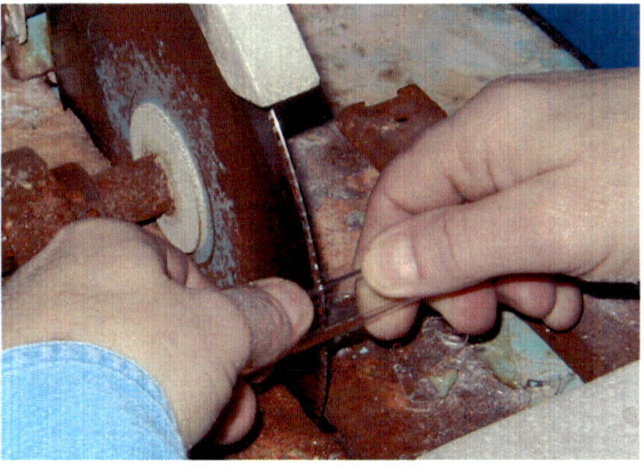

Figure 3.8 *Cutting with a mechanical diamond saw. safety glasses are a must.*

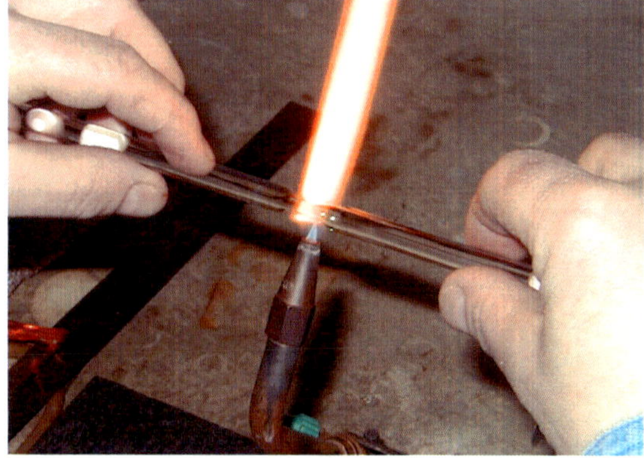

Figure 3.9 *Flame cutting. always started and completed in the flame!*

FLAME CUTTING

Flame cutting is one of the few operations actually done in the flame. When glass is heated strongly and pulled on, the diameter begins to decrease. Continued heating will sever the glass (Figure 3.9). This method is discussed in more detail in Chapter 4 on page 75.

CUTTING HEATED ROD WITH PLIERS

If small diameter rod (up to 6 mm) is heated for a few seconds with a hot flame, it can be snipped off conveniently with the cutting edge of a pair of pliers (Figure 3.10). This method is especially useful for removing a small amount of glass from the end of a rod. Little or no shattering occurs since the outside surface of the rod is soft and plastic. Special hot glass scissors can be purchased, but these pliers seem to work just as well with small diameter glass. Be sure to do all cutting over a metal waste container which is free of any combustible materials.

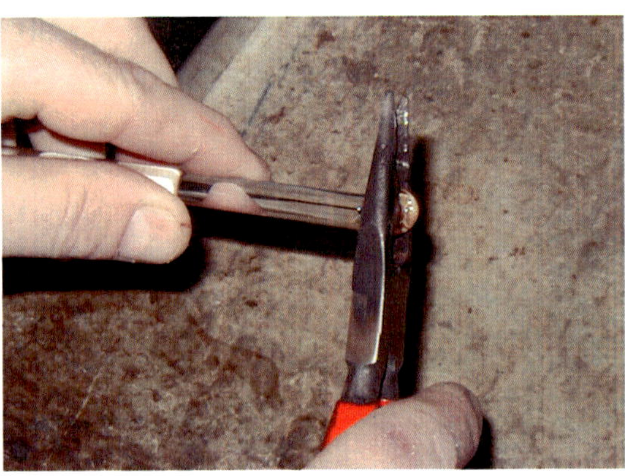

Figure 3.10 *Cutting heated rod with pliers.*

OTHER METHODS

Many other methods of cutting have been developed and used by glassblowers over the years. In most cases, a particular method is useful only under special circumstances or a method is favored by certain workers. Obviously, the more methods you make available to yourself, the better prepared you will be for any situation that arises.

LABORATORY EXERCISE TWO

CUTTING GLASS ROD AND TUBING

1. Take a two foot piece of 4 mm rod and cut two or three 6 inch pieces using the triangular file. Save the pieces for later exercises. Remember, if you need to exert a lot of pressure on the glass, you are doing something wrong. Small diameter rod and tubing should break with ease. Use the "stomach" technique if necessary until you feel comfortable making these cuts.
2. Finish cutting the 4 mm rod into pieces using your glass knife. Then repeat this procedure with a two foot piece of 5 mm rod using only your glass knife. Save the pieces for use later.
3. If these cuts go well for you, try one or two cuts on 6 mm rod, 8 mm rod, 6 mm tubing, and 10 mm tubing. Be sure to save all the pieces.

FIRE POLISHING

With the exception of flame cutting, any time that rod or tubing is cut, sharp edges will be produced. When working with tubing, it is always wise to fire polish all cut edges, even if you plan to join them again. This is not only for reasons of safety, but it turns out that the fire polished ends make better joints. Rod should also be fire polished to remove sharp ends, but in reality, glassblowers rarely take the time to do this. Special care should be directed to the handling of such unfirepolished pieces. Certainly, all finished ends, tubing and rod, must be fire polished. An item is fire polished by melting the sharp edges in the flame. Surface tension draws the softened glass into a smooth, rounded contour (Figure 3.11). Care must be taken so that the piece is not heated too strongly or too long, and during the process, the glass should always be rotated. With rod, one must avoid getting a "ball" of larger diameter than the

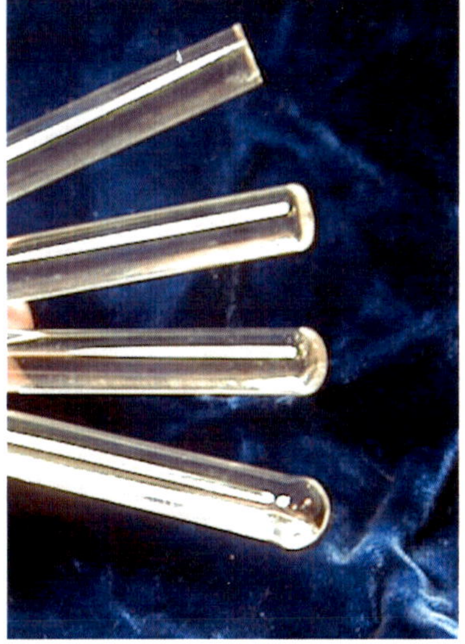

Figure 3.11 *Rod fire polishing.*
Top: *Not fire polished.*
Second: *Partially fire polished.*
Third: *Properly fire polished.*
Bottom: *Heated too much.*

rod. With tubing, special care must be taken to insure that only the wall edges become rounded (Figure 3.12). The tubing should never begin to close up! You may find that doing a good job of fire polishing is not quite as easy as it looks. Be sure to use the right size flame and keep the glass rotating at all times.

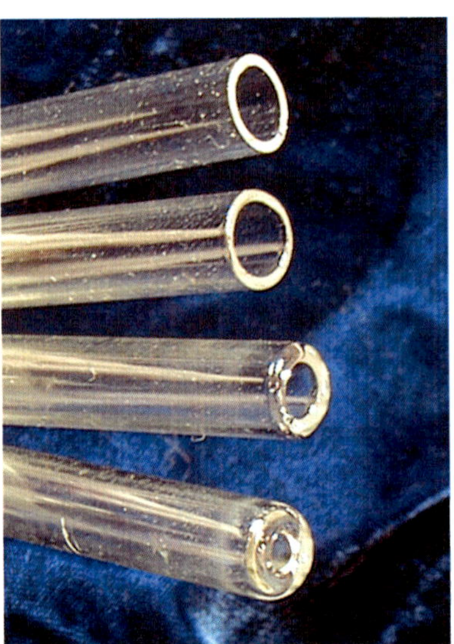

Figure 3.12 *Polishing tubing.*
Top: *Not fire polished.*
Second: *Properly fire polished.*
Third: *Heated a little too much.*
Bottom: *Heated too much.*

ROTATION TECHNIQUES

One of the most important and fundamental skills that must be acquired by a glassblower is that of rotating the glass while working with it in or outside the flame. Rotation is important for a number of reasons. First of all, it allows uniform heating of the tubing or rod. Secondly, it serves to cancel out any gravitational effects on the softened glass. Thirdly, it allows for uniform cooling of the tubing or rod when it is removed from the flame. Remember that heat rises, and therefore the lower surfaces of the glass cool considerably more rapidly than do the upper surfaces.

In reality, the glassblower may not always rotate the glass at a uniform rate. One side of the glass may call for additional heating. In this case, the flame will then be played on this side more than on the other. Or, one may choose to utilize gravity to make a particular shape or bend. Or, the worker may note upon blowing or working the glass that one side was not sufficiently softened. This side should then be turned upward so that the rising heat can soften the area as work is continued, even though the glass may be outside the flame. Proper rotation, therefore, either constant or selective, is important both in and outside the flame.

No matter what nature of rotation is required, good coordination of the hands is a necessity. The glass should not be pushed or pulled unless thickening or constricting is required. The speed of rotation of the right and left hand must be synchronized so that twisting does not occur. Furthermore, the pieces in both hands must be held in a straight line. All of this may seem awkward or even impossible to the beginner, but after some practice it will become second nature.

In rotation, the glass is controlled by the action of the thumb and forefinger with the other fingers helping slightly. The palms may be up or down, but it is common for a right handed person to have his left palm down and right palm up (although at times it may be advantageous to have the right palm down). A good way to practice rotation is to connect two pieces of glass tubing or rod with a piece of cloth attached to each glass piece with a rubber band. Practice rotating the two pieces of glass so that no twisting or pulling or pushing occurs. Once some confidence is gained, try it with glass in the flame.

LABORATORY EXERCISE THREE

FIRE POLISHING AND ROTATION

1. Light your torch and set up a normal working flame (an 8 to 10 inch yellow flame followed by enough oxygen to get a half inch cone). Be sure to wear your glasses (this will be assumed in all further exercises). Take a short piece of 6 mm glass rod that you cut in Exercise 2. Place it in the flame slightly above the blue cone. Note the color of the flame and the glass. Remove your Didymium glasses for a moment and again observe the color of the flame and the glass. (What causes the yellow?) Note that by now the end of the rod has rounded.

2. Repeat this with a second piece of 6 mm rod after placing the hot end of the first rod away from you in a "special area" on the lab bench. This time rotate the rod and carefully watch the glass as it becomes rounded. Remove it from the flame, continuing rotation for a few seconds, and note its shape. A properly fire polished rod should be smooth and round and no larger in any place than the diameter of the original rod.

3. Now repeat this with smaller rod (4 or 5 mm) and then also with larger rod (8 mm). Note the length of time needed for the fire polishing in each case.

4. Do the same with several pieces of glass tubing (also from Exercise No. 2). These will fire polish very quickly. Remember that you do not want the ends to close up at all.

5. Once you have mastered this, take one piece of tubing and allow the end to remain in the flame for a longer period of time (with rotation). Note carefully what happens each step along the way. (How would you describe the resultant product?)

ANNEALING

If a piece of glassware is removed from a hot flame immediately after completion, chances are that it will cool too quickly, develop stresses, and then begin to crack in an attempt to reduce these stresses. Even if the glass does not crack right away, it may do so later, when even the slightest additional stress is imposed. Touching or moderate warming can provide more than enough additional stress.

Stresses occur for a number of reasons. In thick pieces of glass, especially those items made solely from glass rod, the outside surfaces cool very quickly and thus contract slightly. The inside remains hot. Sometime later, the inside also cools and also tries to contract, although now an outer shell of rigid glass prevents this from happening. Thus internal stress is created. To some degree this type of stress is good. In fact, sometimes glass is deliberately "tempered" by this method. This compressive stress can be strengthening, but it must be uniform and controlled in order to be effective. Uneven internal stresses are usually destructive.

One can also think of stresses in molecular terms. When the various glass molecules in a disturbed high energy state are "frozen" or trapped (due to sudden cooling) in some unfavorable positions, the result is a stress. Glass molecules are disturbed like this every time any kind of joint or seal is made between two pieces of glass. Again, sudden cooling is the culprit.

Ideally then, glass products should be cooled very slowly from the intense temperatures needed to make joints and bends. This controlled treatment is called annealing. Correct annealing of hot glassware really involves two stages. First, a rather high temperature (called the "annealing point") is maintained. Although this is very high (1040°F or 560°C for borosilicate glass), it is considerably below the temperature necessary for normal working of the glass (2286°F or 1252°C for borosilicate glass). During this stage of annealing, the glass molecules are given sufficient time to reorganize and shift to more favorable and more stable positions. The second stage of annealing consists of the actual controlled cooling. Ideally this is done in two steps. The first step takes the glassware to about 75°F below the annealing temperature (approximately 965°F for borosilicate glass), and the second step brings the glass down to room temperature.

In practice, one usually flame anneals the product immediately after it is completed or oven anneals it at a somewhat later time, usually at the end of the day. In most cases, a combination of the two methods is used.

To flame anneal, the finished product is heated uniformly with a large bushy flame. This can be achieved right after completion of the product by increasing the gas flow considerably (about one additional full turn on the gas valve) while keeping the oxygen flow the same. After a while, the oxygen level is decreased slowly until finally it is turned off completely. At this time a fine layer of soot will begin to accumulate on the glass surface. Do not allow this to become very thick, as the black surface will actually cause the glass to lose heat even faster than before. Only a very light coating is needed to indicate that the glass object is now "cool" enough. Be careful to keep the product away from all cold drafts and off of cold table tops! If it is to be oven annealed, the best place to set it down would be in the oven. Excess soot should always be wiped off the cool item before oven annealing.

Remember that it is a good rule of thumb that the amount of time spent in flame annealing should be approximately as long as it took to make the object, and that if the glass is to be oven annealed later, approximately half the construction time is sufficient. Keep in mind, however, that this is still a rather long time!

In oven annealing, of course, one additional stage is necessary in the annealing process. The glass must be reheated to the annealing temperature. This cannot be done too quickly, as rapid heating can cause severe thermal stresses which may crack the glass. The actual times required for each stage in the annealing process depend on a number of factors, the most important being the type of glass (although in this book it is assumed that only borosilicate glass is used) and the thickness of the glass. The graph in Figure 3.13 shows the relationship of temperature and time in a normal annealing cycle. From this, one can get an idea of the approximate times required. Rather complex mathematical formulas have been developed to calculate the actual times necessary for each stage of the annealing process[5], but one can make some estimates of the time for normal glass products. Some reasonable times would be a heating phase of 30-60 minutes, an annealing phase of 15-20 minutes, an initial cooling (down to 75° below the annealing temperature) of 10-20 minutes, and a final cooling of 1-2 hours. Thicker glass may require a longer annealing and initial cooling phase; glass with thinner walls may require shorter times.

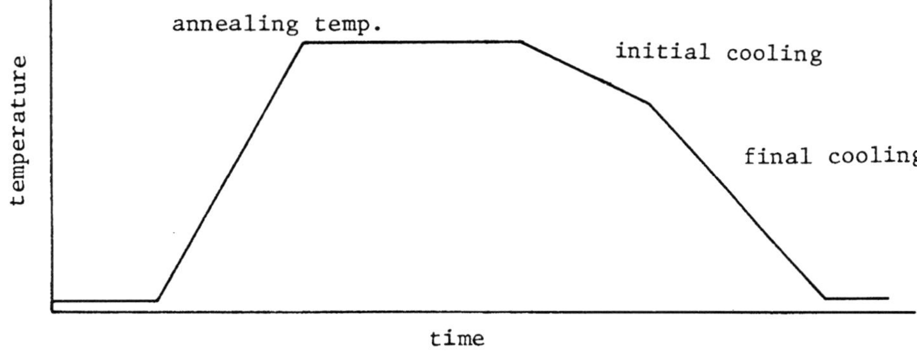

Figure 3.13 *Temperature-Time Graph showing proper cycle for annealing borosilicate glass. Note that initial cooling rate is very slow.*

In actual annealing practice, one normally raises the oven temperature slowly until the annealing temperature is reached,allows it to anneal for about 20 minutes, and then turns the oven off allowing the entire cycle (both phases) to extend over a period of three to four hours. An excellent article on the annealing process has appeared in *Fusion*.[6]

Figure 3.14 *Cooling glass item under a layer of vermiculite in a fireproof pail.*

If an annealing oven is not available or if you are working with glass having parts which have considerable thickness, a very simple yet extremely effective annealing unit can be utilized. This is simply a large metal can (such as a coffee can or old cleaned up paint can) filled with vermiculite. After a thorough flame annealing of the object, it is placed in a depression in the vermiculite (Figure 3.14). More is then poured on top to cover the object. Vermiculite is such an excellent insulator that the object will cool very slowly and very constantly, much as it would in an annealing cycle in an oven. The glass may still be too hot to remove even after 30-60 minutes. It is best to keep the glass covered for at least an hour. It is wise, therefore, to have several such annealing cans available for use. One word of caution: Always flame anneal the object thoroughly first. Do not immerse pieces that are still above the working temperature, as the vermiculite could leave marks on the soft glass.

It is important to note that safety glasses should be worn whenever handling vermiculite because the small mica particles in it can cause severe irritation to the eyes.[7]

REMOVING EXCESS GLASS

It is not uncommon to discover that you need to remove a small hunk of glass from the piece you are working on. This may be due to a jagged or uneven edge resulting from a poor cut, or there may be a small "dimple" of excess glass on a test tube end. Likewise, you may find it necessary to remove a glob of glass resulting from careless contact with another hot piece of glass.

There are a number of ways that such small excesses can be removed. Sometimes jagged edges on tubes or rods can be literally cut off with the cutting edge of a pliers. Or a wire screen can be used to “sand” the protrusions down. In other cases where the small glob of unwanted glass appears on a product, strong heating can be used to make the excess glass melt into the rest of the glass. If the glob is too large, however, as much as possible should be removed first. This can be done by wiping . The excess glass is heated with a small, hot flame. When it becomes soft, a cold glass rod (6 mm or larger) is brought up to it and is used to pull off the excess. The glob can be heated with care while the excess is being removed with the rod, but caution should be exercised so as to prevent heating too large an area. Also, the wiping rod must be cool. Once it is heated, it too may be joined to the object, and then you will have more glass than you had in the first place! It is sometimes useful to rotate the rod which is used to pull off the excess glass. After the excess has been removed, the glass product should be reheated slightly in the affected area in order to smooth out the surface. A very large excess, once softened, can also be removed quite effectively with a pair of tweezers. The excess is simply pulled out and removed in a manner similar to that described above.

Either method can also be used to advantage in removing the "dimple" of excess glass from test tube ends. Likewise, this wiping technique can be used as an alternate way to remove jagged edges from the ends of tubing. Practice will enable you to use these methods easily and effectively whenever the need arises.

CLEANING GLASS

It is important that glass be clean and dry before it is used. Dust or other dirt can cause permanent surface defects or devitrification. In some cases, products may even crack after completion as they cool. This can happen even if the item has been properly annealed.

In actual practice, cleaning is rarely needed when relatively new glass stock is used. Normally, precautions are taken to keep the glass clean and free from dust. As mentioned previously, glass should be stored flat in a dust-proof cabinet and should not be allowed to lay around the laboratory in any quantity.

However, at times it will be obvious that the glass is really dirty and does need to be cleaned. Rod can be readily cleaned with a rag dampened with distilled water. Tubing offers more of a challenge, especially if it has been stored vertically, allowing dust to get inside. In this case, in addition to wiping the exterior surface, a damp rag should be forced through the tubing. Never use a metal object to push the rag, as this may scratch the glass. Both interior and exterior surfaces should then be dried with a clean, dry, dust-free cloth. A detergent solution can be used for extremely dirty glass.

It is also important to have clean hands while glassworking. Even fingerprints can pose a problem when they become worked into the glass with a flame.

Cleaning becomes especially important to those who are involved in repair of scientific apparatus, or for that matter, in repair of any glass objects. In both of these cases, in addition to dirt that may be present, there is also the likelihood that the glass surface has aged or decomposed somewhat. This can happen simply by reaction with the moisture and other vapors in the air. In the case of chemical glassware, further reaction may have occurred by direct interaction of the glass surface with the chemicals. The sodium and calcium oxides found in the glass are especially soluble and reactive. If these are removed from the glass surface, the glass composition and therefore the glass strength is changed.

For such pieces of glassware, it is important to do a very thorough job of cleaning. In fact, it is best to remove the surface of the glass so as to once again expose fresh glass of constant composition. This can be accomplished by soaking the glassware for about twenty minutes in a 2% water solution of hydrofluoric acid for cleaning glass. Protective gloves and eye wear must be used, and the solution should be stored in a plastic pail. Hydrofluoric acid is an extremely dangerous acid and can cause very severe burns.[8] Only authorized persons should use this solution, and only a knowledgeable chemist or glassblower should dispense the concentrated acid (See Appendix A).

After cleaning in the hydrofluoric acid solution, the glass can be immersed for several minutes in a 5% solution of sodium hydroxide and then thoroughly rinsed with distilled water.

Special caution should be exercised if organic solvents (e.g. acetone) are used to clean the glassware. It is very important to make sure that the solvent is totally evaporated before heating the glass surface. Remaining solvent may form an explosive mixture with the air. Never use benzene, carbontetrachlorde or trichloretylene (old solvents once utilized) to clean glassware!

No matter how much effort is spent in cleaning old glass surfaces, it should be remembered that there is no substitute whatsoever for fresh, clean glass stock.

GLASS DEVITRIFICATION

Some operations you perform while glassblowing may produce a condition known as devitrification. Generally this appears as a whitish coating on or near the place you just finished working. Some glass workers choose to describe this process as "wrinkling" rather than devitrification.

Whatever it is called, one generally wants to avoid its formation and one needs to know how to remove it.

Just as there is controversy as to its name, there is also disagreement on the exact cause of this phenomenon. Some proposals include chemical changes such as reduction of the glass or decomposition of the glass (loss of sodium). But the author-chemist-glassblower believes that the evidence favors that it is simply a physical change. This phase change occurs when conditions cause the normally amorphous glass to begin to crystallize on the surface. In other words, the normal chaotic, nonuniform internal structure of the glass begins to become well ordered (crystallized). Thus, for purposes of this book, we will define devitrification as undesired microcrystallization on the glass surface.

This usually shows up when glass is manipulated at a temperature below its normal working range. Let us briefly consider an analogy to the situation in a supersaturated solution. Such solutions actually have been tricked into allowing more solute to dissolve than normally permitted at that temperature. These can remain as supersaturated solutions for long periods of time, but if these are stirred, crystallization occurs immediately.

Glass is analogous to the supersaturated solution as by all rights, it really should crystallize, but it doesn't. It remains "stuck" in this amorphous form (without regular internal structure). Manipulating it below its working temperature (too cool) is like stirring the supersaturated solution, as the movement allows some of the "glass molecules" to become ordered (crystallized). Since the surface cools and solidifies more rapidly, this causes the crystallization to remain.

Whatever its true cause, we need to discuss how to avoid it, and this can be stated quite simply. Don't perform operations on the glass when it is too cool to be worked. Never force glass to bend or stretch when it does so reluctantly. This resistance is telling you that you are working (manipulating) the glass at a temperature which is too cool. It might be noted that although we will focus on avoiding devitrification, some art workers try to stimulate its formation to produce an opaque surface.

Fortunately, should devitrification occur, it is quite easy to remove. Generally, a light "brushing" of the surface with a small hot flame will cause the milky whitish surface to become clear once again.

IDENTIFICATION OF BOROSILICATE GLASS

It is assumed throughout this entire book that borosilicate glass will always be used. The reasons for the superiority of borosilicate glass have already been discussed. Also, it must be emphasized that one never mixes two different types of glasses in constructing a product. Probably no one would do so knowingly, but it has happened many times that someone has inadvertently placed a piece of soft glass on the laboratory bench. After a product is completed is a bad time to discover that part of it was made from soft glass! Always be wary of unfamiliar glass stock.

Also, at times a person may be faced with repair of an artistic object or a piece of scientific apparatus. In each of these cases it is wise to take a few minutes to test the glass to see if it is really borosilicate. There are a number of different methods that may be used.

LIQUID METHOD

Probably the simplest method involves immersing the glass in question in a liquid that has exactly the same index of refraction as does borosilicate glass (n_D=1.479).[9] Years ago, the most commonly used liquids were solutions containing 59 volumes of carbon tetrachloride and 41 volumes of benzene or 16 volumes of methanol and 84 volumes of benzene.[10] However, we now know that both of these pose very serious health concerns. Carbon tetrachloride and benzene should never be used in any glass lab.[10]

A reasonable substitute would be pure trichloroethylene (n_D=1.4773).[11] This has essentially the same index of refraction as does borosilicate glass. Keep in mind that this is still a rather dangerous organic compound, as it is known to be a kidney and liver toxin.[10] Thus if used, keep in a closed bottle and use only with great caution and with productive gloves. Some workers have also used pure dimethyl sulfoxide (since it has the same index of refraction), but this is not only a smelly substance, but now recognized to present other health hazards.

When borosilicate glass is placed into the trichloroethylene, it seems to disappear. Other types of glasses remain clearly visible. It is a good idea to keep a piece of borosilicate glass and a piece of soft glass immersed in your test solution at all times to aid in determining the nature of the questionable piece of glass. But keep the bottle closed tighly!

PHENOLPHTHALEIN METHOD

A small amount of a phenolphthalein-ethanol solution is evaporated on the unglazed reverse side of a porcelain spot plate. A drop of water is then added to the area, and the questionable piece of glass is drawn briskly across the spot. The rough porcelain surface fractures the glass surface. If the glass was soft glass, enough alkali will be released to turn the phenolphthalein pink.[12] Borosilicate glass shows no such color development.

GAS-AIR FLAME TEST METHOD

A third method to test for borosilicate glass is to attempt to work it in a gas-air flame. (Be sure to use a gas-air tip on the torch for the test.) If a seal can be made between the unknown piece of glass and a known of soft glass (don't misplace the soft glass!) then it can be certain that the unknown piece of glass was also soft. If the glass was borosilicate, it simply will not soften enough to make a seal in the gas-air flame.

GLASS SPHERE TEST METHOD

Another method of testing involves the sealing of a small piece of unknown glass to the end of a borosilicate rod using the usual gas-oxygen torch. The mixture is then heated so as to form a small glass sphere. A stream of air is then passed over the hot sphere. If the unknown piece was also borosilicate, nothing will happen. If the unknown piece was not borosilicate, the sphere will show numerous cracks upon the sudden cooling

THREAD METHODS

Two other techniques involve the formation of thin threads made up of a mixture of glass known to be borosilicate and the unknown sample.

In the first method, a piece of known borosilicate is held alongside the unknown glass. The melted junction is then grabbed with a pair of pliers or forceps and pulled into a small fiber (Figure 3.15). If upon cooling, the drawn glass fiber remains straight, both pieces were the same composition, implying that the unknown sample was also borosilicate. If it curves, (Figure 3.15b) the glasses were different; thus the sample was not borosilicate (the glass on the inside of the curve has the higher coefficient of expansion).

In the second method, the ends of both pieces of glass (a known borosilicate sample and the unknown sample) are heated until they melt (Figure 3.16a). They are then overlapped and physically joined by using a pair of pliers or forceps (Figure 3.16b). Then without twisting the junction, the center of the joint is heated strongly (Figure 3.16c) and then rapidly stretched out (Figure 3.16d) to a very long thread (over 24 inches). The smaller the diameter of the thread, the better the test. Again, the formation of a straight thread

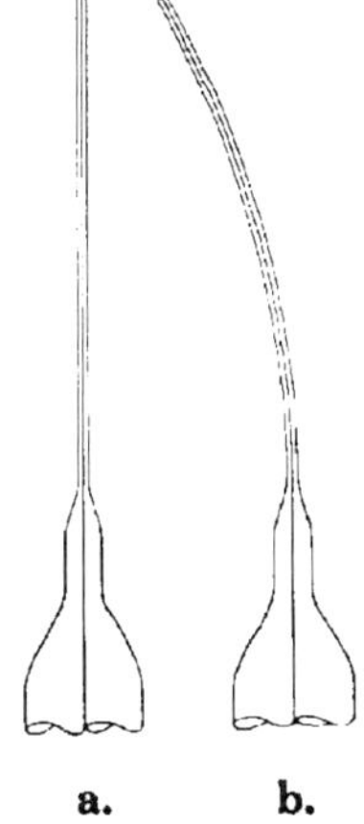

Figure 3.15 *Thread method one.*
***a.** Same glasses.*
***b.** Different.*

(3.16e) indicates that both glasses were of the same type. A curling of the thread (3.16f) indicates that the samples were different.

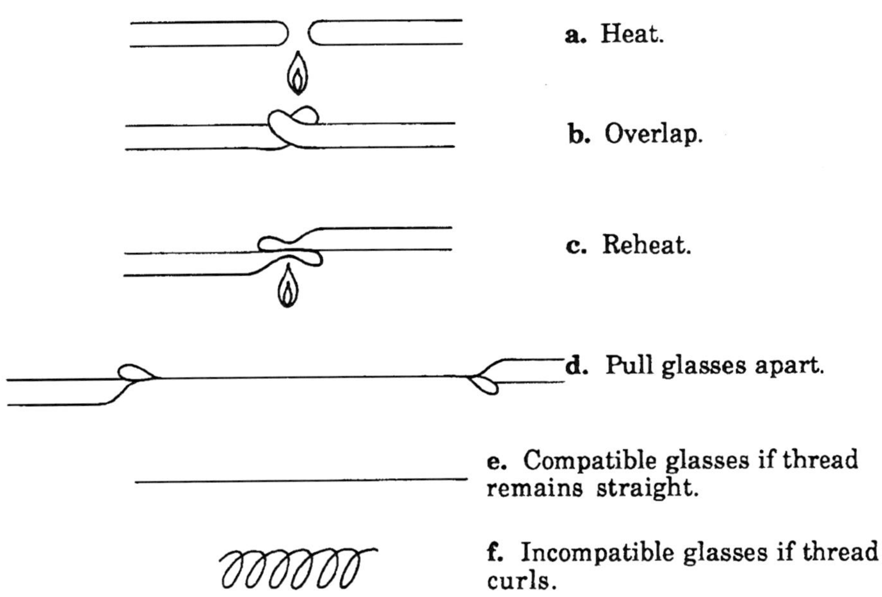

Figure 3.16 *Thread method two. Another method for testing to determining whether two glass samples are of the same type of glass.*

ENDNOTES

1. J. H. Pirolo, "The Color, Composition and Tempertures of Flames Most Commonly Used for Scientific Glassblowing", *Proceedings of the 38th Symposium on the Art of Scientific Glassblowing, American Scientific Glassblowers Society,* pp 42-47, 1993.

2. T.A. Michalske and B.C. Bunker, "The Fracturing of Glass", Sci. Amer., Vol. 257, 1987, pp 122-129.

3. L.H. Milligan, *J. Soc. Glass Technol.*, Vol. 13, 1929, p. 351.

4. T.A. Michalske and B.C. Bunker.

5. F. Schuler, *Flameworking: Glassmaking for the Craftsman*, 1968, p. 122-126.

6. M. Olsen, "Holding and Annealing Oven Techniques", *Fusion*, Aug., 1988, pp. 26-29.

7. A.G. Macenski, *Fusion*, Nov., 1981, p.45.

8. Hydrofluoric acid burns should be washed with cold water for at least 15 minutes. After drying the skin, a gel containing 2.5% calcium gluconate is then applied. Contact a physician immediately. (M.J. Lefevre, *First Aid Manual for Chemical Accidents*, Dowden, Hutchinson & Ross, Inc., Stroudsburg, PA, 1980, p 171).

9. The index of refraction of any substance is a measure of the extent to which light is bent by the substance. All substances bend light to some degree and most substances do so to a different degree. Thus most substances have different indexes of refraction. The index of refraction of borosilicate glass is 1.479.

10. G.E,Meyers and J.S. Gregar, Health Hazards in the Glass Shop, Proceedings of the 35th Symposium on the Art of Scientific Glassblowing, American Scientific Glassblowers Society, pp 19-23, 1990.

11. Laboratory Glass Blowing with Corning's Glasses, Corning Glass Works, 1969, p. 2.

12. W. H. Brown, *J. Chem. Ed.*, Vol. 56, 1979, p. 692.

Chapter 4
FLAMEWORKING WITH SOLID ROD

One normally associates rod flameworking (glassworking) with products such as artistic knickknacks or glass sculptures. This is certainly true to some degree, but even scientific glassware occasionally requires the use of rod. Furthermore, the principles of rod working are important to all students of glassblowing. Therefore, it is wise for even the purely scientific worker to become acquainted with at least the basic operations of rod working.

EFFECTS OF SURFACE TENSION AND GRAVITY

Since rod is solid glass, a significant amount of mass is involved in any simple operation. Thus, when in the molten state, it is especially important to understand and to utilize the natural forces that are acting. The two most important forces to consider are surface tension and gravity.

Surface tension is the force that causes the surface of any liquid to contract to the smallest possible area. Ideally this minimum area would be a sphere. All of us are familiar enough with gravity. It would tend to flatten out a liquid drop, making its surface area a maximum. Therefore, with both gravity and surface tension acting, the result may be anywhere between the extremes. For example, very few raindrops that fall on your car are ever seen as perfect spheres, nor are they totally flattened out.

EFFECTS OF ROTATION AND SLOPE OF GLASS

The mark of a successful glassblower is that he or she has learned not only how to combat the forces of surface tension and gravity when necessary, but also how to use them effectively whenever possible. We have just seen that without gravity, any liquid would assume the shape of a sphere. But gravity is real, and therefore, to get a perfect sphere, one has to negate it, at least to some degree. This is done by controlled rotation of the glass rotation (this takes care of gravity compensation in two dimensions) and by changing the slope or slant of the rod with respect to the flame (slope adjustment is much the same as rotation about the third axis). Sometimes it is more difficult to change slope than it is to rotate, but it is just as important.

Experience is, of course, the best teacher. Several weeks of work is often sufficient to begin to acquire this feel for glass and the forces acting on it. Thus, the best way to learn about rod working is to experiment. For this reason, much of what we want to say about rod will be done by means of laboratory exercises.

LABORATORY EXERCISE FOUR

EXPERIMENTING WITH EFFECTS OF SURFACE TENSION, GRAVITY, ROTATION, AND SLOPE

1. Light your torch and adjust it to a standard flame. Heat the end of a 6 inch piece of 5 mm rod in the flame (always slightly above the blue cone), but do so without rotation. The rod should be held in a position perpendicular to the flame. As the glass softens, gravity begins to act on it. Soon a piece of glass will dangle from a thread of glass (Figure 4.1). Finish breaking the 4 mm rod into pieces using your glass knife. Then repeat this procedure with a two foot piece of 5 mm rod using only your glass knife. Save the pieces.

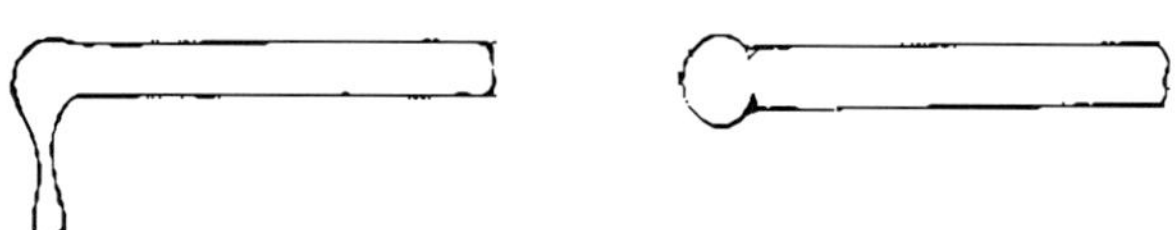

Figure 4.1
Left: *Glass heated strongly without any rotation.*
Right: *Glass heated strongly with proper rotation.*

2. Knock this end off in the waste container and now repeat the experiment with rotation. If you slope the rod upward slightly (hand slightly lower than the rod tip) and if you rotate evenly, you should note that the molten glass begins to flow toward you, thickening the rod and taking the shape of a sphere (Figure 4.2b). The rotary motion, together with the slight slope allows gravity to exert its pull evenly.

3. Now repeat the procedure using another rod, but slope the rod downward (hand higher than the rod tip). Rotate in such a way so as to keep the glass shape on the axis of the glass rod. Rotate whichever direction and as rapidly as needed to keep the shape along the axis. Constant rotation may not be required; only rotate as much as necessary. Do not allow the glass to become too thin so that it begins to drop off. Note the resulting teardrop shape (Figure 4.2c). You will discover that in order to make a larger teardrop shape, it will be necessary to gather a sufficient amount of glass by first forming a spherical or even squat shape (i.e. by holding the rod, with rotation, at an angle of 45° upward). Then, when enough glass has been melted, the rod is sloped downward, as done previously, until the desired teardrop shape is attained. A similar procedure will be necessary to produce large spherical shapes.

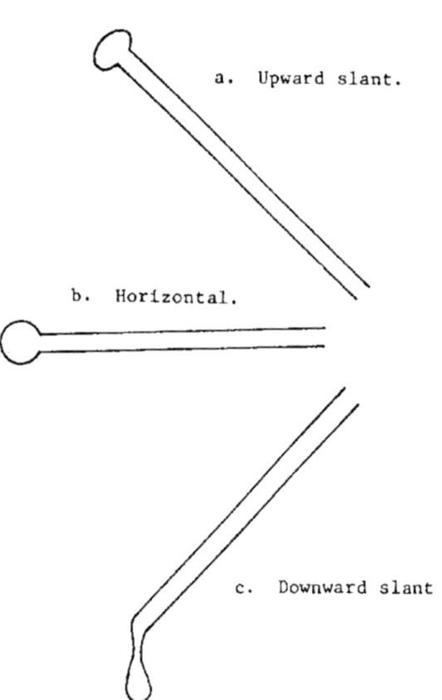

Figure 4.2 *Effect of rotation and slope on masses of hot gathered glass.*

4. Repeat once again, but now slope the rod sharply upward. Again rotate so as to keep the glass shape along the axis of the rod. After a while, a doorknob or squat shape should form on the end of the rod (Figure 4.2a). Do not try to make this shape overly large at this point. If you have trouble obtaining this squat shape, it is likely that your flame is not large enough or hot enough.

5. Start again using a new piece of rod (6 mm) and first make a definite, knob shape (slope up). Then attempt to convert this shape into a perfect sphere (some downward slope will be necessary at first). Finally, convert this sphere shape into a teardrop form, keeping the shape along the axis of the rod. Once this has been accomplished, try to go back to a spherical form (change to slope upward again). Heating and rotation should be done as necessary during the entire exercise. This cycle should be repeated several times until you feel that you can go from one shape to another with ease and confidence. Take a two foot piece of 4 mm rod and cut two or three 6 inch pieces using the triangular file. Save the pieces for later exercises. Remember, if you need to exert a lot of pressure on the glass, you are doing something wrong. Small diameter rod should break with ease.

THE CONSTRUCTION OF MARIAS

END MARIAS

Often it may be desirable or necessary to have a flattened end on a rod. Such shapes find extensive use as an intermediate step in many scientific and artistic glassworking procedures. These flattened portions or disk-like bulges are called marias.

The so-called end marias are quite easy to form. The end of a glass rod is uniformly heated to softness. The rod is then pushed straight down onto a graphite plate (Figure 4.3). If a graphite plate is not available, any fire resistant board can be used, but quite often such boards leave a pattern on the glass or small loose pieces of fiber may become incorporated into the maria. For these reasons, a graphite plate is strongly recommended. Never form marias by pressing hot glass onto the top of the glassworking bench. Always use a separate plate.

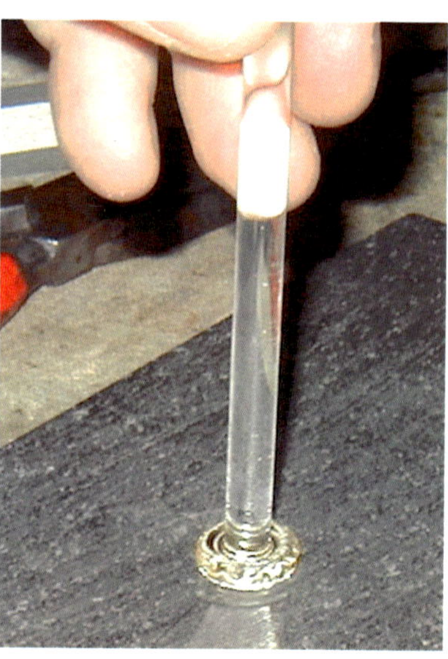

Figure 4.3 *Making an end maria on a graphite plate.*

The size of the maria is determined by the size of the rod, the amount of rod softened, and the amount of pressure used to form the maria. The downward pressure must be exerted in such a way so as to keep the rod perfectly straight up and down, otherwise the maria will not be centered. Care must also be taken to prevent sliding or slipping of the maria as it is being formed, or else one part of it will become thicker than the rest. However, if it is seen that the maria being formed is off center or is developing a thicker portion, sliding may be encouraged so as to re-center or shift some of the glass.

LABORATORY EXERCISE FIVE

CONSTRUCTION OF END MARIAS

1. Carefully soften the end of a 5 mm rod and try to form a well-centered end maria. Be sure to press evenly while keeping the rod absolutely perpendicular to the graphite plate.

2. After forming the maria, cut it off using the cutting edge of your pliers (see instructions for this kind of cutting on page 51).

3. Repeat the process, making such marias until you become confident with the method. Try to vary the size of the maria by heating a larger (or smaller) rod area or by pressing harder (or softer) on the graphite plate.

   Be certain that you are controlling the size of the maria and that differences do not occur simply by chance. (How would you describe the actual shape of the maria? Is it perfectly flat and disk-like?)

4. Make some additional marias from 4 mm and 6 mm rod.

INTERMEDIATE MARIAS (BULGES)

An intermediate maria is very similar to the end maria, except that it occurs in the middle of a piece of glass rod. It too is used extensively in the construction of a wide range of artistic and scientific products. Undoubtedly, one could form such an intermediate maria by first making an end maria, and then adding a second rod to the flattened side. In fact, in some cases this is done, but most often such marias are formed in one step. This is done by heating an intermediate zone of glass rod (with rotation), removing it from the flame (still rotating in order to keep the temperature uniform), and then gradually pushing the ends of the rod together while continuing rotation. When completed, examination of the work at eye level should reveal a uniform maria as well as aligned rods on either side of the maria (Figure 4.4).

Unfortunately, these intermediate marias are not as easy to make as the end marias. Sometimes the glass rod slides while the maria is being formed, causing the maria to be uneven. This also makes the rods on either side nonlinear. Probably the most common errors are caused by overheating the rod before pushing together or by failing to rotate the glass while pushing together. Such errors can be corrected (as with end marias) by making the rod slip over on purpose while the glass is still hot. This should return the rods to linearity once again and may also redistribute the glass from the uneven portions of the maria. If necessary, completed marias can be carefully reheated to allow correction of some of the errors.

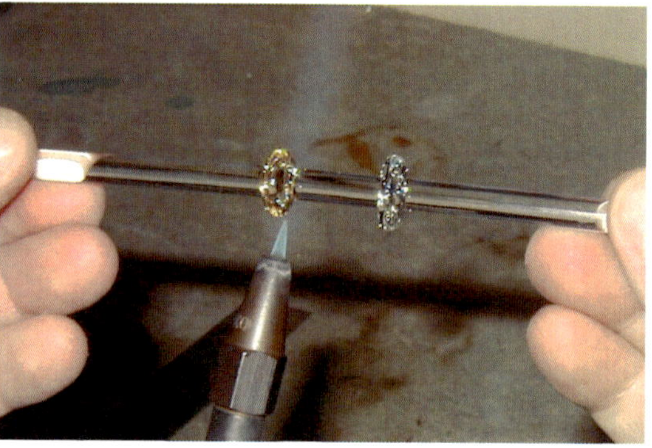

Figure 4.4 *Making intermediate marias.*

LABORATORY EXERCISE SIX

CONSTRUCTION OF INTERMEDIATE MARIAS

1. Start with a 12 inch length of 6 mm rod. (Smaller rod will be more difficult to control.) Follow the instructions given above to form a well centered and uniform maria. Take care to realign the rods while they are still hot.

2. Repeat by making a second maria about 1 inch to the right of the first, and then a third maria about 1 inch to the left of the first.

3. Once you get the feel of the pushing procedure and are able to control the sliding, try to regulate the size of the maria formed.

Heat a larger area (or smaller). Push together harder (or softer). Then attempt to make marias that are exactly twice the diameter of the rod.

4. Now try to make intermediate marias from 5 mm and then 4 mm rod.

FLAME CUTS, CONSTRICTIONS, AND DRAWING OUT

FLAME CUTS

In actual practice, flame cuts are used extensively, although seldom discussed. In this method, the tubing or rod is separated by melting the glass. This is one of the few operations that is done in the flame. In most other procedures, the rod or tubing is heated in the flame, but manipulation is done outside of the flame.

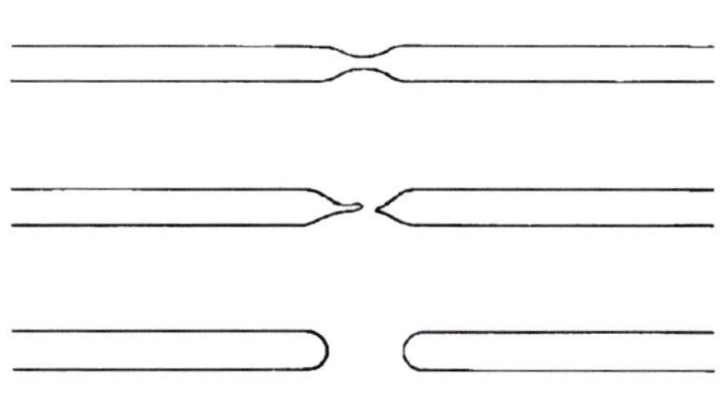

Figure 4.5 *The three distinct steps in making a flame cut. The first two steps are done in the flame. Finished ends are then fire polished.*

A rather hot flame is required, but the piece must be heated gently at first in order to prevent shattering due to sudden thermal stress. After the glass becomes thoroughly softened, a slight outward pull is exerted (Figures 4.5 - 4.8). The middle of the heated portion will shrink considerably and then finally "burn off" (become detached). If the "flame cut" is done incorrectly (outside the flame), a long, thin thread of glass will form between the two pieces. Avoid producing these thin strands of glass!

Figure 4.6 *Beginning the flame cut (Out of flame only for photo!)*

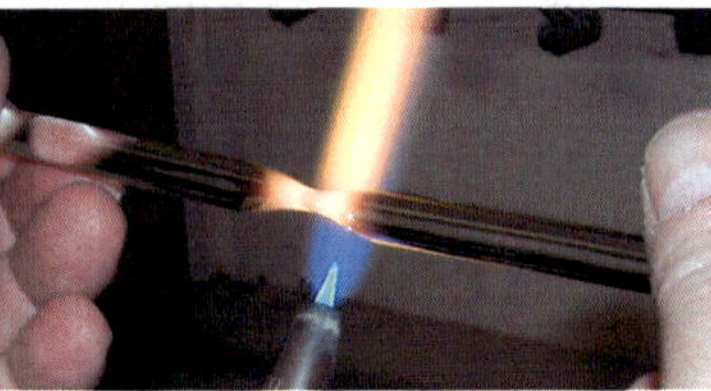

Figure 4.7 *Continuing the flame cut (Out of flame only for photo!)*

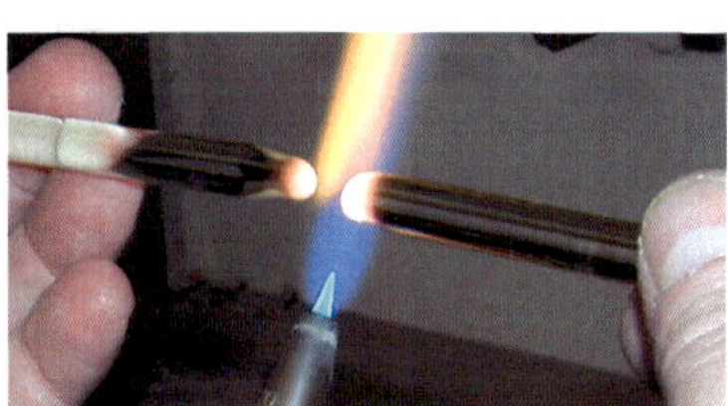

Figure 4.8 *The completed flame cut.*

LABORATORY EXERCISE SEVEN

FLAME CUTTING

1. Take a piece of 5 mm rod and gently heat the middle portion. Be sure to preheat the glass to prevent cracking.

2. Now lower the rod to the hottest part of the flame (slightly above the blue cone), rotate the glass, and then pull out the ends of the rod while keeping the middle portion of the rod in the flame. (Do not pull the rod very strongly. In this exercise stretch it a maximum of 3/4 to 1 inch.) Note that as the glass rod is pulled out, the middle section becomes thinner and hotter.

3. Soon, without any additional pulling, the glass will "burn" apart and the two severed ends will become fire polished (Figure 4.8). Uniform rotation must be maintained throughout this entire exercise. Repeat this several times using different diameter rod.

CONSTRICTIONS

In many cases it is necessary to reduce the rod diameter or to draw out a piece of glass from a larger rod. Often the drawn rod is shaped with graceful curves by manipulation just before the rod cools. Such is the case in the fashioning of animal tails and pump handles.

Constrictions in the middle of a piece of rod are done rather easily by heating the rod uniformly at the place to be constricted, taking the glass out of the flame, and then carefully pulling outward. Uniform rotation must be continued in every step of the process. Flame cutting is somewhat similar, but with flame cutting, the pulling is done in the flame. In making constrictions, the pulling is done outside of the flame. The thickness and the length of the constriction depend on the area of rod heated, the intensity of the heating, and the rate of the pulling motion.

Many times constrictions are made to serve as a handle. This is usually referred to as pulling a point (Figure 4.9). The procedure outlined above is followed; the resulting thin section should be about 4 mm in diameter as it must be strong enough to serve as a handle. The point is flame cut at approximately 4 inches (or longer or shorter as desired). It is quite common to pull a point on both sides of a piece of thick rod (Figure 4.10). In this way one can work on the necessary portion of the rod while not wasting a larger amount of it. For such cases, a point may be pulled close to the end of the rod by using a pair of pliers or forceps to hold on to it and pull.

Figure 4.9 *Pulling a point or constriction on a glass rod.*

Figure 4.10 *Pulling a point or constriction on both sides of a section of rod.*

LABORATORY EXERCISE EIGHT

CONSTRICTIONS AND PULLING POINTS

1. Uniformly heat the center portion of an 8 inch piece of 8 mm rod; remove from the flame and pull on the ends. Note that the thinnest section cools more quickly and becomes rigid first. Also note that the glass will continue to be "pulled out" of the hotter section where the rod is thicker.

2. Repeat the process a number of times, paying particular attention to the feel of the glass and the color of the flame which is a reflection of the temperature. Try to control the diameter so that it is exactly 2 mm (measure it). Then try to control the length of the constriction so that it is exactly 4 inches long. Eventually, try to control both the diameter and the length simultaneously.

3. Make several two-sided points with 1 inch of 8 mm rod in between. Use a forceps or pliers to aid in the making of points near the end of the rod.

DRAWING OUT AND FORMING SHAPES

Drawing out rod involves a technique similar to that of making constrictions, but is better described as a longer constriction which is often fashioned into designs as cooling occurs. Drawn glass is usually made by softening a large amount of glass at the end of a rod, attaching this to another piece of glass, and then pulling this out. The thinner rod is then continually drawn out of the thicker mass of glass and may be fashioned as it cools. Needless to say, this technique requires a little more practice than does the formation of a simple constriction. The technique, however, is used widely in artistic glassworking and therefore, must be mastered.

One very common problem encountered when a large length of glass is to be drawn out is that the resulting constriction may be lumpy. This is due to cold spots in the rod interior and is a reflection of incorrect heating procedures. Perhaps the rod was not rotated evenly, or the rod may not have been heated strongly enough or long enough. But most often the error is due to heating with too strong a flame. This causes the outside of the rod to heat up very quickly. In fact, some bubbling due to overheating and thermal decomposition of the glass may be evident. The glass may feel very soft, but the fact is that insufficient heat is transferred to the rod interior. This will almost always result in a lumpy product. Thus, a somewhat cooler flame should be used, and heating should be continued for a slightly longer period of time.

LABORATORY EXERCISE NINE

DRAWING OUT RODS
MAKING SCROLL SHAPES

1. Soften a one-half inch area at the end of a 6 mm rod by heating it while holding and rotating it with your right hand. Heating should be continued until the glass glows with a uniform redness over the entire heated area. It is neither necessary nor desirable to continue heating beyond this point. This rod will be called the working rod.

2. Meanwhile, preheat a small area of a second 6 mm rod (this will be called the base rod) at a point about one-half inch from the end.

3. Once the glass on the working rod is sufficiently heated, heat the end of it one last time, and then attach it to the side of the base rod in the flame (Figure 4.11).

4. Remove the rod from the flame and immediately begin to pull it slowly outward (Figure 4.12).
5. When you feel that it has hardened, flame cut the piece at the point where it begins to thicken again. Obviously, the longer or larger the drawn out spike you wish to make, the greater the length of glass that will have to be heated and softened on the working rod.
6. Repeat the process by attaching and drawing out a second glob of glass at a point just below the first drawn rod (or spike). Continue this exercise a number of times, but each time study the effect of heating, rate of pulling, and amount of softened glass.
7. Once you begin to get the feel of the glass, try to shape the drawn portions. Just before the drawn rod hardens, push the working rod downward and inward. A scroll shape should result (Figure 4.13). Experiment with this and other shapes until you feel confident that you could make the shapes desired and reproduce the same shape, the same size, a number of times.

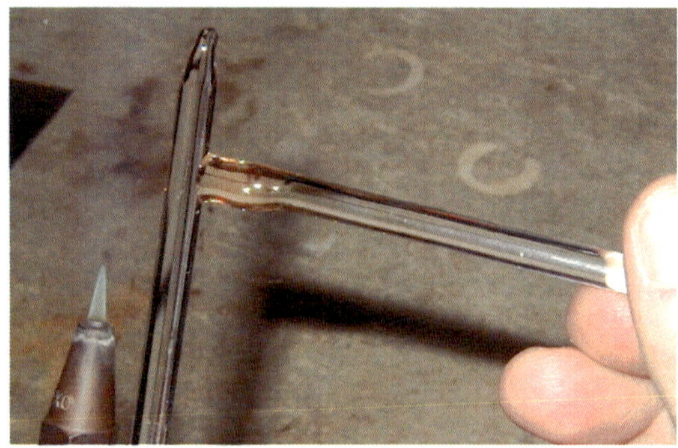

Figure 4.11 *Softened rod is attached to the side of the base rod. This is done in the flame.*

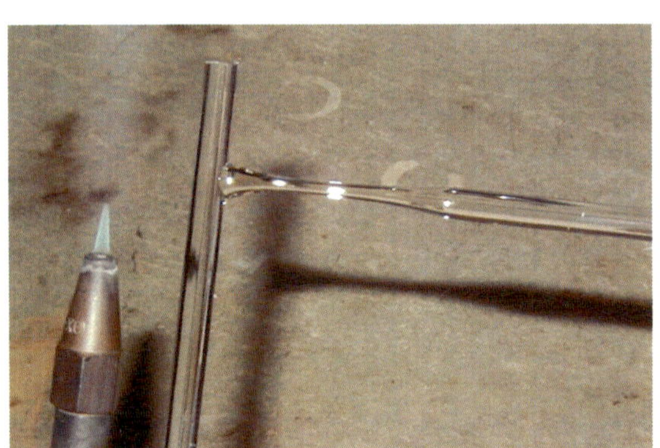

Figure 4.12 *Softened rod is pulled outward. This is done outside the flame.*

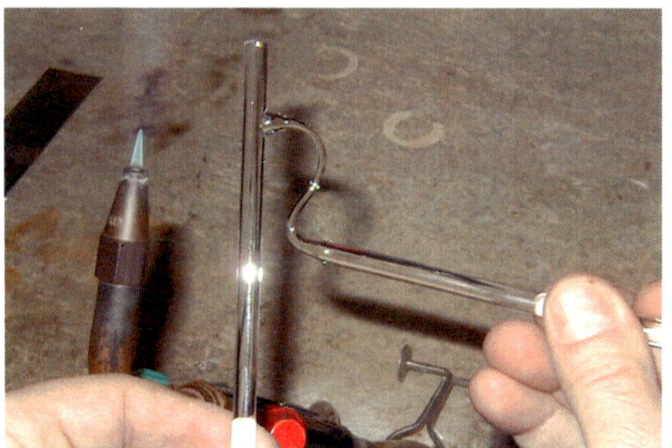

Figure 4.13 *Scroll shape is formed outside the flame. The working rod is then flame cut.*

INCREASING ROD DIAMETER

The formation of marias certainly is one way of increasing rod diameter, but sometimes a larger bulge or mass of glass is required, as in the formation of heads on small glass animals or in more complex rod sculptures. In these cases, the glass rod is heated strongly with rotation until the end becomes uniformly soft. Then the ends are pushed together with continued rotation. In situations where a very large amount of glass is to be built up, the pushing can be done (always with rotation) while the glass rod is held in the flame. In fact, the hottest part of the flame should be directed continuously at the junction of the bulge with the rod (Figure 4.14). In this way, the softened glass can be continuously pushed into the bulge until the proper size is obtained.

.

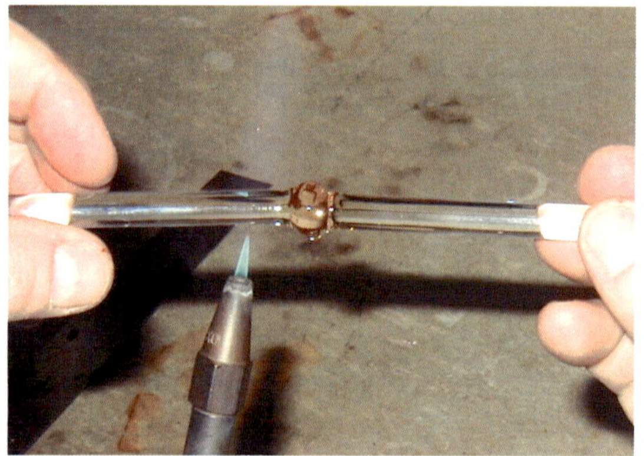

Figure 4.14 *Increasing rod diameter by pushing in while rotating in flame.*

Figure 4.15 *Forming point handles on thickened portion of rod.*

It is very common to do this type of thickening on a rod furnished with points as handles (Figure 4.15). Care must be taken to prevent the handles from being heated; otherwise they will become soft and useless in your shaping efforts. One or both of the points can later be removed if desired. Remember that very thick glass must be annealed immediately or else it must be cooled very slowly in a can filled with vermiculite.

LABORATORY EXERCISE TEN

THICKENING ROD

1. Heat a 6 inch piece of 6 mm rod in the middle with rotation.
2. After it becomes softened, push the ends in while continuing to heat the enlarging bulge.

3. Now direct the heating to one side at the junction of the bulge and the rod. Continue rotation and pushing.

4. Now reheat the entire thick portion to make it uniform, as the original bulge may be far from uniform.

5. Remove the shape from the flame and continue rotation until the glass has cooled with the protruding rods linear to one another.

6. Repeat this exercise using one of the 1 inch 8mm rod Points constructed in Exercise No. 8. Use care in heating so that the point handles do not become softened. Often it is wise to tilt the glass piece so that the point closest to the heating is aimed downward. This will allow the flame to play directly on the rod/bulge junction and keep the handle as cool as possible (since heat rises).

   Try to form a sphere between the two handles. This may be quite difficult. One of the handles should then be removed by flame cutting, and the end rounded by continued heating and rotation.

7. Repeat the exercise again using another 8mm Point, but now try to make the shape oblong.

USE OF TOOLS FOR SHAPING

So far we have examined the methods of making the most common and most useful shapes. The teardrop (oblong), doorknob (squat), sphere, maria, bulge, and constriction will each prove to be the basis of many artistic and scientific products. Various combinations or variations of these can yield an almost unlimited variety of shapes and forms.

But there is another endless category of shapes that we have not yet discussed. These are made with the help of various tools, and almost anything can be considered to be a shaping tool. Pliers, forceps, wire brushes, edges of files, ends of files, or edges and ends of almost anything nonflammable can be used to impart patterns into the glass. The possibilities are limited only by your imagination. Furthermore, the shapes or patterns you impart to the hot glass can be changed or modified by using some of the shaping methods described previously. For example, a piece of glass scored with the edge of a file can be drawn out and become the wing of a bird.

Let's look briefly at a few specific tools and some possible uses, but remember that these are only suggestions to whet your imagination. No doubt you can come up with many more, but be sure to remember that only clean, nonflammable objects should be used.

MARVER (CARBON PADDLE)

The marver is one of the simplest shaping tools and is basically just a portable graphite plate. Obviously, this tool produces flat surfaces. When it is difficult or impossible to lower the hot glass to a graphite plate, bring the graphite plate (marver) to the glass. Or, if you wish to flatten a piece of rod along the axis, the rod can be heated and pressed between the marver and a graphite plate (Figure 4.16).

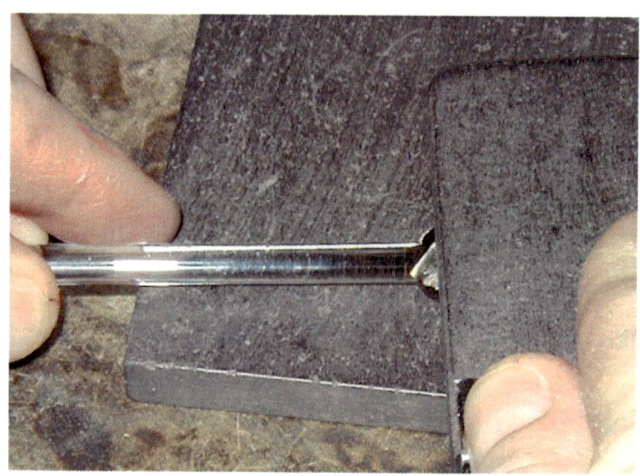

Figure 4.16 *Flattening a piece of rod with a marver on a graphite plate.*

PLIERS OR FORCEPS

Usually the tips of needlenose pliers and forceps are patterned. These patterns, as well as the shapes of the plier or forcep tips, can be imparted with ease to softened rod (Figure 4.17). Glass shaped in this way has a number of uses. With a little imagination, the rod becomes a leaf on a tree or a petal on a flower. The possibilities are endless.

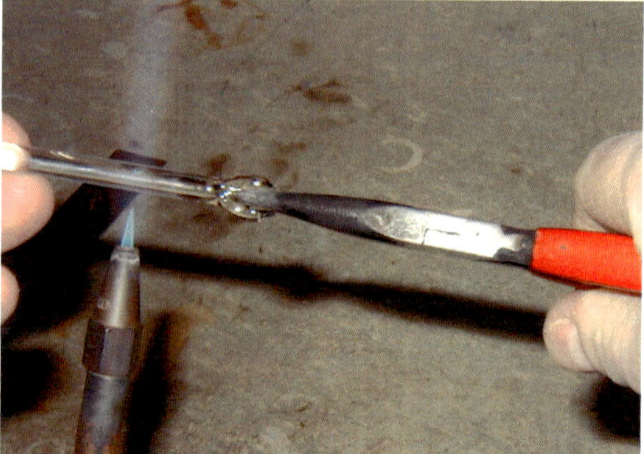

Figure 4.17 *Imparting a pattern on a piece of rod with a pair of needlenose pliers.*

TRIANGULAR FILE

Even if the triangular file is not used for cutting (since one probably uses a glass knife), such a file may be one of your most important tools.

One of the more popular uses has already been mentioned. Wings of birds, wings of angels, flower petals, or leaves can be fashioned by scoring the end of a hot glass rod two or three times with the plain edge (the handle) of the file (Figure 4.18), sealing this scored edge to another piece of glass, reheating it, drawing it out, and finally flame cutting it at the proper length.

Figure 4.18 *Imparting pattern on a piece of rod with the plain edge of a triangular file.*

With experience, you will discover more and more potential tools. As said before, the possibilities are endless.

JOINING GLASS ROD

Undoubtedly, joining glass rod is one of the most important and one of the most universal operations in glassworking. It can be a very simple procedure, as in joining two rods of the same diameter, or it can be rather complex, as in joining rod to blown glass forms. Right now we will look at the simpler procedure and work up to more complex situations.

SPOT WELDING METHOD

If two rods of the same diameter are to be joined, both ends must be heated simultaneously in the flame. This can be rather tricky since they should not touch one another before making the joint. If you are very steady-handed, or if the flame is quite large, both pieces can be heated at the same time at the same level in the flame. If you are less steady or if the flame is small, one rod can be heated lower in the flame and the other above it. The positions are then changed a number of times in order to insure that both are evenly heated. Uniform rotation is of great importance in this entire procedure. The heating is continued until both tips are softened or fire polished and appear to be the same color. The ends, however, should not become enlarged. Flame color is an important key to knowing flame temperature. Make every effort to become familiar with the various hues of orange and the approximate degrees of softness that they indicate.

Both ends are then removed from the flame and pressed together with care. The rods should meet evenly so that they form a straight line.

They should be pressed together slightly so that the junction forms a bulge somewhat larger than the rod diameter. The junction is immediately placed back into the hottest part of the flame and held without rotation until the glass melts together in that spot. The joint is then removed from the flame for a few seconds, rotated slightly, and returned to the flame so that a second area can be fused in a similar way. Allowing the joint to cool a little between heatings will make the glass easier to control. This is repeated until the rod is joined all the way around. After the final heating, the ends are pulled slightly so that the junction becomes smooth and is returned to the original rod diameter. While it is cooling, continue rotation near eye level and adjust the rod positions so that the resulting product is perfectly straight. For obvious reasons, this is often referred to as the spot welding method of making seals. In the next section, an alternate approach will be discussed.

LABORATORY EXERCISE ELEVEN

JOINING GLASS RODS USING THE SPOT WELDING TECHNIQUE

1. Obtain two short pieces of 6mm rod. Do not use pieces under 3 inches long until you are more experienced. Pieces cut in Exercise No. 1 are ideal for this exercise.

2. Heat the rod tips evenly until fire polished, but do not allow contact. Rotate constantly and uniformly.

3. Remove the glass pieces from the flame when both tips are softened.

4. Join by carefully pushing the ends together.

5. Without rotation, reheat in the hottest part of the flame until fused. The indention will disappear at that point.

6. Remove from the flame, rotate and repeat Step 5 until the glass has been fused together all the way around. Wait a few seconds between each heating.

7. After the final heating, pull outward slightly until the diameter of the joint is uniform with the rest of the rod.

8. Check to make sure that the rods form a straight line.

9. Repeat this exercise several times. Then proceed to 8mm rod, then to 5mm rod, and finally to 4mm rod. Change your flame size and temperature to fit the situation. If your joints appear overly distorted, you may be using too hot or too large a flame. After the glass cools, it can be recut on either side of the original joint. Make a number of joints on the same rod.

IN-FLAME METHOD

Another approach for sealing two rods together involves joining the softened ends of the two pieces of rod directly in the flame. For very small diameter rod, little or no rotation is necessary to complete the seal, and the joint can be removed from the flame almost immediately. Larger diameter rod will require some rotation in the flame to finish the seal all the way around. The rod is then removed from the flame, pulled slightly (if necessary) to reduce the diameter at the joint to that of the original rod, and adjusted for straightness. Once you become somewhat proficient at this, you may prefer this method. Or you may choose to use a combination of the two techniques.

LABORATORY EXERCISE TWELVE

JOINING ROD BY THE IN-FLAME METHOD

1. Once again obtain two short pieces of 6mm rod, and heat the tips evenly until fire polished. Rotate constantly and uniformly.

2. When both tips are softened, join them in the flame, pushing together slightly.

3. Continue rotating, while heating in the hottest part of the flame, until thoroughly fused. Take care to keep the glass pieces linear and to refrain from pushing together or pulling apart.

4. Remove from the flame, and if necessary, pull outward slightly until the diameter of the joint is uniform with the rest of the rod.

5. Check to make sure that the rods form a straight line. Hold the finished piece vertically and turn ninety degrees to check for straightness.

JOINING DIFFERENT DIAMETER RODS

Often it will be necessary to join rods of different diameters. The principles in making these joints are about the same as those just discussed, but keep in mind that the smaller rod will always soften more rapidly. Thus, always try to keep the smaller diameter rod in the cooler part of the flame. Likewise, if any reheating is necessary, direct most of the heat onto the larger diameter rod. Also use care in pulling the rods in the last step. Usually, the joint should be such that there is a uniform change in diameter from the smaller to the larger diameter rod.

LABORATORY EXERCISE THIRTEEN

JOINING RODS OF DIFFERENT DIAMETERS

1. Obtain short pieces of 6 mm and 8 mm rod.

2. Heat the tips evenly until fire polished. Rotate constantly and uniformly. It will be wise to place the 8 mm rod in the hottest part of the flame and the 6 mm rod somewhere above it.

3. When both tips are softened, join them in the flame, directing more of the flame onto the 8 mm rod than on the 6 mm portion.

4. Continue rotating, while heating in the flame, until the rods are thoroughly fused.

5. Remove from the flame and pull outward carefully. Too much pulling may reduce the diameter of the smaller rod to less than it was originally.

6. Check your seal; reheat if necessary. Also, as done in the previous exercise, check to make sure the rods are joined straight.

LABORATORY PROJECT - ARTISTIC ONE

CONSTRUCTION OF A SIMPLE FLOWER

Introduction:

A simple flower can be made by using a combination of several techniques already studied, namely making a sphere at the end of a rod, fashioning shapes with simple tools, making joints between pieces of rod, and modifying the shapes by drawing them out in the flame. (Figure 4.19)

Figure 4.19 *A simple glass flower.*

Materials:

2 pieces of 6 to 8 inch 5 mm rod
(6 mm rod may be substituted)

Special Tools:

Triangular file, graphite plate

Flame:

#5 tip; small to medium flame

Construction Steps

1. Make a spherical ball on a 6 to 8 inch piece of 5 mm rod. The diameter of the finished sphere should be nearly twice that of the rod. This piece of glass will be referred to as the *base rod*.
2. Make a petal by heating the tip of another piece of 5mm rod (the *working* rod) and scoring it once with the smooth end (handle) of a triangular file. Do this by laying the heated glass on a graphite plate and then quickly press down with the file handle. (If too much time is taken, the graphite will cool the glass too much to be worked properly.) Use about 1/4 inch of the file handle to make the mark.

3. Prepare to make a joint between the edge of the petal just constructed and the sphere (which will become the center of the flower) by heating both of them in the flame. The entire sphere should be reheated, but final heating should be focused anywhere along the circumference where the seal is to be made.

4. After the ends of both pieces are softened, make the seal by pushing them together slightly and then pulling apart right away (Figure 4.20). The seal should be made in the flame.

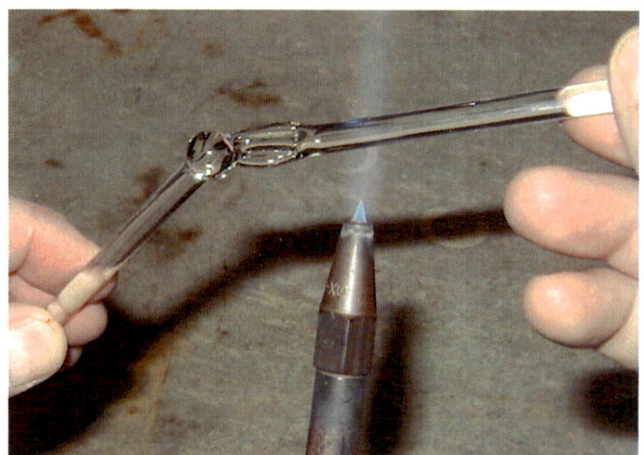

Figure 4.20 *Drawing out petal after joining to sphere at the end of the base rod.*

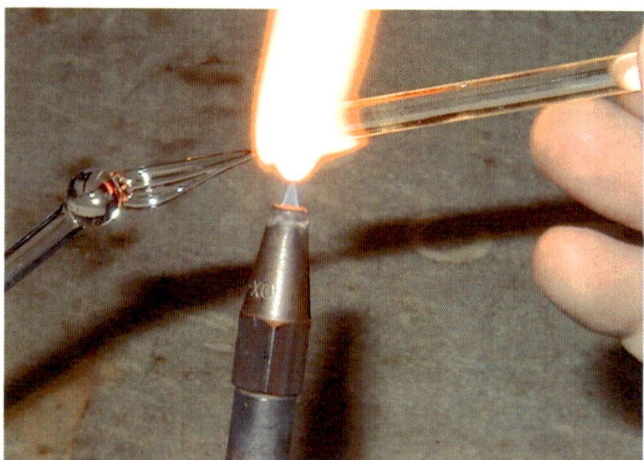

Figure 4.21 *Flame cutting petal after drawing out and shaping.*

5. Now concentrate heating on the scored portion of the petal. While heating, slowly draw the flower (base rod) down and out of the flame. This turns out to be a much more satisfactory procedure than holding the flower and pulling the petals.

6. Flame cut the glass at the proper length (Figure 4.21). The amount of heating and rate of pulling will determine the length of the petals. The direction that the flower is pulled out of the flame will dictate the shape of the petal. If the petal has a very sharp point, it was pulled out of the flame too rapidly. The rate of drawing out should be such that the glass thickness remains good. The resulting cut is usually automatically flame polished. How the flower is pulled from the flame will determine if the petal is straight or slightly curved.

7. Make another petal as you did in Step 2.

8. Now prepare to attach the second petal. If possible, keep all of the partly constructed flower warm by rotating very high in the outside portion of the flame. Then again, heat more strongly at

a spot on the sphere 180° from the first petal, while heating the base of the second petal in your other hand. Great caution must be exercised so that the first petal does not melt. A glancing flame rather than a direct flame is best for use on the sphere.

9. Make the joint as before, keeping the completed petal below the flame; however, make sure the joint is made *in* the flame.

10. Focus heating on the scored portion of the second petal and try to pull out in exactly the same way as was done for the first (Figure 4.22). The two petals should be similar in length and thickness and curvature. Obviously this will take some practice. The first petal is always the easiest since it can be any shape, but the second should match the first (harder!).

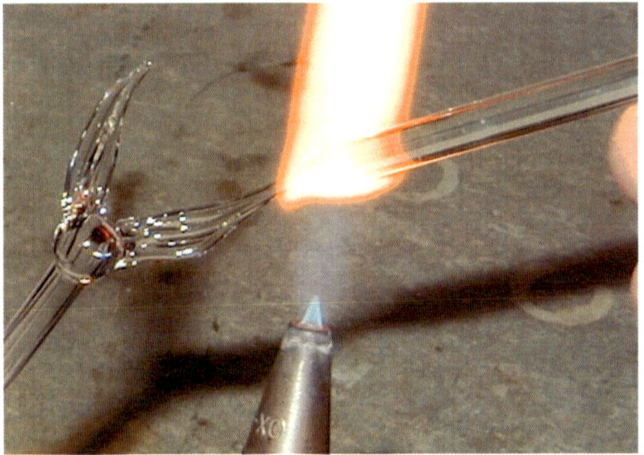

Figure 4.22 *Drawing out, shaping and flame cutting second petal.*

Figure 4.23 *Drawing out, shaping and flame cutting third petal.*

11. Repeat Steps 6-10 for the third and fourth petals. Each petal should be located approximately 90° from the other petals (Figure 4.23).

12. When completed, flame anneal the whole flower for several minutes by turning the gas on at least one full additional turn (Figure 4.24). Rotate the flower high in the yellow portion of the flame. After several minutes, gradually turn the oxygen down. (The gas may also have to be turned down in order to keep the flame from blowing out.) Eventually all the oxygen is turned off and the completed piece is "cooled" in the bushy yellow "gas only" flame. This is continued until a very slight deposit of soot is detected on the flower.

13. Inspect your flower (Figure 4.25). No edges or ends should be too thin or too sharp. If they are, fire polish these and make every effort to make the glass thicker in the future by using a cooler flame and not drawing out as rapidly. All joints should be physically tested. A gentle tap with a pair of forceps or light pressure exerted with your fingers should be sufficient for this test and should not break any joints unless they are poorly joined. All petals and leaves on your flowers should also be tested in this way. If any parts do break off, they can always be rejoined, but it is always best to make the joints properly the first time. Glass joints should always appear to be thoroughly fused together not just stuck together. Such visual and physical examinations should be made on every item you make.

Figure 4.24 *Flame annealing the finished product.*

Figure 4.25 *Although the finished flower is a very simple item, many techniques are used.*

14. The completed flower should be oven annealed when possible; however, it would be very instructive to look at the completed flower with a polariscope both before and after the oven annealing.

You may wish to make more complex flowers of your own design, perhaps by modifying the center portion, adding more petals, bending the stem somewhat, or adding leaves. Be imaginative, but always check your finished piece for safety and strength.

LABORATORY PROJECT - ARTISTIC TWO

MAKING A SMALL DECORATIVE BIRD

Introduction:

These glass birds may be used as decorations for planters or terrariums; a four inch length of rod is left on as a base so that it can be inserted into the ground (Figure 4.26). Or, they may be later incorporated into other projects such as decorative trees or birdbaths. Once again, the construction described is a combination of simple operations. Perhaps the most difficult part is the drawing out of the wings, but this is very similar to that done in the last project in making flower petals. Rod of 5mm diameter is recommended, but larger birds can be made from 6 or 8mm rod or smaller ones from 4mm rod. Obviously the flame size must be adjusted to work with the rod size used.

Figure 4.26 *Glass bird.*

Materials:

Two pieces of 5 mm rod, at least 6 inches long
(6 mm rod may be substituted)
Approximately 6 inches of 4 mm rod

Special Tools:

Triangular file, graphite plate

Flame:

#5 tip; medium flame

Construction Steps

1. Begin forming a sphere of glass at the end of a 5 mm rod. The rod should be pointed upward during this step of melting the

glass. Heating should always be focused at the junction of the sphere and rod whenever wanting to gather more glass.

2. Once the sphere has reached a size of about twice the diameter of the original rod, change the tilt of the rod so that it is pointed downward. Continue heating until a droopy teardrop shape begins to form.
3. At this point, remove the rod from the flame and point it downward at a 45° angle (without rotation). The resultant shape (the body of the bird) is then cooled at this angle (Figure 4.27).
4. The tip of a piece of 4 mm rod is now heated in one hand while the body is kept warm in the flame with the other hand.
5. The top of the body is then heated strongly and a joint is made between it and the 4 mm rod. This is done in such a way that the 4 mm rod is parallel to, but not co-linear with, the original 5 mm rod (Figure 4.28).

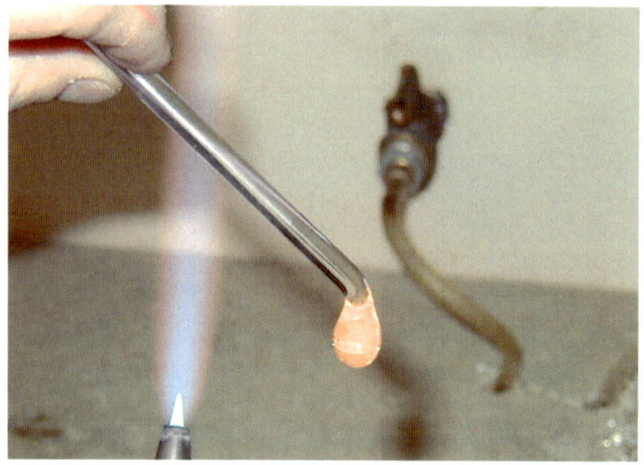

Figure 4.27 *Making the body of the bird by gathering glass, shaping and angling.*

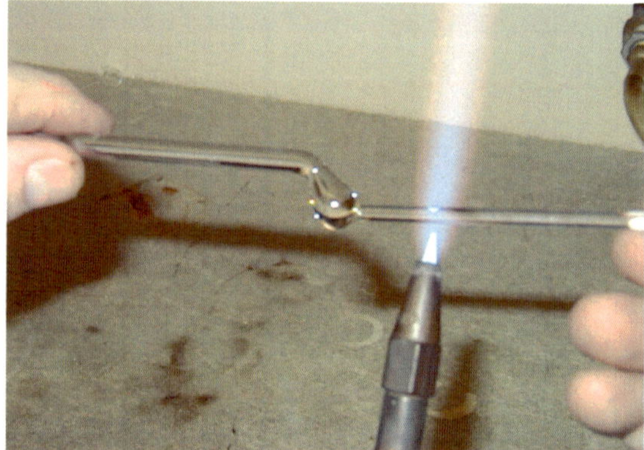

Figure 4.28 *Adding 4 mm glass for the head. Keep this new rod parallel to the base rod.*

6. The 4 mm rod is then flame cut about 3/8 inch from the body. Heating of the piece still attached to the body is continued with rotation (which will seem awkward) until it is transformed into a small sphere which will be the head (Figure 2.29). Gravity should be utilized in such a way so that the head is given the proper shape. It may be necessary to invert the body while it cools. (Alternatively you may choose to heat the head further, fusing it more into the body to give it a more dove-like shape.)

7. The tip of a second piece of 5 mm rod is heated until red and softened. It is then laid on a graphite plate and scored twice with the handle of a triangular file. This piece will become one of the wings.

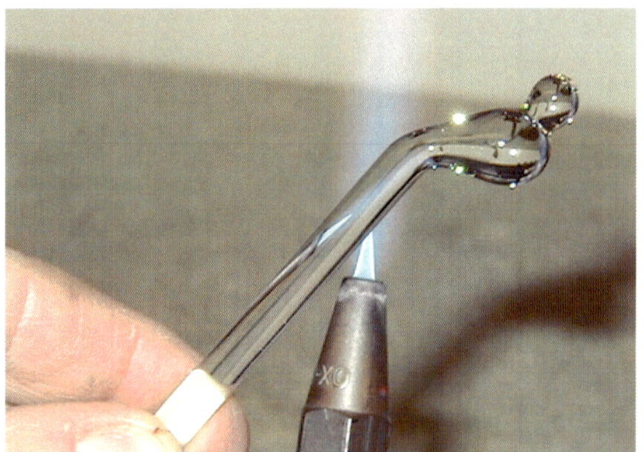

Figure 4.29 *The head of the bird after flame cutting and shaping of the added glass.*

Figure 4.30 *Adding the first wing of the bird. Note that the scored side of the wing is up.*

8. This wing is then immediately prepared for attachment to the body. This is done by heating the tip of the wing while the body is heated to redness at the point where the wing is to be attached. With the bird head pointed away, this first wing is attached to the right side; the scored part of the wing should be facing upward. A seal is made in the flame when both parts are sufficiently softened (Figure 4.30).

9. The joint is allowed to cool for about a second, and the wing is then reheated under the scored portion. When softened, the wing is shaped by drawing the bird slowly out of the flame (Figure 4.31). The rate and direction will determine the size and shape of the resulting wing. When at a proper length, the wing is flame cut and lightly fire polished. The end of the wing should be neither too sharp or too melted down.

10. The partly completed bird is now thoroughly reheated in the upper part of the flame and a second wing is prepared as in Step 7.

11. The second wing is attached as before, but in an upside down position. To do this, the bird is inverted and the wing is attached again from the right side with the scored side of the wing now downward.

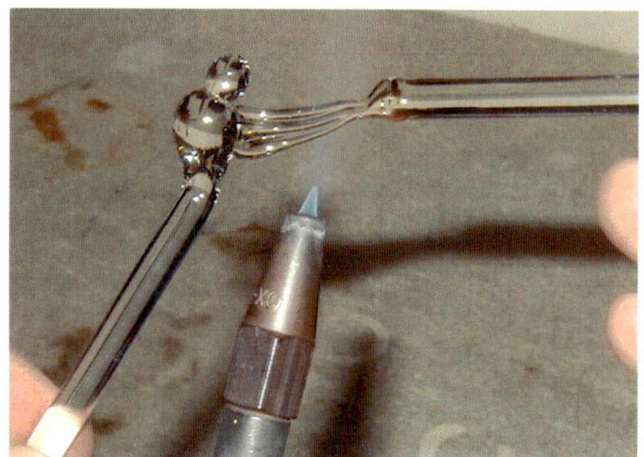

Figure 4.31 *Shaping the first wing of the bird. The scored side of the wing is still up.*

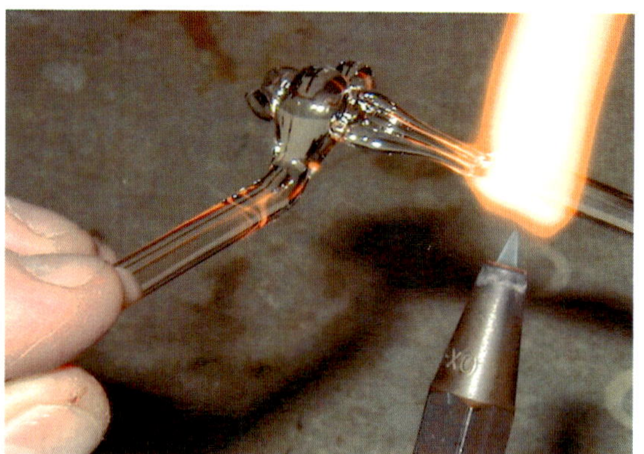

Figure 4.32 *Adding the second wing. Note that the scored side of the wing is down now.*

12. The wing is reheated and drawn out as before. Shaping is done by moving the body of the bird upward out of the flame (Figure 4.32). Every effort is made to make the wings similar in size and shape. While still warm the second wing can be adjusted using the cold portion of the glass rod (Figure 4.33).

13. Tail feathers are added next. The portion of the body directly

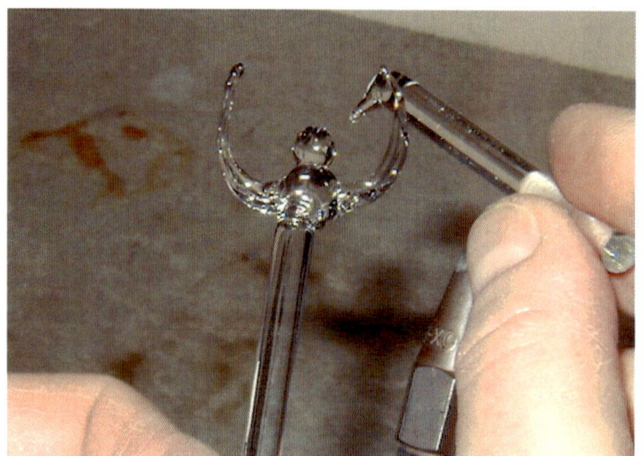

Figure 4.33 *Adjusting the second wing so it matches the first. Use a cold part of glass.*

Figure 4.34 *Adding the first tail feather. The working rod is 90 degrees to the base rod.*

under the wings on the top side of the body is heated briefly but strongly with the tip of the flame. At the same time the end of a 5 mm rod is also heated until a small glob of glass forms. This hot glob of glass is then attached at the back of the right wing (the head of the bird is pointed away) and drawn out (to

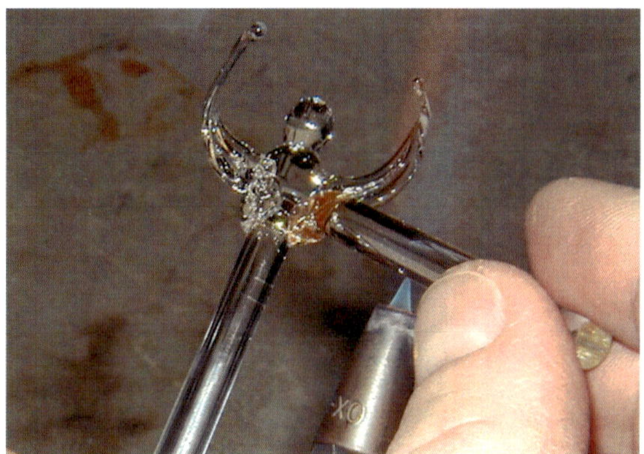

Figure 4.35 *Adding the second tail feather. The working rod is pointed toward the worker.*

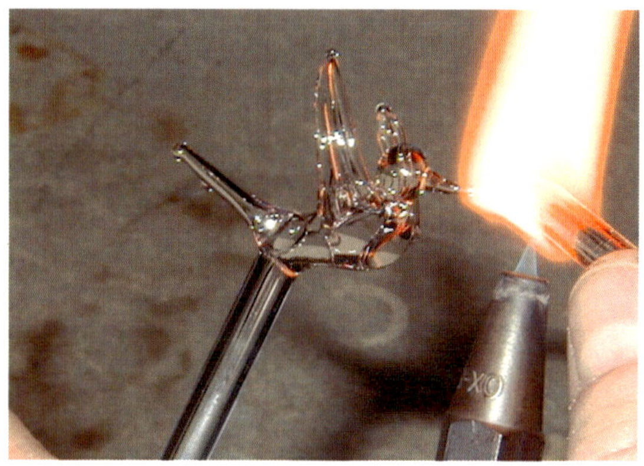

Figure 4.36 *Adding the beak on head. A small amount of glass is added and is flame cut.*

the length of about 0.5 inch) at an angle of 90° to the original 5 mm rod which is now serving as the handle (Figure 4.34). The tail feather is then flame cut. Gravity dictates that the finished tail feathers should be pointed downward until cool.

14. The left side of the body is then heated and another tail feather is added in a similar way with effort made to make both of equal length and shape (Figure 4.35).

15. The beak of the bird is now formed. The tip of a small rod is heated as is the forward portion of the head. The softened rod tip is then attached, and the head is pulled slightly outward (and a little upwards) so that a pointed beak is fashioned (Figures 4.36-4.37).

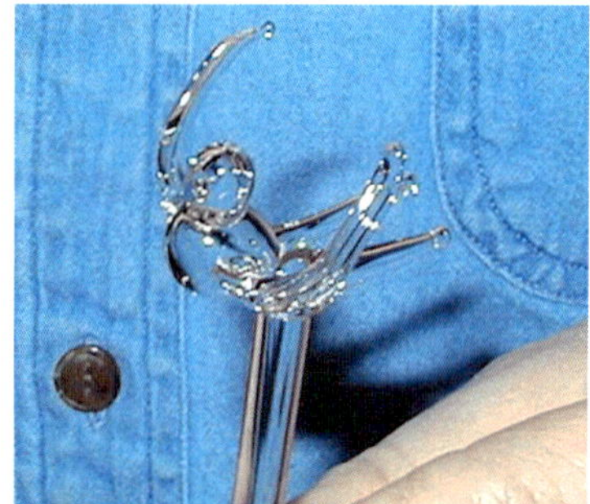

Figure 4.37
Finished glass bird.

16. A pointed tip on the 5 mm handle (for use in a planter) may now be fashioned by making a flame cut about 4 inches below the body of the bird. Or, the bird may be removed from the 5 mm rod handle so it can be used later in other projects. To remove the bird, heat strongly directly below the tail feathers, rotating but keeping the tail feathers downward as much as possible to keep them from melting. Grasp the bird head with a pliers and pull it off the rod when the glass is sufficiently softened. If the resulting stub is too large, excess glass can be removed by wiping (see page 61).

LABORATORY PROJECT - ARTISTIC THREE

CONSTRUCTION OF A DOG

Introduction:

Dogs with a "snoopy-like" nose can also be made by a combination of the techniques already learned. Although these dogs may look complex, they are really a lot easier to make than you might think. In fact, students usually report that they enjoy making these more than any other item. Most have some trouble the first time through, but after that they discover they can turn out very nice looking products (Figure 4.38).

Figure 4.38 *Sitting glass dog.*

Beginners often have trouble the first time because they make the body too large in Steps 1 and 2. Try to *think small* until you feel more confident about the procedures. Likewise, adding the ears (in Step 9) can cause some problems if the working rod and the neck region are not both sufficiently heated. Prepare for this step by practicing on scrap pieces of glass before doing it on the dog you are making.

Materials:

Approximately 12 inches 6 mm rod (although 5 mm or 8 mm could be used for smaller or larger dogs)

Blue borosilicate glass drawn out to 1mm diameter for decoration (if unavailable, use regular colorless 4 mm rod)

Special Tools:

Large forceps, graphite plate

Flame:

#5 tip; small to medium flame

Construction Steps

(All part letters refer to Figure 4.54 on page 102)

1. A 12 inch piece of 6mm rod is heated (with rotation) at a point 4" from the left end until the rod glows with a red color. Then, holding the rod so that it remains straight, move the flame over to a point about 1 to 1.25 inches to the right of the first point (no more!), and heat it in a similar manner until it glows.
2. Return to heat the original spot again; it should still be glowing enough so that is can be easily located. The right side is also heated once again. Move back and forth. Then fold the rod at these points so that the resulting glass piece (Figure 4.39) has three thicknesses in the middle (Part A in Figure 4.54). Enough of the rod should remain at both ends so as to be used for handles. This triple thickness is then heated with rotation in order to fuse the glass together to some degree (Part B). Try to keep the three thicknesses flat, or as flat as possible. If necessary, the piece can be taken out of the flame and flattened with a marver, but don't do this unless absolutely necessary.
3. Make a flame cut on the rod in your left hand at a point rather close to the triple thickness. As it is being cut off, move the rod more to the middle of the thicknesses (Figures 4.40; Part C).

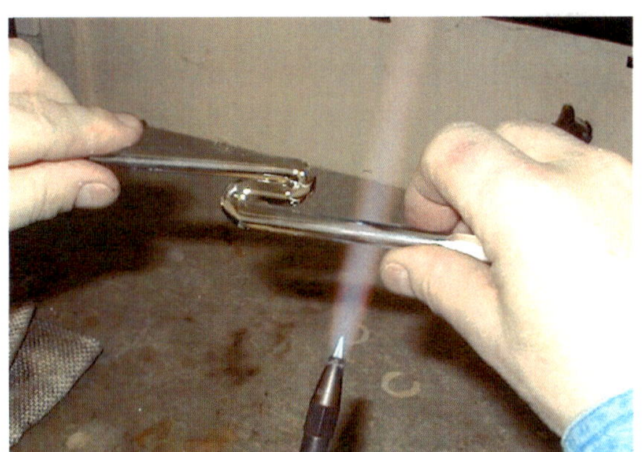

Figure 4.39 *Folding the rod to make a center with three thicknesses of glass (the Body).*

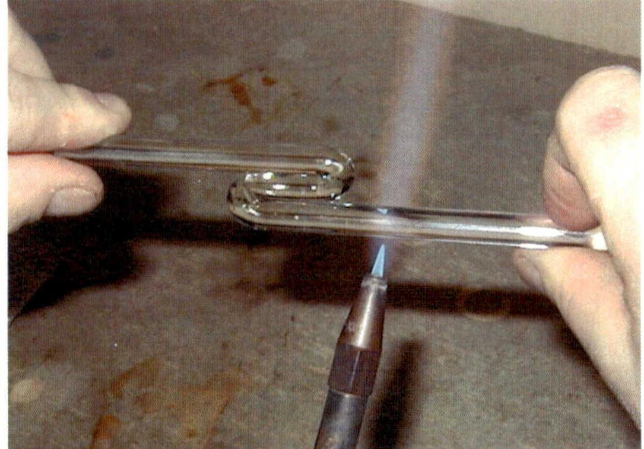

Figure 4.40 *Heating excess rod on the part which will become the bottom of the dog.*

4. Repeat heating of the entire thicknesses, but finally concentrate heating over the bottom portion (Figure 4.41) while drawing off the rod which is not the body (in this case, the left part).

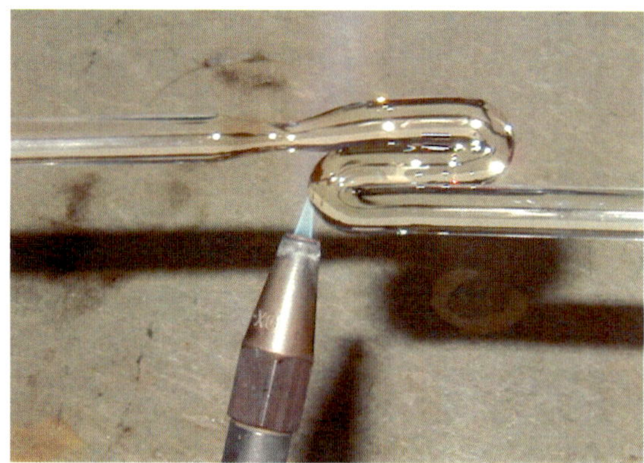

Figure 4.41 *Flame cutting excess rod. Before the cut, the glass is pushed onto the body.*

Figure 4.42 *Flattening the bottom of the dog on a graphite plate (may devitrify).*

Figure 4.43 *Adjusting the neck to improve the final center of gravity (looks better too).*

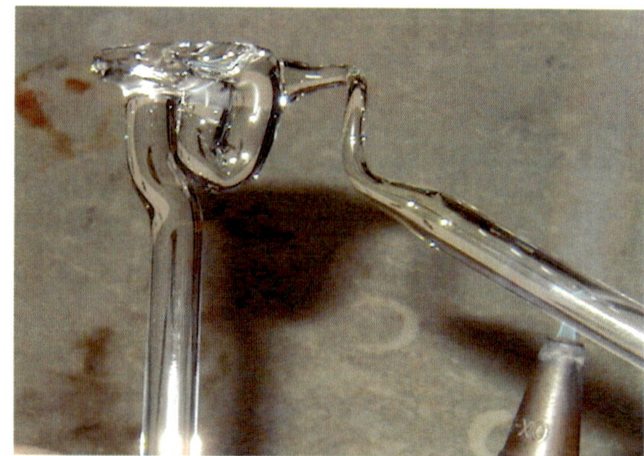

Figure 4.44 *Drawing out and shaping the tail on the back of the dog body.*

5. Remove from the flame. Then, holding the 6mm rod in a vertical position press down firmly onto a graphite plate so as to flatten the bottom of the dog (Figure 4.42 and Part D). Immediately return to the flame and gently reheat the whole piece in order to prevent cooling too rapidly and subsequent cracking. It is likely that devitrification will occur along the bottom during the flattening operation. This can be easily removed by heating the whitened areas with the very tip of the flame

6. Now reheat the neck portion (the 6 mm rod handle) closest to the body (use large forceps to hold the glass) and place on the graphite plate. Move the neck rod so it is straight up and down, and also push slightly toward the center of the body (Figure 4.43, Part F).

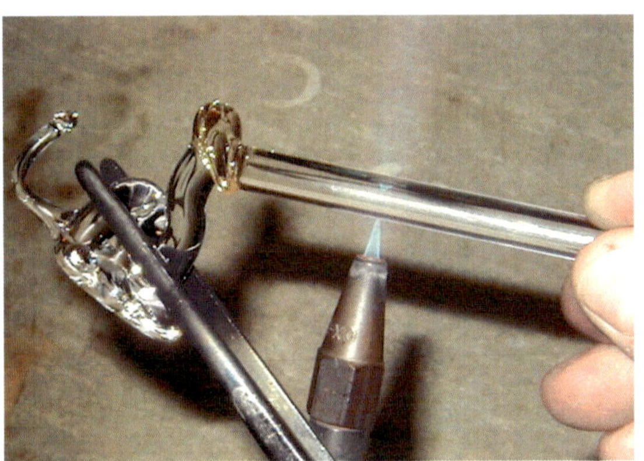

Figure 4.45 *Immediately after the formation of the head. The rod has been bent and pushed.*

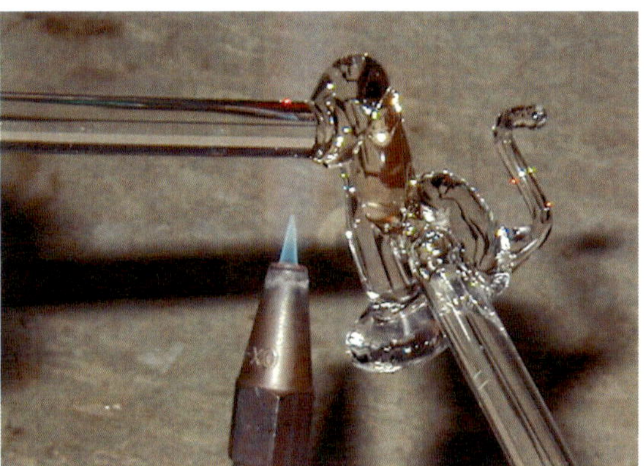

Figure 4.46 *Attaching the first ear to one side of the dog head. Heat both pieces sufficiently!*

7. The tail is fashioned next using the 6 mm rod that had been flame cut in Step 3. Heat the rod strongly while also heating the back of the dog's body (diagonally from the 6 mm rod handle). A joint is now made in the flame. The rod is then drawn out, forming the tail, and just as it begins to harden, it is curled upwards close to the body and then flame cut at a reasonable length (Figure 4.44 and Part E).

8. Next, heat the neck all around at about 3/4 of an inch above the top of the body (it is important to heat all around the rod). Once the glass becomes fluid enough so that the body weight is no longer supported, grab the body as done before with the forceps. Then with a single motion, which is both pushing down from the front and pushing backward slightly, the head and forehead are formed (Figure 4.45). The dog's snout (the remaining 6mm rod handle) should be at about 120° from the body of the dog (Part G).

9. The ears are now added. The neck is heated below the head on both sides. Care is taken so as to prevent the flame from playing on the body too much, as it has now cooled enough so that reheating the body will cause cracking. Meanwhile, an additional piece of 6 mm rod is heated very strongly in your other hand until the glass is very soft and very molten. Attach this piece slightly below the head, move the glass upward until it touches the head and then immediately pull downward along the neck and finally out at a right angle to the neck. Don't hesitate (Figure 4.46). Flame cut immediately. This entire procedure should be done in one single, continuous motion. If the

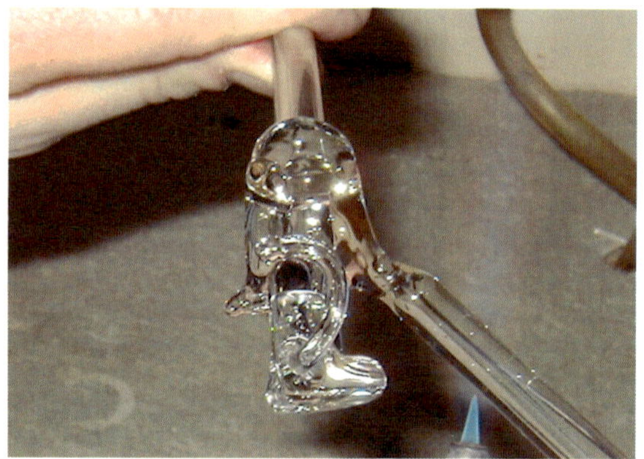

Figure 4.47 *Forming the second ear. Note the position of the dog body.*

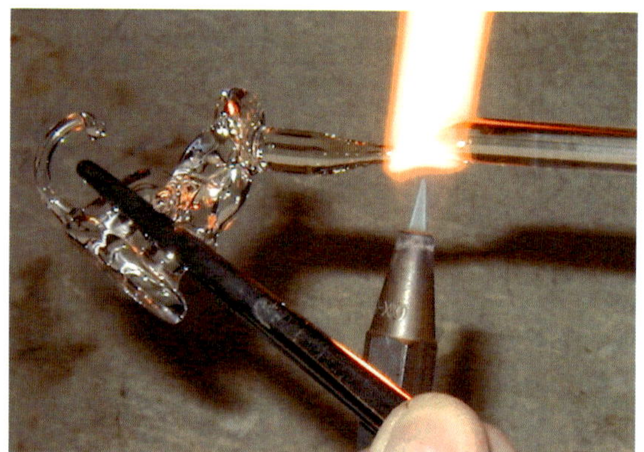

Figure 4.48 *Flame cutting the base rod, which will become the nose. Note position of forceps.*

neck was not heated sufficiently or if too much time is taken to do this step, the glass will become solid too quickly. The same operation is repeated for the second ear (Figure 4.47, Part H).

10. The nose is now cut off and shaped. At a point 3/4 of an inch beyond the forehead, heat the rod (the nose) all around. Once it becomes very soft, grab the body firmly as done before with the forceps. Next, the nose is flame cut (Figure 4.48) and immediately heated thoroughly. The snout should be directed upward slightly, allowing gravity to shape it properly (Figure 4.49). Turn and heat whenever necessary. When finished, the end of the nose should be slightly thicker and pointed upward (Part I).

11. The eyes and nose are added next. Reheat the forehead and the end of the snout area with a medium to strong flame (Figure 4.50). Then with a smaller flame, heat again more directly and add two blue spots of borosilicate glass (from a thin, drawn out piece of blue borosilicate rod) evenly spaced on the forehead for the eyes (Figure 4.51) and on the tip of the snout for the nose. Once placed, add enough heat to melt the blue glass so that it makes a good seal with the clear glass. (Heating too strongly will cause the two glasses to coalesce too much; insufficient heating will not join the blue glass, making the eyes and nose appear as if they are just sitting on the surface.)

12. Oven anneal the final product (Figure 4.52 and Part J) as soon as possible.

Figure 4.49 *Shaping the nose of the dog.*

Figure 4.50 *Heating the head before placing the first eye.*

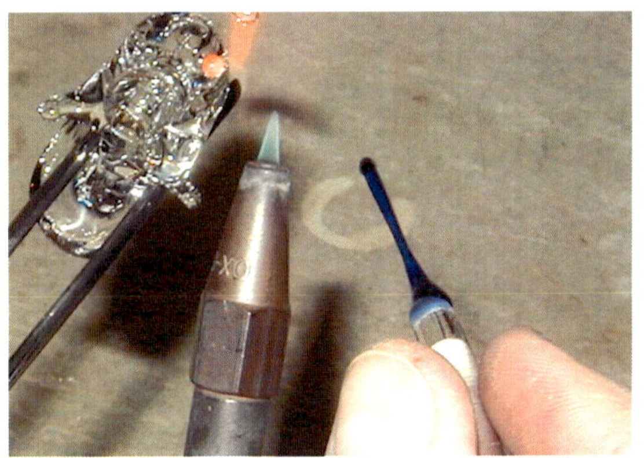

Figure 4.51 *Adding the eyes and heating to insure good attachment to the head.*

Figure 4.52 *Two finished dogs made with two different sized rods.*

Other similar animals such as cats or panthers can be made in much the same way as was this dog (Figure 4.53). Simple variations can be made by making the greatest changes to only the heads and necks. But, certainly there are many other creative approaches to making animals. Once you are familiar with the basics of glassworking you will be urged to pursue almost any creative ideas that you may have.

Figure 4.53 *Cat and panther.*

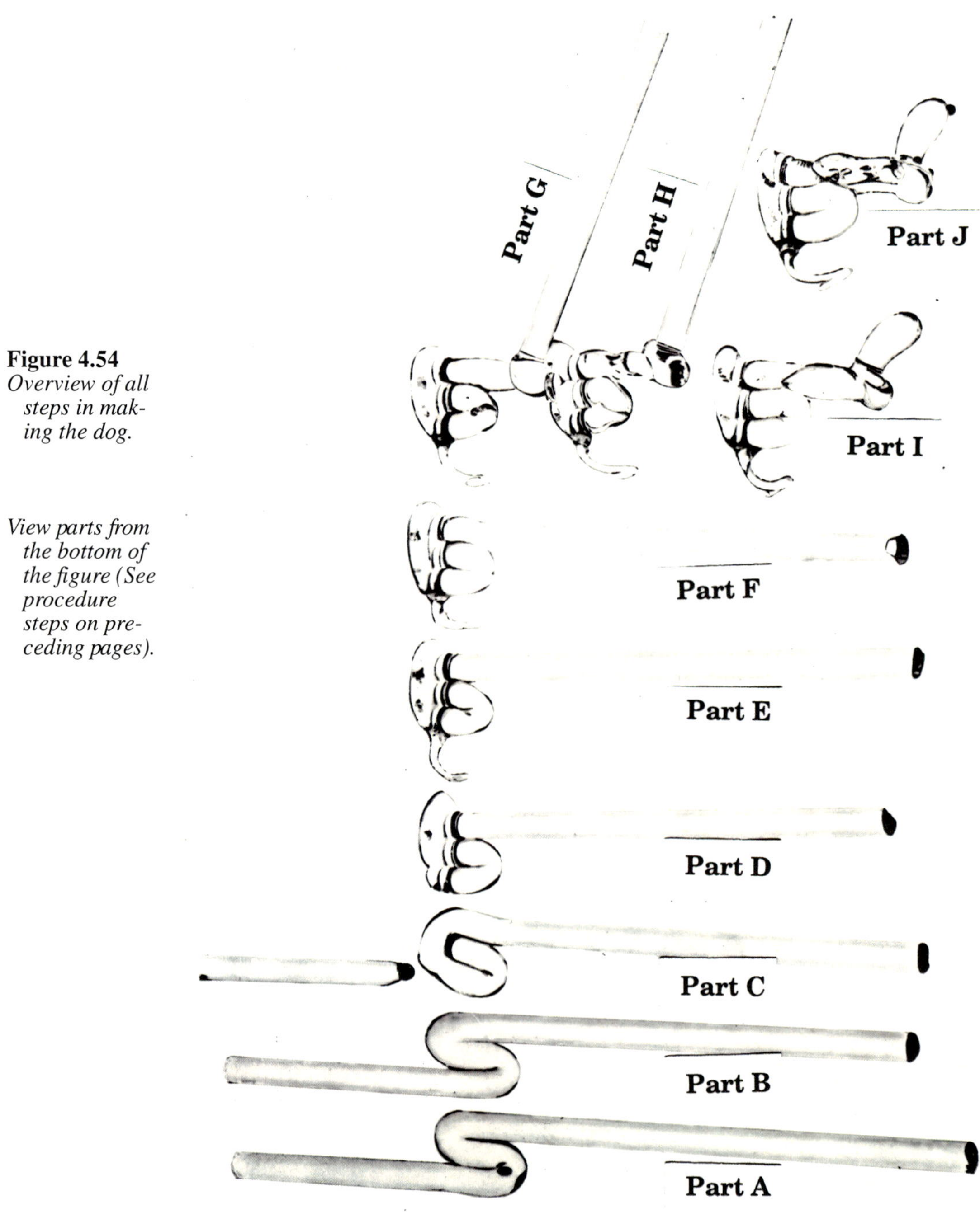

Figure 4.54
Overview of all steps in making the dog.

View parts from the bottom of the figure (See procedure steps on preceding pages).

LABORATORY PROJECT - ARTISTIC FOUR

MAKING A DECORATIVE HAND PUMP

Introduction:

An attractive and graceful old fashioned hand pump can be made out of glass rod by a combination of elementary steps. The construction of the handle is the hardest part since a large amount of glass needs to be gathered, drawn out, and shaped in a single, continuous operation. The completed pump may be used as a unique decoration for planters and terrariums (Figure 4.55) or a lace base can be added (as described on page 131) so that it may stand independently.

Figure 4.55 *Decorative hand pump in planter.*

Materials:

About 12 inches 5 mm rod

About 12 inches 8mm rod

Special Tools:

Marver, graphite plate, pliers

Flame:

#5 tip; adjust for rather small, hot flame (1/2 inch cone)

Construction Steps

(All part letters refer to Figure 4.74 on page 110)

1. In the middle of a twelve inch piece of 5 mm rod make an intermediate maria about 12 mm in diameter (see Part A); continue to rotate and adjust so that the rod ends are linear.

2. Make a flame cut about 1 to 1 1/4 inches to the side of the maria (Figure 4.56 and also Part B). The end of the remaining piece in your right hand is heated in the flame so that an end maria of the same diameter as the intermediate maria can be formed. When sufficient glass is softened, form the maria using a graphite plate (Part D). Set this piece aside for later use.

3. The remaining glass piece with the intermediate maria is heated strongly at he end where it had been flame cut (Figures 4.56 and 4.57). This is heated and rotated in such a way that it forms a spherical shape (Figure 4.58 and Part D). The flame tip should be played on the junction where the rod and forming sphere come together. Care must be taken so that the sphere does not touch the intermediate maria. Thus, proper rotation is very important. When it nearly touches the maria, continue to heat it strongly. It may be necessary to make a doorknob shape to get the glass close enough to this maria. If this is the case, invert the piece while still hot to reform the spherical shape. The glass may be reheated if necessary to obtain this shape.

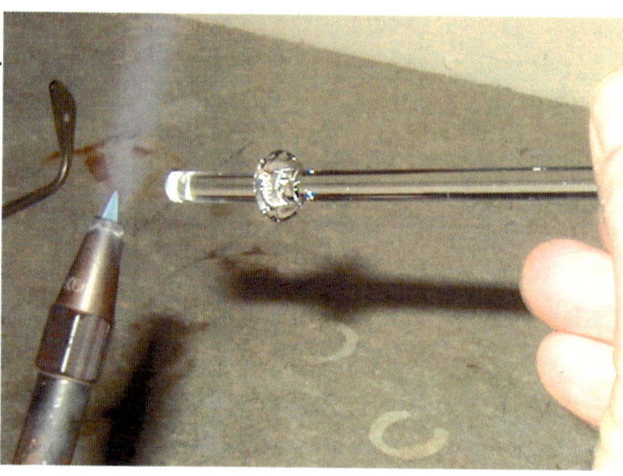

Figure 4.56 *After making a flame cut a small distance from the intermediate maria.*

4. Now take the end maria that was made in Step 2 and reheat it quite strongly on the flat part. At the same time reheat the sphere and prepare to make a seal between the two in the flame (Figure 4.59). Push these together slightly (Figure 4.60), and then hold up to eye level in order to see if the rods are again linear. Rotate, reheat and adjust (Part E).

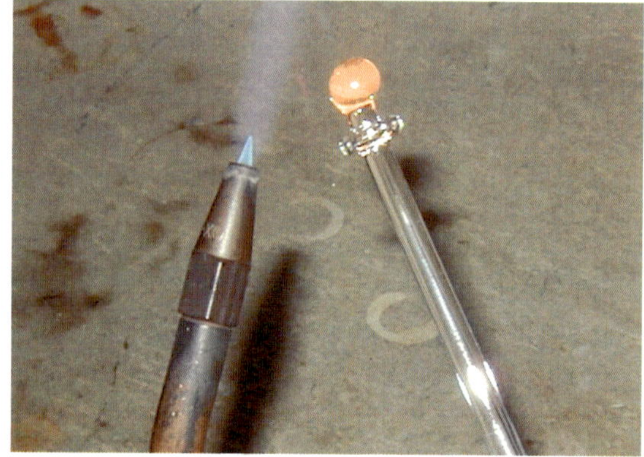

Figure 4.57 *During the formation of a sphere just above the intermediate maria.*

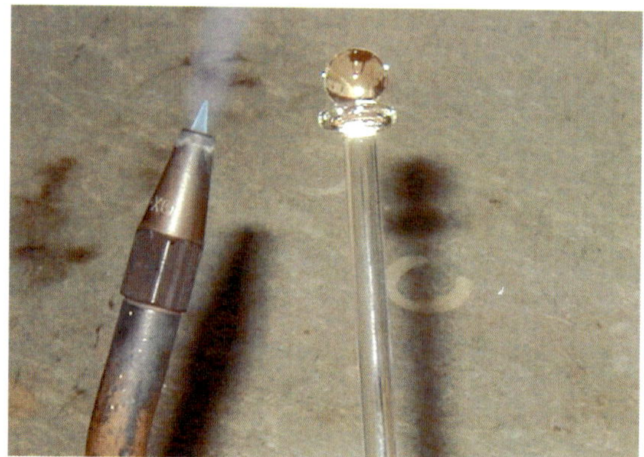

Figure 4.58 *After forming and shaping the sphere just above the intermediate maria.*

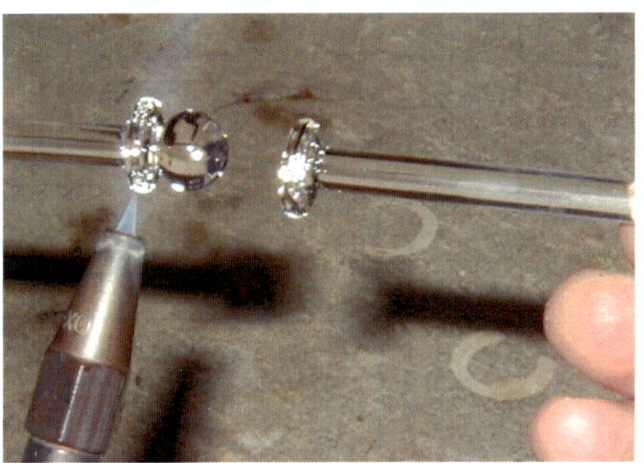

Figure 4.59 *Attaching the end maria to the sphere just above the intermediate maria.*

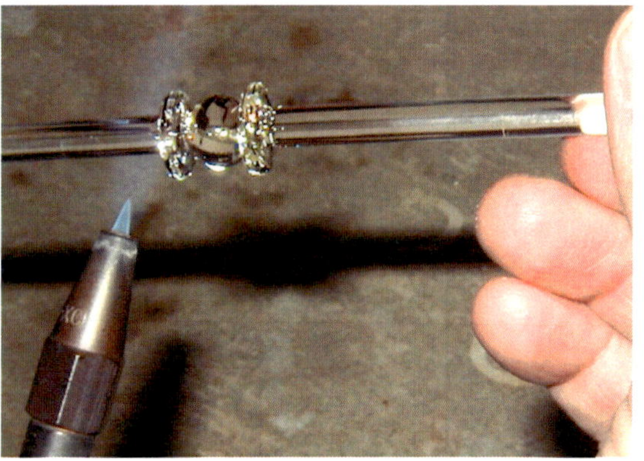

Figure 4.60 *Completing the seal between the end maria and the sphere.*

5. Now heat the rod at a point about two inches above the second maria and make another flame cut (Part F). Hopefully the piece being cut off is long enough to be held in the right hand; otherwise, use forceps or pliers.

6. The spout is then added to the sphere between the two marias. The end of a separate 5 mm rod is heated while also reheating the entire sphere. Finally concentrate the heating on one side of the sphere. It is a good idea to choose a portion on the sphere which has some imperfections, or where the marias are spread slightly (Figure 4.61). The spout will tend to hide any of these imperfections. Then, join the sphere and rod, taking care that the spout rod does not attach itself to either maria. As soon as a good seal is assured (the joint may need to be

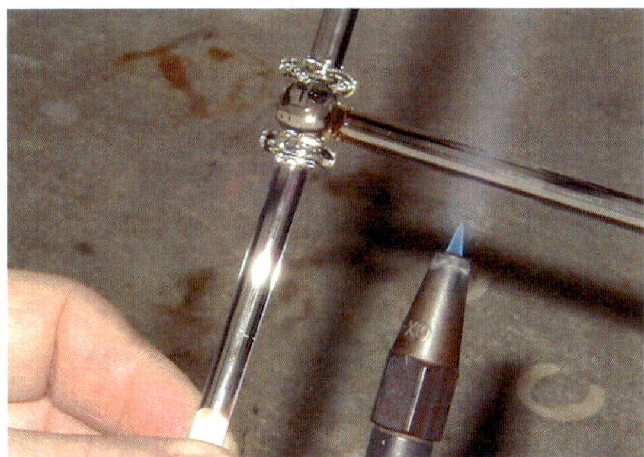

Figure 4.61 *Adding a rod to the sphere. This will become the Spout of the Pump.*

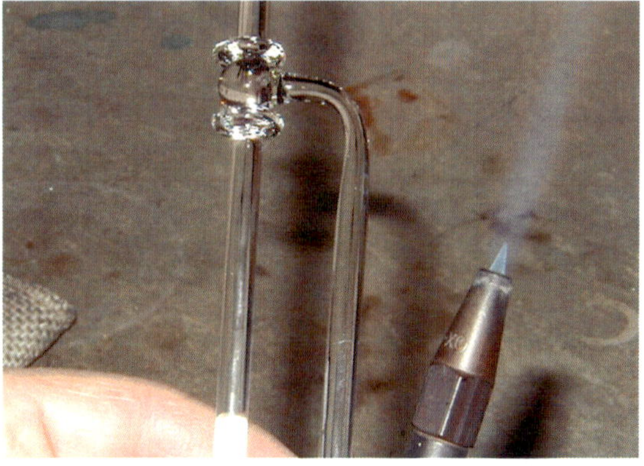

Figure 4.62 *Making the bend on the spout. The rod is slightly drawn out and bent down.*

Figure 4.63 *Using a marver to form a small flat flange at the bottom of the spout.*

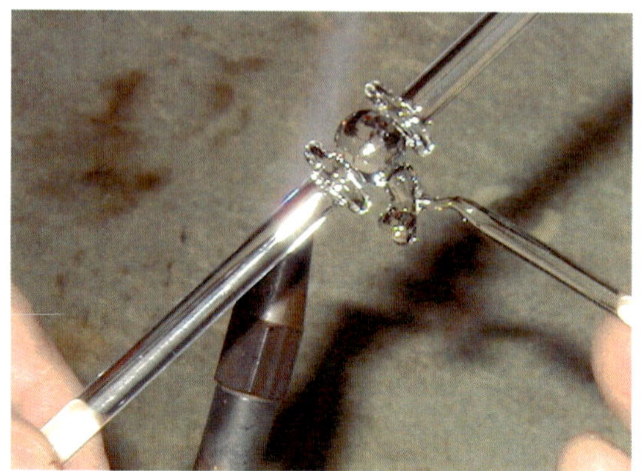

Figure 4.64 *Adding a small piece of glass on top of the spout at the bend (to hold pail!).*

be reheated), the rod is pulled out straight, at a right angle from the pump. It is then heated about 0.5 inch from the joint and bent downward so that the rod becomes parallel to the pump (Figure 4.62).

7. The excess spout rod is now removed by making a flame cut about 0.5 inch below the bend. The glass hanging down from the spout is then heated rather strongly. It will tend to thicken and climb up as it is heated. A marver is used to flatten the bottom part of the spout (Figure 4.63). Devitrification may appear on the spout at this point. Remove any such milkiness by strongly heating with the tip of the flame. A small hook can be added to the top of the spout if desired (Figure 4.64;Part H).

8. Now, heat the end of the rod at the top of the pump in order to gather enough glass so that a rather large end maria may be formed. Again use a graphite plate, being careful not to press too hard. The end maria should remain quite thick (Figure 4.65 and part G).

Figure 4.65 *Making a maria on the top of the pump. The handle will attach here.*

9. The pump handle holder is fashioned next.

Another piece of 5 mm rod is heated along a length of approximately 0.5 inch; meanwhile the top portion of the pump above the spout and opposite to it is heated briefly. Strong heating of the pump must be avoided or it will bend when making the joint. The rod is then joined and formed into a scroll shape (Figures 4.67 - 4.68 and Part I of Figure 4.74). Any needed adjustments should be made right away. Be sure to check to see that the holder is flat and untwisted. Incidentally, this "handle holder" is purely decorative and will not actually be connected to the actual handle.

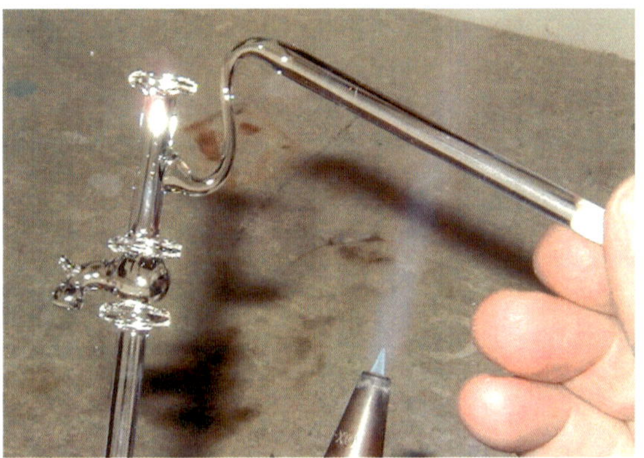

Figure 4.66 S*haping the scroll pump handle holder (purely decorative).*

Figure 4.67 *Flame cutting the excess glass rod from the scroll pump handle holder.*

10. Now glass is gathered for the formation of the pump handle. This is without doubt the most difficult step in this project. Thus it is important that the student practice this operation on scrap pieces of glass having a maria on the end. Practice often before trying this on your nearly completed product!

    Begin to heat the end of a separate piece of 6 mm rod (8 mm rod may be better). A larger and hotter flame will be needed, but be aware that if the flame is too hot, only the exterior of the rod will be heated. The interior will remain cooler and upon drawing out, a very non-uniform, lumpy piece of glass will be produced. The end of the rod should be heated strongly and quite a bit of glass should be gathered. It will be necessary to tilt the glass upward so that a sphere of glass develops. If the accumulation of glass is not spherical, but distorted, this means that the glass is not being heated strongly enough. If this is the case, use a larger flame.

    An alternate way to gather sufficient glass is to heat the 6 mm rod over a larger area at the end of the rod. Heating should be continued until the glass glows with a uniform redness over the entire heated area. It will become much like a large wet noodle. Do not heat beyond this point. (This method is similar to the procedure used to make scroll shapes as described on page 79.) In this method, it is not necessary to build up a large sphere of glass; the same amount of glass is gathered in a longer length of the rod. Many students report that this method is somewhat easier.

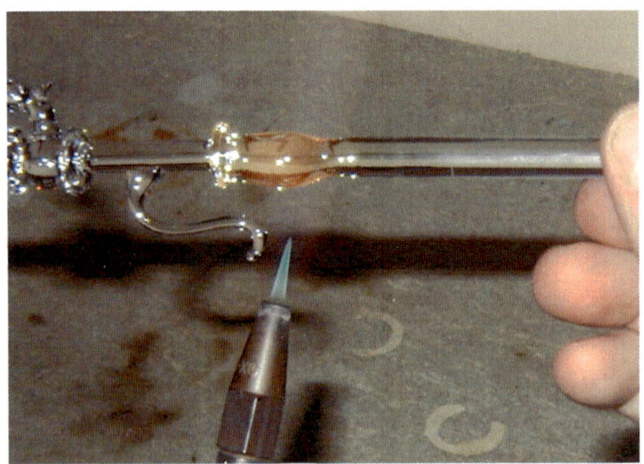

Figure 4.68 *After attaching the gathered glass, the thickest portion is reheated.*

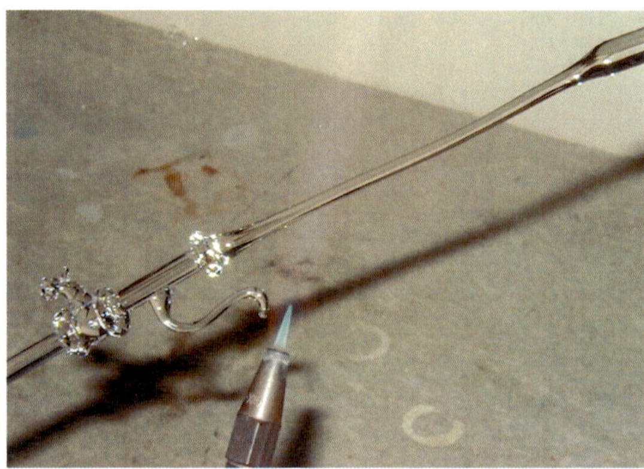

Figure 4.69 *After sufficient heating, gathered glass is slowly drawn out before shaping.*

11. Now the pump handle is drawn out. This is the most difficult step. When sufficient glass is gathered, heat the top maria of the pump so that a good seal can be made. (Do not heat the maria too strongly, and also take care so that the handle holder does not become reheated and bent.) Join the gathered glass to the maria in the flame. The sphere (and the whole pump) is rotated and heated at the thickest part (Figure 4.68). Then the handle rod is pulled up slowly and outward. The thick parts are lightly reheated whenever necessary. When about 6 inches of glass of uniform thickness is drawn out (Figure 4.69), the glass is brought downward and bent upward at the bottom (Figure 4.70). This final position is held for several seconds to allow the glass to cool. The handle is then flame cut (Figure 4.71) and rounded slightly (Part J). If the handle holder becomes bent or distorted in this last operation, reheat it over a wide area, and reshape it using a pair of pliers. Practice this operation often.

12. The bottom of the pump, about 5 inches below the lowest maria, is now heated and a pointed tip is added by drawing off the small remaining piece with a pair of pliers. Hold the pump

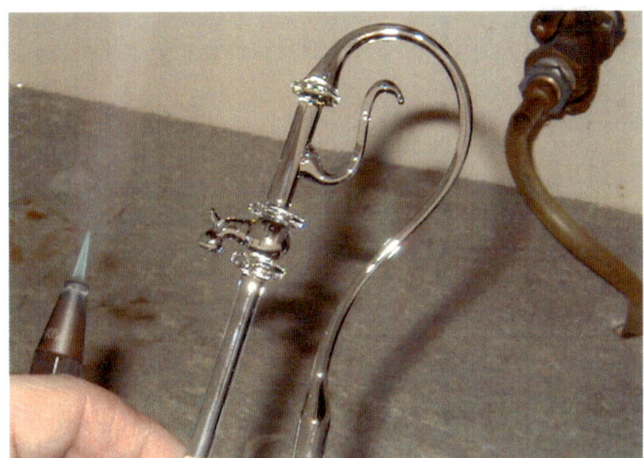

Figure 4.70 *Finishing the pump handle. Be sure to make the bend gracefully and keep in the plane of the rest of the pump.*

Figure 4.71 *After the handle has cooled somewhat, the excess glass is removed by making a flame cut. Make sure the end is not sharp.*

in an area midway between the lowest maria and the place where the point is being fashioned. The pump is now completed (Part K of Figure 4.74) and can be put on a lace stand (Figure 4.73) or into a household planter for decoration (see Figure 4.125 at the end of the chapter).

13. Oven anneal the product when possible.

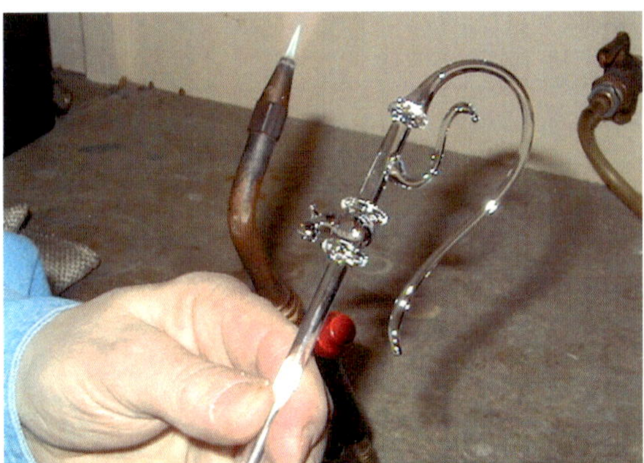

Figure 4.72 *The completed hand pump. A pointed end may be added to the bottom so the item can be placed in a planter (for decoration) or a lace stand may be made so it will be free standing. lace stands are discussed in a Chapter Five.*

Figure 4.73 *A completed pump attached to a lace stand.*

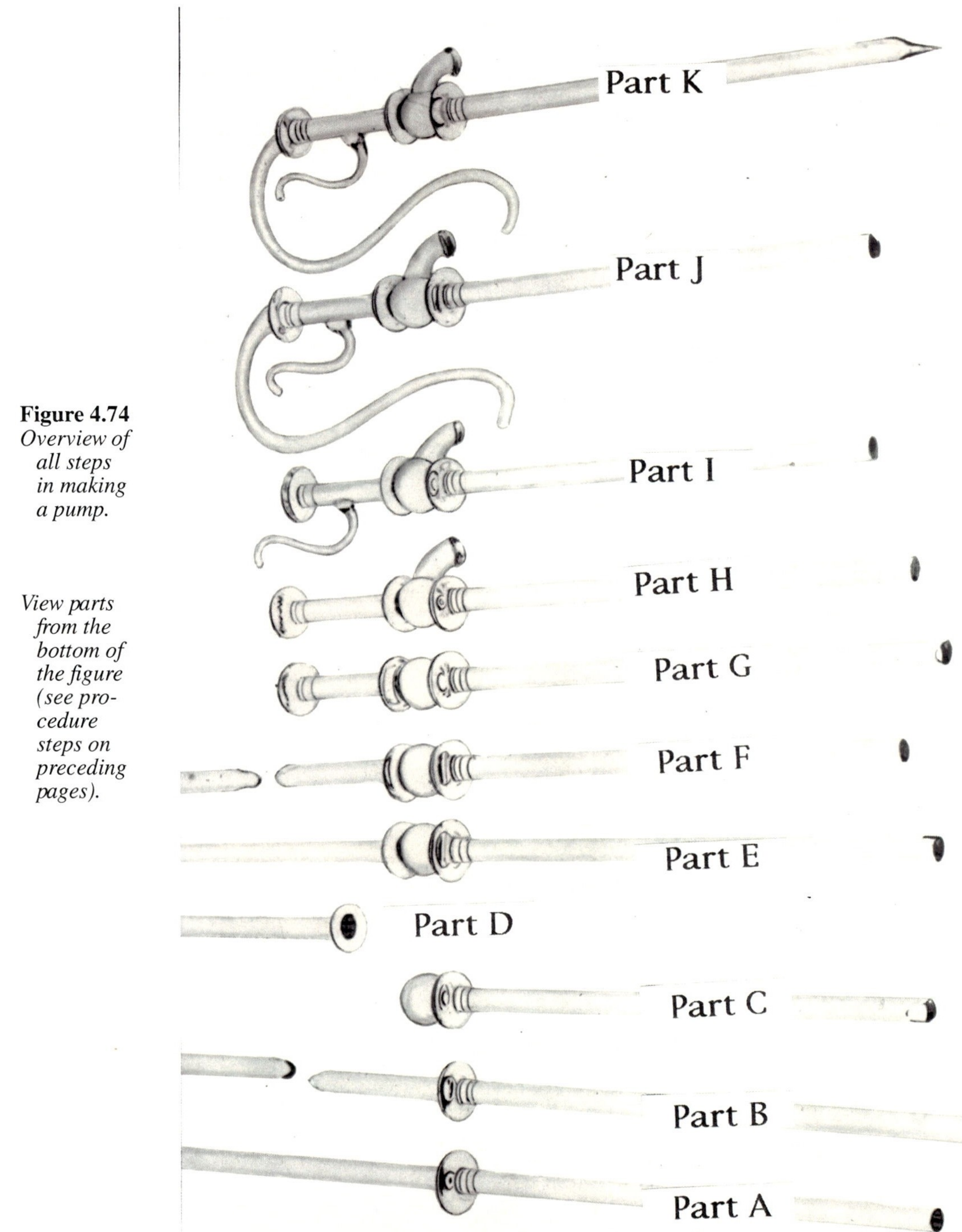

Figure 4.74
Overview of all steps in making a pump.

View parts from the bottom of the figure (see procedure steps on preceding pages).

LABORATORY PROJECT - ARTISTIC FIVE

DECORATIVE TREE BRANCH WITH BIRD

Introduction:

A "two dimensional" glass tree branch is rather easy to make and is also a beautiful addition to any planter in your home (Figure 4.75). The trunk, branches and leaves are all fashioned out of 6 mm rod. A glass bird (Project Artistic Two) is placed in the branch, and the leaves and bird can be colored with glass stain if desired. Special should be given to the symmetry and flow of lines in the product as it is being made.

Figure 4.75 *Branch and bird as decoration in planter.*

Materials:

Approximately 24 inches of 6 mm rod

Special Tools:

Needle nose pliers

Flame:

#3 tip; small bushy flame

Construction Steps

1. A piece of 6 mm rod, approximately 12 inches long is heated over a wide area about one third of the way from the end. Once softened, the rod is bent gracefully (utilizing gravity) to an angle of about 90°.
2. The rod on the end is then heated over a broad area and drawn out to some degree so it is gradually tapered and continues a gradual downward bend (Figure 4.76). A flame cut is made at a point four or five inches from the middle of the bend. Be sure that the drawn glass does not get too thin at the end.

3. The end of a second piece of 6 mm rod is now heated while also reheating the curved rod at the middle of the bend region at a point opposite to the direction of the bend. A seal is made with the second piece being added in the same plane as the first (Figure 4.77).

Figure 4.76 *Making the initial bend, which will become the main branch.*

4. This added rod is then heated over a wide area (a shorter area) and drawn out so it too is gradually tapered and directed slightly downward.

5. A small bird is constructed (see Project Artistic Two on page 91) and placed near the end of the bend on the larger branch (Figure 4.78). During this operation, the bird is held with a forceps or modified pair of needle nose pliers (see page 37). Be sure that a good seal is made and that the bird is positioned in an attractive way.

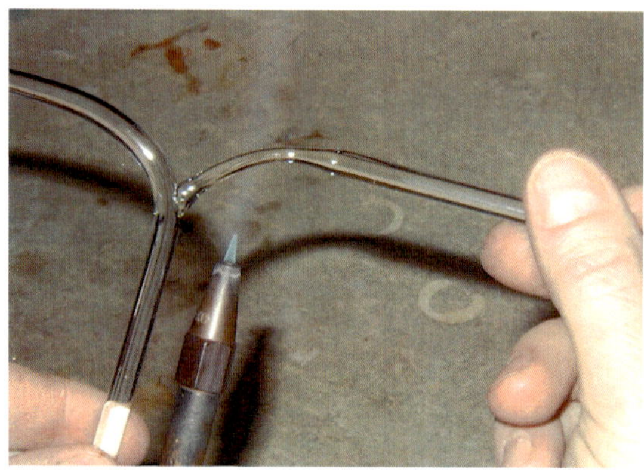

Figure 4.77 *Attaching smaller main branch to the larger branch in the plane of the bend.*

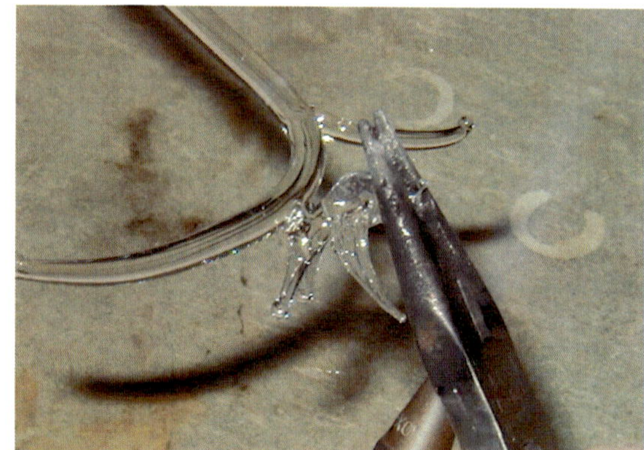

Figure 4.78 *Connecting and positioning a small bird to the larger branch.*

6. Smaller branches and stems for leaves are now added to both of the larger branches in any pattern that is pleasing to the eye (Figures 4.79 and 4.80). Once again, be sure that all branches and stems remain relatively thick at the ends.

7. Next, leaves are made by heating the ends of small pieces of 6 mm rod and then imparting a pattern onto each with a pair of clean needle nose pliers (Figure 4.81). As you impart the pattern, pull slightly to thin the region between the pattern (the leaf) and the rod (which will serve as a handle when sealing the leaves onto the branch). Make as many leaves as are required for your particular branch. Usually about eight to ten will look nice on a small branch.

8. The leaves are now joined (Figures 4.82 - 4.83) to the smaller branches and stems constructed in Step 6. After each is sealed and properly adjusted, the flame is directed to the thin region on the rod handle, and a flame cut is made. Be sure that these ends are lightly fire polished and not too pointed.

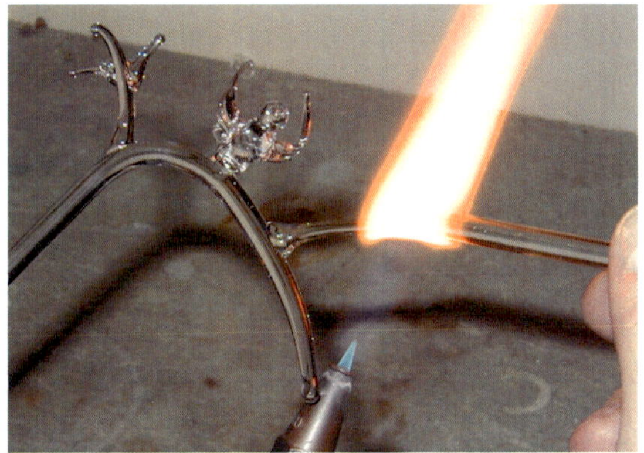

Figure 4.79 *Adding smaller branches to the larger ones.*

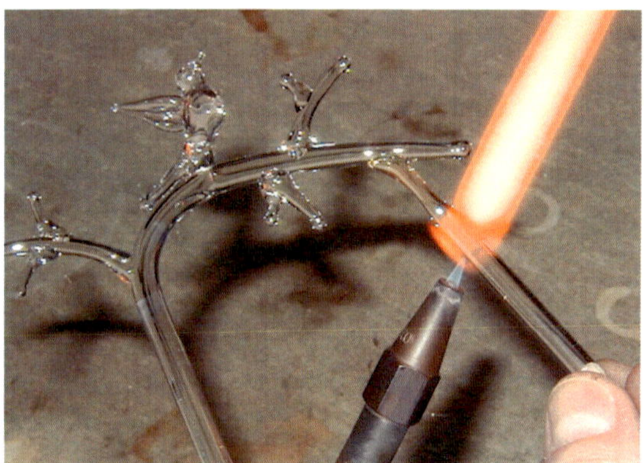

Figure 4.80 *Completing the addition of smaller branches. Give consideration to balance.*

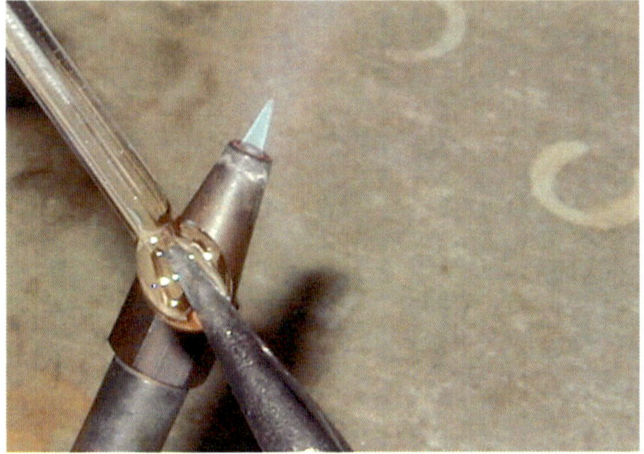

Figure 4.81 *Make leaves by imparting a pattern with pliers. The rod will be the handle.*

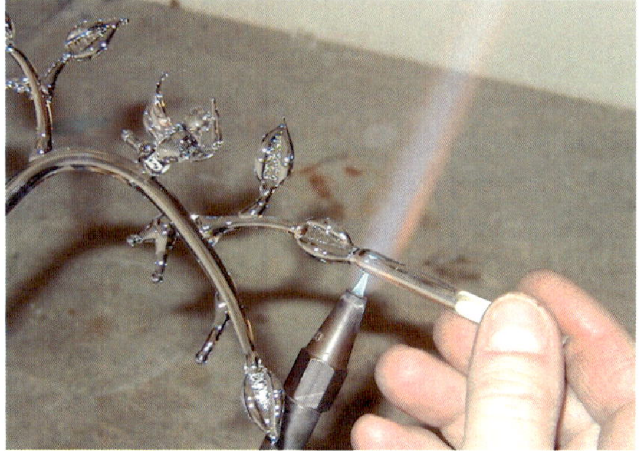

Figure 4.82 *Adding leaves to the ends of the branches. Then the handle is flame cut.*

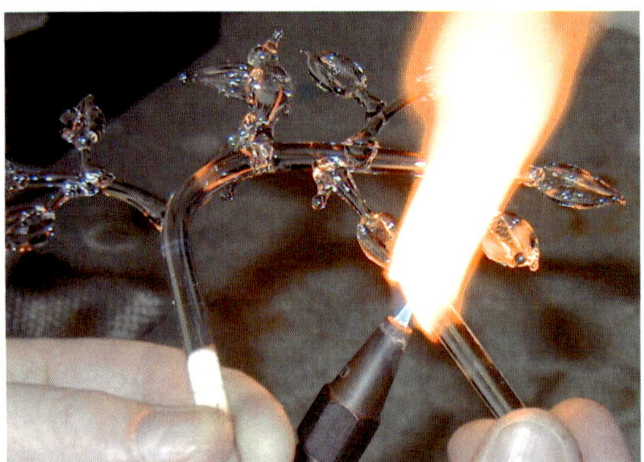

Figure 4.83 *A Closer look at flame cut of the rod handle. Ends must not be too pointed.*

Figure 4.84 *The finished branch and bird. Leaves can be rearranged to improve look.*

9. At this time, carefully check each joint for physical strength and also look over the distribution of the leaves on your branch and make any desired changes (Figure 4.84).
10. The bottom of the branch, about 5 inches below the bend, is now heated and a point is added by drawing off the small remaining piece with a pair of pliers (Figure 4.85). The branch is now completed and can be put into a household planter for decoration.
11. Oven anneal the completed product.
12. If desired, the leaves and bird can now be colored with glass stain. (See page 20 in Chapter 1.)

Alternately, one can construct larger trees which are also "two dimensional" in design. In this case, the trunk can be made of larger rod (8 mm) and numerous branches added where desired. These larger trees can be made to be free standing by adding a tripod-type base (roots) which may be made of either 6 or 8 mm rod,

Figure 4.85 *Making a pointed bottom on the branch. May then be put into planter.*

depending on the size of the tree.

The general sequence of steps should begin with the shaping of the trunk (the lower part serving as the handle), adding the branches and secondary branches, forming leaves, adding the leaves, cutting off the trunk at the desired length and finally adding the base (three drawn rods which are nearly 90° to the main trunk and 120° from one another). One or more birds can also be added (Figure 4.86).

Figure 4.86 *A More elaborate, stand alone tree utilizing steps similar to those described in this project.*

LABORATORY PROJECT - ARTISTIC SIX

SNOWFLAKE CHRISTMAS ORNAMENTS

Introduction:

Beautiful and delicate looking snowflake ornaments can be made by a method that involves only the most basic of techniques (Figure 4.87). The six facets of the snowflake are made one at a time and then joined together. In this way a smaller and closer patterned snowflake is possible; otherwise heat from the flame would easily melt the neighboring parts that are already completed.

Figure 4.87 *Glass snowflake.*

Most beginning students err in making the knobs too large on each of the snowflake's "spokes". Think small! Even the smallest knobs will look surprisingly beautiful when the whole snowflake is assembled.

Materials:

About 36 inches of 4 mm rod

Special Tools:

Marver, graphite plate and pointed graphite rod

Flame:

#3 tip; small pin-point flame

Construction Steps

(All part letters refer to Figure 4.99 on page 120)

1. Form a small sphere at the end of a 6 to 8 inch length of 4 mm rod.

2. While the sphere is still hot, flatten it between a marver and a graphite plate. The flattened disk will be the center of the snowflake, and the rod will become one of the spokes of the snowflake (Part A).

3. Carefully preheat the area two inches below the flattened disk by passing the rod through the flame rapidly for no more than 1 to 2 seconds.

4. While doing this with one hand, heat the tip of a piece of 4 mm rod until it becomes softened.

5. Join the rod, draw it out, and flame cut it as is shown in Figure 4.88 (and Part B). This is done in the same plane as the center disk . These drawn out knobs should be very small!

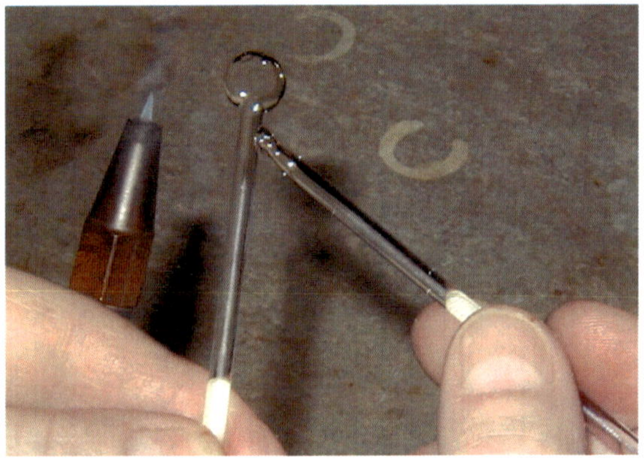

Figure 4.88 *Joining the first knob of the snowflake pattern.*

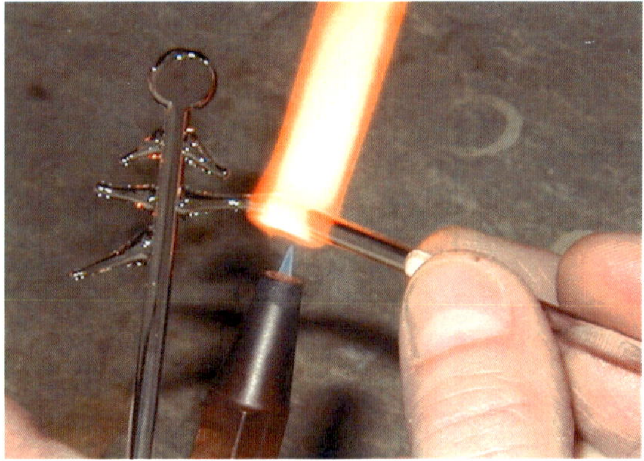

Figure 4.89 *Continuing with the pattern on the first part of the snowflake.*

6. Now proceed to complete the pattern as shown in Figures 4.89 - 4.90 and Part C. Set this completed spoke aside for use in Step 8. The rod may need to be reheated briefly from time to time, but probably for sure by the time you get to the fifth or sixth knob on the spoke.

7. With another piece of 4 mm rod, construct a similar pattern on it by repeating Steps 3 through 6. No disk should be made at the end of this rod.

8. When completed, join this piece to the first spoke by heating the flattened disk at a point directly opposite to the first spoke. Simultaneously heat the tip of the newly constructed spoke (Figure 4.90). It is neither necessary nor desirable to heat the entire flattened disk. Make all of these joints by using the

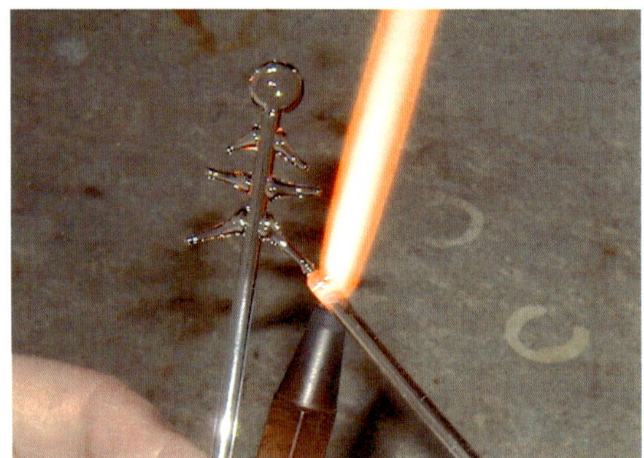

Figure 4.90 *Completing the pattern on the first part of the snowflake.*

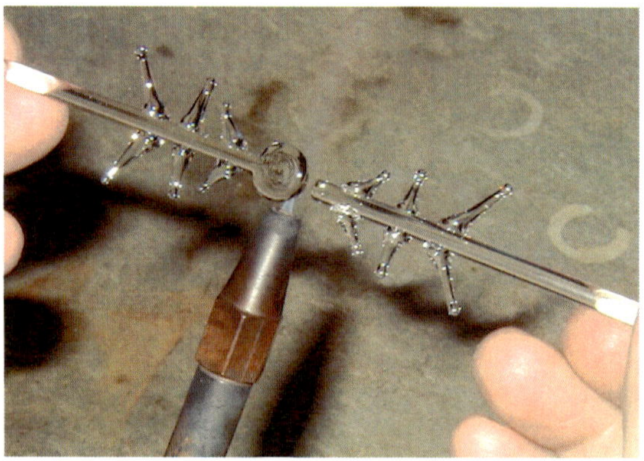

Figure 4.91 *Joining a second part of the pattern to the first part (to the center flat disk.*

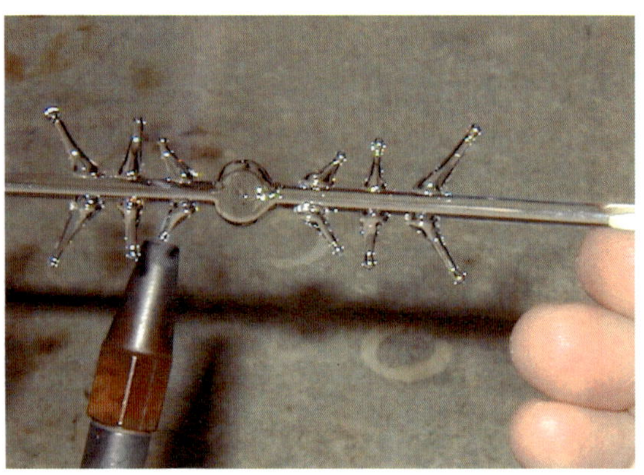

Figure 4.92 *After the second part of the pattern is joined to the first part.*

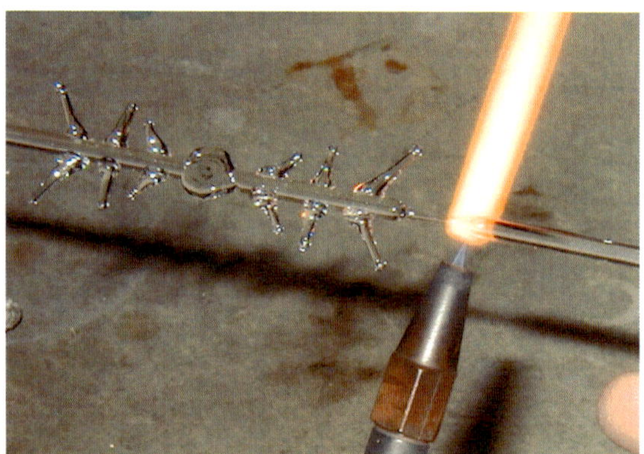

Figure 4.93 *Making a flame cut on the rod with the second part of the pattern.*

in-flame technique (seal together while both parts are in the flame). Try to work quickly, but accurately. Make certain that the two spokes (Figure 4.92) are positioned in a straight line and that the pattern on each spoke remains in the plane of the center disk.

9. Remove the excess 4mm rod handle from the second spoke by flame cutting (Figure 4.93 and Part E). The first spoke is kept long to serve as a handle.

10. Repeat Steps 7 and 8 until a total of 6 evenly spaced spokes (including the handle) are attached to the central disk. Each should be the same length and be located at 60° from one another (Figures 4.94 - 4.96 and Part F).

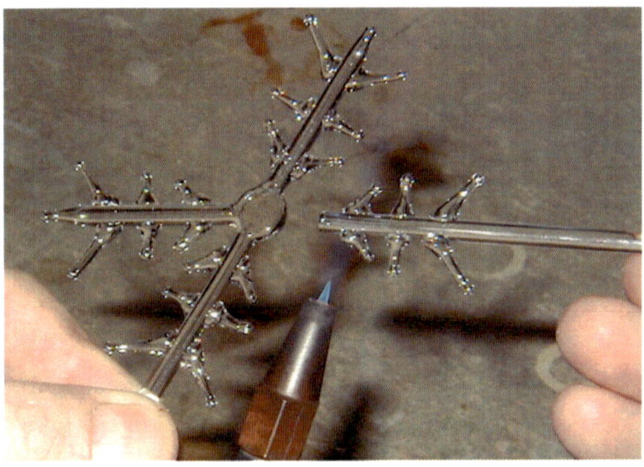

Figure 4.94 *Joining a fourth part of the pattern to the first part (to the center flat disk).*

Figure 4.95 *Joining a fifth part of the pattern to the first part (to the center flat disk).*

11. When completed, allow the snowflake to cool.

12. Make a thorough physical inspection of each joint, by pressing slightly and carefully with your fingers. The joints should easily withstand this gentle pressure. If any parts break off, the probable cause was insufficient preheating of the rod spokes before making the joints. Make any necessary repairs.

Figure 4.96 *Joining the last part of the pattern to the first part (to the center flat disk).*

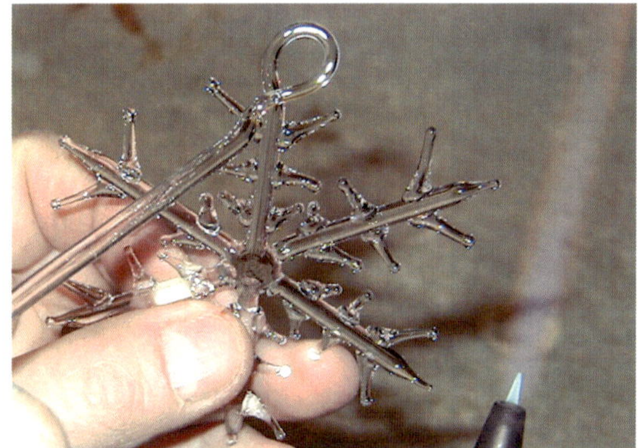

Figure 4.97 *Forming the loop off of what was previously the base rod.*

13. Now the hanging loop is formed. Hold on to the body of the snowflake and heat the excess rod previously used as a han-

-dle. The heating should be focused just above the last of the patterns on this spoke. When it becomes sufficiently softened, remove from the flame, draw out, and fashion a loop (Figure 4.97). Remove any of the extra rod by doing a flame cut as close to the loop as possible. Be sure to seal the ends so as to make a good joint. Pressing the hot ends together with the flat end of a graphite rod will prove helpful. Use a small carbon rod to make the loop circular (Figure 4.98). The finished product is shown in Part G of Figure 4.99 and in Figure 4.87 at the beginning of this project.

Figure 4.98 *Finishing the loop on the top of the snowflake.*

4. Oven anneal when possible.

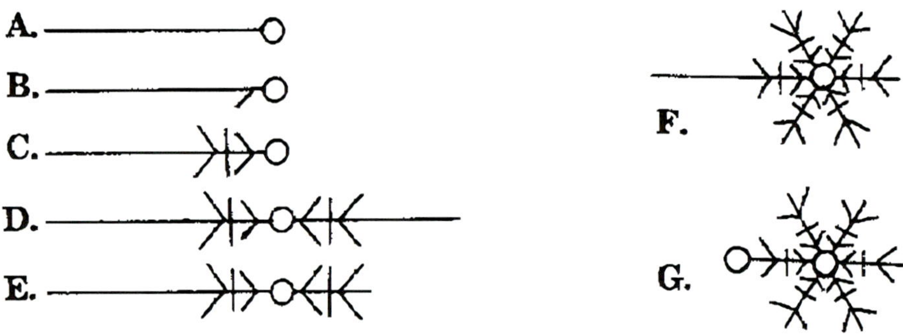

Figure 4.99 *Summary of the steps in the construction of a snowflake ornament.*

LABORATORY PROJECT - ARTISTIC SEVEN

ICICLE CHRISTMAS ORNAMENTS

Introduction:

Attractive old fashioned icicle Christmas ornaments (Figure 4.100). can be made by a combination of simple techniques. One new technique employed here, the twisting of flattened rod, is easy to learn and can be very useful in a number of other artistic projects.

Figure 4.100 *Old fashioned icicle ornaments.*

Materials:

Two pieces of 6 mm rod, appproximately 6 inches each
(8mm rod may be substituted for larger icicles)
Colored borosilicate glass optional

Special Tools:

Marver, graphite plate, small carbon rod

Flame:

#5 tip; hot, medium sized flame

Construction Steps

1. A rather large sphere is formed on the end of a piece of 6 mm rod (Figure 4.101).
2. When the sphere is large enough, it is flattened by pressing it with a marver onto a graphite plate (Figure 4.102). If desired, add one or two kinds of colored glass to the edges of the

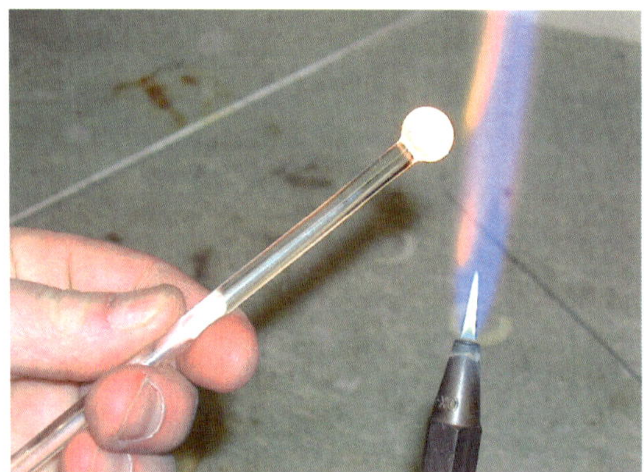

Figure 4.101 *Forming a large sphere of glass at the end of a 6 mm rod.*

Figure 4.102 *After flattening the sphere of glass with a marver.*

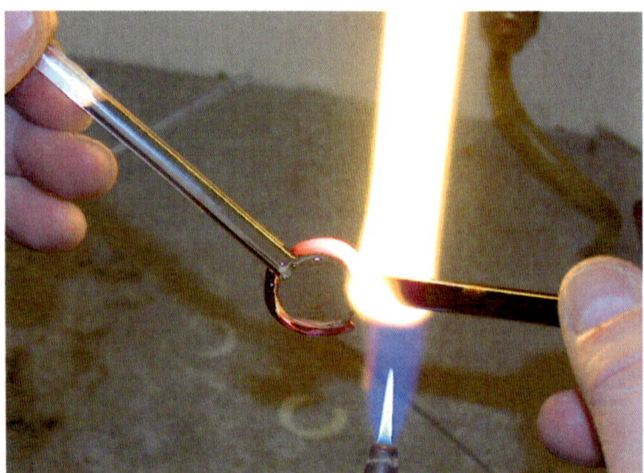

Figure 4.103 *Adding blue borosilicate glass to the edges of the flattened glass disk.*

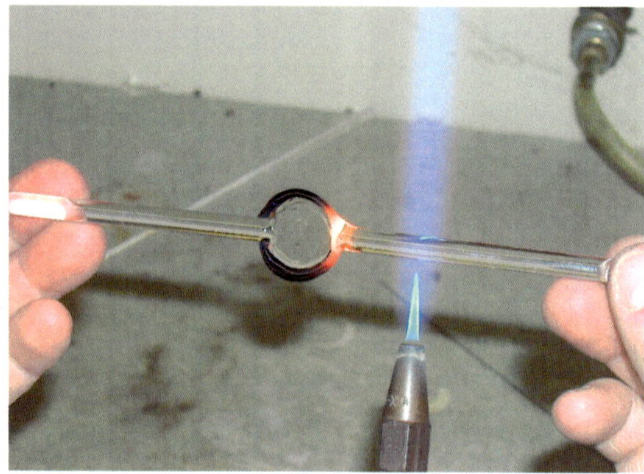

Figure 4.104 *Adding a second 6 mm handle to the opposite side of the flattened disk.*

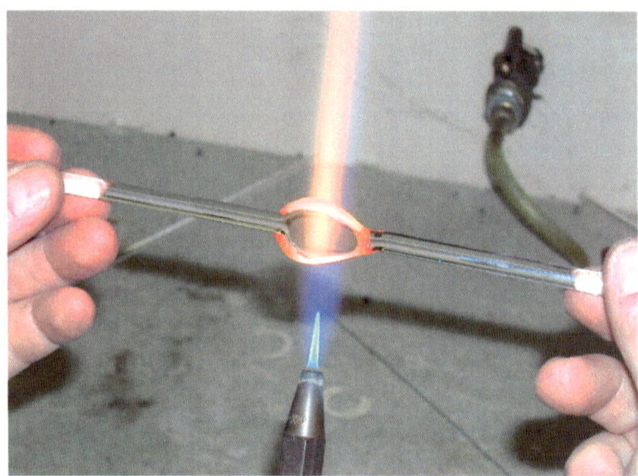

Figure 4.105 *Heating the flattened disk.*

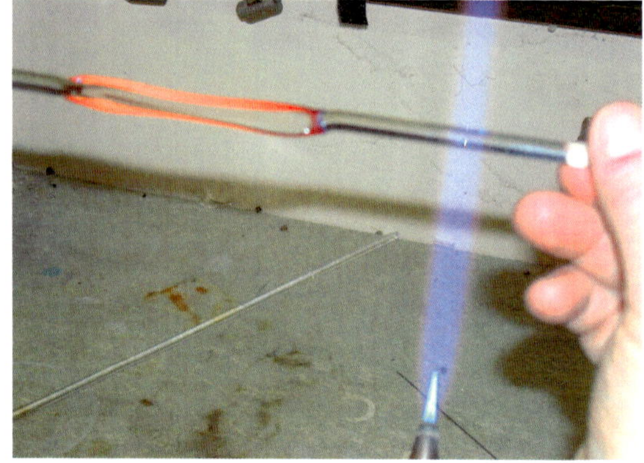

Figure 4.106 *Beginning to stretch and twist the disk.*

flattened disk (Figure 4.103). The colored glass will produce an interesting pattern in the finished product.

3. A second 6 mm rod is then added to the opposite edge of the flattened disk (Figure 4.104). Take care to make a good joint. This will serve as a second handle.

4. This disk is now reheated strongly until it becomes quite soft (Figure 4.105). Remove from the flame and simultaneously pull and rotate the handles in the opposite direction (Figures 4.106 - 4.107). Control the rate of pulling and the rate of rotation so that the desired thickness, length, and spiral design is attained. Keep tension on the finished product until it becomes cool, thus keeping the twisted portion straight.

5. If the twisted area is sufficiently long, make a flame cut in the middle (Figure 4.108) and allow the pieces to cool. Make certain that the cut does not result in a sharp edge. This will make two equal length icicles. Icicles of 4-6 inches in length are recommended. Otherwise make a flame cut at the desired length if a single, larger icicle is desired.

6. Reheat the glass right above the twisted portion until it becomes softened (Figure 4.109). Then draw it out and at the same time form a small loop (Figures 4.110 and 4.111). The excess rod should be removed with a flame cut. While still hot, the ends are pressed into the glass with the flat end of a small carbon rod (Figure 4.112). Then reheat again. If necessary, the loop can be reshaped with the same rod (Figure 4.113).

7. The finished product (Figure 4.114) should be oven annealed.

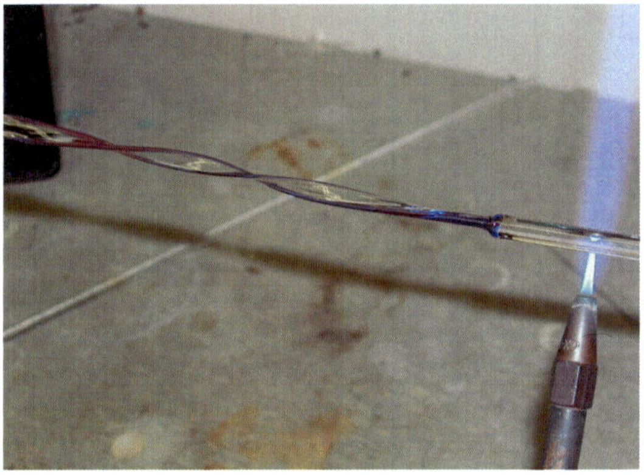

Figure 4.107 *Completing the searching and twisting of the disk.*

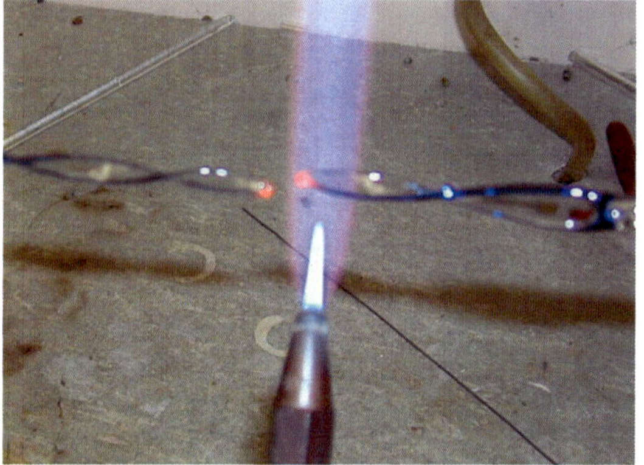

Figure 4.108 *Flame cutting in the middle.*

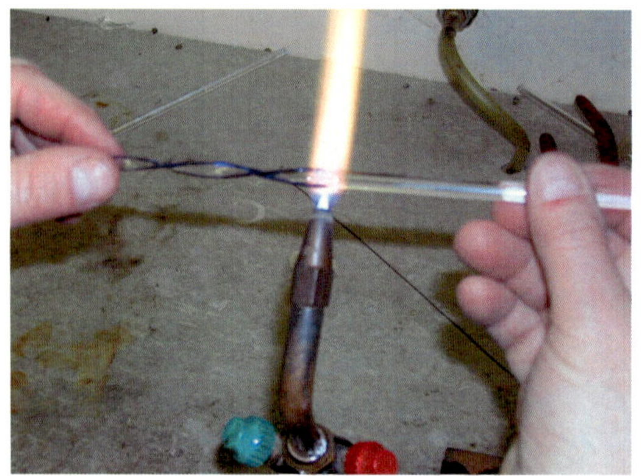

Figure 4.109 *After the flame cut has cooled, the top is heated and drawn out.*

Figure 4.110 *After the top is heated, it is drawn out in order to form the loop.*

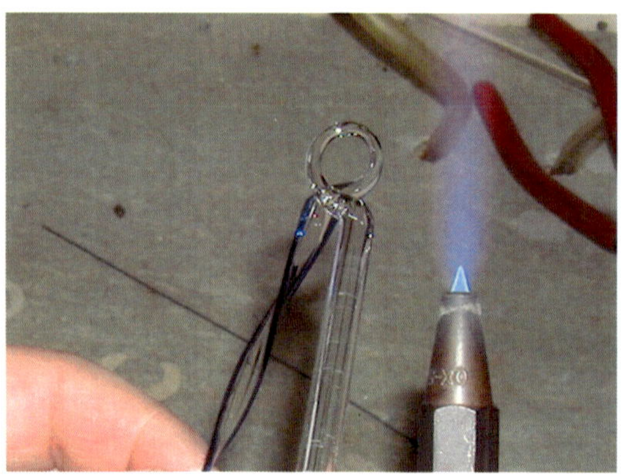

Figure 4.111 *Forming the loop.*

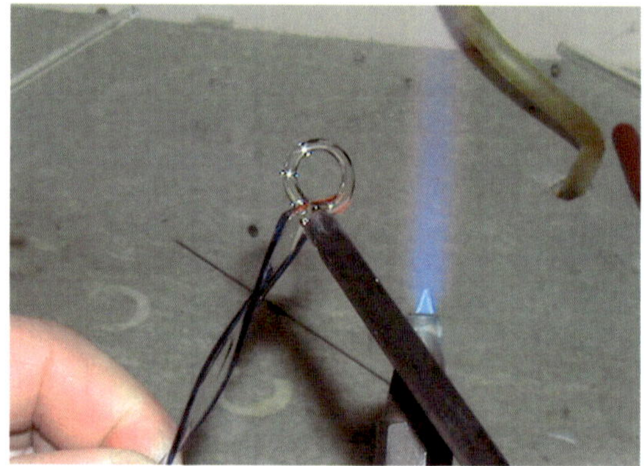

Figure 4.112 *Closing the loop with end of the graphite rod before reheating.*

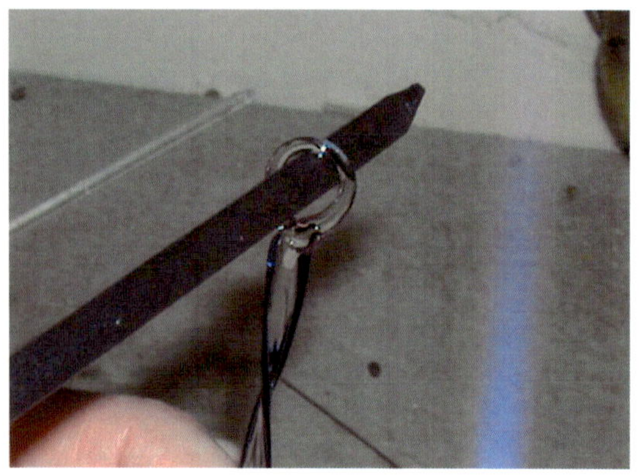

Figure 4.113 *If necessary, the loop is reheated and reshaped.*

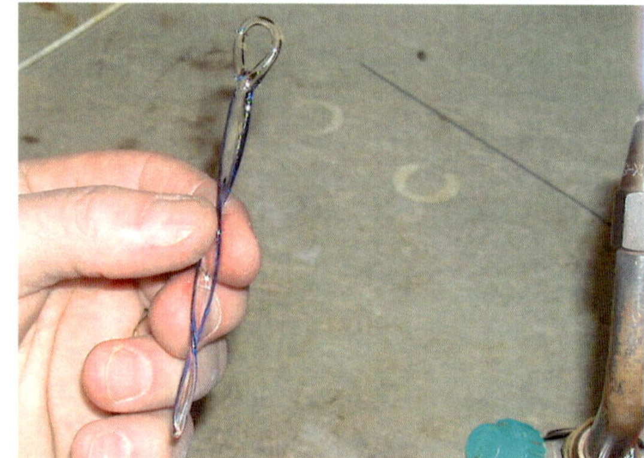

Figure 4.114 *The finished icicle ornament.*

More Ideas for Items To Make From Rod

A number of additional items made entirely from rod are shown in Figures 4.115 - 4.130. Try to analyze the items to determine the probable steps involved in their construction. Some can be made by beginners, but some require advanced skills. Easier items are indicated.

Figure 4.115 *Solid swan and fish. Each can easily be analyzed and made by the beginner.*

Figure 4.116 *Small bear & octopus (with top hat). Again, can be made by the beginner.*

Figure 4.117 *Sea gulls on a piece of driftwood. Each of the birds is a simple modification of those made earlier. White glass can be used.*

Figure 4.118 *A Windmill that works, Made of 4 mm rod. A vine with leaves and a small pump on a stand are added.*

Figure 4.119 *Beautiful colored flowers in a white vase. Flowers made by attaching the hot glass to piano wire. (See Endnote 1 concerning the famous Blaschka glass flowers.)*

Figure 4.120 *Mouse, rabbit and cat. Once again, these are items for the beginner.*

Figure 4.121 *Bicycle. This is a little tricky, only because of the round tires.*

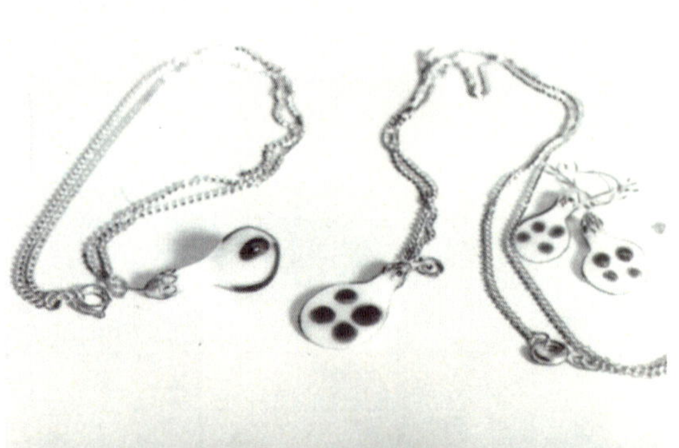

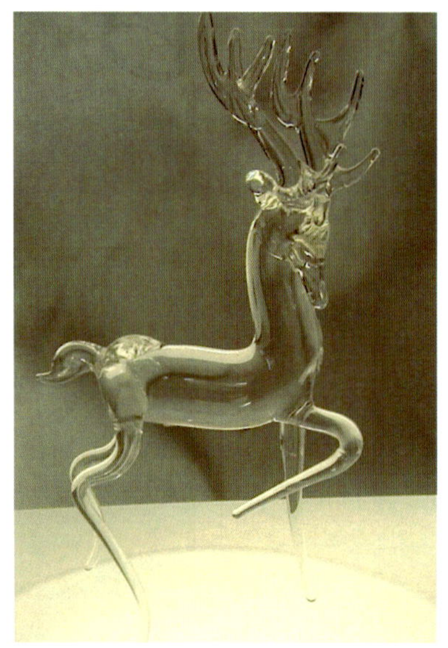

Figure 4.122 (Above Left) *Use your imagination to make glass pendants to fashion into necklaces or earrings. The metal parts can be purchased from craft stores. These are more items for the beginner.*

Figure 4.123 (Above Right) *These shamrocks are similar to the flowers made in the first project. Add a few leaves.*

Figure 4.124 (Left) *A solid reindeer, perfectly balanced on delicate legs. This is definitely for the advanced worker.*

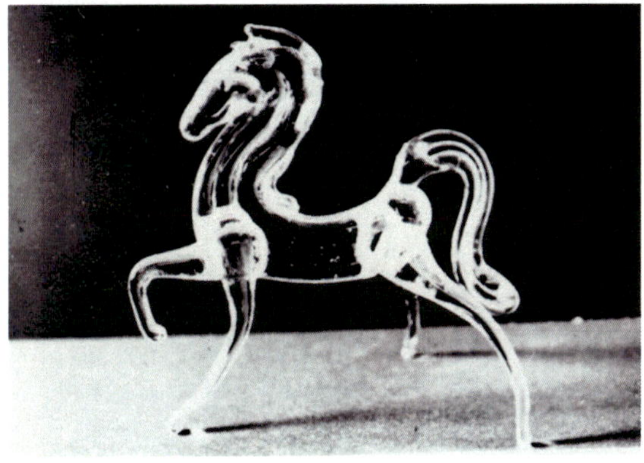

Figure 4.125 (Left) *Bird and pump in planter.*

Figure 4.126 (Above) *A solid horse. Another perfectly balanced item on delicate legs. This is definitely for the advanced worker. Made by Joe Wheeler.*

Figure 4.127 *A graceful figure skater. Her body and skates are etched to give a special effect. This is definitely for the advanced worker. Made by Gordon Smith, Rochester, MN.*

Figure 4.128 *Christmas tree fashioned entirely with loops of glass attached from limbs radiating from a central trunk. Ornaments and a star are then added. Glass stain adds color to the product.*

Figure 4.129 *Another beautiful Christmas tree made in a different manner. In this tree, limbs radiating from the central trunk are formed in such a way that small hooks are made at the ends. Individual ornaments with loops are placed on each hook. A removable angel is placed on the top.*

Figure 4.130 *This elaborate candelabra would be remarkable in its own right if it were made of borosilicate glass, but this wonderful combination of marias, twists, curlicues and leaf petals was made entirely from quartz glass by the glassblowers at the Mendeleev Institute of Chemistry in Moscow, Russia. It was presented as a gift to the author. Expert glassblowers in the united states admit that such a creation made entirely of quartz is generally regarded as "nearly impossible". Thus, beginners are encouraged "not to try this at home"!*

ENDNOTES

[1] An assemby of more than 3000 fantastic Blaschkas glass flowers, dating from 1887, is on permanent exhibit at the Ware Museum at Harvard University. The exact method of the construction of these very remarably detailed and accurated models of botanical species has been lost, although several have tried to explain the "magic" of these life-like specimens. For example, see (a) S. M. Rossi-Wilcox, "The Blaschkas as Scientific Glassblowers," *Proceedings of the 35th Symposium on the Art of Scientific Glassblowing, American Scientific Glassblowers Society*, pp 2-6, 1990 and (b) D. Gover, "The Blaschka Glass Blowers: Proposed Methods of Construction, *Proceedings of the 38th Symposium on the Art of Scientific Glassblowing, American Scientific Glassblowers Society*, pp 23-34, 1993. Make it a point to visit this exhibit when you are in the Boston area!

Chapter 5
LACE TECHNIQUES

The lace, or network, technique is widely used and is incorporated in making a great range of artistic items. Often it is used simply as decoration on other items, but sometimes items such as glass ships are made almost entirely of lace and drawn glass (Figure 5.1). There are a number of different ways to fashion glass into a lace-like appearance. Probably the most popular approach is that which is often referred to as the running stitch (Figure 5.2). This produces a rather dense and strong product (Figure 5.3 top). A more elaborate and difficult technique involves a network of closely spaced loops (Figure 5.3 bottom). This is done by rotating the hand back and forth while making the network. In this book, only the running stitch will be considered.

Figure 5.1 *A large, intricate glass lace ship built by the author.*

Quite a variety of different rod diameters can be used, and different workers will certainly have different preferences. It is probably easiest to start off with 6 mm rod, but more experienced glassworkers often choose 8 or 9 or even 10 mm rod. The lace may be formed not only along a rod but also in a circular fashion at the end of a rod (Figures 5.3 and 5.4), or both can be combined to make larger, more complex objects. We will focus our attention on the making of circular patterns, as these are relatively easy to make and are extremely useful as portions of items or as bases for many other items.

Figure 5.2 *Making a simple running stitch.*

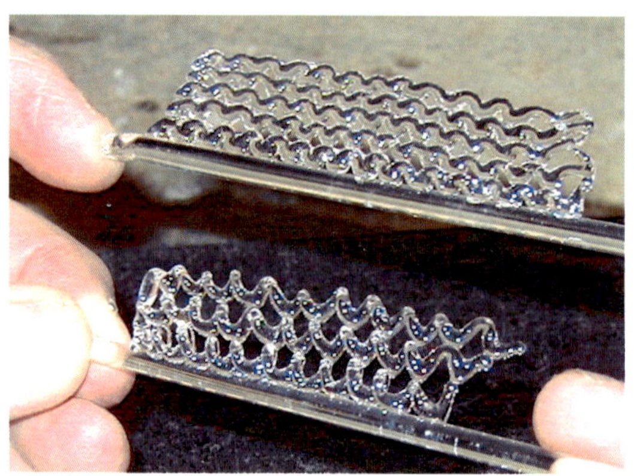

Figure 5.3 *Samples of running stitch (top) and looped stitch (bottom).*

Once you learn how to make these, it will be easier to apply the technique to non-circular patterns.

Regardless of the type of lace, rod size or shape of the pattern you select, you should realize that this technique will require more practice to master than any of the other techniques described so far. An hour of practice may be all that is necessary for some simple projects for some students, but it is more likely that many, many hours of practice will be necessary before you begin to feel any confidence with making attractive lace. At any rate, don't become discouraged. Stick with it, and you will be pleased with your results.

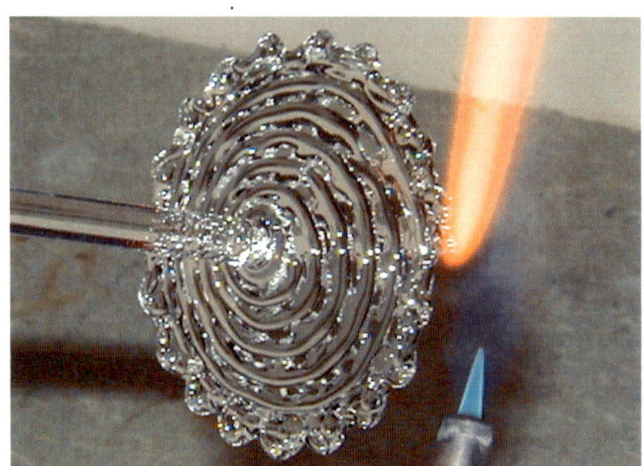

Figure 5.4 *Finishing off five rounds of running circular lace with one row of looped stitch lace. The last stitch is carefully sealed to the base and fire polished.*

Figure 5.5 *The cut off circular lace piece, ready to be attached to another item.*

LABORATORY EXERCISE FOURTEEN

THE CIRCULAR RUNNING STITCH: MAKING CIRCULAR BASES

1. The burner is adjusted for a small, bushy flame having a triangular blue cone no larger than 1/4 inch. This flame is fine for small areas of lace. For larger items or for more advanced work or more advanced workers, a larger, hotter flame should be used.

2. An end maria is formed on an 8 inch piece of 5 mm rod. Once completed, switch this to your left hand. This is to be the base rod, on which the lace will be built. The tip of an 8-12 inch piece of 6 or 8 mm rod (the working rod) is softened in the flame at the same time with the right hand. At this point, the maria on the base rod is positioned in such a way so that it just touches the outer left hand portion of the flame. The base rod itself should be nearly perpendicular to the flame.

3. When the tip of the working rod is sufficiently softened, it is touched to the tip of the base rod and then immediately pulled out slightly to form a small area of constricted glass. While still hot, it is then reattached a small distance from where it was pulled out, producing a small loop.

4. The base rod is rotated counterclockwise slightly, and the procedure is repeated. The left hand turns the base rod while the right hand moves in and out to fashion the lace loops. The working rod should pass through the hottest portion of the flame as it is moved in and out (Figure 5.6).

5. Adjust the position of the glass in the flame as necessary. If the lace is too thick or the loops are too large, the working rod is not being heated sufficiently. Move the tip of the working rod closer to the tip of the blue cone and work slower. If the lace is too thin or the loops are too small, the working rod is being heated too much. In this case, move the tip of the working rod slightly higher in the flame. Such corrections may need to be made constantly, and they should be made while the lace is being formed. Do not stop either of the motions; eventually you should attain a regular rhythm. The lace should have small noticeable holes. It may be necessary to adjust the loop size by moving the working rod in and out either more or less. The main thing is to try to form loops of uniform size with glass of uniform thickness.

6. As the circular pattern becomes larger (Figures 5.7 and 5.8), it will become necessary to add a few more loops to each layer to compensate for the increased diameter of the piece. It is likely that the circular shape being formed may not be flat, but somewhat concave in nature. This is usually ideal for bases to put on other items. Eventually you will be able to make flat or even convex shapes if desired. The beginner is advised to limit the diameter of completed networks to an inch or two. Larger products are much more likely to crack.

7. The entire lace should be carefully reheated to remove the stresses within the piece. The flame should be gradually increased in size and hotness and the lace held high in the flame and rotated rapidly. Eventually the entire piece should become somewhat reddened.
It may be a good idea to make certain that the bottom sits flat by pressing the finished hot product on a graphite plate (Figure 5.10). Check that the rod is pointing straight up when this is done. Afterwards, it will be necessary to reheat the item once again. Do this slowly and carefully.

8. At this time, flame annealing is begun by adding at least one full turn of gas to the flame. After a while, the temperature of the flame is slowly reduced by turning down the oxygen until eventually it is completely off. The finished piece should then be immersed in vermiculite (Figure 5.11) and later oven annealed.

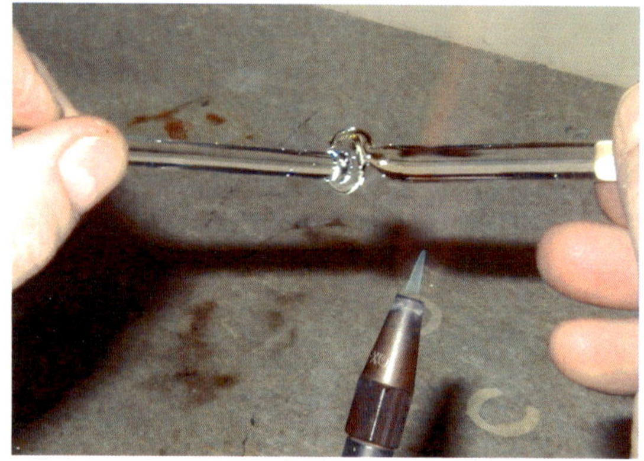

Figure 5.6 *Starting the circular running stitch.*

Figure 5.7 *Continuing the circular running stitch.*

Once you become somewhat proficient with this technique, you may wish to add one extra row of decorative looped lace along the circumference of your circular base, but at right angles to the original lace (Figure 5.9). This will give the piece a more finished look, adding much to the overall appearance. Be sure that the base is adequately preheated before beginning. When finished, be sure that you take extra care to make a good seal to the base after making the flame cut (shown in Figure 5.4). Once completed, the piece should be reheated again and then thoroughly flame annealed. Again, it is wise to flatten larger bases on a graphite plate immediately after the final reheating before flame annealing (Figure 5.10).

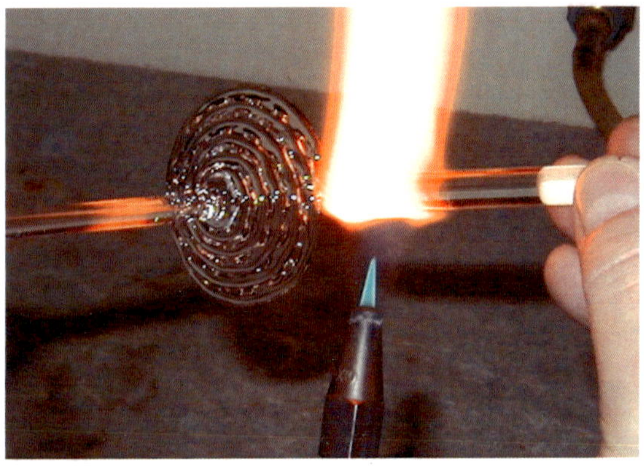

Figure 5.8 *Further continuation of the circular running stitch.*

Figure 5.9 *Adding the last row of looped stitch to the circular running stitch.*

Figure 5.10 *Flattening the finished circular running stitch on a graphite plate.*

Figure 5.11 *Placing the finished circular running stitch into a can filled with vermiculite to allow it to cool slowly, preventing excess stresses in the finished product.*

LABORATORY PROJECT - ARTISTIC EIGHT

HAND PUMP WITH LACE BASE

Introduction:

Circular bases (Figure 5.5) can be added to many of the items you make. A good example is the addition of a base to one of the hand pumps you made in Project Artistic Six.

In this specific case, the joint between the pump and the base is made directly below the bottom maria. This serves to hide the joint and makes the finished product look more attractive (Figure 5.12).

Figure 5.12 *Hand pump.*

Materials:

Approximately 12 inches of 5 mm rod

Special Tools:

Graphite plate

Flame:

#5 tip; medium flame

Construction Steps

1. Make a hand pump as described in Laboratory Project Artistic Five.
2. Once the pump is cool enough, score with a glass knife and cut directly below the bottom maria, just below the spout.
3. Construct a lace base as described in Exercise 14 on page 131. The base should be at least two inches in diameter.

4. When the lace base is cool, clean it off thoroughly. Use your glass knife to score and cut the rod at a distance of about two inches above the base.

5. Heat the end of this rod and also the bottom maria on the hand pump (Figure 5.13). Join these in the flame and reheat if necessary to make a good seal.

6. Be sure to check that the pump stands straight. Do this by placing the pump on a graphite plate (Figure 5.14). Oven anneal as soon as possible.

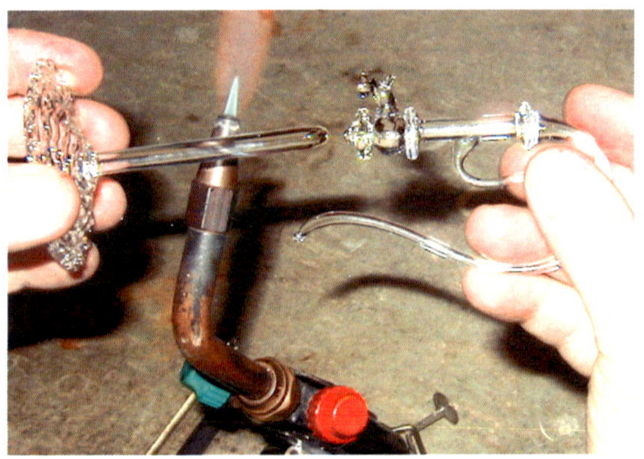

Figure 5.13 *Attaching the pump to the lace base (circular running stitch piece).*

Figure 5.14 *Straightening the finished pump on the lace stand.*

LABORATORY PROJECT - ARTISTIC NINE

LACE TEA POT

Introduction:

A delightful lace teapot can be made by anyone who has gained some proficiency in forming lace. The item starts out as a cone shape. The teapot lid is added later. With some imagination you will be able to think of numerous other products that could be made from the basic cone shape utilized in this project.

Figure 5.15 *Lace tea pot (color added)*

Materials:

Approximately 8 inches of 4 mm rod
Approximately 15 inches of 6 mm or 8 mm rod

Special Tools:

Graphite plate, needlenose pliers, small carbon rod

Flame:

#5 tip; medium flame

Construction Steps

1. Form an end maria at the end of a 4 mm rod. The bottom of the teapot will be built around the maria. The rod will serve as a handle and base rod during this construction.

2. The bottom of the teapot is fashioned first. Keep the maria warm while softening the end of a 6 mm rod. A small, cool flame should be used. As soon as the rod is softened, begin to form a tight, flat circular pattern of glass (not lace) around the maria. This can be done simply be rotating the working rod and wrapping the softened glass onto the maria. A solid base

should result. Every effort should be made to avoid forming any holes during this part of the construction. (In Step 10, the base will be strongly heated again and flattened. Any holes would quickly enlarge during this step.) Continue the wrapping procedure until the base is slightly more than an inch in diameter.

3. Now the sides of the teapot are begun. This is done without disconnecting the working rod from the finished bottom. Instead, the base rod position is changed so that the lace can be built up on the upper portion of the flat disk. Rotation of the base rod by about 90° toward you should position the glass properly. The sides are built up of running stitch lace with uniform holes throughout the pattern. The technique here should be the same as used in making the circular bases in Exercise 14. (Some of the pictures in Figures 5.6 - 5.8 beginning on page 131 may also be helpful for this project.)

4. After several layers are added, begin to decrease the diameter of the sides so that the product takes on the appearance of a cone. The finished cone should be approximately 1.25 inches in length. After completing the lace work, position the working rod so that it is attached to the tip of the lace in such a way that the two rod handles are now linear with one another.

5. Increase the flame size and reheat the entire lace portion in the flame with constant rotation. This should be continued until the piece becomes uniformly red in color. Any shaping can be done at this time by selectively pulling or pushing the handles. A slight pulling will always tend to remove irregularities and make the piece more symmetrical.

6. The right hand rod is now flame cut at about 1/4 inch beyond the lace point. This is then shaped into a sphere by proper heating and rotation.

7. The flame size is reduced again and two layers of lace are added on to the side of the cone below the spherical knob about 1/3 of the way down the side. This is best done by holding the product in the left hand so that it is just below the bushy part of the flame. A 6 mm working rod is then heated and allowed to pass through the flame. The base rod is rotated counterclockwise and lace is added until both layers are completed. (The result will be the "lid" lip of the teapot.) When finished, the working rod is flame cut, and the remaining end on

the product is strongly heated in order to permanently seal it to the rest of the glass.

8. The teapot handle is now added. The lace form is kept warm by rotation in the upper part of a strong flame while a 6 or 8 mm rod is softened over a rather large area. The locations for the spout and handle are mentally selected; choose any irregularities in the lid as an ideal place to add the handle. The handle is added by joining the rod just underneath the lid, drawing it outward for about 1 1/4 inches, and then pushing inward toward the base forming a loop. Just before the drawn rod touches the base during the pushing inward, the points where attachment will occur are heated briefly in the flame to insure a good seal. The excess drawn rod is then removed by flame cutting. All of this should be done in one single smooth operation. Any reshaping necessary can be done at this time with a small carbon rod.

9. The spout is added in much the same way. The entire piece is kept warm while a 6 or 8 mm rod is softened. A larger amount of glass is gathered for this step by holding the rod upward while heating. When ready for attachment, the thickened rod is touched to a point on the base opposite the handle. Then it is drawn outward and downward slightly, and finally upward and in slightly to give the spout its proper shape. It is flame cut and fire polished.

10. The product is now held firmly with a pair of pliers by the knob at the top of the pot. The 4 mm handle is removed by doing a flame cut as close to the flat bottom as possible. Any remaining excess is wiped off. A somewhat larger flame is used for these operations. No doubt some cracking of the base will be heard during these operations, but as soon as the handle has been removed, the entire solid base is reheated until it is uniformly red. This should repair any cracks that may have formed. The product is then pressed down firmly on a graphite plate to flatten the bottom.

11. The product should be immediately flame annealed and then immersed in vermiculite or placed between heat resistant gloves until cool. Oven anneal as soon as possible.

LABORATORY PROJECT - ARTISTIC TEN

BIRD IN A BIRD CAGE

Introduction:

A beautiful bird in a cage can be made once you have gained some confidence with the circular lace technique. The bird is made first by methods described earlier (Artistic Two). A lace bottom to the cage is then built around the base of the bird, and finally the cage spokes and top loop are fashioned by drawing out and shaping hot glass rod.

The completed cage makes an attractive Christmas tree ornament, or a cage stand can be constructed so the item may be enjoyed all year round.

If you wish, 5 mm rod can be used in place of 6 mm and the lace could be made from 6 mm rod instead of 8 mm.

Figure 5.16 *Bird cage on lace stand.*

Materials:

Approximately14 inches of 6 mm rod
Approximately 8inches of 8 mm rod

Special Tools:

Needlenose pliers, small carbon rod, marver, triangular file

Flame:

#5 tip; medium flame at first, but flame varies in each step

Construction Steps

1. Make a small bird out of 6 mm rod by the method described previously in Laboratory Project Artistic Two. Ideally, this

should be done at the end of a rod at least twelve inches long in order to allow an adequate handle for the procedures described in the following steps.

2. Once the bird is cool enough, an intermediate maria is made by heating the rod (small hot flame) uniformly at a distance of about a half inch below the tail feathers. The head of the bird can be held in the right hand and used as a handle. This end should be held lower while the rod handle end is held higher. In this way the bird should remain cool and your fingers should be far enough away from the flame. Care should be taken so as to prevent the tail feathers from becoming softened. Most heating on the rod to form the maria should be done with the tail feathers in a downward position.

3. As soon as the intermediate maria has been formed (outside the flame as usual), return it to the flame and heat briefly just below the maria and pull out so that a slight constriction is formed. This will make it easier to flame cut the cage when it is finished.

4. Reduce the intensity of the flame. Reheat the maria and begin to soften the end of an 8 mm rod which is at least 8 inches in length. Begin to form the cage bottom by using the methods described previously for making circular lace bases. The lace should be started with the bird head down and away from you with the maria just brushing against the bottom portion of the bushy flame. The 8 mm working rod is fed through the flame to the top of the maria while the base rod (the maria and bird) are rotated counterclockwise. Try to make the lace thicker and a little more solid than usual lace. This is done by using a somewhat cooler flame. (Note that this cage bottom is truly a lace bottom and not solid as was the case for the teapot.) Continue until four or five rows of lace are completed, keeping it as uniform as possible. Then flame cut the leftover 8 mm rod and heat the remaining end on the lace strongly enough so that it melts into the rest of the base.

5. Immediately reheat the entire base by rotating close to the flame until it becomes uniformly red in color. Take care to keep the heating off of the constricted area or else the bird and base will bend. If this does happen, use a pliers to correct the situation immediately. Likewise, if the lace bottom itself becomes distorted, use a marver to reflatten it.

6. Increase the intensity and size of the flame. Begin heating the end of an 8 mm rod while keeping the base hot by rotating it in the upper portion of the flame, about 8 inches above the tip of the torch. The base must be kept hot throughout the rest of the steps, otherwise cracking is certain to occur.

7. The first of the four "cage bars" is fashioned by touching the softened 8 mm rod to the top of the base lace at a point on the right front (when the bird cage is positioned upright and facing you). The rod is then drawn upward at a slow rate so that it forms a rather thick piece of glass approximately 3 inches long. Just as it begins to harden, it is bent inward so that it passes directly above the bird's head. A slight downward pressure at this point will cause the bar to assume a graceful curved shape. All of this should be done in a single motion outside of the flame. Reheating of the drawn bar should not be necessary.

8. As soon as this has hardened, heat the drawn rod at a point directly above the bird's head and pull the rod straight upward and flame cut.

9. Immediately return the base of the cage to the upper portion of the flame to reheat it. Also begin to reheat the 8 mm rod again in preparation for making the next bar.

10. The second cage bar is made on the left front in the same way as described in Step 7 above. Be sure to space the bars evenly along the bottom of the cage and make the bars so that they are about the same thickness. The end of the drawn rod should touch the end of the first bar at a point directly above the bird's head.

11. The end of the second drawn rod is then reheated and wrapped around the upright portion of the first bar.

12. Repeat Step 9.

13. Repeat Steps 10-11 (do the left rear bar next).

14. Repeat Steps 9-11 (doing the right rear bar last). The more rapidly all four bars can be added, the greater will be your chances of success with this project. Eventually you should be able to add all four bars over a period of less than 3 minutes.

15. As soon as the last bar is finished, turn the gas down (keeping the oxygen on) so as to make a small, intense flame. Transfer

the handle to your right hand and heat the mass of tangled ends at the top of the cage until they melt and coalesce into a single sphere. Take great care to prevent any of the thin bars from becoming melted or distorted. After the sphere is formed, invert the entire bird cage to allow the sphere to harden in a centered position.

16. Now, the top loop for hanging is fashioned. Immediately begin heating a piece of 6 mm rod. It may be wise to switch the cage back to your left hand. Also keep the top sphere heated. Turn the bird cage upright and with the bird pointing away from you, attach the 6 mm rod to the right side of the top sphere and draw it out very slowly, keeping it thick. Loop it around so that it touches the left side of the top sphere and do a flame cut. Use a small carbon rod to push the hot glass end into the sphere. Reheat the sphere to complete the seal, reshaping the loop if necessary with the carbon rod.

17. Use a pliers to hold on to the head of the bird. Tilt the cage so that it is down below the flame, and carefully flame cut the base rod. Keep the flame away from the bottom lace or else it will crack!

18. Oven anneal as soon as possible. Color may be added to the wings, tailfeathers and beak, if desired, after annealing.

LABORATORY PROJECT - ARTISTIC ELEVEN

BIRD WITH A LACE BODY

Introduction:

An attractive decorative bird with large, graceful wings and tail feathers and a lace body can be made by using the techniques already studied. If desired, the wings, tail feathers, eyes and beak may be colored with glass paints.

If you wish, 5mm rod can be used in place of 6mm and the lace could be made from 6mm rod instead of 8mm.

Figure 5.17 *Bird with lace body.*

Materials:

Approximately 16 inches of 6 mm rod
Approximately 8 inches of 8 mm rod

Special Tools:

Needlenose pliers, small carbon rod, marver, triangular file

Flame:

#5 tip; medium flame at first, but flame varies in each step

Construction Steps

1. The end of a 6 mm rod is softened, placed on a graphite plate and scored twice with the handle of a triangular file. Ideally, this should be done over a 3/4 inch length of rod. The flattened portion (which will later be drawn into the shape of a tail) is then aligned with the rest of the rod.
2. This piece now becomes the base rod. It is kept warm in the flame while the tip of a second piece of 8 mm rod is heated in a

small, rather cool flame. This will become the working rod in the formation of the lace body. If desired, 6mm rod can be used for the working rod.

3. Once the working rod is softened, a cone of lace (closely formed running stitch) is added at the end of the flattened part. This is built up, increasing the diameter of the cone slightly with each added layer until the diameter becomes slightly greater than that of the flattened portion of the tail. The diameter of the cone is then decreased again until an egg shape results. The total length should be just less than an inch. The working rod now becomes a second handle.

4. The lace body is strongly reheated with rotation until it becomes uniformly red colored. Any shaping is done at this time by pushing or pulling while rotating.

5. The flame is now increased in size and intensity. The handle in the right hand is flame cut about one inch beyond the body. This is formed into a sphere by rotation at an upward angle in the hottest part of the flame. This will become the head.

6. Once the sphere is completed and joined to the lace body, the product is held without rotation so that the scored part of the tail is pointed downward. This will cause the head to droop, eventually insuring that it will be pointed upward when the bird is completed.

7. The body and head are kept warm in the upper part of the flame while the end of an 8mm rod is softened. Once the rod is softened over a 3/4 inch area, it is placed on a graphite plate and scored three times, making the flat portion nearly twice as wide as the original rod. This will become one of the wings.

8. The end of the wing is heated while the body is kept warm, and it is attached to the right side of the body when the head is pointed away from you. Once joined, the flattened portion is reheated over the entire area and then drawn outward and upward. Shaping is done by heating when necessary and pulling out at the proper rate. The 8 mm rod is then flame cut. The completed wing should be about 1 1/2 inches long and approximately 1/2 to 3/4 inch wide at the junction with the body.

9. The 8 mm rod is heated again and scored. This will become the second wing. (To do this operation, you may need to put the body on your support for a second–no longer.) The completed

portion is gradually reheated in the upper portion of the flame while It is attached to the body on the right side again but this time with the body upside down. It is drawn outward and down, while every effort is made to match the first wing in width and length. When flame cutting each wing, make sure that the resulting ends are not sharp. Allow them to become somewhat fire polished.

10. Eyes are now added. The head is reheated, and two small amounts of glass are added. These are then heated until they become firmly sealed to the head. The beak is fashioned by attaching a small amount of glass and then drawing the bird out of the flame with a slight downward motion.

11. The base for the bird is constructed next. A piece of 8mm rod is strongly heated while the bottom portion of the bird is kept hot in the upper portion of the flame. Once a good amount of glass is softened, it is added to the bottom of the bird. The extra 8 mm rod is then flame cut.

12. The base is then heated strongly until it becomes nearly white hot. The bird is then pressed downward on the graphite plate in the manner that the bird is to sit when completed. The tail may be slightly lower than the head.

13. The flattened area of the tail is now heated carefully. Caution must be exercised so that the junction of the tail with the lace body does not crack. Just before the area is thoroughly softened, the bird is inverted and the head is firmly held with a pair of pliers. When the scored tail portion is softened, it is slowly drawn out and downward. Shaping is done by proper heating and pulling. The resulting tail should be a little over an inch in length.

14. Oven anneal as soon as possible. Color may be added to the wings, tail feathers, eyes and beak, if desired, after annealing.

LABORATORY PROJECT - ARTISTIC TWELVE

CHRISTMAS ANGEL WITH LACE BODY

Introduction:

A wide variety of angel Christmas ornaments can be made using a method quite similar to that described in the construction of lace teapots (Laboratory Project Artistic Nine). Various musical instruments or other Christmas articles can be fashioned and substituted for the praying hands described in this project. Any of these products make excellent ornaments for the tree or decorations for the home at Christmas time. See additional variations on this design in Figures 216-218.

Figure 5.18 *Lace angel.*

Materials:

Approximately 12 inches of 4 mm rod
Approximately 12inches of 8 mm rod

Special Tools:

Graphite plate, needlenose pliers, small carbon rod, triangular file

Flame:

#5 tip; medium flame at first, but flame varies in each step

Construction Steps

1. Form an end maria at the end of a piece of 4 mm rod. The bottom of the angel will be built around the maria. The rod will serve as a handle and base rod during its construction.
2. Keep the maria warm while softening the end of an 8 mm rod in a small, cool flame. As soon as the rod is softened, begin to form a flat, circular pattern of glass around the maria, continuing until four complete layers are made (Figure 5.19). This bot-

Figure 5.19 *Forming the bottom of the angel.*

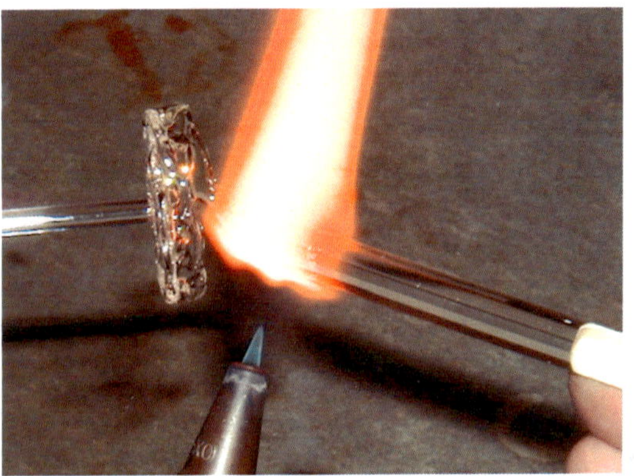

Figure 5.20 *Adding layers of lace (ninety degree angle from base).*

Figure 5.21 *Adding additional layers of lace, forming the body of the angel.*

Figure 4.22 *Continuing the formation of the lace body.*

tom should be like that made for the teapot, without any holes in the pattern.

3. The body of the angel is then begun without disconnecting the working rod from the finished bottom portion. This is done by changing the base rod position by about 90°. The working rod hand stays in nearly the same place. (Figure 5.20).

4. After several layers are added, begin to decrease the diameter of the body so that the product takes on the appearance of a cone (Figures 5.21-5.23). The finished cone should be approximately 2 inches in length. After completing the lace, position the working rod so that it is attached to the tip of the lace in such a way that the two rod handles are now linear with one another.

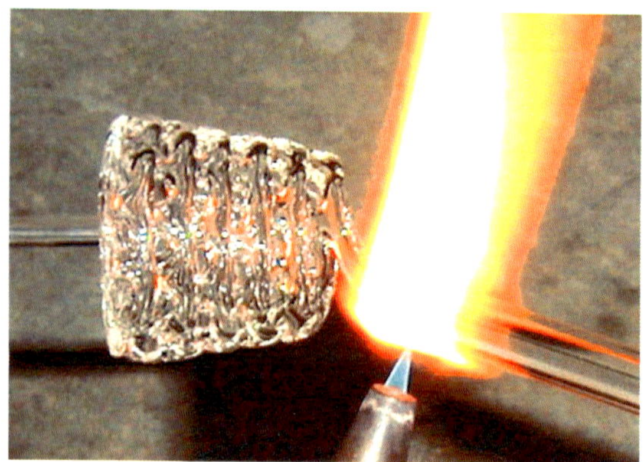

Figure 5.23 *Continuing the formation of the lace body.*

Figure 5.24 *Reheating the entire lace body.*

Figure 5.25 *Making a flame cut on the 8 mm base rod. This glass will become the head.*

Figure 5.26 *After strongly heating this piece of glass, it is formed into a sphere–the head.*

5. Increase the flame size and reheat the entire lace portion in the flame with constant rotation (Figure 5.24). This should be continued until the piece becomes uniformly red in color. Any shaping can be done at this time by selectively pulling or pushing the handles. A slight pulling will always tend to remove irregularities and make the piece more symmetrical.

6. The 8 mm rod is now flame cut at about 1 1/4 inch beyond the lace point (Figure 5.25). This is then shaped into a sphere by proper heating and rotation (Figure 5.26). This will be the head of the angel.

7. The body and head are kept warm in the upper part of the flame while the end of an 8 mm rod is softened. Once the rod is softened over a 3/4 inch area, it is placed on a graphite plate

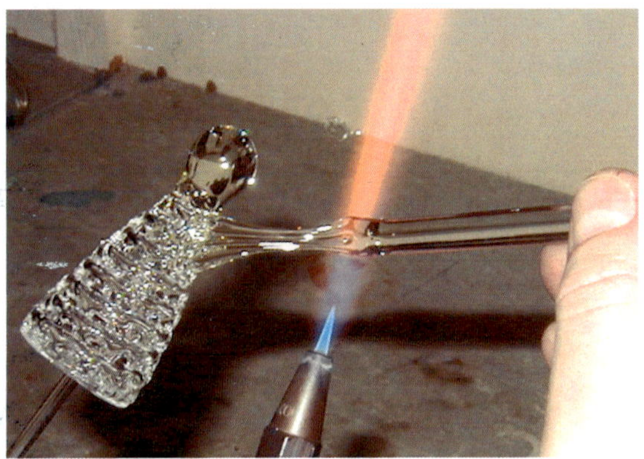

Figure 5.27 *Adding the first wing to the angel body. The working rod is drawn out and up.*

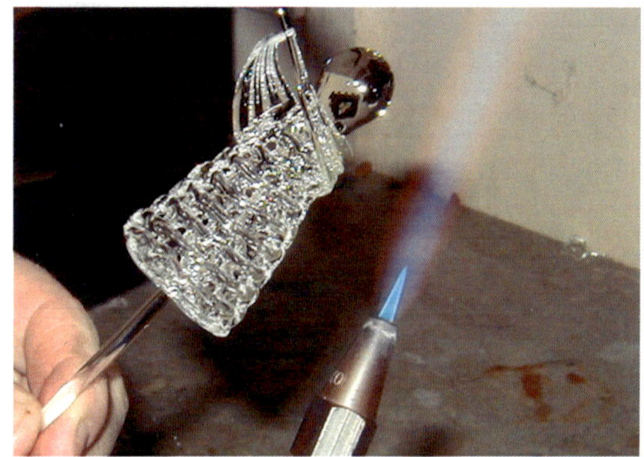

Figure 5.28 *After adding the second wing and after making the flame cut, tips are joined.*

and scored three times, making the flat portion nearly twice as wide as the original rod. This will become one of the wings.

8. The end of the flattened glass is heated, while the body is kept warm, and it is attached just below the head, with the scored pattern facing you. Once joined, the flattened portion is reheated over the entire area and then drawn outward and upward while the angel is rotated slightly clockwise (Figure 5.27). The excess 8mm rod is then flame cut. The completed wing should be about 1 1/2 inches long and approximately 1/2 to 3/4 inch wide at the junction with the body.

9. The completed portion is kept hot in the upper portion of the flame while the 8 mm rod is heated again and scored as in Step 7. This piece is then attached at a point about 90° from the first wing with the back of the angel facing you. This time the scored pattern is faced away from you. Once joined, the added glass is reheated and drawn outward and up, aiming the thin portion to touch the tip of the first wing. The flame cut should then also serve to join the two wing tips, making a sturdier product (Figure 5.28).

10. The entire piece is briefly reheated with rotation in the flame.

11. Arms are fashioned next. Keep the entire angel body hot in the upper part of the flame while an 8 mm rod is heated. Once a small amount of glass is softened, attach it to the left front of the angel body, just in front of the wing. Heat the rod while drawing out toward the center of the angel's front (Figure 5.29). Make a flame cut and repeat the operation adding the second

Figure 5.29 *Adding the first arm to the body front. Again, the rod is drawn out and up.*

Figure 5.30 *Adding the second arm to the body front.*

Figure 5.31 *After heating joined rods, hands are formed using pliers - outside flame.*

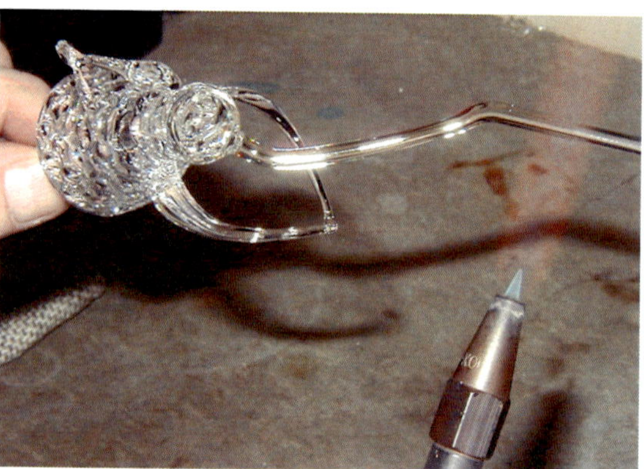

Figure 5.32 *Forming the halo from heated rod on the top and back of the head.*

arm in a similar manner (Figure 5.30). Bring this arm so that it connects to the first arm and flame cut. Heat the glass where the arms join, remove from the flame and use the tip of the pliers to grab onto the glass and pull slightly upward (Figure 5.31). This will form the folded hands.

12. A halo is now added. Heat the back of the head with a medium flame while also heating the end of a piece of 4 mm rod. Join in the flame and then proceed to heat a 1 1/2 inch portion of the 4mm rod closest to the head. This should be done with a back and forth motion until the rod glows red uniformly. When this occurs, remove from the flame, draw out slightly, and form a loop (Figures 5.32-5.33). Make a flame cut to remove the excess 4mm rod. Use the flat end of a graphite

Figure 5.33 *Completing the halo loop. The extra rod will be flame cut next.*

Figure 5.34 *After sealing the halo and reheating the joint, the halo position is adjusted.*

rod to push the glass together, and then reheat until a good seal is made. Use your pliers to adjust the position of the halo (Figure 5.34).

13. The 4 mm handle is now removed, and the bottom of the angel flattened. Carefully heat the bottom of the angel with a rather cool flame. Gradually increase the size and hotness of the flame. As the rod handle softens, hold the angel firmly by the neck with a pair of needlenose pliers or forceps. Focus the heating at the base of the 4 mm rod and make a flame cut (Figure 5.35). Some cracking of the base may occur during these operations, but now the base is reheated with a more intense flame (Figure 5.36). This should repair any cracks.

14. Once the bottom is sufficiently heated, the angel is pressed

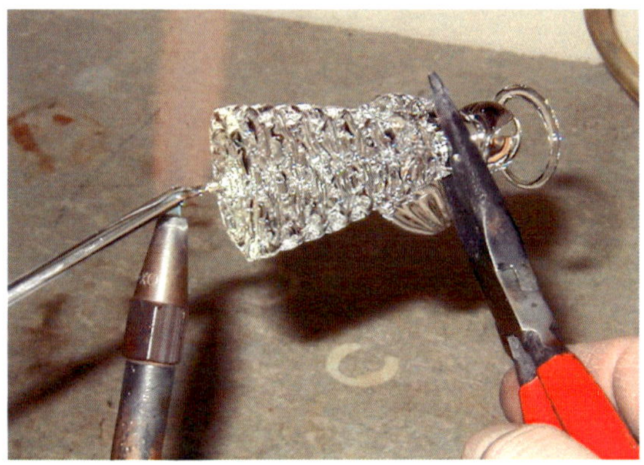

Figure 5.35 *Making a flame cut close to the bottom to remove the 4 mm rod handle.*

Figure 5.36 *Strongly heating the angel bottom before flattening on the graphite plate.*

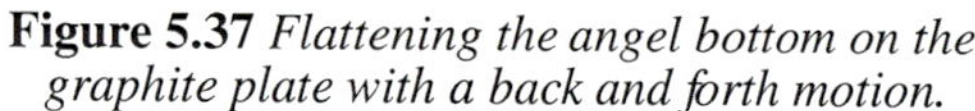

Figure 5.37 *Flattening the angel bottom on the graphite plate with a back and forth motion.*

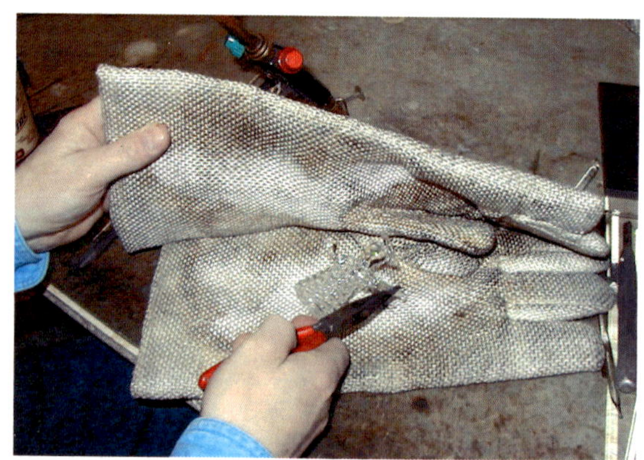

Figure 5.38 *Placing between heat resistant gloves to slow down the rate of cooling.*

down firmly on a graphite plate to flatten the bottom (Figure 5.37).

15. Immediately flame anneal the bottom and then immerse the angel in vermiculite or place between heat resistant gloves until cool (Figure 5.38). Oven anneal as soon as possible.

Figure 5.39 *The finished praying angel.*

Figure 5.40 *Angel playing tambourine.*

Figure 5.41 *Angel holding shamrock.*

Over a period of twenty six years, the author has designed and made a different angel for each year – many with musical instruments and some with items having personal significance. All of the “Carberry Christmas Angel Collection” are pictured in the photographs on the following pages (Figures 5.42 - 5.47).

Figure 5.42 *String instruments: violin, lute and harp.*

Figure 5.43 *Percussion instruments: tambourine, drum, cymbals, bell and triangle.*

Figure 5.44 *Horn instruments: trumpet, saxophone, clarinet, french horn, flute, and the conductor.*

Figure 5.45 *Angels with heart, candle, gift, Christmas tree and Russian icon.*

Figure 5.46 *Angels with shamrock, red rose, choir book, white dove, praying and white flower.*

Figure 5.47 *Creche (manger) scene with Mary, Joseph and Baby Jesus on a bed of spun glass.*

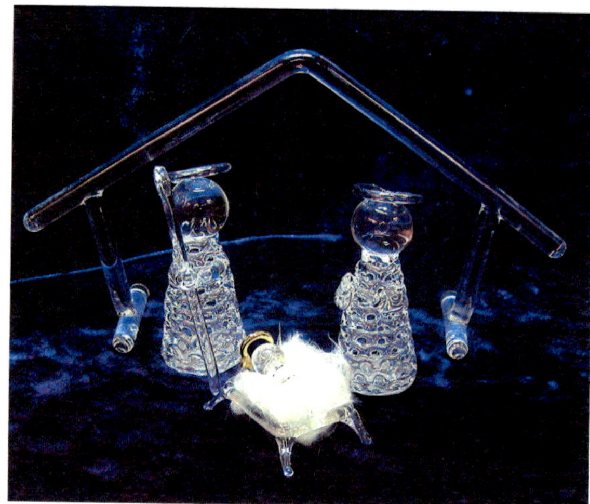

LABORATORY PROJECT - ARTISTIC THIRTEEN

LACE BELLS

Introduction:

A sturdy bell that actually rings can be fashioned from lace, with each layer slightly larger in diameter than that preceding it (Figure 5.48). This is built around an intermediate maria to which a loop has been added for the clapper, which is made separately and added later. If made correctly, the bell will have a beautiful ring to it. The shape of the handle can be as simple or as complex as desired.

Figure 5.48 *Lace bell.*

Materials:

Approximately 14 inches of 6 mm rod
Approximately 12inches of 8 mm rod

Special Tools:

Graphite plate, needlenose pliers, small carbon rod

Flame:

#5 tip; medium flame at first, but flame varies in each step

Construction Steps

1. Form an end maria at the end of a 6 mm rod which is at least 8 inches long.
2. A loop for the clapper is now fashioned on the bottom of the maria. (This will eventually be inside the bell.) Heat the end of another short piece of 6 mm rod while reheating the bottom of the end maria. Once both pieces are sufficiently hot, join them and draw out the second piece of rod in such a way as to form a loop under the maria (Figures 5.49-5.50). Remove the

excess 6 mm rod by flame cutting; reheat the end and push in with the flat end of a small graphite rod (Figure 5.51). Reheat the ends again to insure a good seal. Reshape the loop itself with the same graphite rod (Figure 5.52).

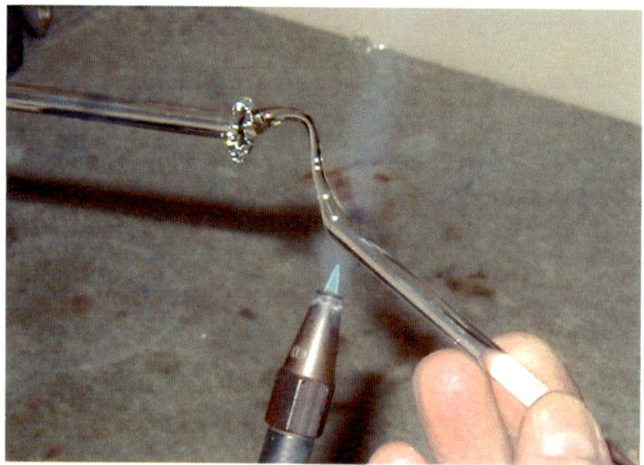

Figure 5.49 *Beginning to form the loop, on which the ringer will hang when completed.*

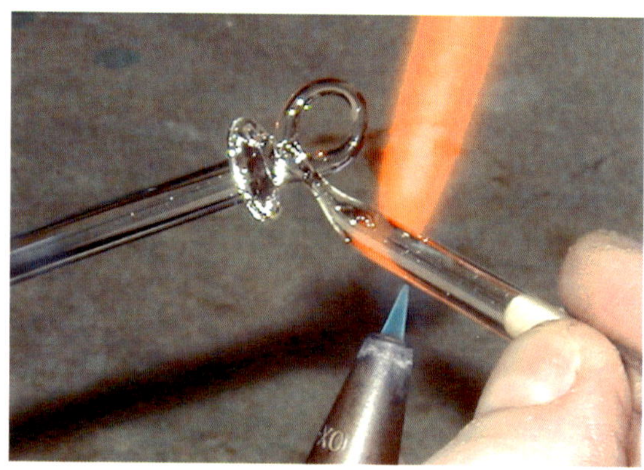

Figure 5.50 *Finishing to the loop, on which the ringer will hang.*

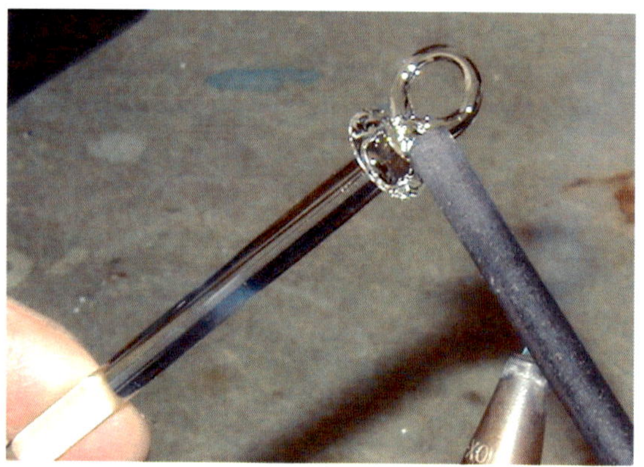

Figure 5.51 *Forcing the heated glass loop together by pressing with a graphite rod.*

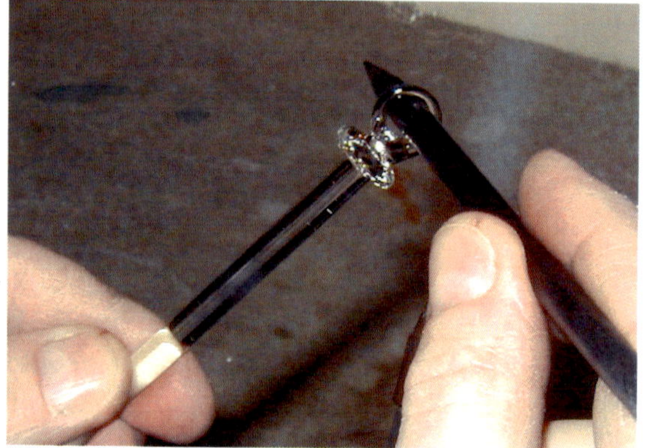

Figure 5.52 *Reshaping the loop with a graphite rod, after reheating the glass.*

3. Keep the maria warm while softening the end of an 8 mm rod in a small, cool flame. As soon as the rod is softened, begin to fashion lace around the maria, making each layer slightly larger in diameter than the last and making each layer slightly lower and more away from the base rod (Figure 5.53).

4. Continue this process until about nine or ten complete layers of lace are made (Figures 5.54 - 5.55). It is wise to reheat the entire lace portion after finishing.

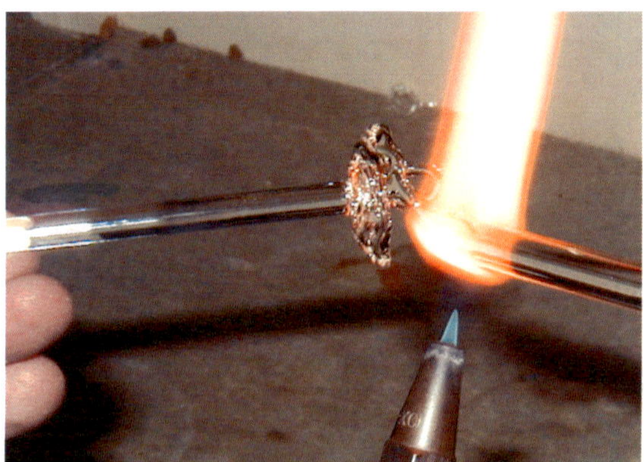

Figure 5.53 *Beginning the lace portion of the bell.*

Figure 5.54 *Continuing the lace portion of the bell.*

Figure 5.55 *Continuing the lace.*

Figure 5.56 *Adding a row of looped lace.*

5. If you wish, you may add an extra row of looped lace around the circumference of the bell, over the last layer of the regular lace (Figures 5.56-5.57). This will give the piece a more finished look. Once completed, the entire piece should be reheated again and then thoroughly flame annealed.

6. While still hot, the bottom of the bell is flattened on a graphite plate and then thoroughly flame annealed.

7. Immerse the bell in vermiculite or place between heat resistant gloves and allow it to cool completely.

8. Once the bell is cool, make a flame cut on the base rod, about two inches above the lace portion. After the cut is made, continue heating to form a sphere from about half of the rod; this

Figure 5.57 *The finished bell with lace edge.*

Figure 5.58 *Gathering glass for the handle.*

Figure 5.59 *Using gravity to shape handle.*

Figure 5.60 *The finished bell and handle.*

will serve as the handle (Figure 5.58). Shape, as necessary, using gravity (Figure 5.59 - 5.60). Allow the product to cool once again.

9. The clapper is now formed by making a sphere at the end of another piece of 6 mm rod. Once formed, set aside to cool. After cooled, grab the sphere with a pair of pliers or forceps and then heat the rod about one inch from the sphere. When softened, draw it out and form a hook (Figures 5.61-5.63).

10. Use your needle nose pliers to insert the cooled clapper into the bell. If necessary, reheat and reshape the hook to fit properly (Figure 5.64).

11. Try ringing the bell. If it rings nicely, you have been totally successful (Figure 5.65). If the finished bell rings poorly, some of

the lace may not be properly joined. Next time, reheat the entire bell more thoroughly in Steps 4 and 5.

Figure 5.61 *Beginning to form the ringer.*

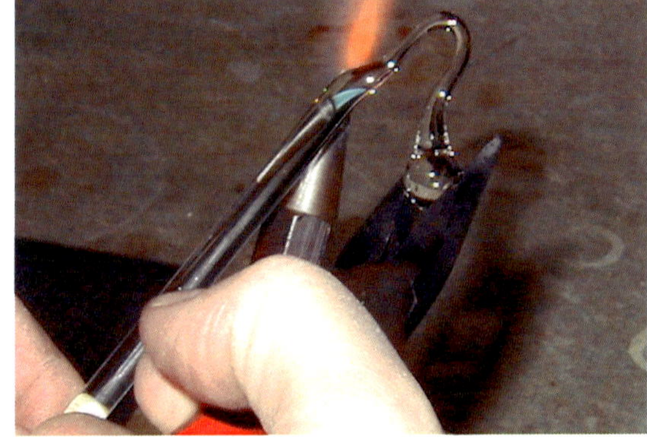

Figure 5.62 *Finishing the ringer for inside the finished lace bell.*

Figure 5.63 (Right Top) *The finished ringer.*

Figure 5.64 (Right Bottom) *Inserting the ringer.*

Figure 5.65 *The finished lace bell. (These usually have a wonderful ringing tone. If the ring is poor, the lace may not be properly welded together. Strongly reheating may help.)*

LABORATORY PROJECT - ARTISTIC FOURTEEN

LACE CHRISTMAS TREE

Introduction:

An attractive glass Christmas tree can be made in much the same way as were the teapot and angel ornaments (Figure 5.66). Of course, because the size of the lace portion is larger, this should only be attempted by those proficient in the construction of teapots and angels. A circular lace base is added to allow the tree to be free standing. After the tree has been completed and annealed, the ornaments can be accentuated by painting with various colored glass stains.

Figure 5.66 *Lace Christmas tree with gold ornaments.*

Materials:

Approximately 12 inches of 6 mm rod
Approximately 18 inches of 8 mm rod

Special Tools:

Graphite plate, needlenose pliers

Flame:

#5 tip; medium flame at first, but flame varies in each step

Construction Steps

1. Form an end maria at the end of a 6 mm rod. The bottom of the tree will be built around this maria. The rod will serve as a handle and base rod during its construction.
2. Keep the maria warm while softening the end of an 8 mm rod in a small, bushy flame. As soon as the rod is softened, begin to form a flat, circular pattern of glass around the maria, continuing until four or five complete layers are made. This bottom

Figure 5.67 *Building up the base of the tree.*

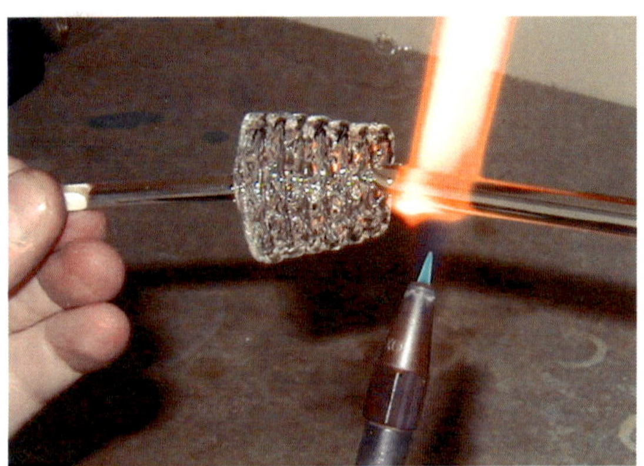

Figure 5.68 *Building up the sides of the tree.*

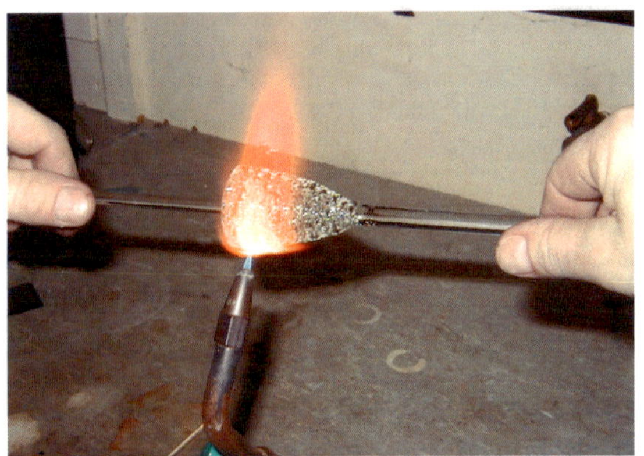

Figure 5.69 *Reheating the lace portion of the tree.*

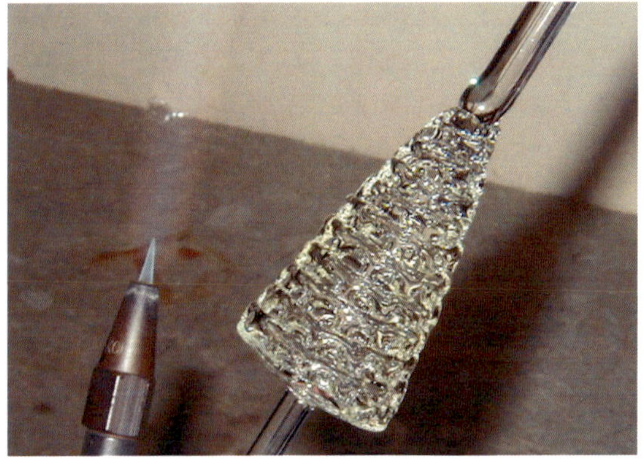

Figure 5.70 *Shaping the tree by a slight pull outward after reheating.*

should be like that made for the teapot and angel, without any holes in the pattern (Figure 5.67).

3. The body of the tree is then begun without disconnecting the working rod from the finished bottom portion. This is done by changing the base rod position by 90°. The working rod hand stays in nearly the same place.

4. After several layers are added, begin to decrease the diameter of the lace pattern so that the product takes on the appearance of a cone (Figure 5.68). The finished cone should be anywhere from two to four inches in length. After completing the lace work, position the working rod so that it is attached to the

tip of the lace in such a way that the two rod handles are now linear with one another.

5. Increase the flame size and reheat the entire lace portion in the flame with constant rotation. This should be continued until the piece becomes uniformly red in color (Figure 5.69). Any shaping can be done at this time by selectively pulling or pushing the rod handles. As usual, a slight pulling motion will tend to remove irregularities and make the piece more symmetrical (Figure 5.70).

6. The 8 mm rod is now flame cut just beyond the lace point (Figure 5.71). This spike can serve as the tree top, or if you wish you can add some glass to make it into a star-like shape (Figures 5.72 - 5.73).

7. Ornaments are now added to the tree. The entire tree is reheated and kept warm in the upper part of the flame while the end of a 4 mm rod is softened. Once the rod is softened, it is used to add small amounts of glass at random places all over the tree surface (Figures 5.74-5.75). Immediately after each is added, it is briefly heated to shape it. From time to time, it may be necessary to reheat the entire tree again and pull it out to keep it straight and correctly shaped.

8. When finished adding ornaments, flame anneal the entire tree and then immerse it in vermiculite or place it between heat resistant gloves until cool.

9. Make a lace base, approximately two inches in diameter (See Exercise 14 on page 131). The base rod should be 6 mm.

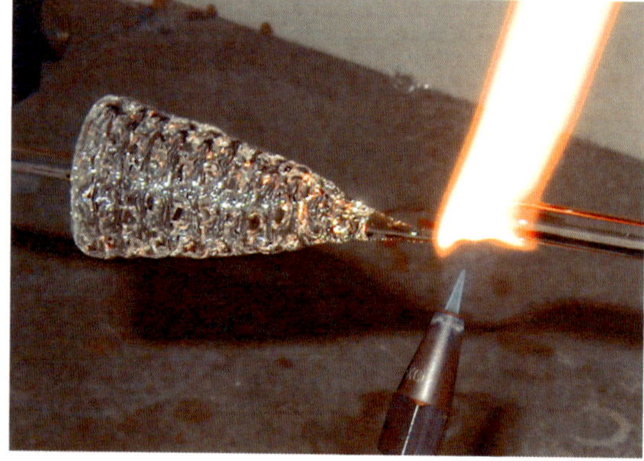

Figure 5.71 *Flame cutting the top rod.*

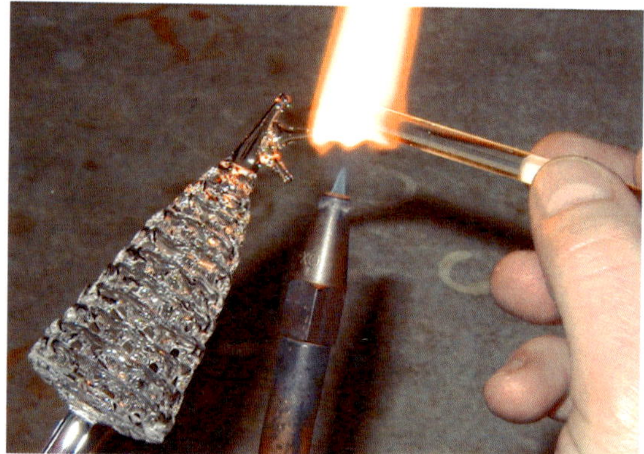

Figure 5.72 *Beginning the star.*

Figure 5.73 *Finishing the star.*

Figure 5.74 *Adding ornaments to the tree.*

Figure 5.75 *Adding the last ornaments.*

Figure 5.76 *Straightening out the tree shape.*

10. Flame cut the 6 mm rod on the tree about 3/4 of an inch below the flat bottom, keeping the lace tree down as low as possible to prevent it from becoming reheated again (Figure 5.77). If the base is reheated, it would probably crack.

11. Flame cut the 6 mm rod above the lace base about 1/2 inch from the lace portion.

12. Heat the 6 mm rod on both the tree and base, rotating to keep the glass from drooping. Once sufficiently heated, join the two in the flame, and push together to form an intermediate maria (Figures 5.78-5.79). The maria will serve to hide the joint and will look more attractive than a regular butt joint.

13. Check to make sure that the tree stands straight. Reheat and adjust if necessary (Figure 5.80).

14. Oven anneal as soon as possible. After annealing, the ornaments may be colored with various colors of glass stain or with gold or silver.

Figure 5.77 *Flame cutting the base rod.*

Figure 5.78 *Joining a lace base to the tree.*

Figure 5.79 ***(right top)*** *Forming a maria at the joint.*

Figure 5.80 ***(right bottom)*** *Straightening.*

Figure 5.81 ***(below)*** *The finished tree (with gold trim added later).*

MORE IDEAS

A number of additional items which incorporate lace in their construction are shown in Figures 5.82 - 5.102. As usual, try to analyze the items to determine the probable steps involved in their construction.

Figure 5.82 *Colored flowers in lace basket.*

Figure 5.83 *Bird and bird nest with eggs.*

Figure 5.84 *Birds on bird bath. (This is another example in which the top & bottom parts are made separately and then joined as with the pump.)*

Figure 5.85 *Small lace ship. (This ship is about four inches tall.)*

Figure 5.86 *Decorative top for a wedding cake. (Many different variations on this design are possible. Be sure item is very well constructed if to be used on a cake!)*

Figure 5.87 *Ballerina.*

Figure 5.88 *Stork with baby.*

Figure 5.89 *Pony with lace body.*

Figure 5.90 *Two Birds on very small branch.*

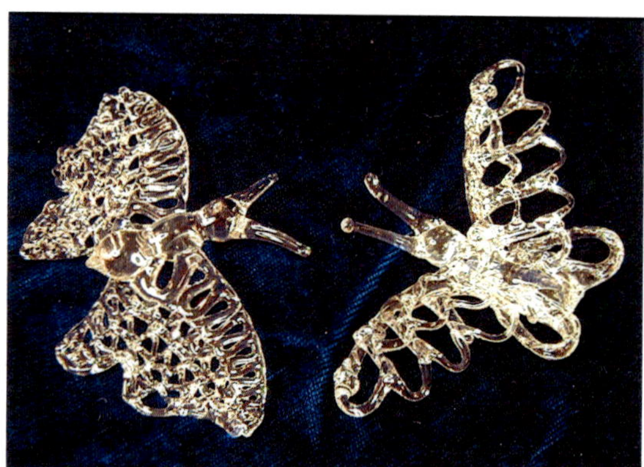

Figure 5.91 *Two lace butterflies.*

Figure 5.92 *Old fashioned candle holder.*

Figure 5.93 *Swan with lace body.*

Figure 5.94 *Wishing well with vine.*

Figure 5.95 *Large urn with two birds.*

Figure 5.96 *Candle Christmas ornament.*

Figure 5.97 *Lace basket with colored glass eggs.*

Figure 5.98 *Two birds in lace cage on stand.*

Figure 5.99 (Left)
Small lace creche Christmas ornament.

Figure 5.100 (Right)
Another variation of a small lace creche Christmas ornament.

Figure 5.101 *Intricate lace ship standing 18" high with three main mast. (Made by the author.)*

Figure 5.102 *Another lace ship standing 17" high with two main masts. (Made by the author.)*

Chapter 6
ARTISTIC GLASSBLOWING

AN INTRODUCTION TO WORKING WITH TUBING

Even though this entire book deals with the subject of glassblowing, the student should have noticed by now that no blowing has been involved up to this point. This term "glassblowing" has come to refer to the entire subject of working with glass. But it isn't until we discuss tubing that the name really becomes strictly correct. Up to this point, we have actually been talking about "glassworking".

In addition to the natural forces (gravity and surface tension) and the applied forces (pushing, pulling, and bending) that one must be aware of and use to advantage when working with solid rod, an additional aspect is critical in the working of tubing. This, of course, is the use of air, or blowing. Likewise, there are a number of unique things about working with tubing that need to be discussed. First, let us look at some physical aspects.

Like rod, tubing usually is purchased in four foot lengths and the diameters that are referred to are always outside diameters. Normal tubing has a wall thickness of about 1 mm, although heavier walled tubing can be obtained. The inside diameter is therefore usually approximately equal to the outside dimension minus 2 mm for the two walls.

But the real differences in working with tubing occur because of what happens when it is put into a flame. The openings at the end of the tubing tend to close upon heating, whereas openings fashioned on the sides of tubing tend to widen upon heating. In general, heating glass tubing decreases the diameter and increases the wall thickness. Pulling on heated tubing also decreases the diameter but in this case also decreases the wall thickness. Pushing on heated tubing increases the diameter and likewise increases the wall thickness. Blowing on heated tubing also increases tubing diameter but decreases the wall thickness.

Much important information is summarized in the above paragraph. It is well to reread it and to think about each part of the material. All of this will become more reasonable as you become more and more experienced. Until that time, however, it may be wise to memorize those general principles.

In rod working, you probably thought that the amount of working time was short enough. One has to make quick decisions and take corrective measures almost immediately before the rod becomes cool and unworkable. But when working with tubing, the amount of working time is usually significantly less and repairs may be impossible or, at best, very difficult to make. The problem stems from the fact that the thicker the glass, the longer the heat is retained. This means that the glassblower has more time to manipulate the glass when rod is used. You have probably discovered that an 8 mm rod holds quite a bit of heat for quite a long time. However, tubing is essentially only 1 mm thick. Needless to say, such thin glass cools very quickly and thus makes the working time extremely short. With tubing work, rotation and uniformity of heating become not only desirable and important, but essential.

Cutting, fire polishing, and other basic operations have already been discussed in previous sections in Chapter Three. You are strongly encouraged to review these before proceeding further.

DRAWING OUT POINTS

Nearly every artistic item made of blown glass begins as a "Point". The term Point refers to a piece of glass made up of a drawn out region (point) on either side of a smaller length of tubing. In this book we will be referring to the drawn area on one side of a piece of tubing or rod as a point (with a small letter p) and the total piece consisting of a length of tubing or rod with drawn areas on both sides as a Point (with a capital letter P).

Just as in rod working, the points serve as convenient handles, but now the handles serve an important second purpose. They are the blowpipes that allow the shaping of the heated tubing. Needless to say, learning to construct Points (often called pulling points) in the correct manner is quite basic to artistic glassblowing and must be mastered before attempting elaborate projects.

Although the exercise that follows is designed for use with 15 mm tubing, any diameter tubing can be used as long as the proper flame is used. Larger tubing, however, is much more expensive and requires more skill, and therefore should not be used until you are proficient with 12 to 15 mm tubing.

Making good Points is somewhat of an art. Thus, do not get discouraged right away! With more and more practice, your proficiency will increase. Try to learn from your mistakes. Analyze each Point you make and then try to decide what steps you could take to make them more symmetrical and more linear.

LABORATORY EXERCISE FIFTEEN

PULLING POINTS FROM TUBING

1. The center portion of a piece of 15 mm tubing (at least two feet in length) is heated with constant rotation approximately 1/2 inch above the blue cone of the flame (Figure 6.1). You may wish to substitute 12 mm tubing. Both hands are held above the tubing, and both aid in the rotation.

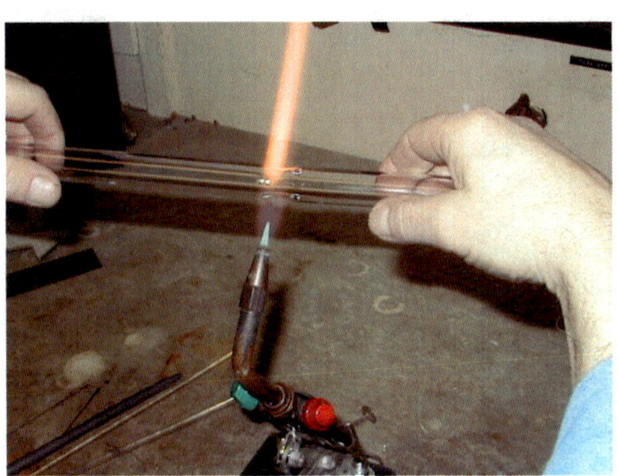

Figure 6.1 *Rotating the tubing to soften the glass so the point may be drawn out.*

2. Continue heating and rotation until the flame becomes orange-yellow in color and the glass begins to attain a reddish glow. The glass should then be quite soft, but make every effort to hold the tubing in a straight line, neither pulling nor pushing on the ends.

3. Remove the tubing from the flame and continue to rotate it uniformly. Pull on the ends and continue uniform rotation until the constricted portion is about 10 inches in length (Figure 6.2). Keep the ends taut so that the constricted areas remain linear with the tubing. Hold this position until the tubing is cooled.

4. After the glass has sufficiently cooled, make a flame cut on the constriction area (Figure 6.3). The drawn portion of the piece which will become the Point should be approximately 5 inches long.

Figure 6.2 *Pulling the softened glass (outside the flame) to form the first side of the Point.*

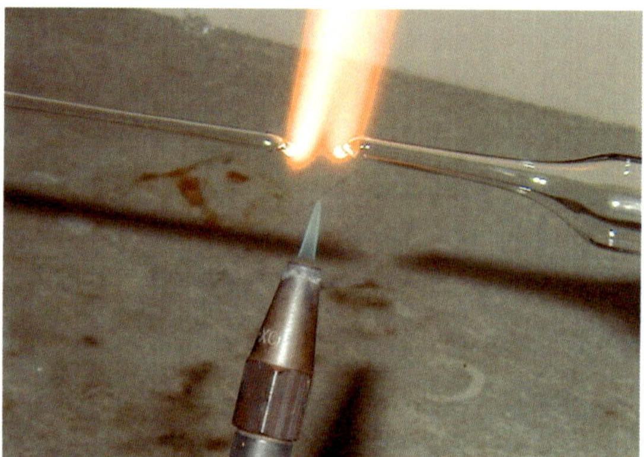

Figure 6.3 *Making a flame cut to the left of the piece which will become the Point.*

5. Once the point is sufficiently cool, the second drawn out portion is formed. This is done by holding the thick end of the tubing in the in the right hand and the drawn portion (the point) in the left hand. The glass is returned to the flame and heated with rotation at a distance of about 1 1/2 inches to the right of the first drawn out section. (All rotation should be done with the right hand which should be held above the tubing. The left hand serves only as a guide to keep the piece in a straight line. Longer or shorter lengths of tubing can be made between the point handles, but when practicing the construction of Points, the shorter the length of tubing the better.)

6. Once the tubing is softened, it is removed from the flame. Rotation is continued, but now both hands are used. The glass is drawn out as before to a length of approximately 10 inches (Figure 6.4). Make every effort to keep the constriction and the tubing linear. There should be no wobble when the piece is rotated.

7. When sufficiently cooled, the constricted area is flame cut at the desired spot (Figure 6.5). It is actually advantageous to make the flame cut two thirds of the distance to the right of the tubing. When done in this way, the completed Point will have one handle longer than the other. The longer end is always used as the blowpipe.

8. The longer point is carefully scored near the end with a glass knife (Figure 6.6) and opened up and very lightly fire polished. This should be done immediately after the Point cools sufficiently.

If not done immediately, one may forget and when later reheated to make another item, the softened glass will expand and cause the glass to bubble and break since it a closed system.

In Steps 3 and 7, it may be desirable to draw out a point with a piece of tubing that is too short for safety. In these cases, instead of holding the short piece of tubing with your hands, use your needlenose pliers, but be sure to get a firm grip so when drawn out, you don't drop that end (Figure 6.7).

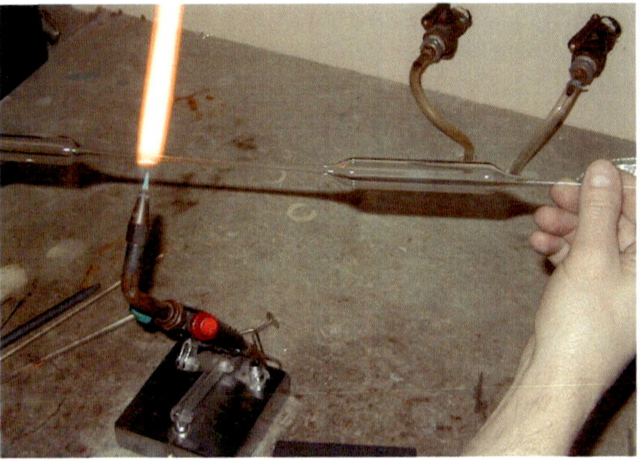

Figure 6.4 *Pulling the second side of the Point.*

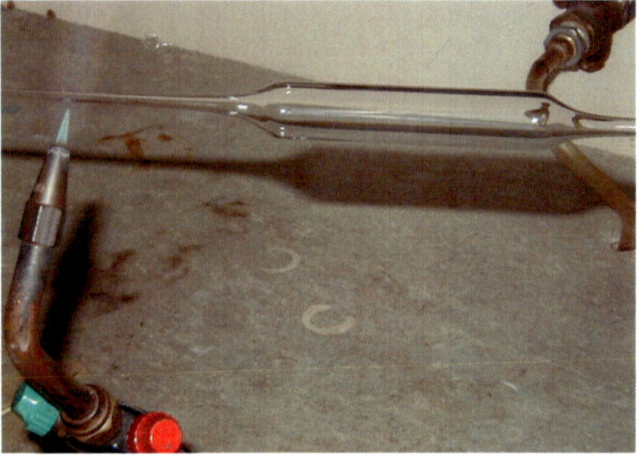

Figure 6.5 *Removing the excess glass by making a flame cutting.*

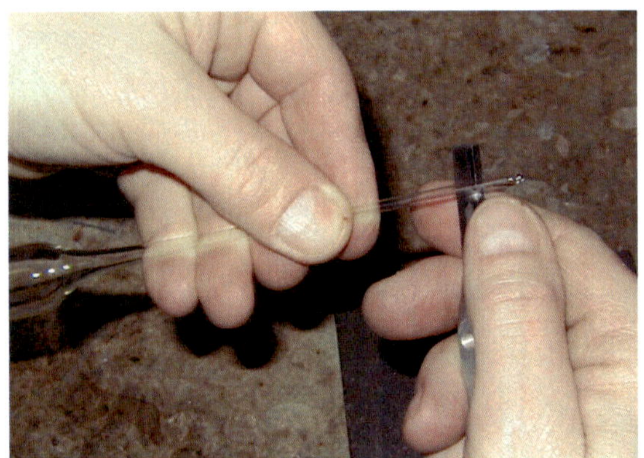

Figure 6.6 *After the point is cool, the end is removed using a glass knife.*

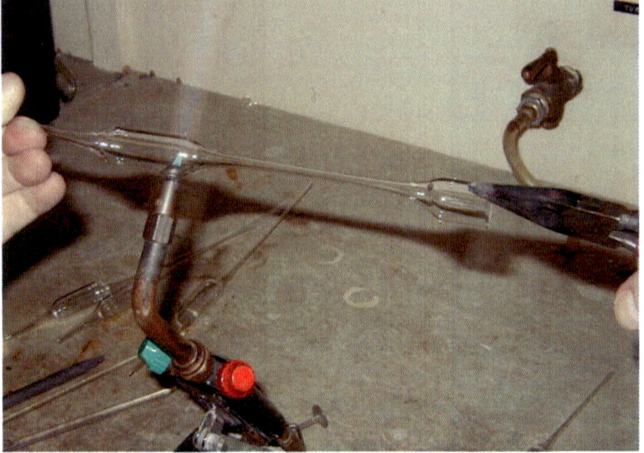

Figure 6.7 *Using a needlenose pliers to pull points when short pieces of tubing are used.*

BLOWING GLASS SHAPES

Blowing glass is something that can be learned only through experience. It is difficult to explain in words exactly what you will see and feel while handling the glass. Perhaps nowhere else is the feel of the glass as important to the glassblower. Nonetheless, it is wise to go into your first exercises with several things in mind.

Uniform heating is a very important part of the process. Constant left and right lateral motion of the full length of the tubing across the flame and constant rotation are the important keys here.

But uniform cooling is probably even more important! All blowing is done outside the flame. Therefore, during the actual blowing, the glass is in the process of cooling. Rotation, once again, insures cooling in a uniform manner. If the tubing was heated properly in the beginning, rapid rotation (as fast as you can turn it) with controlled blowing will always guarantee a nearly perfectly shaped product. Without proper rotation, the heat becomes concentrated on the upper portions of the glass because heat always rises. This more heated portion will then preferentially become blown out, and the product will look distorted. It should be noted, however, that sometimes this principle can be used to advantage. If, during blowing, it is obvious that one side was overheated (that is, the bubble begins to grow larger on one side of the tubing), lower this side and continue blowing. This should help in evening out the blown form. Rotation should rarely, if ever, be stopped completely, but in these cases the hotter side is favored in the downward position.

Knowing how hard to blow is something else that can only come from experience. However, one can generalize to some degree. The first blowing is usually hardly blowing at all. At best, it is only a slight positive pressure. Or, as I like to tell my students, just "think" about blowing. Then as the shape develops (while rotating the piece as fast as you can), and as the glass becomes cooler, the pressure of blowing is increased steadily until the proper size is attained. Quite often the last blowing is done as hard as you can. Thus, the blowing pressure depends markedly on the temperature of the glass and therefore increases throughout the entire procedure, which incidentally may not be more than 5-10 seconds!

Blowing too hard on glass that is too hot (too soft) will result in an irregular bubble of paper thin glass which will probably burst. On the other hand, blowing too softly on the glass that is too cool (too hard) will not produce a bubble at all. Very soon you will become experienced enough to recognize the proper temperature (by judging the color and softness of the glass) at which to begin blowing, and likewise you will sense the right pressure needed at each moment during the process. The procedure is best summarized by stating that glassblowing is a study of controlled blowing.

Ideally, the walls of the blown shape should be the same thickness as the wall thickness of the original tubing (or close to 1 mm). In order to accomplish this, the glass has to be thickened before blowing. This is done almost automatically, since when glass tubing is heated, it tends to thicken. Thus, continued heating after the glass is first softened serves to increase the thickness of the walls before blowing. However, another more direct approach can be used when working with tubing. The thickening can be hastened by exerting a slight inward pressure during the heating process. Although the thickened glass may not appear to be very uniform, proper blowing and rotation can produce a very uniform product. This happens because the thicker glass retains the heat longer and thus continues to be blown out even after the thinner portions have cooled.

More needs to be said about the nature of the blowpipe used. In some cases the blowpipe may be the opened end of a Point. In other cases it may simply be an end of the glass tubing. When the tubing to be worked is very large in diameter, it is wise to draw the end down into a point and then use this for the blowpipe. But regardless of the nature of the blowpipe, be sure to check whether the glass is thick enough so that it will not become crushed while in your mouth. Sometimes drawn points are made incorrectly, and the result is paper thin tubing at the blowpipe end. Such glass should never be used as a blowpipe. You will have a pretty good idea of the thickness of your drawn point when you open the end with the glass knife. Reject any that are not solid. Should glass ever shatter while in your mouth, rinse your mouth thoroughly several times with water from a drinking fountain, being certain not to swallow any water whatsoever.

Likewise, always be sure that the ends of the tubing and points have been lightly fire polished. Remember that you are going to be rotating this glass while holding it in your mouth! Fire polishing takes a just a second, but be sure to wait for the glass to cool before putting it in your mouth.

As you proceed to the exercises that follow, keep in mind that every experience should be a genuine learning experience, and this is especially true of the failures. Ask yourself: Why did it fail? What did I do wrong? What should be done differently next time? Analyze each of your products carefully. The more thinking that you do while working, the less time it will take for you to master a certain technique.

LABORATORY EXERCISE SIXTEEN

EXPERIMENTING WITH BLOWING GLASS

1. Heat the end of a 12 to 18 inch length of 10 mm tubing and close it with the aid of a glass rod. (This can be done by attaching a rod, and then using it to pull off a small piece of tubing. Finally a flame cut is made close to the end.)

2. Check to make sure that the blowpipe end of the tubing is fire polished, otherwise you may end up with cut lips! Let it cool before using.

3. Continue to heat the closed end until it is quite soft.

4. Aim the tube downward into a waste container and blow as hard as you can (no need to rotate). The result will be an irregular bubble of very thin glass which probably will burst into a cloud of iridescent flakes. (Take care to avoid breathing in any of the glass flakes!) This will give you some idea of what uncontrolled blowing will produce.

5. Now repeat the exercise, but continue rotation once the glass is outside the flame and try to control your blowing. Remember, at first, blow only hard enough to get the bubble started. Then slowly increase the pressure until the glass hardens. If you initially heat up a sufficient length of tubing, you should be able to obtain a bulb which is several times the diameter of the original tubing.

6. Hold the completed and cooled bulb over the waste container and try to break it by tapping it with your triangular file. If it breaks very easily, the walls are too thin. To prevent this, do not heat the glass as strongly and do not blow as hard at the beginning. If it does not break very easily, the chances are that the thickness is correct. But is the shape uniform? If not, concentrate on more rapid rotation, both in and out of the flame.

LABORATORY EXERCISE SEVENTEEN

BLOWING BULBS FROM POINTS

1. Construct several 1 1/2 inch Points from 12 or 15 mm tubing.

2. Open one end of one Point and lightly fire polish it.

3. Heat the center portion of the tubing until uniformly reddish in color. Move the tubing laterally in the flame with constant rotation so that all of the area becomes equally softened, but concentrate the heating on the center two thirds of the tubing. Whenever heating near the drawn points, tilt the glass so that the drawn point is low, below the flame. As the tubing becomes softened, push in on the ends slightly so that the glass becomes thickened.

Figure 6.8 *Blowing a spherical bulb from a Point. Constant rotation is a must!*

4. When the tubing area is uniformly red, remove it from the flame while rotating at a rapid, constant rate. Then, immediately blow into the blowpipe cautiously, while concentrating on rapid and uniform rotation. Now increase your blowing pressure until the bulb becomes several times the diameter of the original tubing. Note how quickly the glass cools. Check to see that the completed piece spins true without any wobble. Wobbling may indicate a number of things such as non-uniform heating, non-uniform cooling, or failure to keep the handles aligned.

6. After analyzing your completed piece, repeat this exercise several more times. After several successful attempts, experiment with the effect of pulling and pushing on the ends of the points during the blowing process. (During the heating stage, the ends should always be pushed in slightly.) You will discover that a spherical bulb can be

made by pulling slightly while blowing and rotating. An elliptical bulb can be fashioned by pulling outward harder while blowing. A doorknob or squat shape can be made by pushing inward slightly while blowing (Figure 6.9). Continue this part of the exercise until you feel confident that you can construct a desired shape of a predetermined size.

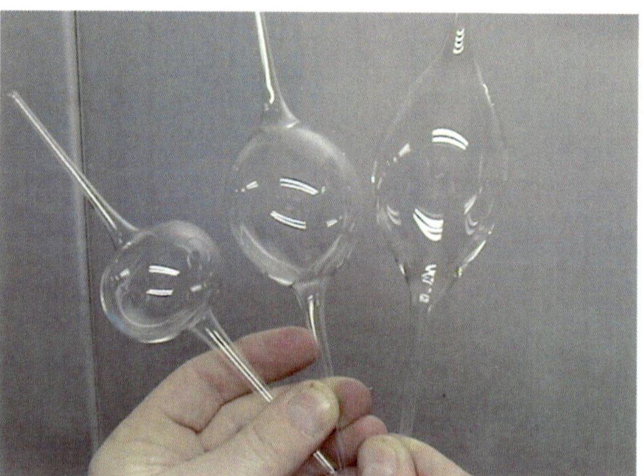

Figure 6.9 *Three differently shaped bulbs. That on the left was made by slightly pushing in while blowing. That on the right was made by slightly pulling while blowing. The middle bulb is spherical because the tubing was neither pushed nor pulled during blowing.*

LABORATORY EXERCISE EIGHTEEN

BLOWING SPHERICAL BULBS FROM ONE-SIDED POINTS

1. Construct a 1.5 inch point from 12 or 15 mm tubing. Open one of the ends and lightly fire polish the freshly cut end.

2. Heat the left shoulder at a point closer to the tubing portion than to the drawn point (Figure 6.10a).

3. Continue heating and remove the left hand drawn point with a flame cut (Figure 6.10b). Undoubtedly a dimple of glass will remain where the drawn point was removed. This is removed by "wiping", that is heating and removing the excess glass with a cold rod or with the thicker portion of the discarded drawn rod (Figure 6.10c).

4. After the excess is removed, reheat the end (Figure 6.10d) and gently blow to make the ending round once again (Figure 6.10e).

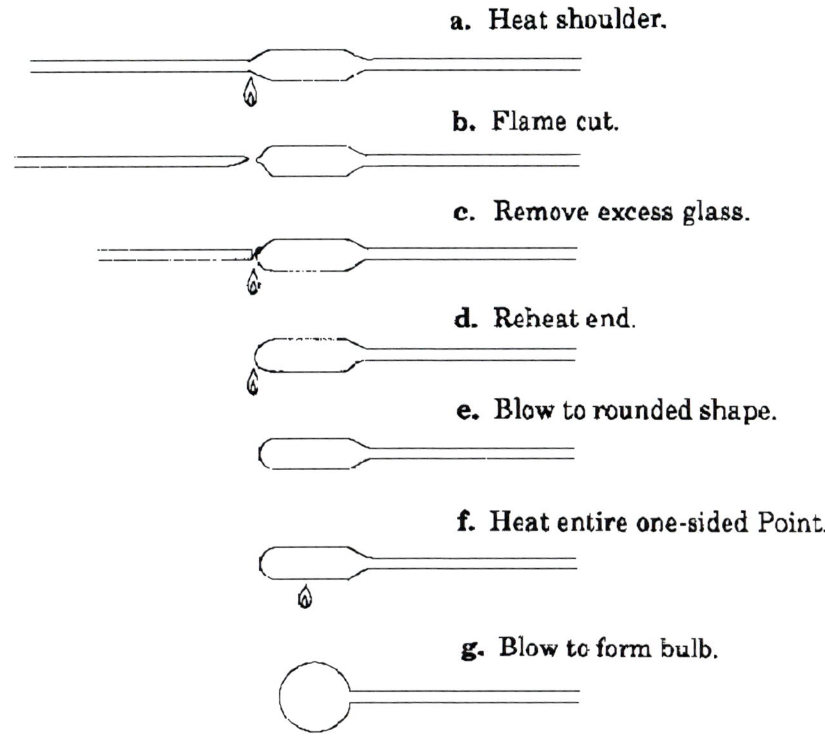

Figure 6.10 *Drawing of steps used in blowing a bulb from a one-sided point.*

This cleaned up, rounded end is often referred to as a "test tube end".

5. Now heat the whole piece of tubing with rotation until it becomes uniformly reddish in color (Figure 6.10f). Remove from the flame and blow with rapid rotation as you did in Exercise 17. Continue until it becomes spherical in shape and is several times the diameter of the original tubing (Figure 6.10g). Check for sufficient wall thickness and wall uniformity with your file as before (over a waste container).

SEALING ROD TO BLOWN GLASS

A special procedure is recommended for attaching glass rod, or pieces of solid glass shaped from rod, to hollow forms. Without this procedure, the glass at the junction would be too thick and would surely crack. In order to avoid this, the hollow form should be blown into immediately after the solid glass is fused to it. The blowing actually starts to hollow out the attached solid glass. What happens is that the hot solid glass heats and softens the blown glass walls which are very thin and thus heat quickly. The blowing forces a bubble to begin forming at the junction. This bubble makes a seal such that the thickness of the solid glass decreases gradually to the thickness of the blown glass wall. Seals made in this way will be markedly stronger than those made without blowing.

LABORATORY EXERCISE NINETEEN

SEALING ROD TO BLOWN GLASS BULBS

1. Make a blown sphere from a point made of 15 mm tubing by the procedure discussed in Exercise 17 or 18.

2. Heat the tip of a piece of 6 mm rod until softened over a 1/2 inch length. Reheat the end once more and attach to the bulb anywhere around the circumference (Figure 6.11). The position isn't important right now, as you are just practicing.

3. Immediately move the blowpipe to your mouth. Blow rather strongly while pulling outward on the rod. When you see that a very small bubble has started to form, cease blowing (Figure 6.12).

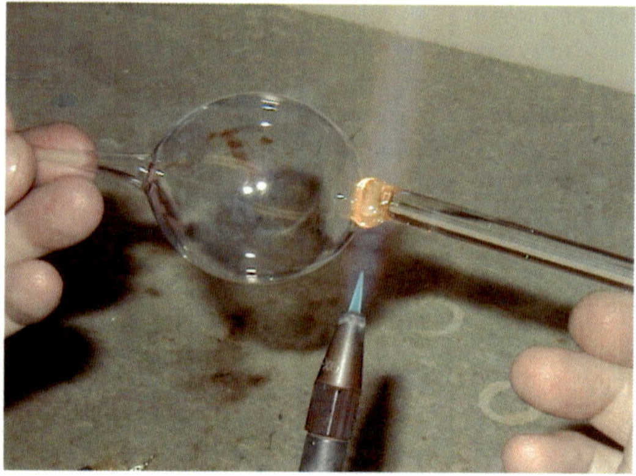

Figure 6.11 *Attaching the softened end of a rod to a blown bulb.*

4. Remove the blowpipe from your mouth and continue to pull and shape the rod. Flame cut where desired. (This exercise is concerned with making proper joints, not in constructing any particular item. Therefore, any shapes may be fashioned with the rod.)

5. Repeat Steps 2-4 as many times as there is room for rods on the same sphere.

6. Examine your joints carefully to see if, indeed, a good seal was made between the rod and the bulb.

This operation is important to remember whenever attaching any rod to a hollow form in order to make the rod to bulb seal stronger.

BLOWING ROD INTO HOLLOW FORMS

A logical extension of the above procedure is to deliberately blow harder and longer so that the rod is substantially transformed into a hollow form. This method can be used in the construction of many novelty items such as blown animals or fancy Christmas ornaments. It is also one way to transform colored glass rod into colored blown forms, since colored borosilicate tubing is not normally available.

LABORATORY EXERCISE TWENTY

CONVERTING ROD INTO HOLLOW FORMS

1. Make a blown sphere from a one-sided point made out of 15 mm tubing by the procedure discussed in Exercise 18.

2. Heat the tip of a piece of 8 mm rod until softened over a 1/2 inch area. Reheat the end once more and attach to the bulb at the point opposite to the blowpipe (Figure 6.12).

3. Immediately move the blowpipe to your mouth. Blow moderately hard until you see the bubble fill the diameter of the original rod. Pull the rod outward while blowing. Blow strongly enough to cause the bubble to advance, but not so strongly as to cause the rod to bubble out and burst (Figures 6.13-6.14).

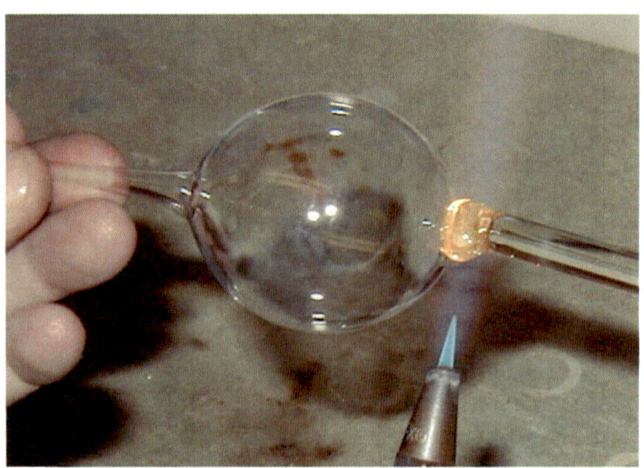

Figure 6.12 *Attaching a mass of softened glass rod to a blown bulb.*

Figure 6.13 *Moderate blowing while pulling the rod results in a hollow glass bubble.*

4. Make a flame cut just beyond the end of the newly constructed bubble.

5. Repeat this exercise, experimenting with both larger and smaller rods. Attach these anywhere around the circumference. Also investigate the effect of pulling versus pushing on the rod while blowing.

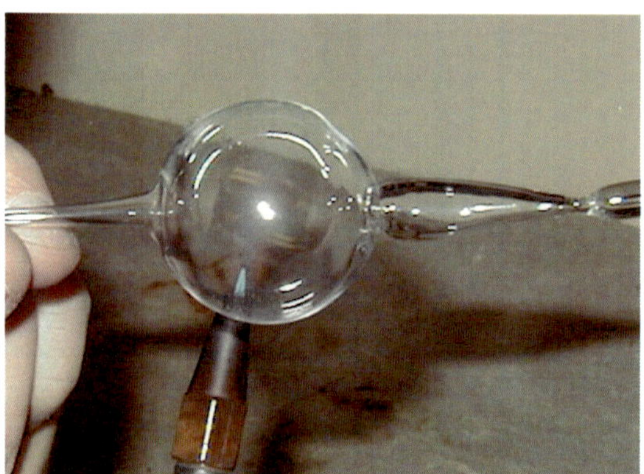

Figure 6.14 *Additional blowing and pulling results in a longer tube bubble.*

LABORATORY PROJECT - ARTISTIC FIFTEEN

BLOWN GLASS MOUSE

Introduction:

A mouse, believe it or not, is one of the simplest blown objects that can be made. Unless a person has a real aversion to mice, these turn out to be rather attractive pieces. The main techniques are those of blowing and attaching rod to blown objects. If desired, 12 mm tubing may be substituted to produce smaller mice.

Figure 6.15 *Blown glass mouse.*

Materials:

One 1.5-2 inch Point made from 15 mm tubing
A thin piece of blue borosilicate glass drawn out to 1 mm diameter
Approximately 12 inches of 4 mm rod.

Special Tools:

Marver, graphite plate, 12 inch stand (optional)

Flame:

#5 tip; small to medium flame

Construction Steps

1. The two ears are fashioned first and are saved for use later in Step 7. The tip of a 4 mm rod is heated strongly so that a small sphere of glass is formed. This is then placed on a graphite plate and immediately flattened with the marver. Just as it is being flattened, and just before the glass cools, pull on the rod firmly, holding the flattened part. This should reduce the rod thickness near the flat part of the ear so that the rod handle can later be removed easily and quickly. This procedure is

repeated in order to make a second ear. The size of the flattened ears is not as important as it is to make the two ears the same size. However, a flattened region of 12 mm in diameter is ideal. The finished ears are placed aside for later use.

2. The right hand two thirds of a 1 3/4 inch long 15 mm Point is heated with rotation in the flame until it becomes uniformly reddish in color. A slight amount of pushing is recommended to thicken the glass.

3. Once uniformly red, the Point is removed from the flame and placed over a graphite plate (ideally near eye level on top of a 12 inch stand). The body is shaped by blowing without rotation. Just as the body approaches the proper size (approximately 30-35 mm in diameter) and just before the glass begins to cool, lower the blown form onto the graphite plate while continuing to blow (Figure 6.16). Do not stop blowing until the glass has cooled.

4. Heat the left side of the point (with rotation) in the area between the blown body and the left shoulder of the original Point.

5. The left handle is now removed by flame cutting, thus forming the head and nose. More specifically, as the glass softens, pull the left handle outward while still rotating the glass in the flame (Figure 6.17). Just before the flame cut is completed, hold the mouse body so that the flattened bottom is upward and stop rotation. Continue to pull outward and now downward until the handle is separated (Figure 6.18).

Figure 6.16 *After blowing a bulb on the front part of the point, the hot bulb is flattened.*

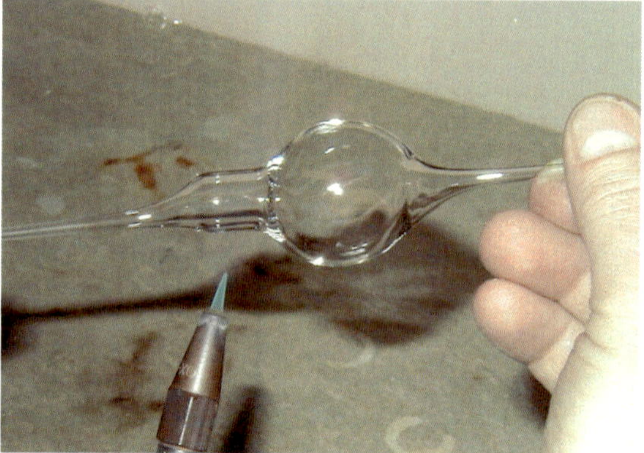

Figure 6.17 *Heating the unblown part of the Point.*

Figure 6.18 *Drawing out the heated glass, forming the nose of the mouse.*

Figure 6.19 *Making a flame cut on the drawn out portion, finishing the nose of the mouse.*

6. Immediately reheat the tip of the nose and wipe off any excess glass using the thicker part of the handle (which was just removed) as the cold rod (Figure 6.19). Continue to hold the body upside down. Heat the tip again and allow the glass at the end of the nose to form a very small sphere.

7. While the head area is still warm, prepare to add the ears which were constructed in Step 1. Heat one ear on the edge opposite to the rod handle while keeping the mouse head warm by holding very high in the flame.

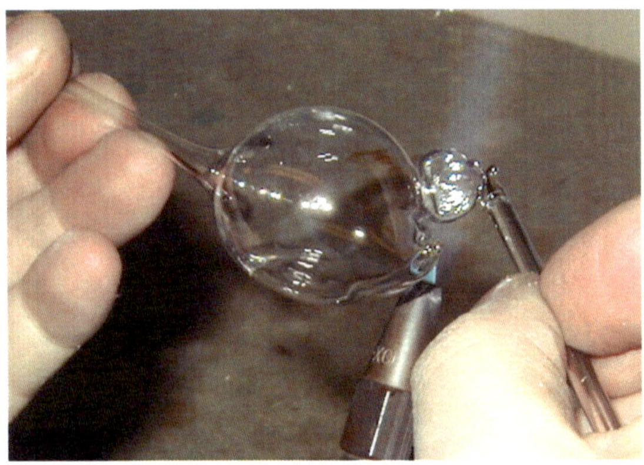

Figure 6.20 *Adding the first ear to the head. After attaching, blow through tail & pull out.*

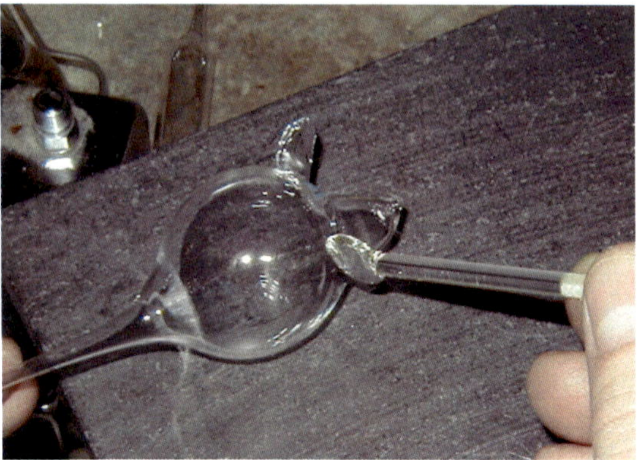

Figure 6.21 *Attaching the second ear while the mouse is held on the graphite plate.*

8. Add the mouse's left ear first. Attach the softened ear to the side facing you at a point where the body begins and the head ends (Figure 6.20). Immediately blow through the tail blowpipe

while pulling slightly on the ear. This will thin out the ear and body junction, making it a stronger and more durable seal (see p 180). Then flame cut the rod handle and heat the ear tip enough so that the remaining knob of glass melts into the flattened disk of glass.

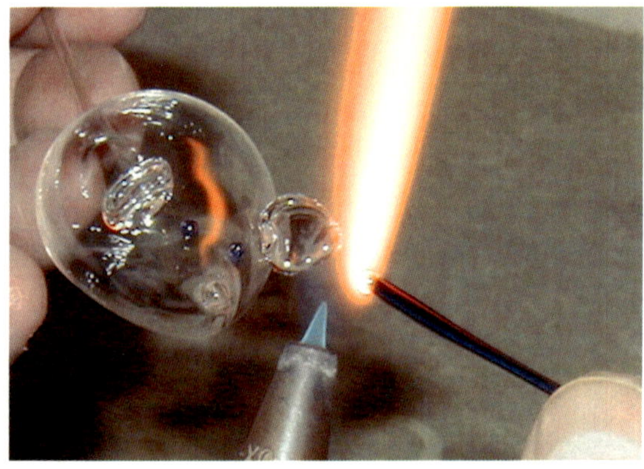

Figure 6.22 *Using a thin rod of blue glass to make the eyes. Reheat to thoroughly fuse to head.*

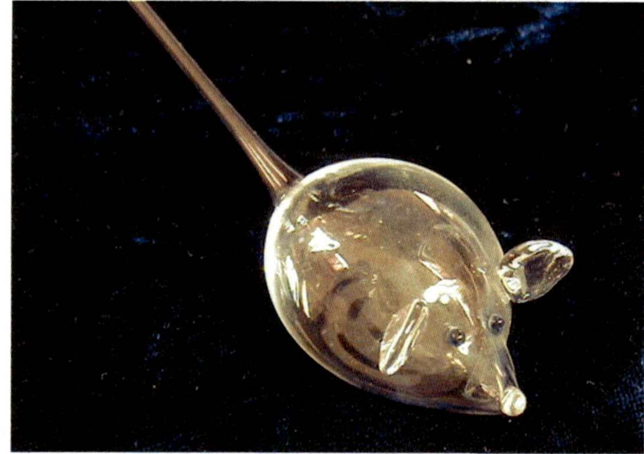

Figure 6.23 *The completed blown mouse.*

9. The second ear is added in a similar manner. To insure proper placement of the ear, put the mouse on the graphite plate on a stand and turn the mouse so that you are facing the side of the mouse with the tail pointing to the left. Now add the softened ear (Figure 6.21). This position will give you a better chance of placing the second ear so that it is in a position which is symmetrical with the first. Likewise, the rod handle is removed by a flame cut.

10. The eyes are added next. The face portion is heated very gently in the upper most part of the flame. Then a thin rod of blue borosilicate glass is heated, and the eyes are placed symmetrically at points in front between the ears (Figure 6.22). The glass is carefully heated to fuse the eyes securely to the blown glass. A slight puff of air may be needed to restore the face contour if the area is overheated.

11. The product should be oven annealed as soon as possible. Be sure to keep the tail open during the annealing process, otherwise the trapped air would expand and break the item. After annealing, the tail can be flame cut where desired. Alternately, a wavy tail can be made by heating the tail portion with a very cool flame and by curving the glass where desired. The end is then flame cut at the proper length - after annealing!

LABORATORY PROJECT - ARTISTIC SIXTEEN

BLOWN GLASS VASE

Introduction:

Useful and attractive flask-shaped vases can be made by blowing spheres from large (15-25 mm) tubing, flattening the bottom, cutting the neck where desired, and flaring or scalloping it. Many interesting variations are possible. Colored glass may be added to the top before making the flares. The necks do not need to be straight, as they can be stretched out to make more interesting designs (see Figure 6.35).

Figure 6.24 *Simple blown vase.*

Materials:

Approximately 18 in of 15 mm, 20 mm or 25 mm Tubing

Special Tools:

Graphite plate, heat resistant gloves, wheel cutter, carbon rod

Flame:

#5 tip; large, hot flame

Construction Steps

1. Prepare to close off the end of an 18 inch length of 15 to 25 mm tubing. A rod can be attached to the tubing to serve as a handle in drawing out the point very close to the end of the tubing (Figure 6.25). Attach a blowpipe hose with a swivel and mouth piece to the other end. If the tubing is sufficiently large, a one-holed rubber stopper will work nicely to add the swivel to the tube.

2. Make a flame cut near the end of the tubing (Figure 6.26) and clean it up to make a test tube end (procedure involving wiping is outlined in Laboratory Exercise 18).

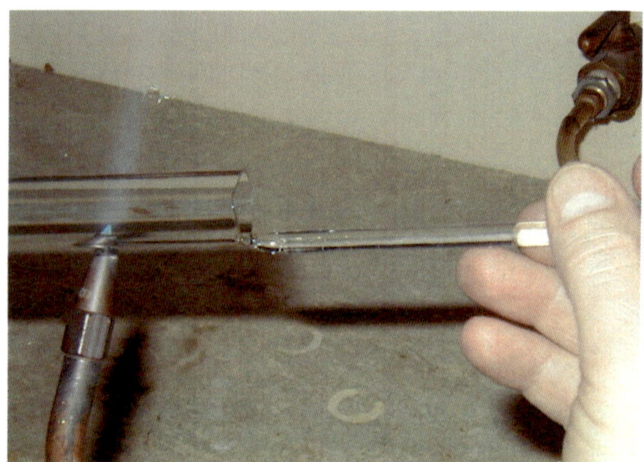

Figure 6.25 *An attached rod to the end of a large diameter tube will serve as a handle.*

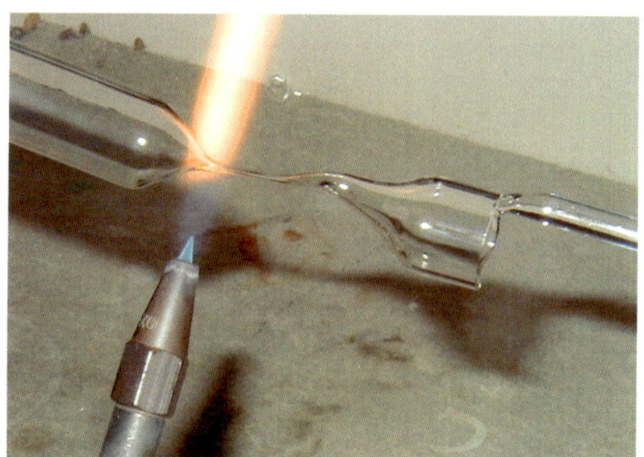

Figure 6.26 *Making a flame cut to the end of the large diameter tubing.*

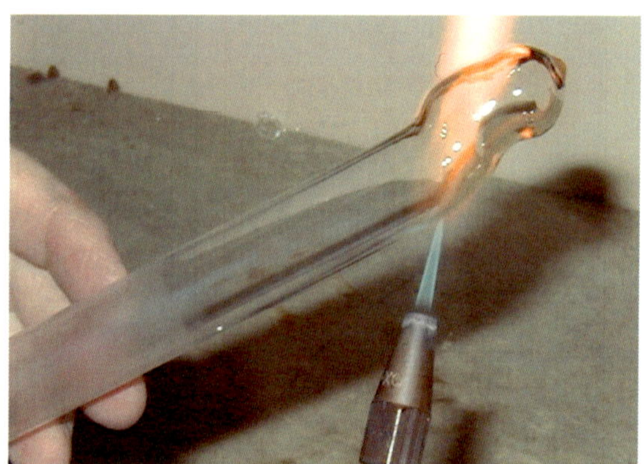

Figure 6.27 *Gathering glass in preparation for blowing the bulb.*

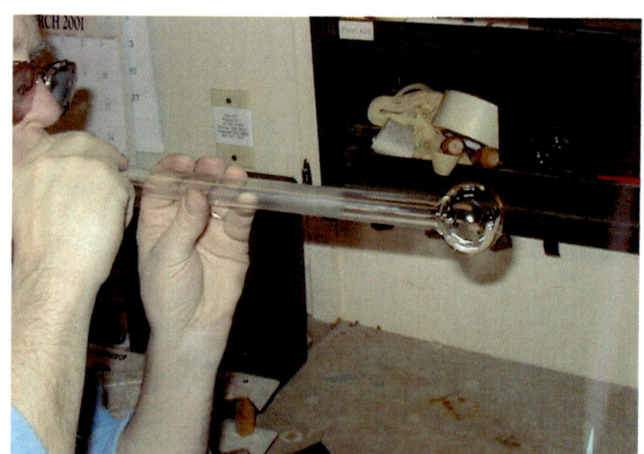

Figure 6.28 *Blowing the bulb outside of the flame. Rotation is important!*

3. Approximately two inches of the end of the tubing are now heated strongly with constant rotation. The tubing will begin to collapse and thicken and will assume a reddish glow. Allow the tubing to be reduced to approximately two-thirds of the original diameter. It is important that the soft glass remains along the axis of the original tubing (Figure 6.27). The glass is removed from the flame while rapid rotation is continued. Do not allow the hot glass to sag, and keep the heated portion along the axis of the tubing. Begin blowing with just enough pressure to begin to shape the bulb. Gradually increase pressure until the proper size (approximately three times the original tubing diameter) is attained (Figure 6.28). The importance of rapid and uniform rotation can not be over emphasized.

Figure 6.30 *Reheating the bottom of the finished bulb in preparation for flattening.*

Figure 6.31 *Flattening the bottom of the finished bulb (vase) on a graphite plate.*

4. Carefully examine the finished bulb and check for uniformity in wall thickness. This can be done both visually and physically with the aid of your triangular file. If the bulb is constructed well and has a desirable shape, proceed with Step 5.

5. Reheat the bottom of the bulb. This is done by rotating the tubing so that the bottom of the bulb just touches the side of the hot flame (Flame 6.30). When sufficiently heated (it may begin to collapse slightly) remove from the flame and press downward squarely onto a graphite plate (Figure 6.31). The long tubing and blowpipe will serve as an excellent indicator as to whether or not the bottom has been properly placed, as it should be pointed straight up at this time. Upon rotation of the piece on the graphite plate, the tubing and point should appear to remain true (that is, no wobble). A properly formed bottom should be uniform and slightly concave, not just flat. There should be no evidence of bumps or cold spots. The piece should be allowed to cool completely. Otherwise heavy heat resistant gloves are needed for the left hand in the next step.

6. The neck of the vase is cut just slightly longer than the finished desired length (anywhere from one half to one and a half inches above the bulb). The best method may be to use the cutting wheel or hot rod technique (procedures discussed on page 51 and page 52). The blowpipe and excess tubing portion are placed aside for use in making additional vases.

7. The freshly cut edge of the vase is heated with rotation (Figure 6.32). Rotation is done as fast as possible with your left hand.

Figure 6.32 *After cutting off excess tubing, the top is heated with rotation.*

Figure 6.33 *When the glass is sufficiently heated, remove from the flame and "flute" with carbon rod. Repeat all around the top.*

8. Scalloped (Fluted) edges are fashioned by using a large to medium sized carbon rod (Figures 6.33 - 6.34). Either three or four scallops can be added. The glass lip will need to be reheated each time a scallop is added. If desired, colored glass can be added to the top of the vase before making the fluted edges (Figure 6.35).

9. It is wise to oven anneal the completed product, although such annealing is not absolutely necessary.

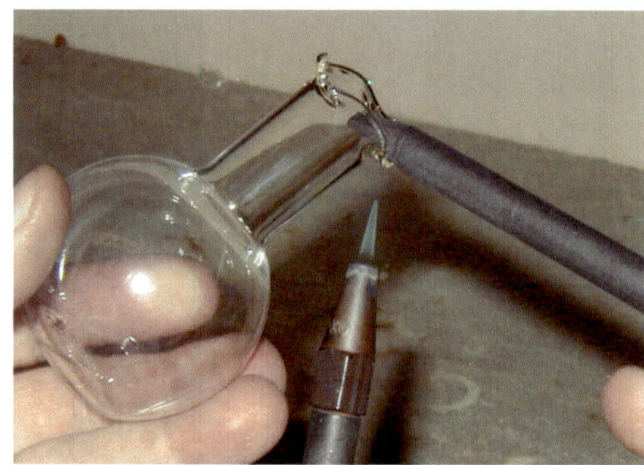

Figure 6.34 *A closer view of making fluted design with a carbon rod. If desired, colored glass can be added along the top edge of the vase before the fluting steps.*

Figure 6.35 *Two finished simple vases. In making the vase on the left, small dots of white glass were added during step 3. Many other "more beautiful" variations on this design are possible. See Figure 6.49 for some examples with elongated necks. Use your imagination!*

LABORATORY PROJECT - ARTISTIC SEVENTEEN

BLOWN SWAN BAROMETERS

Introduction:

Swan barometers are probably one of the first things that come to anyone's mind when artistic glassblowing is mentioned. These always seem to be the focus of much attention wherever itinerant glassblowers demonstrate. Swans look like they should be rather simple to make. There are no joints, and they are made rather quickly. The fact of the matter is that for such simple looking pieces of glass, they are rather difficult to make. They are difficult, that is, until you catch on to how to make them. What is really necessary is to have a real feel for the glass, knowing what to do and when to do it, and knowing how to correct errors as they happen. Certainly such things are important in all glassworking, but in this case, the working time is so short because of the thin walls of the blown glass that even the smallest mistakes become exaggerated and rather obvious.

Figure 6.36 *Blown glass swan. (This Swan was made with amber borosilicate tubing.)*

Many people find swans delightful because of their simple, yet graceful design. Others swear by them as accurate predictors of weather. The fact is that they really are barometers. The level of the water in the neck of the swan is a rather sensitive indicator of atmospheric pressure and therefore of weather. The swan barometer will work best if the water level is about midway in the neck, if the neck is relatively thin, and if there is a large amount of air trapped in the body portion. Let's take a minute to explain how and why they work.

The air trapped in the body of the swan exerts a pressure equal to the atmospheric pressure existing at the time that the swan was filled or set. The level in the neck is, therefore, representative of the weather (really the pressure) at that time. If the present atmospheric pressure is higher, the outside pressure will act to compress the trapped air, and the level in the neck will be lower than it was originally. If the present atmospheric pressure is lower, the trapped air will try to expand, thus causing the level in the neck to become higher than it was originally. High pressure (clear weather) will be indicated by lower levels in the neck; low pressure (stormy weather) will be indicated by higher levels in the neck. Observing changes will be easier if you make a small mark on the neck with a magic marker pen.

Materials:

A three inch Point made from 15 mm tubing
Colored distilled water for filling completed swan.

Special Tools:

Graphite plate, needlenose pliers

Flame:

#5 tip, medium to hot flame

Construction Steps

1. The end of a three inch Point constructed from 15 mm rod is opened and lightly fire polished.
2. The right half of the Point (side closest to the blowpipe) is heated strongly with rotation in a medium flame. As the glass becomes softened, the ends of the Point are pushed inward slightly in order to thicken the glass. Heat all the way to the end of the point, but when heating in that region, keep the drawn point downward to keep the thin portions of the blowpipe from softening.
3. When the glass is sufficiently soft, it should begin to take on a slight reddish glow (Figure 6.37). Be careful not to get the glass too hot; it has to be "just right" and only lots of experimentation will determine this for you.

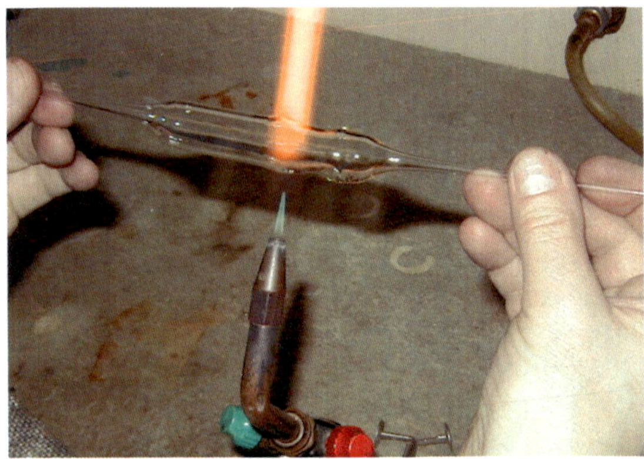

Figure 6.37 *The front half of the point is heated to a reddish glow before blowing.*

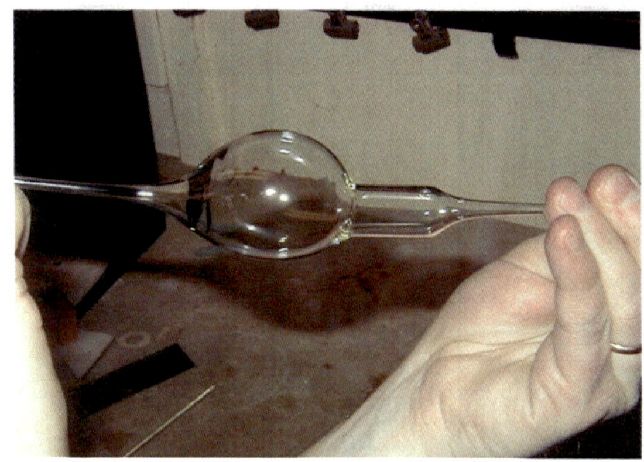

Figure 6.38 *Blowing the front half (the swan body) while rotating to keep shape uniform.*

At this time, the Point is removed from the flame (with constant and rapid rotation) and gentle blowing is begun (Figure 6.38). During rapid rotation and blowing, the ends of the point can be pulled outward slightly, making the product somewhat elongated. This will be the swan's body.

4. Now the neck is fashioned. The left half of the Point is heated with rotation until it becomes softened in a similar manner (Figure 6.39). This time keep the heat away from the shoulder of the Point. Do not overheat this portion of the Point. The glass should become reddish in color as before, but should not begin to collapse significantly.

5. When the glass is sufficiently soft, remove from the flame and

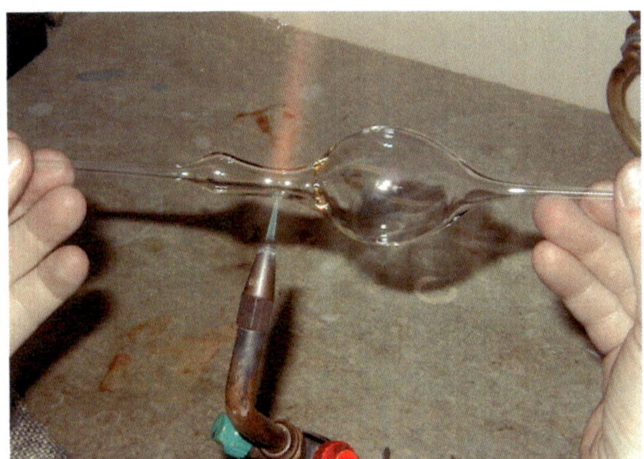

Figure 6.39 *Heating second half to prepare for the drawing out and blowing of head.*

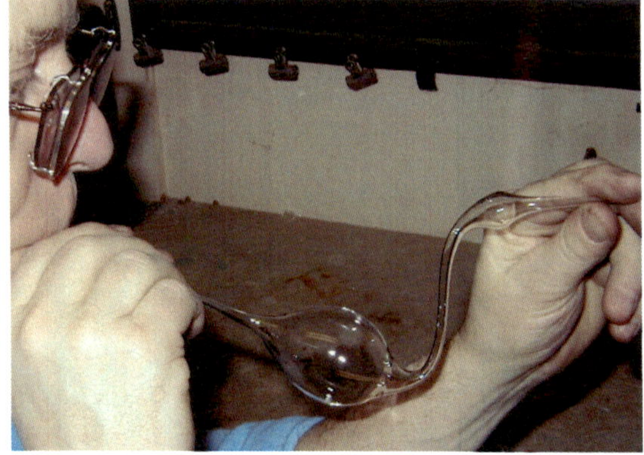

Figure 6.40 *Drawing out and blowing of the neck and head of the swan.*

place the blowpipe in your mouth while holding it firmly in your right hand. The left hand is used to pull the glass outward, approximately 6 inches, and then to move it upward. Finally the end portion is brought downward again while a small puff of air is introduced to keep the neck from collapsing during the bending (Figure 6.40). The final position is held for a few seconds until the glass hardens. The neck portion should be relatively thick. If the neck turns out to be too thin, it is probably because it was heated too strongly.

When cool enough, the body is held in the desired standing position on a graphite plate. Make a mental note where the body should be heated in order to form the bottom. Move it to the flame and heat at the proper spot using a very small, cool flame (Figure 6.41), and then flatten on the board or plate (Figure 6.42).

Figure 6.41 *Reheating the bottom of the swan before flattening.*

Figure 6.42 *Flattening the bottom on graphite plate, taking care that the swan sits straight.*

7. The swan is then allowed to cool. Figure 6.43 shows the swan before filling. Note the flattened bottom. The drawn point on the head end is cut (using a knife or file) as close as possible to the end of the point. Lightly fire polish.

8. The tail is immersed in a container of distilled water (food colors may be added

Figure 6.43 *The completed blown swan.*

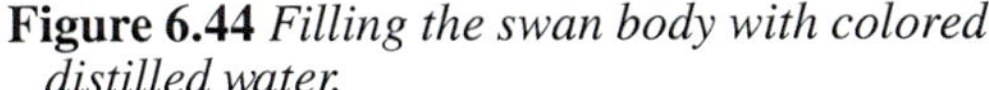

Figure 6.44 *Filling the swan body with colored distilled water.*

Figure 6.45 *Making a flame cut on the swan tail. Keep the water away from this area.*

if desired). The head portion is now used as a suction tube for filling the swan (Figure 6.44). The body portion should be filled about two thirds of the way.

9. Once filled, the body is tilted so the tail is upward. A small flame is used to heat the tail at a point about 3/4 of an inch beyond where the body ends. (Caution: water in the tube may boil and become steam causing the end portions of the tail to become very hot. This can be avoided somewhat by allowing the water to completely drain from the tail by keeping it in the tilted upward position for a few minutes. Working quickly will also decrease the chances of boiling the water.) Once the tail portion is softened, it is flame cut by drawing outward and upward (Figure 6.45). Sharp edges are fire polished.

10. Keep the swan in a tail upward position until the tail region has thoroughly cooled; otherwise the cool water may cause the glass to crack.

11. The nose portion is then cut off again, but this time closer to the head region (Figure 6.46). The cut is lightly fire polished. Make sure it does not become closed (Figure 6.47).

12. Check to see that the swan stands upright without any rocking. The water level in the neck should be adjusted so that the level is about one third into the narrow region of the neck. This can be done by slowly tilting the swan either forward (to raise the level by allowing more air into the body) or backward (to lower the level by removing air from the body).

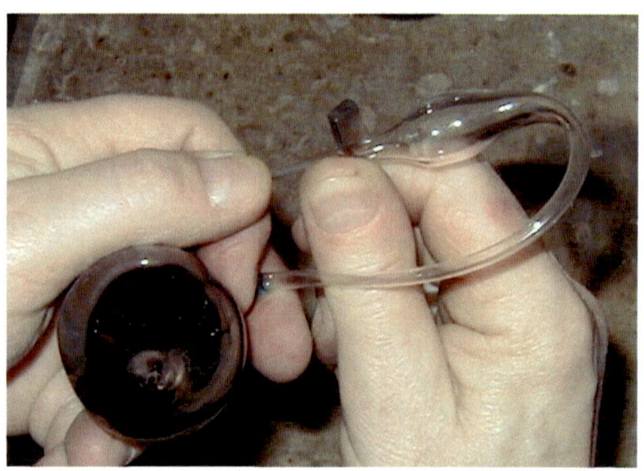

Figure 6.46 *Scoring the glass on the swan beak (previously the item's blow pipe).*

Figure 6.47 *Fire polishing the newly cut end on the head of the swan.*

Figure 6.48 *Sample of finished swan. This particular swan was blown from amber colored borosilicate glass and filled with colorless distilled water.*

Note: Expect to repeat this project *many times* before you obtain a "keeper". Making swans is not as easy as you may think, and numerous failures are common before mastering the technique. A good understanding of glassblowing methods is essential before becoming proficient!

MORE IDEAS

A number of additional items which incorporate blowing in their construction are shown in Figures 6.49 - 6.58.

Figure 6.49 *Additional vases, (These require drawing out the neck before finishing the top.)*

Figure 6.50 *One example of blown "glass sculpture".*

Figure 6.51 *An elegant blown glass bell (Made by Gordon Smith).*

Figure 6.52 *A simple, elegant blown wine glass (Made by Joe Wheeler)*

Figure 6.53 *One example of an oil lamp. This one is essentially a swan vase on a stand.*

Figure 6.54 *A "Little pig" fashioned by techniques discussed in this chapter.*

Figure 6.54 *Another small pig, made similarly, but of blue borosilicate glass (Russian).*

Figure 6.55 (Left)
Figure 6.56 (Right)

These are two examples of antique glass bead Christmas ornaments, probably made in Czechoslovakia in the late 1800's by "cottage craftsmen" and their families. The beads (some being multiple "intermediate maria" bulbs) are strung together in various geometric designs with wire. (Made with soft glass)

Figure 6.57 *This pickle is a modern version of an old German Christmas ornament. It was the tradition to decorate the tree, hiding the pickle. On Christmas morning, the first child to locate the hidden pickle received an extra gift.*

Figure 6.58
Swan vase. This swan is similar to those made earlier but has a hole on the top of its back along with an extra thick neck/head. The beak is closed. Unlike the swan barometers, water in these can be changed if desired. These are used to start plant rootings.

Chapter 7
SCIENTIFIC GLASSBLOWING

TECHNIQUES AND PRINCIPLES

Scientific glassblowing is different in many respects from its artistic counterpart. It may involve the construction or repair of glassware which is often no more than a composite of various commercially available components. These may include stopcocks, standard taper joints, bulbs and flasks, all joined together in a meaningful way for use by the student or scientist. In other cases, the apparatus may be constructed solely from pieces of different diameter tubing, joined together and bent here and there for various functional purposes. Occasionally, the need may arise for construction of simple bulbs, round bottom ends, or other special parts, but usually careful study of almost any complex scientific apparatus will confirm that the glassblower's main job is to join pieces and make bends. Analyze the complex piece of apparatus in Figure 7.1 with these ideas in mind.

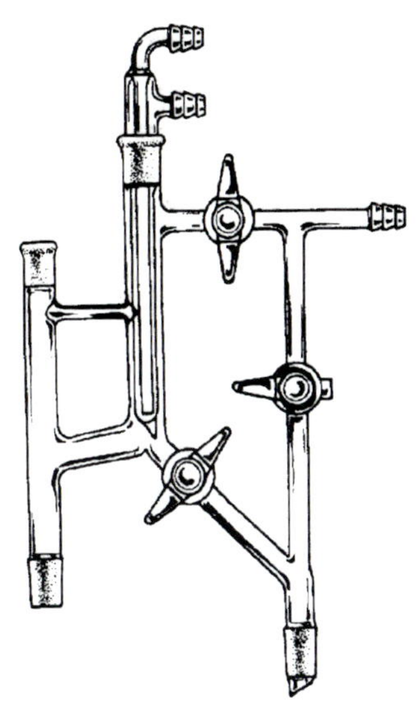

Figure 7.1 *Distillation head (Kimble-Kontes).*

This is certainly not to say that all scientific glassblowers are only joint makers. Professional glassblowers do very much more. Their tasks may range all the way from original product design to blowing large and unusually shaped components. In fact, many operations they perform are extremely complex and require great skill and experience. But the nonprofessional, both student and science professor, will find that 90% of what they need to do will involve making various types of joints and bends and performing other very basic operations.

Joining glass tubing is quite different from joining rod. With rod, the only main concern, other than making a strong seal, is to keep the outside diameter of the rod uniform in the region of the seal. With tubing, of course, one must also be concerned with maintaining the inside diameter. Wall thickness at any seal should always be as close as possible to the original tubing wall thickness. The wall thickness at the seal can always be increased by pushing the tubes together or by continued heating. The thickness can be decreased by pulling slightly on the tubes or by blowing. In actual practice, wall thickness is controlled continuously by a combination of pulling or pushing and heating or blowing.

The blowpipe is an integral part of every scientific operation. All of the openings in the apparatus other than that which will be used for the blowpipe must be closed off by the use of corks or rubber policemen (clamped off rubber tubing) or masking tape. The system should be thoroughly checked before work is begun, as there is nothing so frustrating as to find that when a puff of air is needed at that all important moment, the air escapes from some forgotten passageway.

The blowpipe is often just the glass tubing itself or an opening on another part of the apparatus. Alternatively, it may be a specially attached swivel connected to a piece of rubber tubing and fitted with a mouthpiece. Or, if the glass tubing is large in diameter, a point may be drawn out (see Chapter 6) and opened for use as a blowpipe, much as is done in artistic glassblowing. If given a choice, the beginner should probably always choose the swivel and rubber tubing method since this will allow more attention to be paid to the actual glassblowing and will require much less movement of the glass. Also, with this method, the seal needs to be moved only slightly out of the flame before blowing, and then it can be immediately returned for further heating if necessary. The plastic mouthpiece can be kept in the mouth at all times. When the glass itself is used as a blowpipe, it has to be moved to the mouth after each heating. This may cause the experienced glassblower little or no trouble, but the novice will probably discover that it is very difficult to do such maneuvering without bending or pulling on the pieces, especially since rapid rotation has to be maintained throughout the entire process.

Beginners are often surprised to discover how little pressure is needed during the actual blowing operations. While the glass is red hot, even the slightest pressure may be too much. Thus, special care has to be taken to avoid blowing into the mouthpiece by accident at times when blowing is not required. Usually one never does any blowing while the glass is still in the flame except if you want to form a hole.

Never cover the mouthpiece with the tip of your tongue. This is a rather natural action, but will result in a closed system. Then as the glass becomes heated, the air inside is also heated and expands greatly. This will relieve itself by blowing an unwanted bubble or even bursting a hole in the glass wherever it is hottest.

The swivel can be attached to the desired tubing or opening in a variety of ways. The most common method involves the use of masking tape (Figure 7.2). Tape is first wrapped around the tubing and then flattened onto the swivel. Be sure that the proper end of the swivel, the end that rotates, is taped to the glass.

In other cases involving larger tubing, it may be wise to use a one-hole rubber stopper. But, for very large diameter holes, a pluorostopper or multistopper may be utilized. These are actually a series of many concentric stoppers, the diameters larger than needed being removed (Figure 7.3).

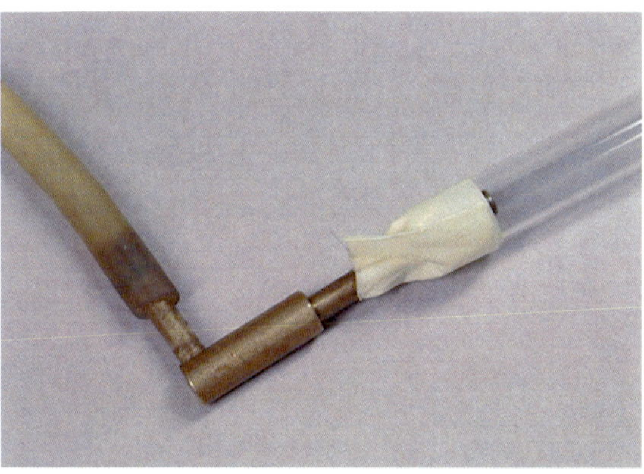

Figure 7.2 *Masking tape connection to swivel.*

Figure 7.3 *Multistopper (Pluorostopper)*

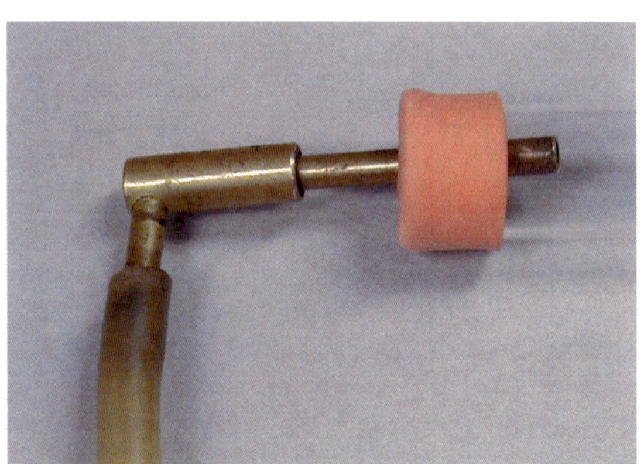

Figure 7.4 *Modified septum connection to swivel.*

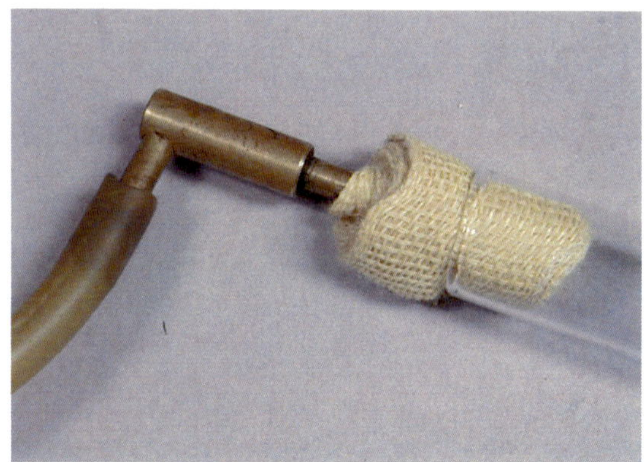

Figure 7.5 *Heat resistant tape connection to swivel.*

These stoppers are quite handy, but very expensive. Care should be taken so that none of the concentric parts are misplaced or damaged.

Modified laboratory septa (Figure 7.4) are also very handy since, with these, either end can be used, and they can be stretched considerably to accommodate a large range of diameters.

In the case of relatively small diameter tubing, a simple rubber hose connector can be used. Or one or more layers of heat resistant tape can be wrapped around the swivel and then fitted snugly into the tubing (Figure 7.5). Another method which is ideal for very small tubing utilizes a rubber stopper as an intermediate is described by Ponton.[1] Rubber "policemen" can be used in a similar way. There are probably many other methods which could also be used. It is wise to use whichever method is most convenient and whatever works best for you.

Brief mention should be made of the fact that most of the methods described above involve substances which are flammable. For this reason, glass tubing should never be heated closer than 2 to 3 inches from the swivel connection. Heating closer than this may cause the tape, stopper, septa, or rubber hose to decompose (actually, to pyrolyze), forming organic products which can then react with the hot glass where the seal is being made. Most glassblowers have experienced this at one time or another. If you ever note that the glass you are working on becomes iridescent red (a darker red than usual), look at your blowpipe connection, as it is probably decomposing from overheating.

If it is absolutely necessary to heat the glass area close to the blowpipe connection, it is best to fit the swivel by packing it with a good quality heat resistant tape (as in Figure 7.5). For larger openings, wrap the stopper or pluorostopper with heat resistant tape.

Care should also be exercised with the rubber blowpipe hose. Be sure to keep it away from the flame and away from hot tubing.

MAKING STRAIGHT SEALS (BUTT JOINTS)

Of all the different types of seals, the straight or butt seal is the most basic and is the one used most often. Technically, it should be the easiest seal, yet many students find that they can make better ring seals or T-seals (described in later sections) than they can butt seals. This may not seem reasonable, but apparently there is some truth in it. The problcm (at least for all but professionals) is expressed quite accurately in the rule of thumb, "the more time spent in making a butt seal, the worse it will look." In contrast, for some reason, the more time spent in making a T-seal, the better it will probably look. Certainly this is not always true (especially for those who really know what they are doing), but you will be surprised at how accurate this axiom turns out to be. The apparent secret for making good butt joints is to make them correctly *as quickly as possible*.

There are at least two different general approaches for making common butt seals. One involves a "spot welding" technique where the tubing is first crudely joined with a "cold seal". Then it is reheated and blown out, area by area, all the way around the joint until it is completely welded together. In some respects, this way may be easier for the beginner and normally produces surprisingly nice results. Structurally, however, the joint may not be as strong as that which is made by the in-flame or hot seal technique, unless it is thoroughly annealed immediately.

In the "hot seal" method, the two tubes are joined in the flame and the joint is heated strongly with constant rotation. In this way the entire seal is made in one operation. In this method, you will see the glass at the joint thicken and collapse somewhat as it is heated and rotated. At that time, it is removed from the flame and, while rotation is continued, a puff of air and a slight bit of stretching brings the diameter back to where it should be. When made properly, such seals can be done very quickly and are very strong.

The best way to understand each method is to try both, but the beginner is urged to start with the "spot welding" or "cold seal" method.

LABORATORY EXERCISE TWENTY ONE

BUTT JOINTS - SPOT WELDING TECHNIQUE

1. The burner is fitted with a #2 or #3 tip. Two pieces of 10 mm tubing, at least 6 inches in length, are readied. The end of one is closed with a small cork, and the end of the other is fitted with a swivel and blowpipe. (It is probably best to use masking tape.)

2. With one tube held in each hand, the open ends are heated with rotation in the flame (Figure 7.6). It will probably be necessary to heat the end of one tube higher in the flame and the other lower. Exchange positions at least one time.

3. When the tubing pieces just become fire polished, remove them from the flame and immediately bring them in contact with one another (Figure 7.7). Do so lightly, yet in such a way so that all parts of the tubing ends touch and become fused. Check to make sure there are no gaps. This is often considered to be a cold seal. But it is not really a seal at all since it has little or no mechanical strength.

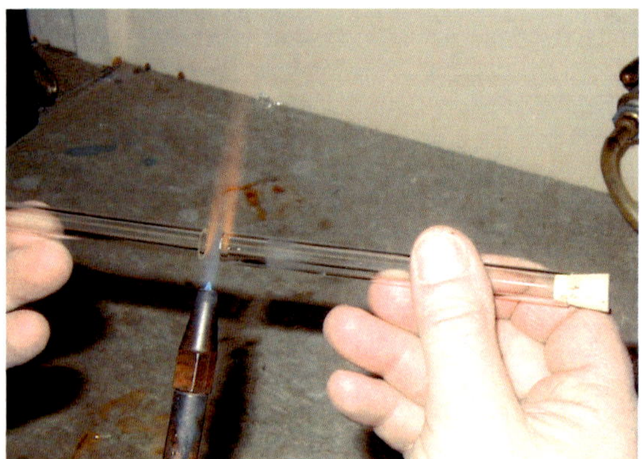

Figure 7.6 *The two glass tubes are heated with rotation in the flame.*

Figure 7.7 *Once brought outside the flame, the tubes are joined to form a "cold seal".*

4. The blowpipe is placed in your mouth at this time, and the cold seal joint is returned to the hottest part of the small flame without rotation. Soon you should see the junction line disappear in the heated region. The glass in this spot melts, collapses, and becomes thickened to some degree. It may appear white hot.

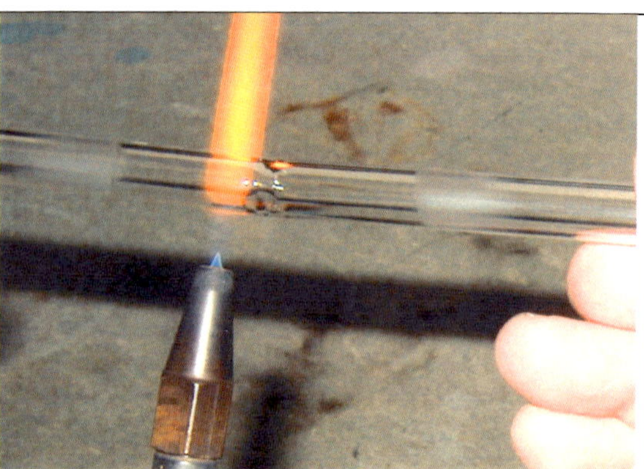

Figure 7.8 *Now the "cold seal" is placed in and out of flame until completely joined.*

5. The joint is moved a small distance out of the flame, and a small puff of air is added to return the depression to the proper diameter.

6. The glass is rotated slightly and a second area is heated, welded, and blown out as described in Steps 4 and 5. This is repeated until the glass is joined all the way around (Figure 7.8). Any necessary adjustments for axial linearity are made during the last heating and blowing. For small diameter tubing, three to four spot welds should be sufficient to complete the seal.

This exercise should be repeated many times with a variety of tubing sizes ranging from 8 to 12 mm in diameter. Several hours of practice may be needed before the joints begin to look good. With this method it is important to avoid overheating and blowing too hard. Don't overwork the joints. Joints made by this technique need to be flame annealed. If the joints are part of a permanent product, they should also be oven annealed.

LABORATORY EXERCISE TWENTY TWO

BUTT JOINTS - HOT SEAL TECHNIQUE

1. The burner is fitted with a #3 tip. Two pieces of 10 mm tubing, at least 6 inches in length, are obtained. The end of one is closed with a cork and the end of the other piece is fitted with a swivel and blowpipe.

2. Place the blowpipe in your mouth but take care not to cover the tip with your tongue. Now heat the open ends of both piece of tubing as done in Exercise 21 with rotation in the flame. Again, it may be necessary to heat the end of one tube higher in the flame and the other lower. Be sure to exchange positions at least once.

3. When the tubing pieces just become fire polished, bring them in contact with one another in the flame while continuing constant rotation. The contact should be done lightly, yet in such a way that all the parts of the edges touch and become fused. Continue heating and rotating.

You will see the junction line between the two tubes disappear. The glass in this region melts, collapses, and becomes thickened. Uniform rapid rotation of the two pieces of tubing is of utmost importance. It is probably best to have both of your hands over the tubing, as this allows for better support for the hot pieces of glass. Remember to keep your tongue off of the tip of the blowpipe, as otherwise, pressure will develop and a hole will be blown in the glass at the region heated.

This whole process will not take very long with small diameter tubing!

4. The joint is removed from the flame while rotation is continued. A puff of air is used to blow the glass in the region of the joint to a slightly larger diameter than the original glass tubing.

5. While the glass is still hot, the ends of the glass tubing are pulled out slightly in order to bring the diameter back to that of the original tubing.

It may be necessary to repeat Steps 3 and 4 order to achieve a satisfactory finished joint.

This exercise should also be repeated with a variety of tubing sizes ranging from 8 to 12 mm in diameter. When working with 12 mm tubing or larger, a #5 tip is needed.

Several hours of practice will probably be necessary before the joints appear to look as you would like them. The glass in the region of the joint will always appear to be distorted to some degree. Experienced glassblowers can make very high quality, good looking joints with this method.

Seals made in this way are often sufficiently annealed during the flame annealing process. Nonetheless, if the joint is part of a permanent product, oven annealing is highly recommended.

CONSTRICTIONS

Many times it is necessary to reduce the diameter of tubing. Such constrictions may be useful in the process of joining a larger tube to a smaller one or in preparing a liquid delivery tip for a piece of apparatus. In most cases, it is desirable to keep the wall thickness of the constriction the same as that of the original tubing.

LABORATORY EXERCISE TWENTY THREE

CONSTRICTIONS
REDUCING DIAMETER OF TUBING

1. Use a medium-hot flame to heat a central zone on a piece of 12 mm glass tubing while rotating. As the area softens, take care to neither push the ends in nor to pull them out. The glass will become very soft and will begin to thicken. Uniform rotation may get very

difficult while the glass is in this semifluid state, but make every effort to keep the tubes aligned and the rotation constant. Also take care that the constricted area does not become twisted. This will be a real test of your rotation skills.

2. When the tubing has shrunk to about two-thirds of its original diameter, remove the piece from the flame, continue rotation, and pull outward until the wall thickness of the constricted area is about the same as that of the original tubing. Once completed, it is best to hold the piece of tubing in an up and down position until it has cooled.

3. Repeat this exercise a number of times, concentrating on controlling the final diameter of the constriction.

4. Cut the tubing at the constriction, and lightly fire polish the ends.

HEAVY-WALL CONSTRICTIONS

In some applications it is necessary to maintain the original outside tubing diameter while constricting the inside diameter. Such is the case in manometers where the heavy walls insure greater mechanical strength. In other cases, it may be desirable to make the wall thickness greater at the constriction, but not necessarily as great as the original outside tubing diameter. This is the case in many seal off tubes for use on vacuum lines. Some extra strength is required, but the walls must be thin enough to allow them to be sealed off by heating and collapsing when necessary.

LABORATORY EXERCISE TWENTY FOUR

CONSTRICTIONS (HEAVY WALL)

1. The central zone of a piece of 12 mm glass tubing is heated with rotation. As the area softens, push inward slightly in order to increase the wall thickness. (If too hot a flame is used, the tubing will thicken and constrict too quickly and may even become solid.)

2. When the proper constriction is attained, remove the piece from the flame. Take special care to prevent twisting at the constriction. (Twisting while the glass is cooling will usually cause devitrification of the glass.) If the inside diameter has reduced too much, blowing can be used to enlarge the diameter, but this should be done only after the outside tubing has hardened somewhat.

3. Heavy wall constrictions should be annealed immediately after they are finished.

ROUND BOTTOM - TEST TUBE ENDS

Often it is desirable to form a round bottom closure on a piece of glass tubing. The round bottom may be the final part of the apparatus itself or it may serve as an intermediate step as in the joining of a very large tube to a smaller tube, or in making the through-seals that are found in condensers and vacuum traps.

Many times it is necessary to construct such round bottom ends near the end of the tubing length. In such cases, for tubing up to 15 to 20 mm in diameter, one can seal a rod to any part of the end of the tubing. This rod will serve as a handle for the flame cutting step. Alternately, especially for very large diameter tubing, the rod can be attached more satisfactorily by a somewhat different technique. The last one-half inch of the tubing end is softened in a large flame. Once softened, it is collapsed using a pair of pliers. The rod is then attached to the center of this collapsed portion, providing a handle having an axis co-linear with that of the tubing. In either case, such handles will make rotation easier, and therefore the subsequent flame heating will be more uniform. By and large, this will lead to a more symmetrical round bottom.

Once a handle has been secured onto the piece of tubing, the tubing is flame cut, drawn off, and blown out to form the round bottom end. Step by step instructions are described in the next exercise.

LABORATORY EXERCISE TWENTY FIVE

FORMING ROUND BOTTOM ENDS

1. A length of 15 mm tubing, about 12 inches long, is held in the left hand while a short length of 6 mm rod, at least 4 inches long, is held in the right hand. The rod is attached to any point on the end of the tubing by using a medium-hot flame (Figure 7.9). The rod will serve as a handle for the flame cut described in the next step. The seal between the tubing and rod should be a good one, not just a cold seal.

2. The left end of the tubing is fitted with a swivel and blowpipe assembly. Hold the mouthpiece loosely in your mouth.

3. The tubing is heated with constant rotation in a medium-hot flame at a point about three quarters of an inch to the left of the attached handle. When the tubing becomes softened, it is drawn off and flame cut (Figure 7.10).

4. The glob of excess glass which remains on the end of the tube after the flame cut is removed immediately by wiping, that is the excess glob of glass is reheated and pulled off with a piece of cold glass. Usually the small piece of tubing at the end of the handle is cool enough to use for this.

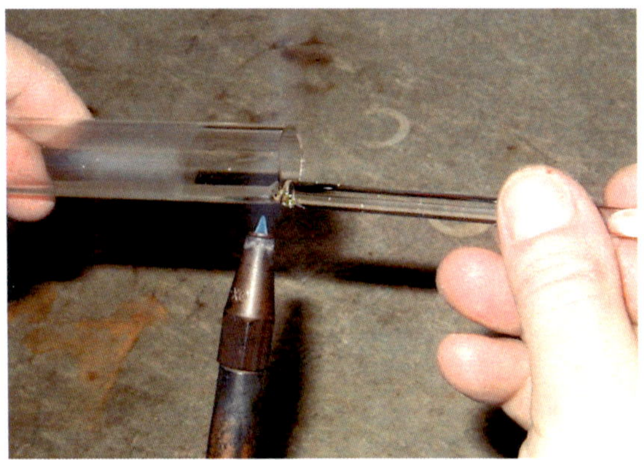

Figure 7.9 *Attaching a rod (which will serve as a handle) to the end of the 15 mm tubing.*

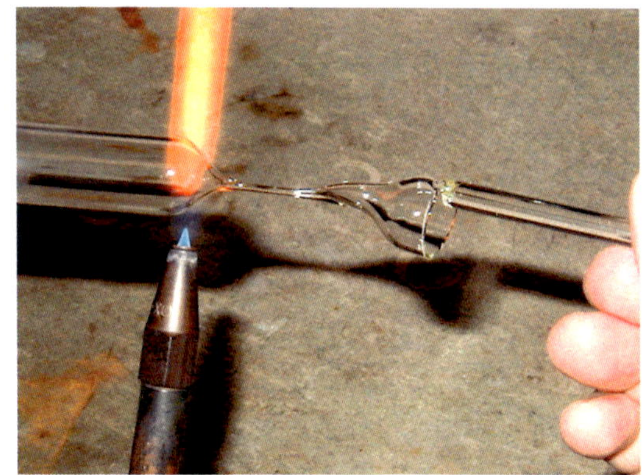

Figure 7.10 *Making a flame cut at the end of the 15 mm tubing.*

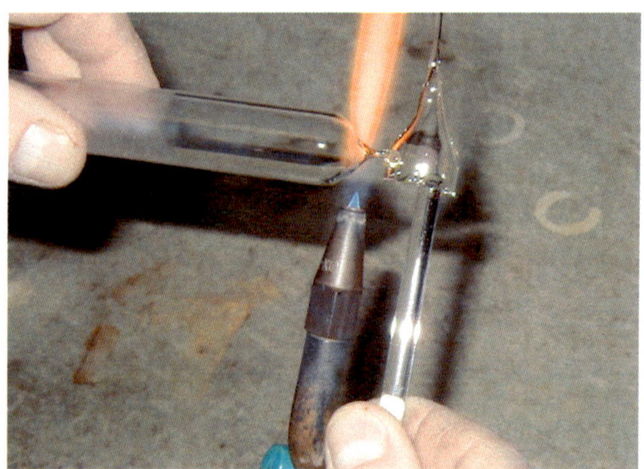

Figure 7.11 *Removing excess glass from the newly closed end using a piece of cold glass.*

Figure 7.12 *Blowing out and shaping the bottom of the round bottom end.*

Since this piece will be discarded, it is ideal for the wiping procedure (Figure 7.11).

5. After most of the excess glass has been removed, the end of the tubing is heated with rotation in the flame. This serves both to redistribute the glass evenly over the end area and to thicken the glass somewhat. This operation may be best accomplished by switching the tubing to the right side of the burner and by using both hands to aid in the rotation. Only the very end of the tubing should be heated.

6. The tubing is removed from the flame while rotation is continued, and one or two puffs of air are used to round out the bottom. Many workers prefer to do all the blowing while the tube is held in a vertical position with the round bottom upward (Figure 7.12). This aids in preventing distortions.

7. If the bottom is not formed properly, the end can be reheated and blown out again. Care must be taken so that the blowing does not expand the shoulders of the tube, as the diameter of the rounded bottom should never exceed the diameter of the original tubing.

8. The bottom should be checked for symmetry and uniform wall thickness. This is done most easily by holding the tube vertically

with the end at eye level. The tube is then rotated while looking through it toward a sunlit window or a bright light. Any inconsistencies should be evident.

Repeat this exercise five or more times or until you feel quite confident that you can get a near perfect round bottom end. Once you have reached this point, you should try to make several round bottom ends on short pieces of 20 mm and 25 mm tubing. You may wish to use the alternate method of attaching a handle when working with the 25 mm tubing.

JOINING TUBING OF DIFFERENT DIAMETERS

Sometimes it will be necessary to join two pieces of tubing of different diameter. If the diameters are quite similar, there is no problem since the methods previously described will be satisfactory. However, if the sizes differ by more than a few millimeters, slightly modified methods should be used. There are at least three different approaches. It will be well worthwhile for you to try each one.

Some workers prefer to draw the larger tubing out until it is reduced to the diameter of the smaller tubing. This is done by forming a constriction of the proper diameter in the larger tubing. The constricted tubing is then cut and sealed to the smaller tubing. Alternately, some workers choose to flare the smaller tube out to the diameter of the larger and then proceed as usual with the seal.

A third method, used most often whenever the diameters differ considerably, involves making a round bottom on the end of the larger tube. This end is then reheated and blown out to give a hole of the same diameter as that of the smaller tubing. The smaller tube is then sealed on by directing the flame only onto the joint area. Some workers prefer to heat the entire shoulder of the larger tubing as well as the joint, subsequently blowing out the entire area to the proper shape.

LABORATORY EXERCISE TWENTY SIX

MAKING SEALS BETWEEN TUBING OF DIFFERENT DIAMETERS

1. A burner with a #3 or #5 tip is adjusted to give a rather large, bushy, hot flame.

2. A round bottom end is fashioned on one end of a piece of 15 mm tubing at least 12 inches in length. Remove the excess glass as usual, and be sure to check the completed round end for uniformity.

3. A smaller flame is now used to heat a spot on the tip of the round bottom end. The glass is removed from the flame. Immediately a cold piece of glass rod is touched to the hot portion and quickly pulled outward along a line on the axis of the piece of tubing. This will serve to remove even more glass (in the form of a thin thread) from the portion where a hole will be blown and the smaller tube will eventually be attached (Figure 7.13). This method should always be used whenever and wherever a hole is to be blown in large tubing. The thin thread is flame cut close to the tubing end and discarded.

4. The slight protrusion is now reheated in a small flame until it collapses and forms a small, white-hot area (Figure 7.14). This area should be just slightly smaller in diameter than the diameter of the smaller tubing which is to be attached, in this case 8 mm. Do not overheat the spot since this will cause the glass to thicken again!

5. Immediately remove the piece from the flame and blow until a very small bubble-like protrusion is produced (Figure 7.15). The end of the small protrusion is reheated until it begins to collapse. The entire protrusion should not collapse; the sides should remain.

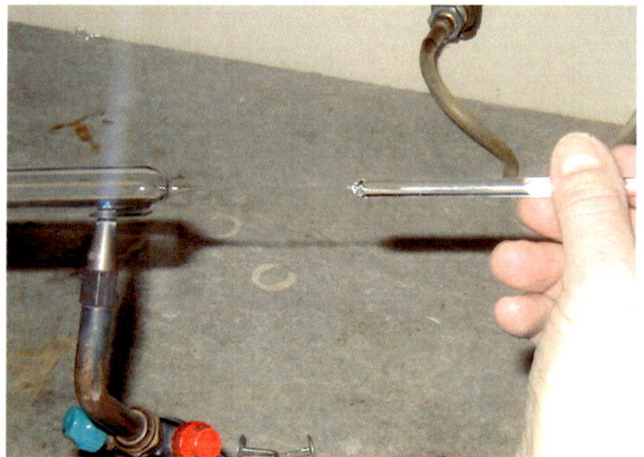

Figure 7.13 *Reducing the amount of glass from the end of closed larger diameter tubing.*

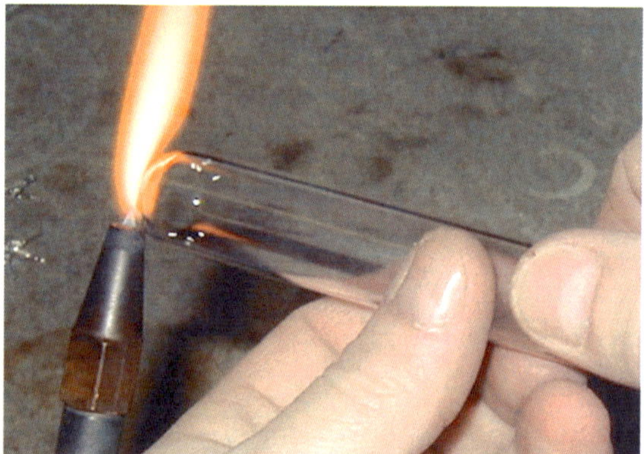

Figure 7.14 *Reheating the end of the tubing to smooth out the area.*

Figure 7.15 *Blowing a small protrusion on the end of the larger tubing.*

Figure 7.16 *After reheating, strong blowing produces a thin bubble of glass.*

6. The piece is removed from the flame once more and blown into rather strongly. An bubble of thin glass (often irregular, sausage-like in shape) should form (Figure 7.16).

7. The glass is held over a waste container (a small aluminum dish is satisfactory), and the thin glass portion is gently removed by breaking it with the edge of a knife or file or by using a wire screen (Figure 7.17). The sides of the original protrusion should remain, as these will be the shoulders upon which the seal will be made.

8. A short piece of 8 mm tubing, at least 3 inches long, is fitted with a cork on one end. If you were using a #5 tip, change to #3. (As you become more proficient, use a #5 throughout.) The two pieces of glass are now heated simultaneously in the flame (Figure 7.18), and a cold seal is made (Figure 7.19). A puff of air through the blowpipe should indicate whether or not there are any holes in the seal.

9. The seal is completed by either the spot welding or hot seal methods previously described.

Repeat the exercise several times until you feel some confidence making these seals. Eventually, switch to 20 mm and 8 mm tubing. A #3 tip may be satisfactory for all parts of the exercise, although a #5 tip may make the initial formation of the round bottom a bit easier. If possible, have two torches ready for use, one with a #3 and the other with a #5 tip.

Figure 7.17 *A wire screen is employed to remove the thin bubble of glass into a waste container.*

Figure 7.18 *Heating the smaller tube and the prepared larger diameter tube.*

T-SEALS

Figure 7.19 *Making the cold seal between the two pieces of tubing.*

The second most common type of seal in scientific glassblowing is the T-seal. Where as a butt seal is usually considered to be any joint made between the ends of two pieces of tubing, the T-seal is nothing more than the same sort of joint made between the end of one piece of tubing and the side of another. Such seals are used widely in construction of scientific glassware.

Basically, there are two approaches to making these T-seals. Most commonly, both pieces are held in the hands while the seal is made by bringing the pieces to the flame in the usual way. Alternately, however, one can rigidly support one piece of the tubing with clamps and hold the second piece in one hand while manipulating the torch with the other hand. Thus, the flame is brought to the glass instead of the glass to the flame. This method may be somewhat easier for beginners, since the flame can easily be directed where needed, and the tubing is unable to bend or sag. Nonetheless, it is wise to learn both methods. Eventually you will probably make most simple T-seals by the tubing-in-hands method, but most T-seals made on large or complex pieces of glassware will probably require the torch-in-hand method.

Quite fortunately, as mentioned before, the old rule of thumb that the longer you take to do the job, the worse it will look is untrue for making

T-seals. Usually one can take as much time as is necessary to work and rework the glass. Even seals that look like disasters in the beginning can be pulled out to look like professional jobs in the end. For this reason, many students enjoy making T-seals more than they do butt seals.

LABORATORY EXERCISE TWENTY SEVEN

T-SEALS - TUBING-IN-HANDS METHOD

1. A six to eight inch piece of 9 or 10 mm tubing is corked on one end and fitted with a blowpipe assembly on the other (masking tape is ideal in this case). A second length of tubing of the same diameter, about 4 inches long, is readied for use in Step 6 by corking one end. A #2 or #3 size tip should be placed on the torch.

2. The center portion of the longer piece of tubing is preheated in a cool flame. Preheating becomes increasingly more important when larger diameter tubing is used. The burner is then adjusted to give a small but hot flame. This is then used to heat one spot in the middle of the tubing (Figure 7.20).

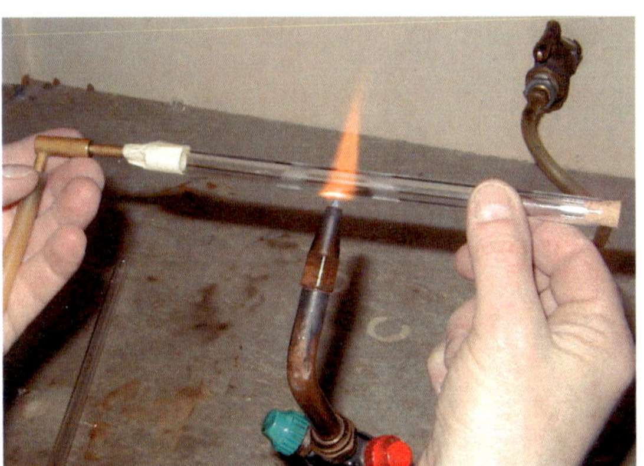

Figure 7.20 *Heating the spot on the tubing where the t-tube is to be attached.*

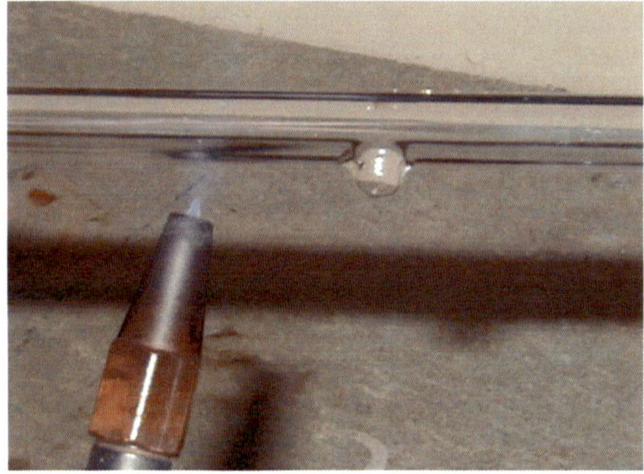

Figure 7.21 *With the tubing out of the flame, a small bulge is blown out.*

3. The heated spot will become whitish in color and will continue to increase in diameter. Continue heating until the diameter of the white spot is about two-thirds of the diameter of the tubing that is to be attached. At that point, immediately remove the tubing from the

Figure 7.22 *After the second heating, a thin bubble of glass is formed by blowing.*

Figure 7.23 *With the bubble directed downward over a waste container, it is removed.*

flame and carefully blow the area out to form a small bubble-like protrusion (Figure 7.21)

4. As before, the tip of the protrusion is reheated, but now it is blown out strongly to produce an irregular bubble of thin glass (Figure 7.22). The glass tubing is rotated so that the bubble is pointed downward. The thin glass is removed by carefully breaking it off into an aluminum pan (Figure 7.23). Care should be taken to remove any small pieces of the thin glass which may become attracted to the surface of the glass tubing.

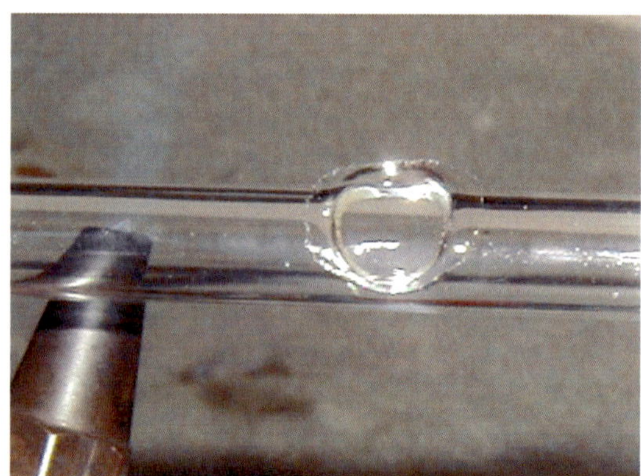

Figure 7.24 *A view of the sides of the protrusion left after removing the thin bubble.*

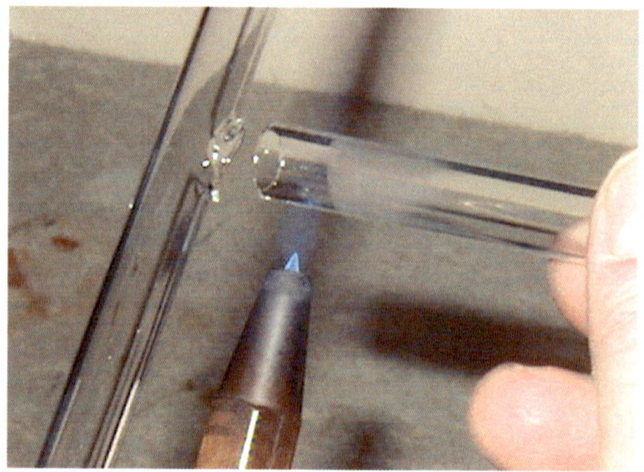

Figure 7.25 *Getting ready to heat both the side hole and a new piece of corked tubing.*

The sides of the original protrusion should remain, as these will serve as shoulders upon which the seal will be made (Figure 7.24).

5. The open end of the short length of tubing prepared in Step 1 is heated simultaneously in the flame along with the shoulders of the hole made in the side of the longer piece of tubing (Figure 7.25). Heating both pieces at the same time may be difficult in a very small flame, but can be accomplished by holding one piece higher and the other lower in the flame.

6. As soon as the edges of both pieces become melted and red in color (do not overheat), the pieces are removed from the flame and joined together to form a cold seal (Figure 7.26). Perhaps the best way to join the pieces is to touch them together at one point on one side and then continue bringing the pieces together as if they were hinged at that first point. This method works especially well even if the hole is slightly larger than it should be. Alternately, if the hole is sufficiently small, the two pieces can be stuck together in a direct manner and then pulled apart slightly as soon as the seal is completed.

A puff of air through the blowpipe should indicate whether or not there are any holes in the seal. If there are any holes, small holes are best repaired by reheating around the entire seal and then forcing the tubing together again. Larger holes have to be repaired with cane (see Figure 7.30 on page 219).

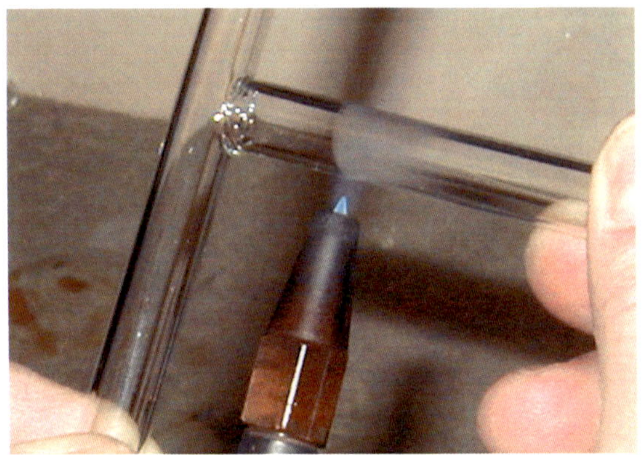

Figure 7.26 *A View of "cold seal" immediately after it was made. (Tubing is outside flame.)*

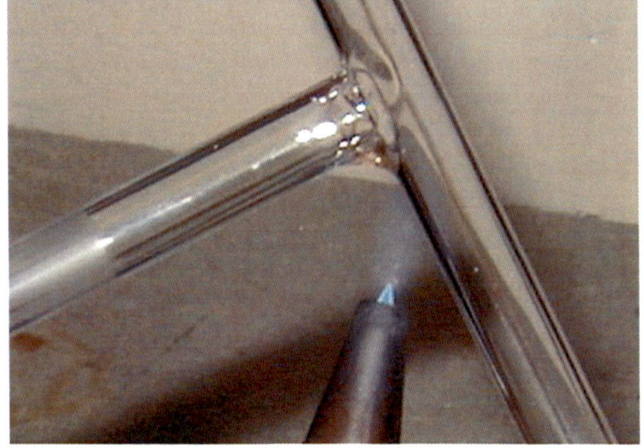

Figure 7.27 *Proceeding to make "spot welds" on the cold seal. This should be begun immediately. Do not allow the "cold seal" to cool!*

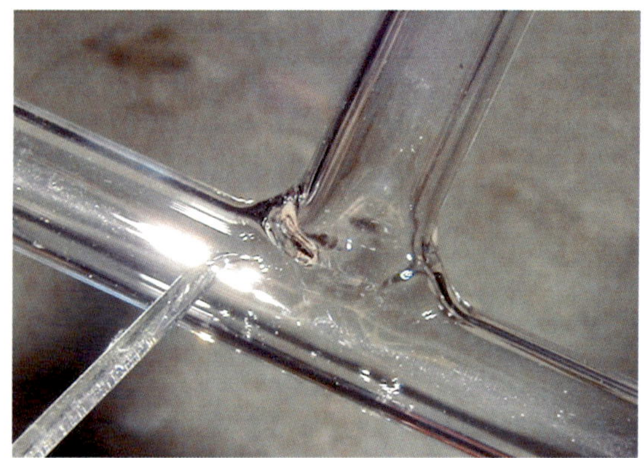

Figure 7.28 *The tip of the glass rod is pointing to a "fold" of glass, indicating that the seal needs further heating.*

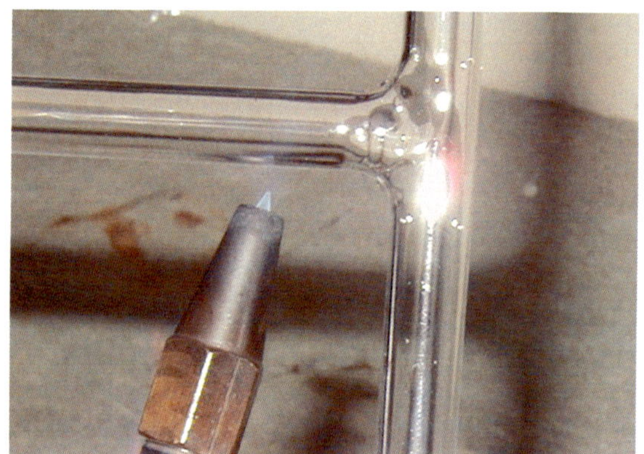

Figure 7.29 *Use the point of a very small flame to get the blue cone of the flame right up to the fold requiring further working. Gently blow ("breathe") in and out while heating.*

8. The seal is made by using the spot welding technique (Figure 7.27). Beginners will find that a very small, hot flame works best. Also, a large number of smaller heating and blowing operations will yield a better looking product.

As you are doing the spot welding technique, look for "folds of glass" within the joint (Figure 7.28). These indicate that the seal needs some additional working. Keep reheating while blowing in and out until these folds are gone (Figure 7.29).

However care must also be taken so that the heated areas are not blown out too much. The seal in the areas of the 90° angle portions should be slightly curved so that if a separate piece of tubing of the same diameter were held at the junction, the tubing's curvature would be close to that of the seal. Likewise, the flat portions of the seal (above and below in the plane defined by the glass pieces) should not be bulged. These areas should remain the same diameter as that of the original tubing.

9. The seal is flame annealed as soon as it is finished. The angles should be checked and adjusted if necessary at this time.

Repeat this many times. Only by lots of practice will you feel confident in making these important seals. Also, experiment by using larger diameter tubing (12 mm) and also smaller diameter tubing (8 mm).

Figure 7.30 *If a leak is detected, one needs to take action right away. As mentioned at the end of Step 7, small holes are best repaired by heating the seal all the way around and then gently pushing the side arm in the direction necessary to close the leak.*

Larger holes will require the use of "cane". Cane is just 2 mm rod (nearly the same diameter as the glass you are working). A very small amount of cane is heated and then pressed into the reheated hole. The cane is then flame cut, and the joint is worked to smooth out the area and spread out any excess glass.

LABORATORY EXERCISE TWENTY EIGHT

T-SEALS: TORCH-IN-HANDS METHOD

1. The torch and glass pieces are prepared as described in Step 1 of Exercise 27.

2. Two ring stands are set up parallel to one another, close to the front of the bench. A small clamp is placed on each ring stand and adjusted to a reasonable height. The ends of the eight inch piece of tubing are then firmly clamped and adjusted so that the tubing is horizontal (Figure 7.31).

3. The torch is removed from its support stand and held in the right hand. The tubing is gently preheated, and a spot is heated strongly as before. The torch is removed while a puff of air is blown to produce a small bubble-like protrusion.

4. As before, the tip of the protrusion is reheated and blown strongly to produce an irregular bubble of thin glass. The glass tubing is rotated so that the bubble is pointed downward. The thin glass is removed by carefully breaking it off into an aluminum pan. Care should be taken to remove any small pieces of the thin glass which may become attracted to the surface of the glass tubing.

5. The open end of the second short length of tubing is heated simultaneously in the flame along with the shoulders of the hole in the side of the longer piece of tubing. This may be somewhat difficult and awkward. A person who is right-handed may be most successful if

the piece of glass is held in the left hand and the torch is worked with the right hand.

6. As soon as the edges on both pieces become melted and red in color, the torch is put aside and the pieces are joined together in the same manner as done before (Step 7, Laboratory Exercise 27).

7. If a puff of air through the blowpipe indicates that no holes are present, the short length of tubing is clamped by means of a third clamp on either one of the ring stands. Alternately, this short length can be supported manually if desired.

8. The seal is completed using the spot welding technique described previously. This time, of course, it is the torch that is moved from region to region until the seal is completed (Figure 7.32). With this method, it is especially important to make a careful inspection of the seal on all sides. Since the T-tube is firmly supported in one position, it is a common mistake to have an excellent looking seal on one side of the T-joint while the other side has been almost completely neglected.

9. The seal should be flame annealed when it is finished, and the angle should be checked and adjusted if necessary.

Repeat this exercise a number of times until you feel some confidence in making the T-seals with this technique. Be sure to experiment with tubing having slightly larger diameters.

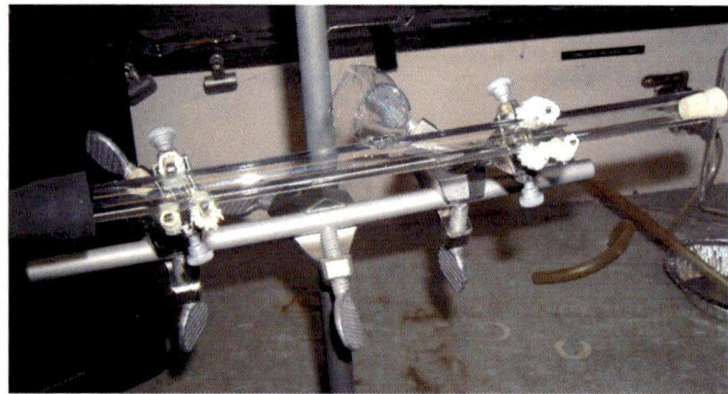

Figure 7.31 *One type of simple set-up for making a T-seal using the torch-in-hands method. Note the policeman (on left) used to attach blowpipe assembly and cork on right end. In this photo, the hole has been blown out, preparing for the T-seal.*

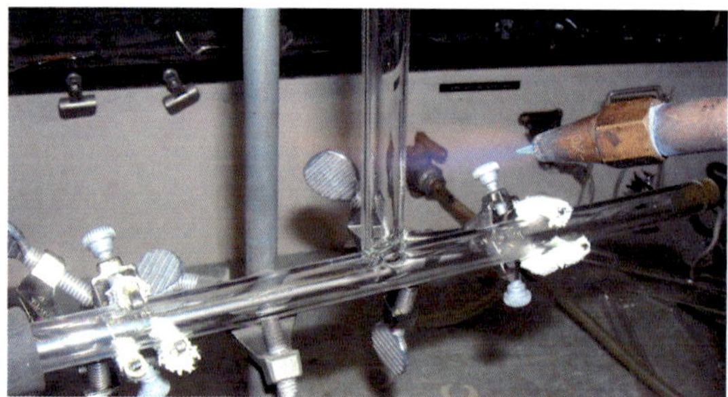

Figure 7.32 *Work is continued on making a T-seal in this torch-in-hands operation. The vertical piece of tubing is held upward by the worker's left hand while the torch is held in the right hand. In this photo, the seal is not yet completed.*

It should be pointed out that there are many instances where the torch-in-hands method is required. If one is building or repairing a large piece of glass apparatus, there may be no choice. In these cases, it many not only be preferable to bring the torch to the project, but it may be impossible to do otherwise. A specific and important situation in scientific glassworking would be when one needs to construct or repair a vacuum line (Figure 7.33). These are large set ups comprised of tubing, bulbs and stopcocks, used primarily in the preparation and study of air sensitive chemicals.

Thus, although the torch-in-hands method may seem unnecessary for making normal T-tubes, it is very wise to practice the method now, as later you will find in to be an invaluable skill. The main difference is that it is usually difficult or even impossible to move the glass pieces when making the seals. It is therefore often rather difficult to make otherwise straightforward joints. Get used to using cane to help in the final joints.

Figure 7.33 *Here the author is using the torch-in-hands method to repair a small leak with cane on a section of a large stationary vacuum line (an apparatus used by many chemists for the handling of volatile air sensitive compounds).*

T-SEALS INVOLVING LARGE DIAMETER TUBING

Whenever the T-seal to be constructed involves very large diameter tubing, it is wise to constrict the end on the side arm down to about two-thirds its original size. The hole in the straight length of tubing is then blown in the usual manner to this size. The pieces are heated, joined, and sealed in the same manner as described for smaller diameter tubing. Likewise, whenever large diameter tubing is used, preheating becomes especially important. Also, in these cases, the initial joining of the two pieces of hot glass is very critical. Every effort must be made to insure complete contact at all points. This is best accomplished by touching the pieces together at one point on one side and then bring the pieces together as if they were hinged at the first point. Any small holes should be detected and immediately repaired. With large tubing, T-seals must be oven annealed as soon as possible.

REPAIRING CRACKS AND HOLES

Thermal stresses can cause hairline cracks to occur in tubing at the most inopportune moments. You may just be starting to heat the tubing ends in order to form a simple straight seal, or more typically you may be putting the finishing touches on a very complex piece of apparatus when such cracks appear. Fortunately, in most cases these can be completely repaired.

In simple situations, as in the first example mentioned above, the crack can often be stopped and repaired by gentle heating beyond the end of the crack. After a little heating, the crack will usually begin to disappear as quickly as it formed. The flame is moved back and forth along the crack region until you are certain it is completely repaired. Some blowing may be necessary in the process. If the crack does not repair in this way, or if it begins to widen, inhale slightly through the blowpipe. This serves to pull the glass inward and therefore bring it together. Sometimes a combination of repeated blowing and inhaling will be especially effective in repairing such cracks.

In more complex situations, as in the case of a nearly completed piece of intricate apparatus, it may be wise to check for stresses in the area around the crack by using a polariscope before attempting a repair. If the polariscope indicates that substantial stresses are still present, any attempts to repair the crack would only result in further cracking. In these cases, it might be best to oven anneal the entire piece first. If no stresses are evident, repairs can be made as described before.

Heating a cracked area too strongly or too quickly sometimes results in widening of the crack. Unfortunately, once a hole or wide crack appears on the side of any tubing, further heating will only cause the hole or crack to increase in size. For this reason, wide cracks or holes must be repaired by a different method.

One approach is to use a tungsten needle to push the heated edges together. Once the crack is filled up again, the area can be heated and blown to redistribute the glass and complete the repair.

A more widely used approach is to use glass cane to fill the crack or hole. In this case, cane is heated with a small, hot flame and deposited in any pattern necessary in order to fill the hole without any overlapping of the cane. The 2 mm rod is used because it is very close to the wall thickness of the tubing. The patched area, which may not look very good at this point, is now heated again with a small, hot flame. Just as the area begins to coalesce or collapse, the heat is removed and a puff of air is used to return the tubing to the proper diameter. The area is worked by repeated heating and blowing steps until the repair is completed. Any small leaks are repaired with additional cane. If done properly, the patch should look pretty good, and in many cases little trace of the original mistake will be evident.

FLARES

Flaring is the process of enlarging the end of a piece of tubing into a funnel shape. Flaring can be accomplished in a number of ways, both with or without the use of special flaring tools.

If a set of ball bearing rollers is available, a flare can be made without other tools. The tube to be flared is supported on the set of rollers and rotated very rapidly while the end of the tubing is heated. The heated ends are literally thrown out to a flared shape. It is imperative to have a clean, straight cut at the end of the tubing. This method works well for small to medium-wide angle flares.

Alternatively, one can use a carbon rod to shape the flare. In this case, rapid spinning is not necessary. The tube can be rotated while it is supported on a roller. The end is heated until it has shrunk several millimeters, which serves to thicken the glass. The tube is then moved out of the flame while still supported and rotated on the roller, and a carbon rod is held at the proper angle against the soft glass while the tube is rotated. This will produce a flare several millimeters larger than the rest of the tubing. In general, one allows the tubing end to shrink about the same amount as the size of the flare desired. Note that the carbon rod is never placed directly into the flame. You may learn the hard way that graphite is a very excellent conductor of heat.

Most workers prefer to rotate the heated glass one way (either in their hands or on a roller) while swinging the carbon rod in an arch in the opposite direction. This takes some practice but tends to diminish any irregularities.

No matter what tools are used, it is important that the tool is not simply pushed into the end of the tubing. This will cause the tubing to fold over instead of flaring out. All flaring operations should involve inserting the tool into the center of the hot glass and lifting the side of the tool onto the inside of the hot portion of the glass tubing while it is being rotated. In this way, the tubing wall is gradually stretched to the proper shape. A number of heatings and flarings may be necessary to give the size and angle flare desired. Brass flaring tools can be used in place of the carbon rod in much the same way. Sometimes the brass tools are preheated slightly and then dipped into beeswax, as a light coating of wax aids in making a uniform flare. As with the carbon rod technique, the brass flaring tools are never placed directly in the flame during the process. Some brass tools have two blades at right angles to one another. These make flaring easier for the beginner since not as much rotation is needed to produce the desired result.

A flare in which the angle is about 90° to the original tubing is often referred to as a flange . Flanges can be made either by the spinning method or by repeated flaring operations where the angle is widened somewhat each time.

As is the case with most operations in glassblowing, the student is urged to try as many different approaches as possible. Often, one method will be easier for one person, while other individuals may favor a different technique. In flaring, this experimentation approach is especially valuable. Although the following exercise describes the most widely used method for making small flares, you will also want to experiment with other techniques.

LABORATORY EXERCISE TWENTY NINE

FLARES USING "IN-HAND" TECHNIQUE

1. Cut some 8 mm tubing into several 8 inch lengths. It is important that the cuts be clean and that the edges are flat.

2. The tubing is held and rotated in the left hand without the use of rollers. Rotation should be such that the top of the tubing is moved away from you. Meanwhile, the end is heated in a medium flame until it has shrunk about 2 or 3 mm.

3. At this time, remove it from the flame while continuing rotation, and insert a small carbon rod into the tubing end as far in as the glass softened. Gently lift upward onto the softened glass and swing in an arch toward you in the direction opposite to that which you are rotating the glass. If necessary, the end can be reheated and the flaring operation repeated.

Repeat this exercise at least ten to twenty times. You should find that flares made in this way can be done quickly and uniformly. During the exercise, the completed flares can be removed by scoring the tubing near the flare with a knife or file and then using the cutting edge.

Also experiment with 10 and 12 mm tubing. Be sure to try using the brass flaring tool on the larger diameter tubing.

FORMING RIMS ON TUBING ENDS

Open tubing ends of most scientific apparatus are normally strengthened with rims. Such rims are made easily by a technique which is just a slight modification of the normal flaring procedure.

The tubing end is heated with rotation until the end melts and begins to contract slightly; this is what happens when tubing is fire polished too much. The hot tube is removed from the flame and is carefully and gradually brought out to the original inside diameter with a large diameter carbon rod by holding the rod flatly against the inside wall and moving it all around the inside circumference of the tubing. It may be necessary to reheat this one or more times to complete the rim formation. Completed rims should always be flame annealed immediately.

THROUGH-SEALS: RING AND INSERTION SEALS

Very often it is necessary to pass a length of tubing through the end of a round bottom or through the side of a larger glass tube. This is the case in making most condensers, vacuum traps, and other similar glassware. We will first examine the through-seals made at the ends of round bottoms. Although the side seals are somewhat similar, they will be discussed separately.

There are two different ways to approach through-seals which pass through round bottoms. In the first method, a short piece of tubing is placed inside a larger tube which has a round bottom end. The end is sealed to the round bottom (a ring seal), and the glass that covers the end is heated strongly and blown out. A second short piece of tubing is attached by making a regular butt seal to the round bottom at the opening. The result appears as if the tubing were inserted through the hole in the round bottom, but in actuality, two separate pieces were joined at the round bottom.

In the second method, a hole which is slightly larger in diameter than the tubing to be passed through is made at the end of a round bottom. An intermediate maria is made on the smaller piece of tubing and is then passed through the hole until the maria and round bottom come in contact. A seal is made by directing the flame onto the maria area of the small tube and the shoulder of the larger tube. The inner tube is centered either by proper rotation of the entire piece as it becomes cool, or by use of a temporary support as will be described later. In this method, the through tube actually does pass through the round bottom. The seal is sometimes referred to as an insertion seal.

Most beginners find the first method, involving an intermediate ring seal, easier than the insertion method. Needless to say, it is wise to try both methods.

LABORATORY EXERCISE THIRTY

THROUGH-SEALS: RING SEAL METHOD

1. A good round bottom end is formed on a piece of 15 mm tubing which is at least 6 inches long (Figure 7.34a). A piece of 8 mm tubing about two inches long is fire polished on both ends. One end can be slightly flared, as this can be of some aid in making the seal. Flaringin this particular case is not absolutely necessary since here the diameters of the inside and outside tubing are so similar.

2. A slight bulge can then be blown into the very center of the round bottom (Figure 7.34b). This bulge should be just large enough so that the tubing (or flare) fits snugly into it. This step is also optional, as many workers are successful by going right to Step 3.

3. The short piece of 8 mm tubing is then inserted into the 15 mm tube. If the piece was flared, the flared end should be inserted first.Of course, the blowpipe stopper will have to be temporarily removed to accomplish this. The inner tube is then allowed to slide down to the round bottom. The tubing end, either fire polished or flared, should fit snugly against the end or into the bulge area.

4. Short pieces of small diameter tubing normally do not require any support, but larger or longer inner tubing can be supported and centered within the outer tube in any one of a number of ways. Corrugated cardboard or heat resistant tape can be wrapped around the tube so that it fits snugly into the larger tube. If too snug, however, it will be difficult to remove. If too loose, the inner tube may slip and move. Corrugated cardboard is often preferred since, if necessary, it can be burnt out in the annealing oven. Obviously this cannot be done with the heat resistant tape. Usually a thin wire with a hook on the end can be used to remove these supports, or in some cases, the supports can be blown out if a side arm is subsequently added to the outer tube at some point between the support and the round bottom.

If a support is used, position the tube carefully so that the end fits snugly against the round bottom or into the bulge area before the blowpipe assembly is reattached. The end of a triangular file or other similar tool can be used to aid in the positioning.

5. A small flame is directed onto the round bottom end or onto the bulge area until it shrinks down and forms a smooth ring seal (Figure 7.34c). Heating should be limited to the inner tubing area on the round bottom. Try to keep the flame from splashing over onto the shoulders of the round bottom, as the shoulder may become distorted and require some blowing in order to be returned to its proper shape. If no support is used for the inner tube, the angle that the tubing is held in the flame will need to be continuously adjusted so that it is sometimes downward and at other times somewhat upward. This is done to reduce the effect of gravity on the tubing against the softened round bottom. If the tubing is constantly held in a downward position, the inner tube will be pulled down and will distort the round bottom considerably.

6. Check the quality of the ring seal. This can be easily determined by looking down onto the inner tube from the outside of the round bottom end. If the ring seal is complete and uniform, the entire ring seal will appear glassy and shiny. Wherever the seal is made incorrectly, the ring will appear less shiny. It is not important to keep the inner tube centered at this time, but this can be easily done by properly rotating the entire glass piece as the seal cools.

7. A small, hot flame is directed within the ring seal area until the glass becomes white hot. Excess glass is removed by pulling out thin glass thread with a cold rod.

8. The area is then strongly heated a second time and is blown out to form an irregular bubble of thin glass (Figure 7.34d) which is removed as usual with the edge of a file or a wire screen.

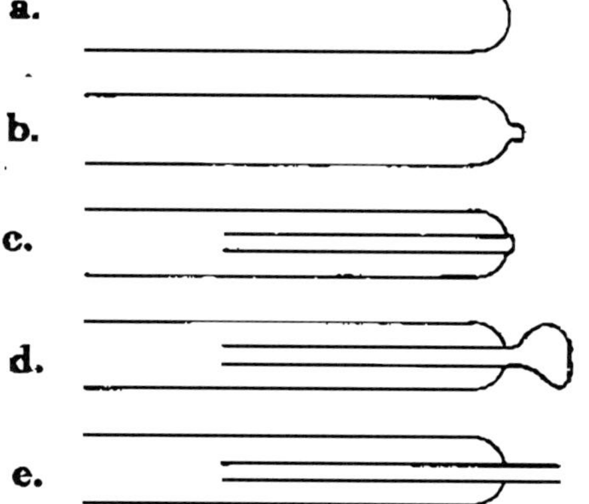

Figure 7.34 *Steps in making a through seal by ring seal method.*

9. A second short length of 8 mm tubing is prepared by corking one end. The remaining open end and the shoulders of the ring seal are heated simultaneously in a medium flame until both appear to be uniformly white hot.

10. Immediately these are moved a small distance out of the flame, joined together firmly, and then immediately pulled outward and blown into slightly.

If done quickly and correctly, especially with small diameter tubing, the seal will probably be complete at this time (Figure 7.34e), and it should look fairly good. Most of the time, however, it will be necessary to spot weld the seal as done with butt and T-seals. This is especially true any time the inner tubing is larger than 8 mm. A very small, hot flame will cause the least distortion of the seal and result in the most professional looking product.

11. The seal should be thoroughly flame annealed. At this time the outer tube should be straightened while the inner tube is centered by proper rotation as the glass becomes cool. Reheating may be necessary if it cools too quickly and the inner tube is in an uncentered position.

Once you feel some confidence in making through-seals in this manner, try using 20 mm tubing for the outer portion and 8 mm tubing again for the inner portion. A support for the inner tube may still not be necessary, but it will be worthwhile to experiment with the various methods. The use of larger diameter inner tubing (10 mm or 12 mm) should also be tried. These should definitely be slightly flared, and an inner support will probably be needed.

LABORATORY EXERCISE THIRTY ONE

THROUGH-SEALS: INSERTION METHOD

1. A round bottom end is formed on a piece of 20 mm tubing at least six inches long.

2. A hole, approximately 9 mm in diameter, is blown into the very center of the round bottom end in the usual manner. The diameter of the hole should always be slightly larger than that of the outside diameter of the inner tubing. In this exercise, 8 mm tubing will be used for the inner portion.

3. A piece of 8 mm tubing approximately eight inches in length is stoppered at one end and fitted with a blowpipe on the other end. An intermediate tubing maria is formed by heating the center portion with rotation in a small flame until it becomes softened. The glass is then blown out slightly while simultaneously exerting a slight inward pressure on the ends. The bulge should be uniform and just slightly larger in diameter than that of the original tube (Figure 7.35). The tubing should remain straight.

4. The blowpipe is removed from the end of the 8 mm tubing and reattached to the end of the 20 mm tubing by some suitable means. The 8 mm tube is inserted through the hole until the maria rests firmly on the outside shoulders of the hole at the end of the round bottom (Figure 7.36). No support is normally needed for the inner tube.

Figure 7.35 *The prepared pieces for making an insertion seal.*

Figure 7.36 *The pieces properly positioned, before making the seal.*

5. After the junction has been carefully preheated, a small, hot flame is directed onto the area where the maria and the shoulder of the outer tube meet. The piece should be rapidly and evenly rotated during this entire procedure.

6. As the junction becomes thoroughly heated and begins to collapse, it is removed from the flame and blown out to the proper size and shape. The glass is continually rotated. This step is really nothing more than an example of the regular hot seal or in-flame method for making butt joints. Thus, in order to succeed with this method, you have to be well acquainted and skilled with the in-flame technique.

7. The completed seal should be thoroughly flame annealed. At the same time, the outer tube should be straightened manually while the inner tube is centered by rotating as necessary. Items involving these seals should also be oven annealed as soon as possible.

INSIDE SEALS

A special case of using a ring seal is that which is sometimes referred to as an inside seal (Figure 7.36). To construct these, the inner tube is flared until it is just slightly smaller than the inside diameter of the larger outer tube. It is then inserted into the larger tube, usually supported by cardboard or heat resistant tape, and the outer tubing is heated until the walls shrink down onto the flare to form a uniform ring-type seal. Blowing returns the outer tube to its original diameter.

These seals find use in certain types of vacuum traps as well as in numerous types of distillation equipment (Figure 7.37).

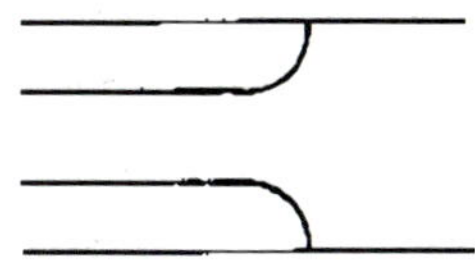

Figure 7.36 *Drawing showing an inside seal.*

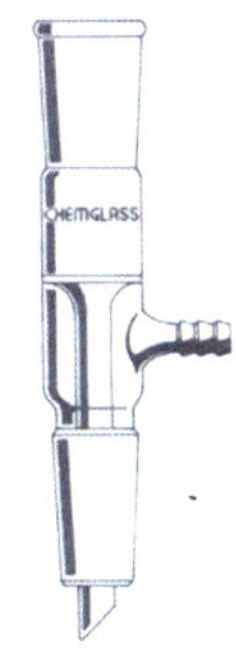

Figure 7.37 *This distillation adapter incorporates an inside seal (Chem-Glass).*

LABORATORY EXERCISE THIRTY TWO

MAKING INSIDE SEALS

1. A short piece of 8 mm tubing is flared until it is just slightly smaller than the inside diameter of 15 mm tubing. The flare should be as uniform as possible.

2. The flared piece of tubing is cut about an inch from the flare, and the cut end is fire polished. (In real applications, the tubing will probably need to be much longer.)

3. The short piece of flared tubing is then placed inside a six inch piece of 15 mm tubing. In this case, because the tubing is so short, no support will be necessary. The larger tubing is then fitted with a cork at one end and a blowpipe assembly at the other.

4. The short flared piece is moved to the center of the 15 mm tube while the region is preheated in a low flame.

5. The area around the flare is then heated strongly with a small flame until the outside tubing collapses and forms a solid ring seal onto the flare. At this point, the piece is removed from the flame (the glass may be very soft) and blown out to the proper diameter while it is straightened and at the same time rotated in order to center the small piece of 8 mm tubing.

6. The entire joint must be thoroughly flame annealed. With these seals, it is important to oven anneal as soon as possible.

When the flared inner piece of tubing is longer than that used in the above exercise, some kind of support will be necessary. If the inner piece is to be shorter than the outer tube, corrugated cardboard or heat resistant tape can be used, but some thought must be given ahead of time as to how these will be removed. Some workers attach a small piece of copper wire to the support. Any extra wire is coiled into the larger tube until the seal is completed. Others use a one hole stopper through which a small diameter rod is placed. This is inserted into the inner tubing and serves to keep it centered, but be sure to keep the stopper away from the region to be heated.

If the flared inner tube is to be longer than the outer piece, a special two holed stopper is fashioned such that the inner tube passes through the center hole. A blowpipe is attached to the inner tube. In addition, a second hole (off centered) is used to attach a second blow-pipe. Both will be needed to blow out the inner tube once the seal has been made. The two blowpipes could be connected by a T-tube so that a single mouthpiece is sufficient.

Try this exercise again, and be sure to experiment with the various types of supports mentioned.

BENDING GLASS TUBING

Students often find that making professional looking bends is one of the harder tasks in glassblowing, and the larger the diameter of the tubing, the more difficult the task. Fortunately, most bends on scientific apparatus involve smaller diameter tubing.

Surprisingly enough, some of the best wide angle bends using small diameter tubing can be made using the humble Fisher burner (see Figure 2.10 on page 33) which is usually found in most analytical chemistry labs. When fitted with a wing top, these burners supply a uniform flame which is sufficiently hot for work on tubing up to about 10 mm.

Some workers are quite successful using a regular hand torch for making bends. One method involves clamping the tubing horizontally on a support and fanning the desired area with a bushy flame, allowing the tubing to bend gradually under its own weight. A puff of air is usually necessary to bring the tubing back to the normal diameter at the bend.

Most often, however, especially for most sharp angle bends, the tubing is held in the hands in the usual manner and heated in the flame with rotation, but over a wide area (at least an inch). This is done by shifting the tubing back and forth lengthwise while it is being rotated. When the tubing just begins to collapse somewhat, it is simultaneously bent by lifting the ends upward (always directing the bend downward with gravity), stretched outward very slightly, and blown out to the original diameter.

Defects are bound to occur once in a while because in all bends one side of the tubing is constricted while the other side is stretched. It does not take much error to get a bend with a flattened or buckled wall. The slight stretching done during the bending procedure should help prevent the buckling, while the blowing should prevent the flattening. Defects that may occur can be corrected to some degree by reheating small areas and blowing them out to the proper shape, but the best looking bends are always made in a single operation.

A special ribbon burner (see Figure 2.11 and 2.12 on page xxx) is by far the best for work on larger diameter tubing or for wide angle bends. The flame length is adjusted so that it is just a little greater than the length of the tubing involved in the bend. This is accomplished by covering the excess burner surface with strips of wet heat resistant tape. Some of the better burners have built in sliding surface covers. The tubing is then heated with rotation as before. When the tubing becomes soft enough, it is allowed to droop somewhat, rocked lengthwise several times to make the glass more uniform, removed from the flame, bent as before by lifting the ends upward, and blown to return the bent portion to the proper diameter. Essentially the same method, using the ribbon burner, can be used to bend rod. Other than omitting the blowing step, everything else remains the same.

LABORATORY EXERCISE THIRTY THREE

BENDING GLASS TUBING USING THE FISHER (MEKER) BURNER

1. A Fisher burner (sometimes called a Meker burner) is fitted with a wing top and then lit. Any necessary adjustments are made. It may be necessary to close off much of the air intake by turning the covers on the sides of the barrel. In some burners, the covers do not cut down the amount of air to a sufficient degree. If this is the case, masking tape can be used to close off additional space. The wing top opening should also be adjusted so that the resulting flame is uniform along the entire length of the burner tip. This can be done by using a pair of pliers to bend the metal where needed.

2. An eight inch piece of 8 mm tubing is heated with rotation just above the blue portion of the flame. It is a good idea to remove your didymium glasses, since the uniformity of the heating can be easily determined by the shape and intensity of the yellow flame. The yellow should appear as a uniform cylinder along the entire length of the heated glass surface. It may be necessary to change the angle or position of the tubing to achieve such uniformity. It is very unusual to use a perfectly horizontal position.

3. Allow the tubing to soften thoroughly. An excellent rule to follow seems to be, "when you think the glass is soft enough, heat it again as long." Only when the tubing is nearly unmanageable is it really ready to bend.

4. While keeping the softened tube in the flame, allow it to droop somewhat and rock it lengthwise several times. This should remove any possible distortions that may have appeared in the glass. Be careful not to stretch the tubing during this procedure.

5. Remove the tubing from the flame and lift the ends upward until the bend is approximately the correct angle. Then as the tubing hardens, it can be lifted to eye level, and the angle more carefully adjusted. The bend should always be pointed downward. Always work with gravity, not against it. Making bends in any other way will result in distortions caused by the action of gravity.

It is a good idea to choose some part of the lab table or the room at about eye level to use as a line of reference when the final angle adjustment is made. Thus, for example, when adjusting a right angle bend, the outline of a block on a concrete block wall could serve as an excellent reference. After some practice, such angles can be estimated with a surprising degree of accuracy.

Repeat this exercise until you feel confident with the method. You will note that the bends made in this exercise are rather wide and graceful. Somewhat sharper bends can be made using the same technique by reducing the width of the flame by placing pieces of wet heat resistant tape over the unneeded parts of the wing top. Try this exercise several times using a flame approximately two inches in length. A blowpipe assembly will probably be needed since sharper bends cause the tubing to flatten and buckle more easily.

SIDE SEALS

A side seal is any seal that passes through the side wall rather than through a rounded end. Such seals are found in many different types of scientific glassware such as adapters, condensers, and other types of distillation equipment.

In most ways, side seals are very similar to the through-seals made by the ring seal method. Nonetheless, most beginners find these especially difficult and frustrating to make. Certainly some of the problems stem from the fact that much greater stresses are incorporated into the glass in side seals than is normally the case in through-seals. Immediate and thorough annealing is an absolute necessity. But getting the air pressure to the right place at the right time is also a problem, and it is common to use two separate blowpipes. In spite of these apparent complications, satisfactory side seals can be made by the beginning student after sufficient practice.

LABORATORY EXERCISE THIRTY FOUR

CONSTRUCTION OF SIDE SEALS

1. A 90° angle is made in the middle portion of a piece of 6 mm tubing which is approximately 8 to 10 inches long. The bend should be quite sharp, yet contain no constrictions or flattened areas.

The bend may be best accomplished by using a medium flame on a regular hand torch. The 6mm tube is stoppered at one end and fitted with a blowpipe assembly on the other end. An area two to three times the flame width is carefully softened. The tubing is removed from the flame, then simultaneously bent, stretched slightly, and blown. The bend can be reworked with the flame wherever necessary.

2. After the glass cools, make a cut quite close to the bend. This cut must be as uniform as possible, and a saw cut may be best. Clean and dry the tuble. The length of the tubing should be adjusted and both ends lightly fire polished. A ten inch piece of 20 mm tubing is fitted with a blowpipe and swivel assembly. The two glass pieces needed in this procedure are shown in Figure 7.38.

3. Now, in order to allow air to be blown simultaneously to all parts of the glass, you need a blowpipe hose to be attached to the inner tube, but it is slightly tricky to accomplish this. First of all, gather the pieces needed. This includes a strip of corregated cardbord (if you can find it), a rubber septum with a hole, and a blowpipe hose assembly (Figure 7.39).

4. The blowpipe hose is now inserted through the hole in the septum. To accomplish this, insert your needlenose pliers throught the inside

side of the septum and reach through and grab the latex rubber blowpipe hose (Figure 7.40). Now pull the hose through (Figure 7.41). Wetting the outside of the hose may facilitate this.

5. The straight end of the bent 6 mm tube is fitted with the blowpipe tubing (Figure 7.42). The 6 mm tube is then wrapped with corrugated cardboard so that it will fit snugly inside the larger tubing. The wrapping should be done midway along the length of the small tube (Figure 7.43).

6. This entire assembly is then inserted into the larger tubing until the whole length of 6 mm tubing is approximately centered (Figure 7.44). The entire setup is shown in Figure 7.45. The blow pipe on the inside tube is then clamped shut (Figure 7.46).

Figure 7.38

The glass pieces involved in making this side seal.

Figure 7.39

Preparing to attach the second blowpipe hose to the inside tube.

Figure 7.40 *Starting to pull the blowpipe hose though the hole in the septum.*

Figure 7.41 *The blowpipe hose pulled though hole in the septum with pliers.*

Figure 7.42 *Adding the blow pipe hose to the tube to be placed inside.*

Figure 7.43 *Wrapping corrugated cardboard around middle of the inside tube.*

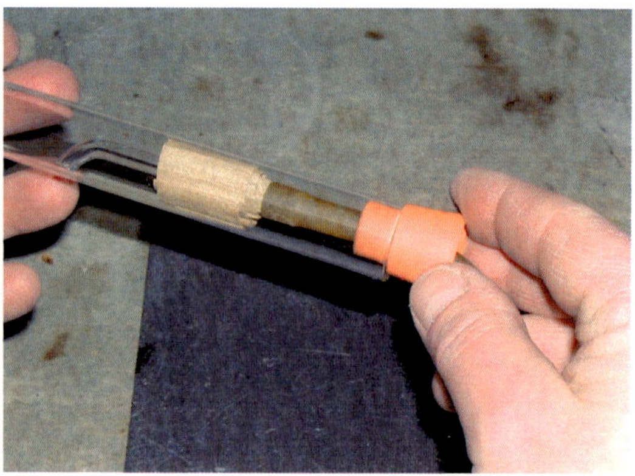

Figure 7.44 *Inserting tube to proper place and fastening septum on larger tube.*

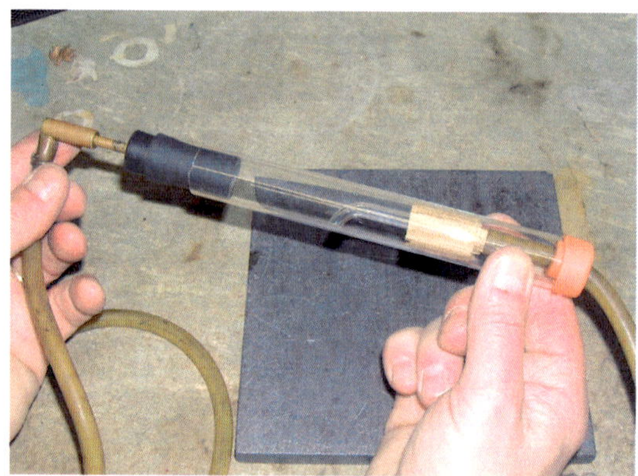

Figure 7.45 *The entire setup showing both blow-pipe hoses. Note the tubing/stopper on left.*

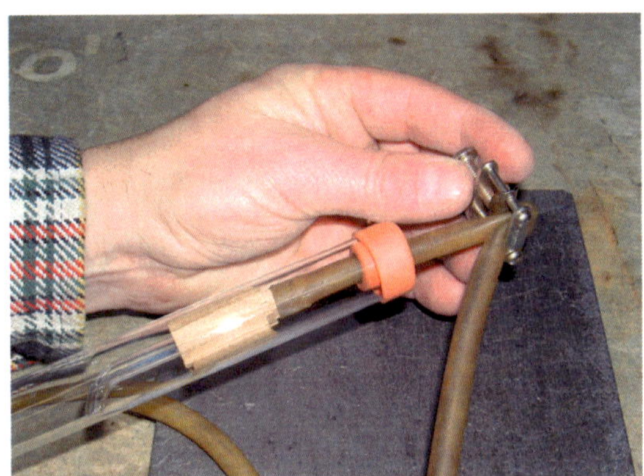

Figure 7.46 *Adding a tubing clamp to the inside tube blowpipe and closing it.*

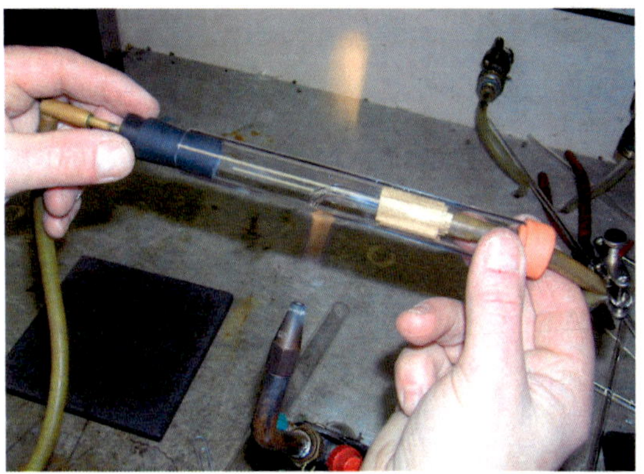

Figure 7.47 *Starting to heat the spot where bent inside tubing contacts outside tube.*

Figure 7.48 *Strongly heating the spot where the inside seal is being made.*

Figure 7.49 *The completed seal, showing a glassy appearance indicating a good seal.*

7. The larger tubing is thoroughly preheated near the area where the side seal is to be made (Figure 7.47). A small, hot flame is then directed onto the spot over the end of the inner tube (Figure 7.48). As the glass softens, it will collapse slightly and fuse to the inner tube forming a ring seal. The glass is removed from the flame and blown out to the original diameter. The completed seal should appear as a glassy-looking ring (Figure 7.49). This indicates that a good seal has been made.

8. The center of the ring seal area is reheated with a small, intense flame (Figure 7.50), and then blown out to form a bubble of thin glass (Figure 7.51) which is removed as usual with the edge of a file or wire screen.

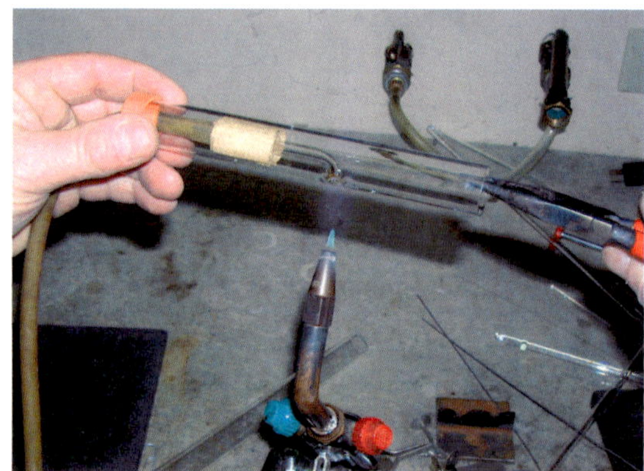

Figure 7.50 *Reheating seal to preparing to blow out the inside seal using inside pipe.*

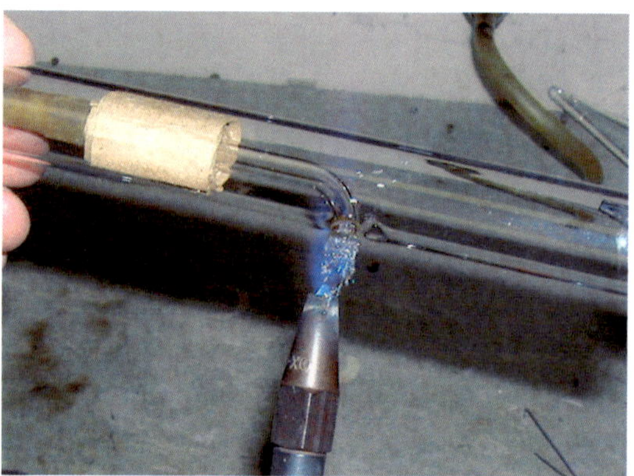

Figure 7.51 *Blowing out the inside seal, forming a thin bubble of glass.*

Figure 7.52 *Attaching a second tube to the hole formed.*

Figure 7.53 *The completed inside seal.*

9. A second short length of 6 mm tubing is prepared by corking at one end. The remaining open end and the shoulders on the blown out ring seal are heated simultaneously until both appear to be unifiormly hot and softened.

10. Immediately, the glass pieces are joined together firmly in the flame (hot seal) and then immediately pulled outward and blown into slightly (Figure 7.52). If done quickly and correctly, the seal should be complete at this point. Most of the time, however, it may be necessary to spot weld the joint in several places. A small, sharp flame should be used for this operation.

11. This seal (Figure 7.53) can be flame annealed, but if at all possible it should be immediately oven annealed. There are lots of stresses in this product! Be sure to remove the cardboard support before oven annealing. Use a wire with a small hook at the end.

It should be noted that corregated cardboard is used "just in case", as in some situations you find it impossible to remove this support. The cardboard should burn up almost completely in the annealing oven, but whenever possible, it should be removed.

As with all the procedures described in this book, keep in mind that there are alternative methods that may work better for you. During your work and experimentation, you will soon discover the procedure that works best for you.

CLOSED CIRCUIT SEALS

Many pieces of scientific glassware involve closed circuits of tubing. A closed circuit exists any time one piece of tubing has both ends sealed to another tube. Such seals are found in pressure equalized addition funnels, soxhlet extractors, distillation heads, and many other similar kinds of apparatus. There are several different ways that such seals can be made, but the method described below seems to be the easiest and most widely used.

LABORATORY EXERCISE THIRTY FIVE

CLOSED CIRCUIT SEALS

1. Two rather sharp 90° angles, approximately three inches apart, are made in the same plane on a piece of 6 mm tubing using a cool, bushy flame. For each bend, heat an area about two times the width of the flame. When softened, the glass is removed from the flame, and then stretched slightly while bent downward and blown into with a blowpipe.

2. After the finished piece cools, the tubing is cut so that a half inch stub remains after each bend. If at all possible, it is a good idea to make one stub slightly shorter than the other.

3. A ten inch piece of 15 mm tubing is fitted with a blowpipe and cork. A bushy flame is used to preheat an area about one third of the length of the tube from one end. The burner is then adjusted to give a small, hot flame and directed onto one spot. The flame is removed, and a bulge slightly larger than 6mm is blown. The bent 6 mm tube is then used to measure where the second bulge should be blown. The 15 mm tubing is preheated at this second spot and the second bulge is blown as before (Figure7.54a).

4. The shorter stub on the 6 mm bent tube is then covered with a piece of masking tape; small corks inflame too easily in this procedure. The end of the longer stub and the shoulders on the blown hole are then heated simultaneously until all the edges become white hot. These are joined together firmly, then pulled outward slightly while blown out to the proper diameter. The bent tube should be oriented so that the second end is directly above the second bulge but about one half inch away from it. At this time, the 6 mm tube will not be parallel to the 15 mm tube, but angled outward slightly (Figure 7.54b).
It may be a good idea for beginners to have a helper with a second torch heat the first seal while you work on the other end of the seal.

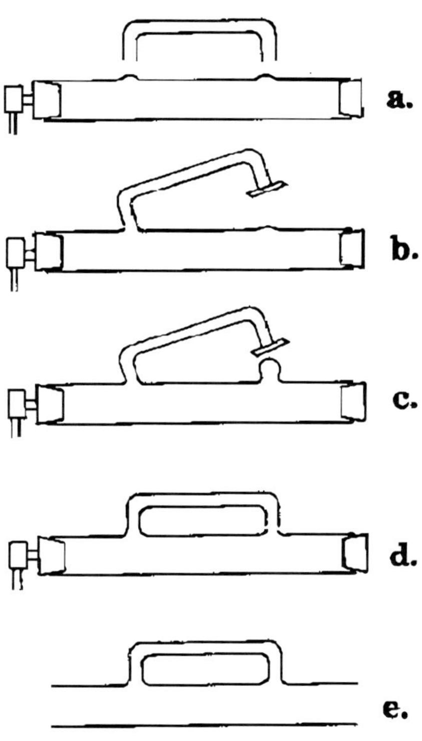

Figure 7.54 *Steps in making a closed circuit seal.*

5. The first joint is now reworked with a very small, hot flame until it is nearly finished. If Step 4 was done properly, very little, if any reworking should really be necessary. When nearly finished, the second bulge is blown out to open it up to the proper size in the usual manner, and the masking tape is removed from the end of the 6 mm

tube (Figure 7.54c). The first seal is then reheated along with the second hole area. The tube is then bent into proper position while the second seal area is heated so that the ends become properly fused.It may be a good idea to have a helper with a second torch heat the first seal while you soften the glass at the ends of the 6mm tubing and the shoulder of the 15 mm tubing so that when the bent tube is lowered into position (Figure 7.54d), a good seal can be made almost immediately. With some practice and dexterity, it is possible for one person to do all of this in a smooth manner.

6. At this point, if necessary the second seal is reworked and partially flame annealed. It may be necessary to use cane to complete the second joint, especially if you are working alone with only one torch.

7. The first seal is then reheated again (to relieve strains) and finally thoroughly flame annealed.

8. After the first seal is cooled, the second is thoroughly flame annealed for a second time. If not properly flame annealed, the system will almost surely crack due to the great stresses involved.

9. The finished piece must be oven annealed as soon as possible.

When you repeat this exercise, you may wish to experiment with larger diameter tubings (e.g. 10 mm and 20 mm).

FORMING HOSE CONNECTOR TUBES

Side arm tubes suitable for hose connections are required on many pieces of laboratory apparatus. Often these contain constrictions or serrations so that the rubber or plastic hose will remain securely in place. These serrations also allow the worker to secure the tubing with wire whenever necessary. The scientific glassblower should always have a number of these tubing connectors ready (Figure 7.55).

Such connectors are commercially available, but the homemade ones work just as well, and they are not that difficult to make. If you make some, remember that it is much easier to make ten or more at one time than to have to go back and make one or two in the middle of a repair or during the construction of a complex piece of apparatus.

There are many different approaches to making such connectors. The method outlined below appears to be a very satisfactory one for most students. Nonetheless, those who have trouble with this method are urged, as always, to try other methods as described by different authors.

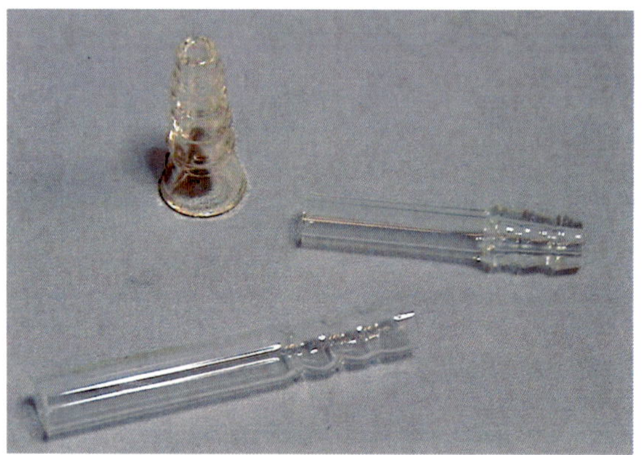

Figure 7.55 *Hose connectors. The two on the top are commercial products. The bottom one is one example of a homemade connector (described in Exercise 36).*

LABORATORY EXERCISE THIRTY SIX

MAKING HOSE CONNECTOR TUBES

1. A piece of 9 mm tubing, about 12 inches long, is flared slightly on one end using the regular method (see page 225). Although 9 mm tubing may be considered a somewhat unusual tubing diameter, it is recommended because the beginner will find it significantly easier to work with than the more common 8 mm tubing.

2. The tubing is placed on a set of rollers with the flared end positioned over an unlighted burner fitted with a #2 tip (Figure 7.56).

3. The tubing is slid out of the way to the left while the burner is lighted and adjusted to give a small, medium-hot flame. .

4. The tubing is rotated continuously while it is moved to the right so that the area about one quarter of an inch to the left of the flare can be

heated. Continue heating and rotation until the tubing becomes softened, but not so soft so that it begins to collapse or droop. A clever way to insure uniform and continuous rotation is to slide a large-size rubber stopper (size 2 or larger) or pluorostopper to the middle region of the tubing between the two rollers. This serves as a fly wheel, allowing rotation of the tube in a uniform manner for some time. Good quality ball bearing rollers must be used. This makes shaping the constrictions in Steps 5 and 6 much easier to do.

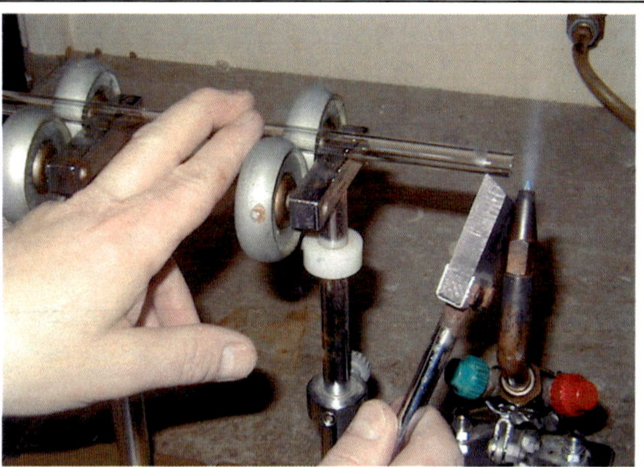

Figure 7.56 *Set up for making tubing connectors.*

5. The tubing is then slid sideways out of the flame. Immediately, the tapered edge of a specially prepared carbon plate (as shown in the above figure) is gradually pressed onto the soft glass while uniform rotation is continued. This should form a circular indention or constriction. Pressure on the graphite edge must be gentle, yet firm.

Too much pressure will cause one side of the constriction to be deeper than the other, or it may force the tubing to bend. Bending can be corrected immediately by using the flat surface of the graphite to straighten out the tubing once again. Normally, the constant rotation during the constricting process should prevent such bending.

6. The procedure is repeated on a similar area another one quarter inch to the left of the first constriction. If desired, a third constriction can be made in a similar way.

7. After cooling, the glass is cut so that about two additional inches of straight tubing remain attached (Figure 7.57). This additional length will serve as a handle when sealing the flared end onto the desired piece of

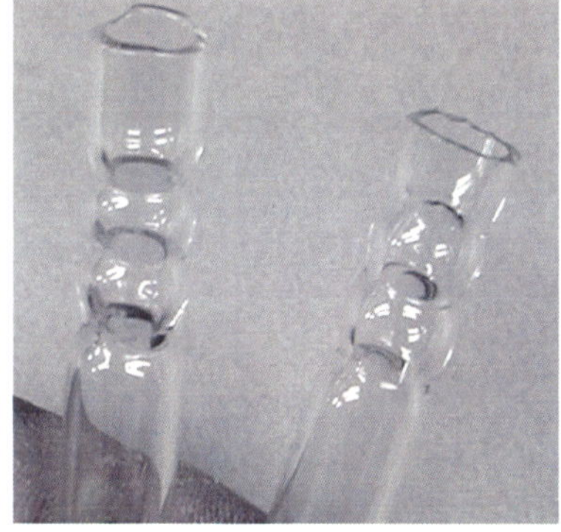

Figure 7.57 *Completed hose connectors.*

apparatus. When the seal is completed, a scratch is made in the constriction closest to the straight handle. The excess glass handle is broken off, and the end of the hose connection is fire polished.

FLAME CUTS AND BLOWN OUT ENDS

Sometimes it is necessary or desirable to cut a piece of tubing using the flame, just as is done routinely for rod. Obviously, however, there is an additional problem involved when tubing is flame cut, namely that the resulting cut will be sealed off. This closed end has to be blown out again to the original diameter of the glass tubing. Thus, such flame cuts really involve two steps: closing by drawing out, and opening by blowing out. The opening process involves the intermediate formation of a round bottom end. A hole is then blown in this, and after heating, it is flared out to the proper diameter.

LABORATORY EXERCISE THIRTY SEVEN

FLAME CUTTING OF TUBING

1. A piece of 12 mm tubing about 12 inches long is fitted with a blowpipe assembly.

2. The tubing is then heated about midway with rotation. A flame cut is made in much the same way as was done for rod.

3. A good round bottom is formed on the end of one of the pieces obtained in Step 2. Care is taken to remove as much excess glass as is possible.

4. A small area on the tip of the round bottom is heated and blown out slightly so as to form a small bulge. The bulge is then reheated and blown out to form an irregular shaped bubble of thin glass. The thin glass is removed in the usual way.

5. The opening is then reheated and flared out with a graphite rod until it has the same diameter as the original tube.

6. The completed end should be carefully flame annealed. Once you have gained some confidence in the technique, try larger diameter tubing (e.g. 15 mm).

FLAT BOTTOM ENDS

Sometimes a flat bottom is called for on a piece of apparatus. Although these are never as strong structurally as round bottom ends, they are, nonetheless, useful and sometimes preferred. Flat ends are made in much the same way as the round bottom ends, but with these, special effort must be made to be sure to remove all excess glass after the flame cut has been made. A blowpipe assembly is usually not necessary in this procedure.

LABORATORY EXERCISE THIRTY EIGHT

MAKING FLAT BOTTOM ENDS

1. The end of a length of 15 mm tubing is flame cut.

2. All excess glass is removed by repeated heatings and wipings.

3. The end of the tube is heated strongly with constant rotation as was done in making round bottom ends (Step 5 of Exercise 25), but the end is allowed to collapse and flatten by itself. From time to time, the tubing should be held at an angle so that the flat end is directed down into the flame. At other times, the tubing can be held at lesser angles. Care should be taken to keep the flame from heating the sides of the tubing. A uniform, flat bottom should result.

4. The tubing is removed from the flame and checked for uniformity and flatness. If necessary, the hot end can be pressed down gently onto a graphite plate to complete the process.

Repeat the exercise several times and try experimenting with larger diameter tubing (20 mm and 25 mm).

BLOWING SMALL BULBS FROM TUBING

Usually, when special glassware is constructed, it is common to use commercially available flask blanks wherever such bulbs are required. But sometimes, especially in the case of very small bulbs, it may be worthwhile for the glassblower to make the bulb himself. When making these, always start out with tubing approximately half the diameter of the bulb desired.

LABORATORY EXERCISE THIRTY NINE

BLOWING SMALL BULBS

1. Make a round bottom end on a ten inch piece of 15 mm tubing.

2. The end area is then carefully heated again and rotated until it thickens considerably. The amount of tubing heated near the end depends on the size of the bulb desired. In this exercise, heat about 1 1/2 inches. During the heating process, puffs of air are used to keep the full diameter as the glass thickens.

3. After sufficient glass has been gathered, the thickened tube is removed from the flame and blown to the desired diameter (about 30 mm) with rapid and uniform rotation. The angle at which the tubing is held during the blowing step depends on the distribution of the thickened glass immediately before blowing. If inspection indicates that the thickened glass is heavier near the end, blowing should be done with the tubing end somewhat upward. If the thickened glass is thinner near the end, blowing should be done with the tubing end downward.

Larger bulbs are made in a similar manner, but the thickening process and uniform rotation of the softened glass is complicated considerably due to the greater weight of the glass. For this reason, it is often advantageous to attach a rod handle to the round bottom end of the glass tube. The handle will aid in the thickening process since it will allow the worker to apply some constrictive pressure as the glass is heated. A handle also serves as a guide for keeping the bulb in line with the axis of the tube during the entire process, especially during the blowing step. After the blowing is completed, the bottom of the bulb is finished by removing the rod handle and completing the bulb as you would in thc construction of any round bottom tube.

Needless to say, blowing uniform bulbs having the proper wall thickness can be a very difficult task, especially when the bulb needs to be a definite size.

Bulbs can also be constructed in the middle of a piece of glass tubing by essentially the same process. The center section of tubing is thickened by heating and rotating. As the tubing diameter shrinks, the ends are pressed inward slightly. The outside diameter is held constant by blowing whenever necessary. When sufficient glass has been gathered, the tubing is removed from the flame and blown to the proper shape. Rapid and uniform rotation is again very important. Some workers choose to gradually enlarge the bulb in the flame during the thickening process, making the final blowing step somewhat easier.

JOINING DIFFERENT TYPES OF GLASSES

In the construction of some kinds of scientific apparatus, it may be necessary to join together two different types of glasses. For example, experiments utilizing ultraviolet radiation may require a length of quartz tubing to be attached to a system which is otherwise entirely borosilicate. A direct seal between the borosilicate parts and the quartz tube would not be possible because their coefficients of expansion differ significantly. However, a seal like this can be made by using an intermediate piece of special glass called a graded seal (Figure 7.58). These seals are a series of disk-like slices of glass tubing fused together. The first slice is pure borosilicate; the second has a slight amount of quartz included. The third has more quartz and less borosilicate and so on until the very last piece which is pure quartz. In this way, the borosilicate part of the apparatus can be joined successfully to the first end of the graded seal while the quartz tube can be joined successfully to the other end. Such seals are available commercially, but they are expensive and are used only when absolutely necessary. Graded seals are also made for other types of glasses, but in scientific glassblowing, the borosilicate-quartz seal is the most important and most widely used.

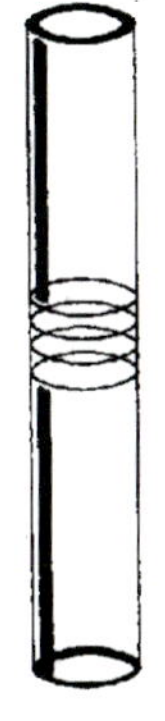

Figure 7.58 *A commercial graded seal.*

LABORATORY PROJECT - SCIENTIFIC ONE

SIMPLE VACUUM TRAP

Introduction:

Vacuum traps (cold traps) are used to remove condensable liquids from a flow of gas. The trap described below is one-piece in construction, but standard taper joints could be added to the outer tube to permit easy removal of any condensed liquids collected (Figure 7.59). For some applications it may be desirable to use a larger diameter inside tube (e.g. 10 mm) in order to help prevent blocking in the trap due to freezing of the liquid within this inner tube.

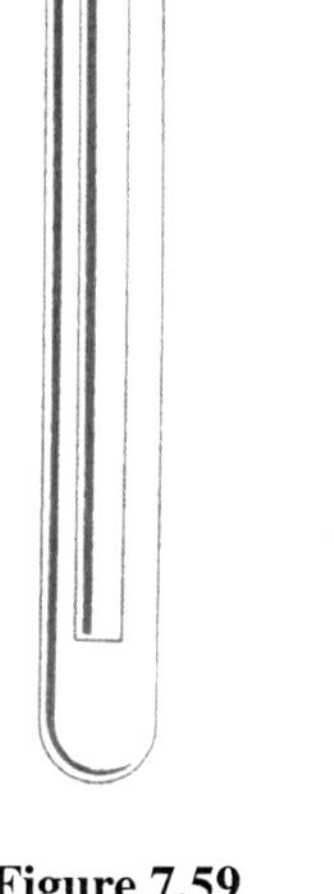

Figure 7.59
A simple vacuum trap

Materials

About 12 in of 8 mm tubing
About 12 in of 10 mm tubing
About 12 in of 20 mm tubing

Special Tools

Flaring Tool, corrugated cardboard or tape

Flame

#2 and #5 tips; size of flame varies

Construction Steps

1. Form a round bottom end near the end of a length of 20 mm tubing (procedure described in Exercise 25 on page 208).
2. A bulge approximately 9 mm in diameter is formed in the middle of the round bottom end. A 6 inch piece of 8 mm tubing is fire polished on both ends and fit into the 20 mm tube so that the end fits snugly into the bulged area. Corrugated cardboard or flame resistant tape should be used to hold and center the smaller tubing.

3. After replacing the blowpipe assembly, a ring seal is made. As the seal cools, the apparatus is rotated so as to keep the 8 mm inside tube centered so that it does not press too tightly against the support material. The glass area inside the ring seal is then heated with a very small flame and blown out. A 2.5 inch length of 8 mm tubing is added to complete the through seal.
4. After careful preheating, a hole is blown into the side of the 20 mm tubing at a distance of about 1 inch from the shoulder of the through-seal. A 2.5 inch length of 8 mm tubing is then added as a side arm.
5. The cardboard or other support is removed. If fire resistant tape is used, it can usually be easily removed by applying air pressure to the side arm. Otherwise, use a wire with a hook at the end.
6. The 20 mm tubing is then flame cut at a point about 1 inch beyond the end of the inner tube and is made into a round bottom end.
7. Both the inlet and outlet tubes are cut off at 1.5 inches and fire polished. The finished item should be oven annealed at the earliest possible opportunity.

SUPPLEMENTARY PROJECT

An Alternative Simple Cold Trap

A much simpler cold trap has been suggested by Gary Coyne, glassblower at California State University, Los Angeles[1]. His students are asked to construct the item shown, telling them only that the item should be configured as drawn and that it must fit into a standard dewar flask. Each student then decides on the required measurements. This seems like an excellent challenge for all scientific students at this point in their study. The various products could be discussed and analyzed by the entire class.

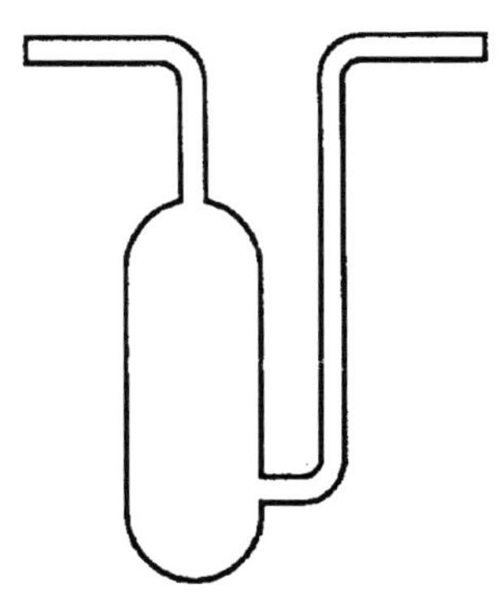

1. Personal communication.

LABORATORY PROJECT - SCIENTIFIC TWO

GAS BUBBLER TUBE

Introduction:

Although this trap is somewhat similar in construction to the one described in Project Scientific One, it is particularly well suited as a mineral oil or mercury bubbler vent for apparatus which requires an inert atmosphere since the reservoir head prevents the oil or mercury from being sucked back into the system. It can also be used as a vacuuum trap or as an air trap in winemaking.

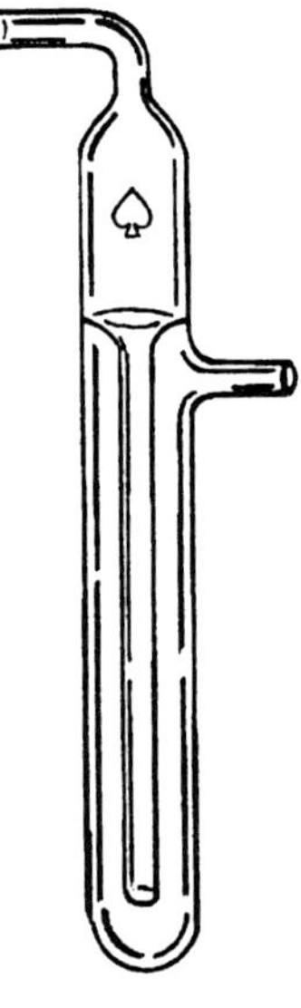

Figure 7.60
Gas bubbler tube (another type of vacuum trap)

Materials

About 12 in of 8 mm tubing
About 12 in of 10 mm tubing
About 12 in of 20 mm tubing

Special Tools

Flaring Tool, corrugated cardboard or tape

Flame

#2 and #5 tips; size of flame varies

Construction Steps

1. Form a round bottom end close to the length of 20 mm tubing (Procedure described in Exercise 25 on page 208).
2. A 2.5 inch length of 8 mm tubing is joined to the end of the round bottom in the usual manner for joining two tubes of different diameters (procedure described on page 211).
3. A large, uniform flare or flange is prepared at the end of a 10 mm tube. (This procedure is described in Exercise 29 on

page 223.) This flange should be large enough to fit snugly into the 20mm tubing.

4. The 10 mm tubing is then cut to a 4 inch length and the end lightly fire polished.

5. The flared tube is inserted into the 20 mm outer tube and positioned so that it is about 2 inches below the rounded shoulders. Corrugated cardboard or flame resistant tape should be used to hold and center the tubing.

6. An inside seal (procedure described on page 231) is made, joining the flare to the outer tubing. Be certain to preheat the area carefully and then to thoroughly flame anneal the seal after it is complete.

7. Immediately prepare to join a side arm tube at a point about one inch below the inside seal. The area should be preheated, a bulge formed and blown out, and a 2.5 inch length of 8 mm tubing joined. The cardboard or tape support is then removed.

8. The 20 mm tubing is flame cut at a point about one inch beyond the end of the inner tube and is made into a round bottom end.

9. The inlet and outlet tubes are cut off at about 1.5 inches and lightly fire polished. The finished item must be oven annealed at the earliest possible opportunity.

LABORATORY PROJECT - SCIENTIFIC THREE

SIMPLE LIEBIG CONDENSER

Introduction:

A simple and useful condenser can be made in a way very similar to that used to prepare a vacuum trap (Project Scientific One). In fact, many of the first steps are nearly identical. The major change is that the excess 20 mm tubing is now flame cut at a point directly over the end of the inner tubing, not an inch away. Also, an additional side arm must be added for a water outlet. The design can be modified to make either larger or smaller condensers, or to include standard taper joints on the vapor inlet and condensate outlet tubes. Pre-made hose connectors (Exercise 36 on page 244) can be used in place of the 2.5 inch 8 mm side arms if desired.

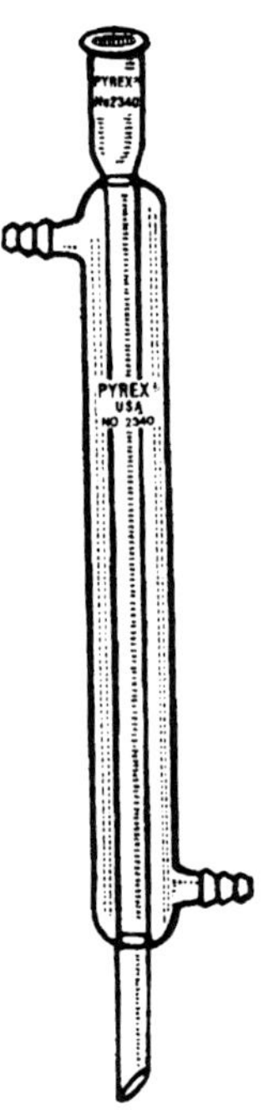

Figure 7.61 *A simple Liebig condenser. Once these were the most widely used condensers in chemistry, now replaced by modifications incorporating standard*

Materials

About 12 in of 8 mm tubing
About 6 in of 10 mm tubing
About 6 in of 15 mm tubing
About 12 in of 20 mm tubing

Special Tools

Flaring Tool, corrugated cardboard or tape

Flame

#2 and #5 tips; size of flame varies

Construction Steps

1. A constriction is formed about 2 inches from the end of a short length of 15 mm tubing. The narrow end of the constriction should be approximately 10 mm in diameter. (Procedure described in Exercise 23 on page 207.) The constriction is cut

in the region having the smaller diameter. A rim is formed on the larger end of the 15 mm tubing (procedure described on page 225). This completed piece is corked on the larger end and then set aside for use in Step 4.

2. Form a round bottom end close to the end of the length of 20 mm tubing (procedure described in Exercise 25 on page 208).

3. A bulge approximately 11 mm in diameter is formed in the middle of the round bottom end. A 6 inch piece of 10 mm tubing is then fire polished at both ends and fit into the 20 mm tube so that the ends fit snugly into the bulge. A cardboard or fire resistant tape support is used to hold and center the 10 mm tube.

4. After replacing the blowpipe assembly, a ring seal is made. As the ring seal cools, the outer tube is rotated so as to keep the 10 mm inside tube centered so that it does not press too tightly against the support material. The glass inside the ring seal is then heated and blown out. The constricted length of 15 mm tubing prepared in Step 1 is then added to complete the through-seal.

5. After careful preheating, a hole is blown into the side of the 20 mm tubing at a distance of about 1 inch from the shoulder of the through-seal. A 2.5 inch length of 8 mm tubing or a pre-made hose connector tube is then added as a side arm.

6. The cardboard or tape support is now removed.

7. A second blowpipe assembly is added to the side arm. This is necessary to form the second shoulder of the condenser.

8. The 20 mm tubing is flame cut at a point directly over the end of the inner tube. Any excess glass is removed, and the end is carefully blown out through the side arm blowpipe until the shoulders become uniformly rounded.

9. The glass inside the ring seal which was formed upon cutting off the 20 mm tubing is heated again and blown out. A 2.5 inch length of 10 mm is added to complete this second through-seal.

10. After careful preheating, a second hole is blown into the side of the 20 mm tubing, this time at a distance of about 1 inch from the shoulder of the second through-seal. The point chosen should be directly in line with the first side arm. Another

2.5 inch length of 8 mm tubing or hose connector is then added as the second side arm.

11. The side arms are cut off at a 1.5 inch length (or hose connectors cut at the last constriction) and are fire polished.

12. The condensate outlet is cut off at a similar length and also fire polished. The finished condenser must be oven annealed as soon as possible.

LABORATORY PROJECT - SCIENTIFIC FOUR

SIMPLE LIEBIG CONDENSER (AN ALTERNATE METHOD)

Introduction:

This condenser is similar in design to that described in Project Scientific Three, but it instead involves an inside seal and therefore somewhat simplifies the construction of the vapor inlet tube.

Materials

About 12 in of 8 mm tubing
About 12 in of 10 mm tubing
About 10 in of 20 mm tubing

Special Tools

Flaring Tool, corrugated cardboard or tape

Flame

#2 and #5 tips; size of flame varies

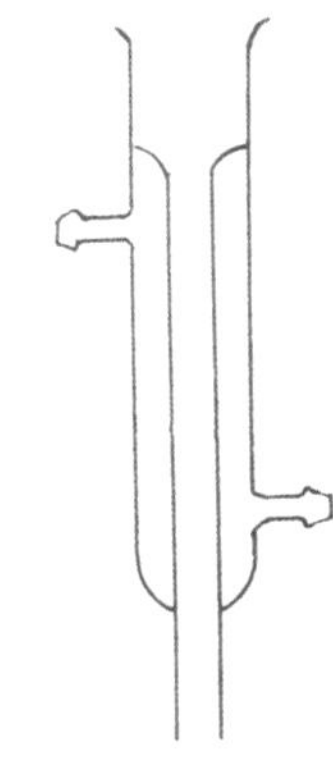

Figure 7.62
A variation on the simple Liegig condenser, utilizing an inside seal.

Construction Steps

1. Form a round bottom end approximately 8 inches from the end of a length of 20 mm tubing.
2. A bulge approximately 11 mm in diameter is formed in the middle of the round bottom end.
3. A rim is formed on the opposite end of the 20 mm tubing (procedure described on page 225).
4. A large, uniform flare or flange is prepared at the end of a 10 mm tube. The flare should be large enough to fit snugly into the 20 mm tubing.

5. The 10 mm tubing is then cut to a 6 inch length.

6. The flared tubing is then inserted into the 20 mm outer tubing in such a way so that the 10 mm end fits snugly into the bulge on the round bottom end. The flare should then be at a position approximately 2 inches from the lip on the end of the 20 mm tubing.

7. After replacing the blowpipe assembly, a ring seal is made to join the 10 mm tubing to the round bottom end. The glass inside the ring seal is then heated and blown out. A 2.5 inch length of 10 mm tubing is added to complete the through-seal. This seal should be thoroughly flame annealed.

8. After careful preheating, a hole is blown into the side of the 20 mm tubing at a distance of about 1 inch from the shoulder of the through-seal. A previously prepared hose connector (or a short length of 8 mm tubing) is then added. Oven annealing is highly recommended at this point.

9. A second blowpipe assembly is now added to the side arm. Both blowpipes will be needed to aid in forming the next seal.

10. An inside seal is now made by joining the flare to the outer tube (procedure described on page 231). Be certain to thoroughly flame anneal the entire area after this seal is completed.

11. A second hole is blown into the side of the 20 mm tubing at a distance of about 1 inch from the inside seal. Another hose connector (or short length of 8 mm tubing) is added.

12. The item must be oven annealed at the earliest possible opportunity.

DESIGN, ANALYSIS , AND CONSTRUCTION OF COMPLEX SCIENTIFIC GLASSWARE

Many times situations arise which call for the design and construction of custom glassware. This is often the case in basic research where unusual requirements, stringent experimental conditions, or difficult procedures are encountered. At other times, the researcher may find it desirable to use certain pieces of glass apparatus that are simply too expensive to be purchased, or it may become necessary to modify pieces of commercially available apparatus for a particular laboratory application. Obviously, a professional glassblower can prove to be invaluable in each of these situations.

In the case of glassware construction or modification, it is usually the person doing the research who has to provide the design for the desired apparatus since he or she is the person most aware of the basic requirements for the particular applications. But it is the glassblower who must be called upon to propose the best possible way to approach the actual construction. Some ideas proposed by the researcher simply may not be physically possible, or perhaps some necessary commercial components may not be available at that particular time. Thus, it is important for both the researcher and glassblower to work closely with one another. Obviously, the situation can be greatly simplified when the researcher has some background in glassblowing or, better yet, is able to do the glassblowing himself. The latter situation is a real benefit whenever time is an important factor.

A thorough discussion of apparatus design is beyond the scope of this book. The only real way to learn effective glassware design is to be knowledgeable about and actively involved in laboratory research. Likewise, judgements as to the best possible way to go about the actual construction can only be made after having some experience in actual glassblowing practices. Nonetheless, even the beginning student can come to appreciate what is reasonable and what is not by a careful analysis of the probable steps necessary to construct the glassware in question. This too is mostly a matter of experience. Therefore, from the very beginning, scientific glassblowing students are urged to look at glassware with an analytical mind, mentally determining the most probable sequence of steps that were used to construct it. Such an approach to viewing glassware can prove to be extremely worthwhile to the student, especially if practiced routinely over an extended period of time. You will find it both interesting and valuable to discuss and compare your ideas concerning a particular piece of apparatus with those of your classmates.

Commercial components such as stopcocks and standard taper joints are important parts of most scientific glassware. If you are somewhat unfamiliar with these items, you are urged to read both Appendix C and Appendix D before continuing with this chapter. In addition, Appendix E will give you an overview of many of the important types of scientific glassware commonly used in research laboratories.

LABORATORY EXERCISE FORTY

ANALYSIS OF COMPLEX SCIENTIFIC GLASSWARE (Part One)

1. Carefully examine each glassware drawing shown below in Figures 7.63 - 7.68.

2. Make a list of the steps that you believe would be best followed in order to construct a similar piece of apparatus. Give as many specific details as possible, but do not worry about specifying actual sizes and lengths.

3. What do you think each piece of glassware is used for?

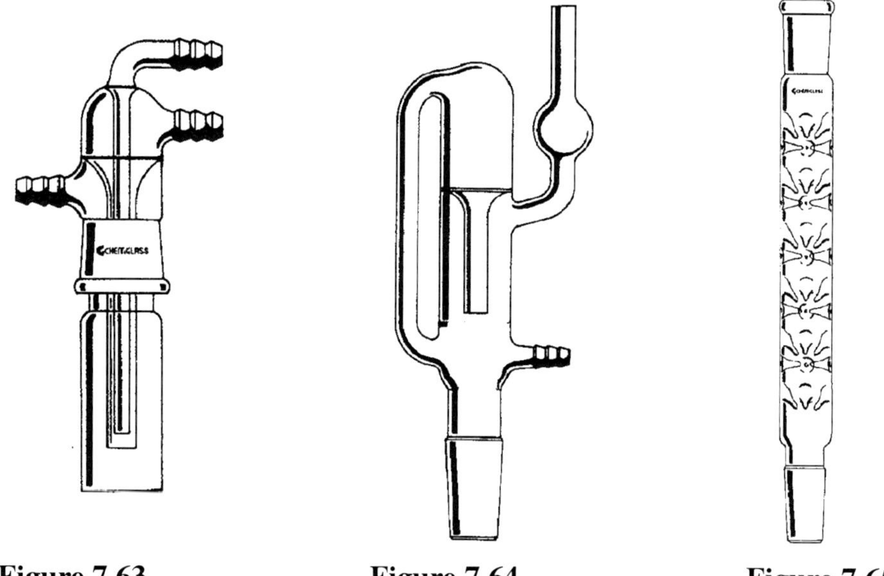

Figure 7.63 **Figure 7.64** **Figure 7.65**

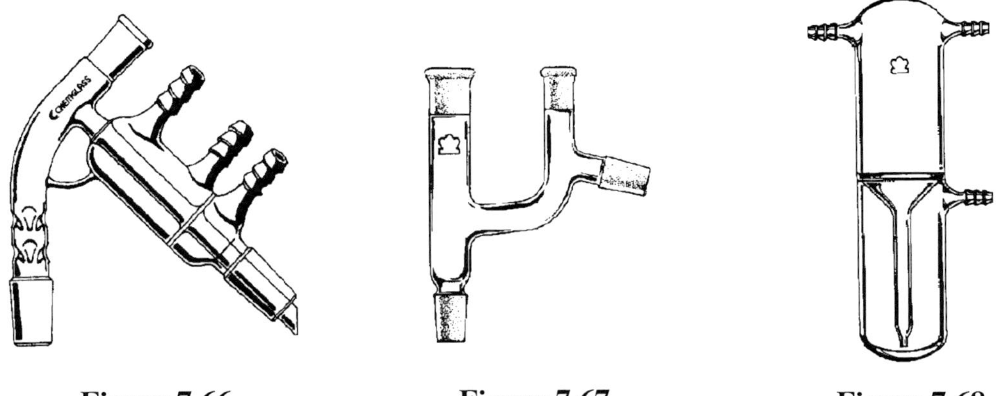

Figure 7.66 Figure 7.67 Figure 7.68

LABORATORY EXERCISE FORTY ONE

ANALYSIS OF COMPLEX SCIENTIFIC GLASSWARE (Part Two)

(This exercise is designed for a classroom setting. It does not apply to those learning on your own.)

1. Your instructor will provide anywhere from two to six actual pieces of scientific glassware for you to examine. Otherwise, try to locate as many pieces as possible yourself. Look at each carefully and analytically.

2. In a manner similar to that described in Exercise 40, make a list of the steps that you think would best be utilized in the construction of a similar piece of apparatus. This time, however, be as specific as possible, including actual sizes and dimensions.

Certainly a thorough analysis and a written outline of possible steps should precede the actual construction of any piece of complex scientific glassware. However, in some cases, a number of additional steps should be considered. For example, for rather complex glassware, it may be wise to prepare a scale drawing. If at all possible, this should be done carefully with the use of a straight edge and other simple drafting tools. All dimensions and parts should be clearly labeled.

In addition, it is a good idea to make a cost estimate. This should itemize the various commercially available components, along with their current prices. The amounts of tubing or rod should just be roughly estimated, and an approximate dollar value assigned. In addition, it will be both beneficial and more realistic to include a labor cost factor, especially if the time involved would normally be spent doing other tasks that would need to be covered by another individual. The point is that your time is worth something and should be included in the estimate. The full estimate should be compared to the current cost of the item if purchased commercially from a scientific supplier. In some cases, such a cost analysis may show that it would be more worthwhile to purchase the item. Of course, the time required for purchasing and delivery must also be considered.

In summary then, there are a number of important steps that should be followed whenever contemplating the construction of any major piece of glassware. The extra time taken will prove worthwhile in the long run. Adequate planning is a crucial phase in any glassblowing endeavor.

LABORATORY PROJECT - SCIENTIFIC FIVE

DESIGN, ANALYSIS AND CONSTRUCTION OF SCIENTIFIC GLASSWARE

In this project, the student is asked to construct a piece of scientific glassware of his or her own choice. The item may be one that is normally commercially available, or it may be one that is of the individual's own design. However, the item should be one that is not too complex. It should be one in which there is a very high probability for real success, yet it should be complex enough so as to be a challenge. In addition, the item should have some potential for actual use in the laboratory. Obviously, it is always true that some students are more skilled than others. Therefore, some projects are bound to be more involved than others. All project proposals should be approved by the instructor before proceeding. The time lines for each phase of the project and for its completion should be determined by consultation with the instructor. Likewise, it should be decided if all of the following steps are to be completed or if some should be deleted because of time constraints. Whenever possible, however, students are urged to complete each part of the total assignment listed below.

1. A crude drawing and description of the proposed project should be submitted for approval.
2. A proposed sequence of detailed steps for its construction should be written up and submitted for approval. Simple drawings should accompany each step.
3. Difficult seals or parts of the apparatus that pose potential problems should be practiced. The actual practice pieces should be saved and handed in for evaluation and approval before proceeding to the final construction.
4. A detailed scale drawing should be prepared. All dimensions and specifications for parts should be clearly indicated.
5. A detailed cost estimate should be made, itemizing all commercially available components and estimating the value for the tubing and rod involved. An estimate for labor can be made if

desired. This should reflect actual construction time. A reasonable, but conservative rate would be $50 - $75 per hour.

6. The item should be constructed and handed in for evaluation. The initial construction should proceed according to the steps proposed in Part 1of this assignment, but the worker should be open to changes. Actual attempts to construct the item might indicate, however, that the proposed sequence was unreasonable, or a better or simpler method may be discovered. Any changes should be accurately recorded for use in Part 7.

7. The proposed sequence of steps should be revised to conform to the steps actually used. Once again, drawings should be included alongside each step. This revised listing should be typed and handed in.

ENDNOTE

1. R. Ponton, *Fusion*, February, 2000, pp 63-64.

Chapter 8
REPAIR OF SCIENTIFIC GLASSWARE

GENERAL INTRODUCTION

Although the scientific glassblower will be called on to do a great deal of original glassware design and construction, an extremely important part of his job will always be the repair of broken glassware. In some respects, the problems involved in the repair of scientific glassware are similar to those encountered in any original construction work. This is especially true if complicated pieces of apparatus are involved. In such cases, it is often necessary to take time to make a careful analysis of the entire piece of glassware. Attempts to repair a single portion of the item without considering the effects of such a repair on the rest of the apparatus will often prove to be futile and frustrating.

Thus, the first step in any repair should always be a thorough inspection of the whole piece of glassware. A list of possible repair steps should then be developed. Special attention has to be given to a number of things which are not normally considered in original construction work. For example, it is very important to thoroughly clean and dry the glassware before starting work on it. Also, it is always wise to check the glassware in the polariscope to see if any stresses remain in the glass, especially in the areas where the work will be concentrated. If stresses are detected, the entire piece of glassware should be oven annealed after cleaning and before proceeding further. Special thought should also be given to preheating steps. This is especially important wherever larger pieces are involved. In some cases, it may be a good idea to preheat the entire item in the annealing oven, as this is a good way to warm the item in a gradual and uniform manner. It is rarely necessary to heat the glass to the annealing temperature unless, of course, it is in need of preliminary oven annealing. In such cases, the item should be allowed to cool considerably before removing from the oven to proceed with the repair procedures. In some special cases, you may even find it desirable to perform the actual repair on the preheated item in the oven itself. This can be done by raising the oven door and proceeding with the necessary repairs using a hand torch and heat resistant gloves. Whenever this is done, special heat resistant stoppers and blowpipe tubing must also be used.

Fortunately, most repairs are not all that complex, as glassware usually breaks in the more accessible areas of the apparatus. For example, the stopcock may be broken off a separatory funnel, or perhaps just the tip is missing. The top of a buret may be chipped, the water inlet tube on a condenser broken, or a standard taper joint on a flask cracked. In these and in other similar cases, the necessary repairs should be rather straight forward and easy to make. Even so, it is important that the glassware be thoroughly cleaned and dried before attempting to repair it. Broken components should be removed with a mechanical saw or other suitable techniques. The new components are then prepared and added. As with any other type of construction, the finished apparatus should be thoroughly inspected and then oven annealed.

In some cases, it is quite possible that you might find it easier to construct a new piece of similar glassware than to repair the broken one. This prospect should always be seriously considered. When this is the case, all unbroken components of the original piece of glassware should be removed and saved for the subsequent reconstruction. For example, if the outer jacket is broken on a coil condenser, it will undoubtedly prove easier to reconstruct than to repair. But the standard taper joints and the inside coil should definitely be removed and incorporated into the new piece of glassware. In most such scavenging tasks, it will prove wise to make extensive use of a mechanical saw. The components, once removed, should be thoroughly washed and dried before they are used again in the reconstruction.

In cases where the glassware cannot be repaired or where reconstruction is not desired, all useful components should be removed and kept for use in construction of other pieces of glassware at a later date. Any remaining glass pieces should be discarded.

Just as in any other facet of glassblowing, experience will prove to be the best teacher. Since there are very few set rules, and since no two pieces of glassware break in exactly the same way, each repair situation will need to be individually assessed. Nonetheless, let's consider a number of specific items and discuss one method of their possible repair.

First, let us take a look at some of the common types of breakage which, for all practical means, cannot be repaired. Too often, lab workers save each and every piece of broken glass, evidently somehow believing that the glassblower can "make them into new" with a few waves of the torch. Thus, even if you never do any glassblowing again, be aware that the following items cannot be easily or economically repaired, and share this knowledge with your colleagues. Beakers with large cracks and graduated cylinders with broken bottoms fit in this category (Figures 8.01 - 8.03). Beakers have no good places to attach blowpipes, and the glass on the bottom a a graduated cylinder is too thick to try to patch by normal reworking methods. (Some workers grind off the remaining base and then use a special epoxy to attach a glass plate which serves as a new base.) Any broken

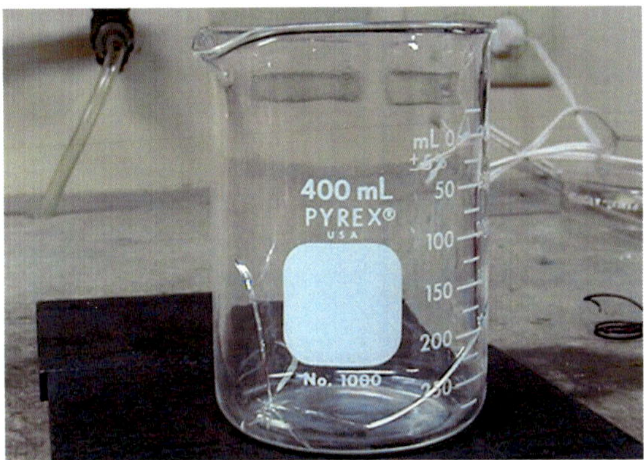

Figure 8.01 *Badly broken beaker, not worth repairing.*

Figure 8.02 *Broken base of graduated cylinder. impossible to repair by conventional glass-blowing methods.*

volumetric flasks with the break below the calibration line also fall in this group. Repairing these would change the volume of the flask. If there are no saveable parts, throw them away!

Of course, there is nothing wrong with getting some practice in repairing broken volumentrics or in trying out some techniques such as gradual preheating, but do not expect satisfactory results, and don't put the repaired the repaired flasks back in a lab that really depends on the accuracy of the glassware.

Figure 8.03 *Bottom of volumetic flask with large cracks. It is not wise to repair these cracks in volumetric flasks.*

Now let's look at some specific representative examples where repairs may be expected to produce acceptable results. But do remember that a certain percentage of repairs do not work, no matter how carefully one proceeds.

LABORATORY EXERCISE FORTY TWO

REPAIR OF STAR CRACKS IN FLASKS

One of the most common and perhaps easiest repairs to make is that of "star" cracks, usually found on the bottom of flasks (Figures 8.4 - 8.5).

Figure 8.4 *Flat bottom flask with star crack on its side.*

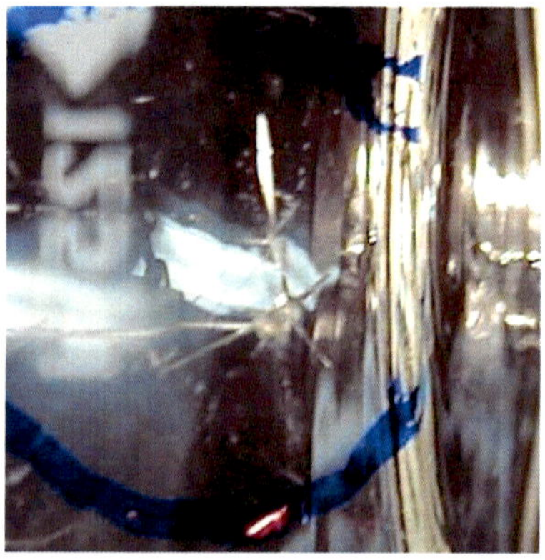

Figure 8.5 *Close up of the same star crack. Note typical shape.*

1. Make sure the flask is clean and dry. Attach a blowpipe and swivel using either a rubber stopper or plurostopper. Take care not place your tongue over the end of the mouth piece.

2. Begin preheating the area with the star crack with a "cool" flame. Move the flask back and forth in the flame until you feel the affected area is heated. Preheat all the area at and around the hairline cracks. Heating the glass too quickly may cause the cracks to spread, perhaps even becoming unrepairable.

3. Once sufficiently preheated, gradually increase the oxygen while still moving the flask around in thc flame. Never keep it in one place.

4. Then with a hot torch, use "brush strokes" with the flame, moving from the outside of each crack to its source in the middle. Repeat this over the entire crack area until all the cracks disappear. Eventually concentrate the hottest part of the flame right on the center of the crack. When the glass begins to collapse a little, remove it from the flame and blow out to the original shape. Sometimes, for larger repairs, it may be necessary to "breathe in and out" with the glass in the flame. This technique causes the melted glass to flow together to complete difficult repairs.

Another method is to attach a piece of "cold glass rod" to the heated region of the star crack and "pull it out" as if removing excess glass from a test tube end.[1] Once reworked, the area will look like new. If you are working on a flat bottom flask (as in this example) and you discover that the bottom of the flask becomes distorted from your repair, it may be necessary to reflatten the bottom with a marver (graphite paddle) as shown in Figure 8.6.

5 When done, immediately flame anneal thoroughly, not only the repaired area, but if possible, the whole region of the flask near the repair.

6. Oven anneal the finished product (Figure 8.7) as soon as possible.

Figure 8.6 *Flattening the bottom with a marver.*

Figure 8.7 *The repaired flask.*

LABORATORY EXERCISE FORTY THREE

REPAIR OF HOLE IN FLASK

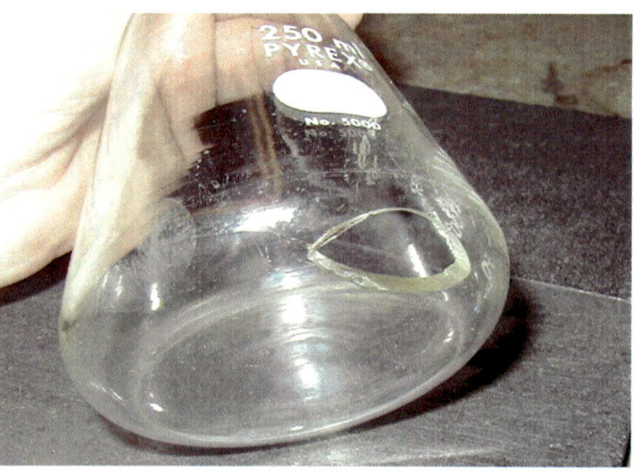

Figure. 8.8 *The rather large hole in the side of this erlenmeyer flask is repairable.*

Another rather typical type of repair is that of a hole in a flask or beaker. Holes in beakers, like the large cracks discussed earlier, are best left unrepaired. Once again, both the lack of a place to insert a blowpipe and the cost of the repair in terms of time dictate that these are best discarded. Holes in most types of flasks, however, are a different matter. Those which occur on the top half of the flask should not be attempted at this time. But those that happen to be on the bottom half are good candidates for repair, and quite honestly, the repair is usually easier than it will appear from the procedure below.

In this exercise, we will address repairing holes similar to that shown in Figure. 8.8.

1. As always, make sure the item is clean and dry, and then carefully examine it, particularly for hairline cracks which may emanate from the hole region. These would need to be repaired before repairing the hole. In the flask we are considering (Figure 8.8), fortunately, there are no such cracks.

2. Attach a blowpipe and swivel using either a rubber stopper or plurostopper. Take care not place your tongue over the end of the mouth piece as you heat the flask in the steps below.

3. Begin preheating the area with the hole with a “cool” flame. To do this, move the flask back and forth in the flame until you feel the entire affected area is heated. Preheat all the area at and around the hole. As usual, heating the glass too quickly may cause the flask to crack.

4. Once sufficiently preheated, gradually increase the oxygen while still moving the flask around in the flame. At this point, never keep the flame in one location.

5. Now, concentrate heating using the hottest part of the flame to move along the edge of the hole.

6. As soon as you see the edges begin to become fire polished, take a piece of cane (2 mm rod) at least 12 inches long, and begin to fill in the hole. Start at one point of the hole, and "paint" on the melted cane along the edge until you have gone "all the way around" the hole. Continue this filling in, keeping the layers of cane as tightly together as possible, without holes (Figure 8.9). Continue this until the entire hole is filled in (Figure 8.10). At this point, the filled in hole will look "terrible", but it will improve in the next steps. Without allowing this completed patch to cool, go on to the next step.

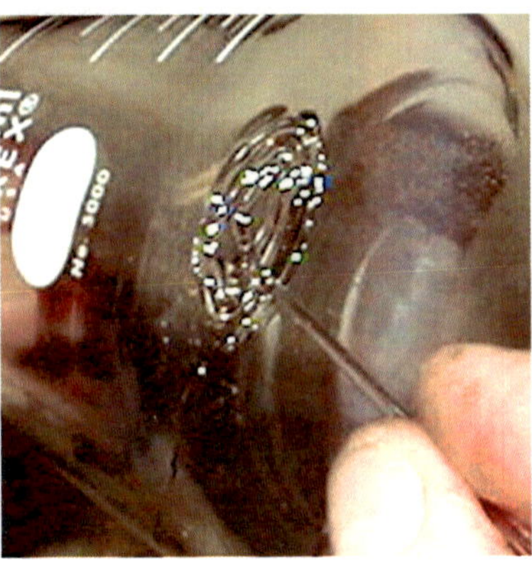

Figure. 8.9 *Beginning to add layers of cane (2 mm rod) to the hole.*

Figure. 8.10 *The totally filled in hole before fusing together.*

7. Gradually increase the amount of oxygen and also the size of the flame, focusing the hottest part of the flame directly onto the patch area (Figure 8.11). As the cane layers begin to fuse together, the flask wall will begin to collapse. When this happens, remove it from the flame and blow out to the original shape. Sometimes, it greatly helps to "breathe in and out" with the glass in the flame. This technique causes the melted glass to flow together to complete uniform fusion of the cane patch.

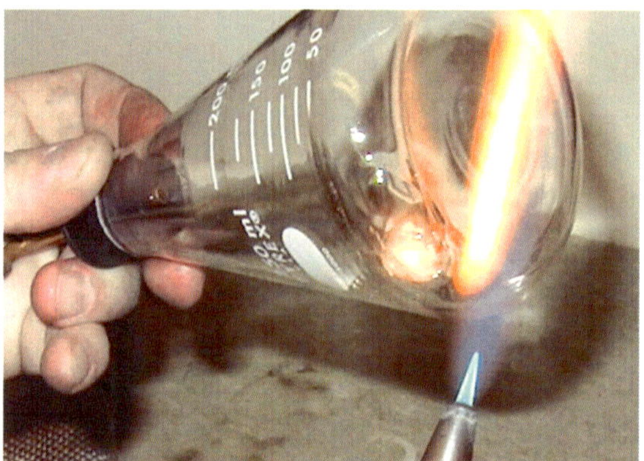

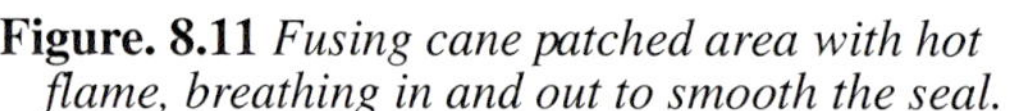

Figure. 8.11 *Fusing cane patched area with hot flame, breathing in and out to smooth the seal.*

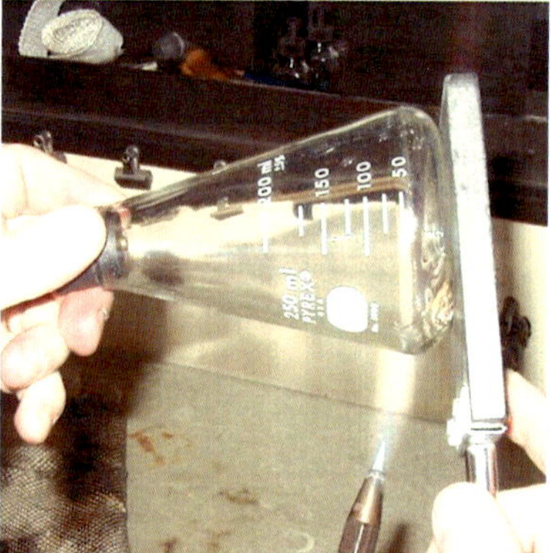

Figure. 8.12 *Flattening out the bottom with a marver.*

8. If you are working in an area of the flask close to the bottom and you note that the bottom begins to become distorted from your repair, it will be necessary to reflatten the bottom with a marver (graphite paddle) as shown in Figure 8.12.

5 When done, immediately flame anneal thoroughly, not only the repaired area, but if possible, the whole region of the flask near the repair.

6. Oven anneal the finished product as soon as possible.

LABORATORY EXERCISE FORTY FOUR

REPAIR OF A BROKEN BEAKER OR FLASK RIM

Consider a beaker with a nick out of the top rim or even with a missing piece as large as that shown in Figure 8.13. This beaker also has some cracking in the area of the break. Thus, in some ways this repair will involve all techniques described in the three previous exercises, plus the additional problem of not having a blowpipe.

1. Make sure the beaker is clean and dry. Then carefully examine it, looking especially for hairline cracks which extend down. Long cracks of this nature are hard to repair, often "spreading" to the bottom of the beaker once any heat is added. The crack to the right of the large chip is about as large as you would normally want to attempt to repair.

Figure 8.13 *It may be possible to repair the crack and hole on the rim of this beaker.*

2. Begin preheating the area with a "cool" flame by moving the beaker back and forth in the flame until you feel the whole area is heated (Figure 8.14). Be sure to preheat the area directly beyond the longest hairline crack.

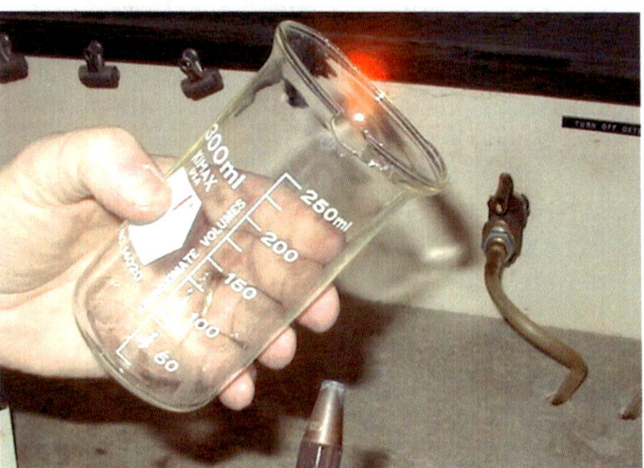

Figure 8.14 *Preheating the area to be repaired in a diffuse flame.*

3. Once the area is preheated, gradually increase the oxygen,

making the flame hotter and hotter. Then begin to move the beaker in a manner so that the flame repeatedly "brushes" the longest crack from below its source to where it ends on the rim. Repeat this for each crack in the area until the cracks disappear.

4. Then move your flame to the second area of repair, the chipped out region, carefully and slowly reheating it if necessary. Finally, heat the edges of the chip with a rather small, but strong, hot flame.

5. As soon as you see the edges begin to become fire polished, take a piece of cane (2 mm rod) at least 12 inches long, and begin to fill in the hole. Start at one side of the rim, and "paint" on the cane along the chip until you reach the other end of the hole. Then perform a similar operation in the opposite direction (Figure 8.15). Keep the layers of cane as tightly together as possible (without holes) until the entire hole is filled. Be forewarned that at this point, the filled in hole "will not look very pretty" (Figure 8.16), but have faith, it should improve in the next steps. Immediately go on to the next step.

Figure 8.15 *Beginning to add layers of cane (2 mm rod) to the chipped out area.*

Figure 8.16 *The totally filled in area. Don't allow the area to cool much before doing the next step!*

6. The filled in area is then immediately reheated. Gradually increase oxygen and also the size of thc flame, focusing the hottest part of the flame directly onto the mass of cane. As it begins to fuse together, it may be necessary to use a large diameter carbon rod to keep the wall of the beaker from collapsing inward (Figure 8.17)

7. If one is fortunate, it may be possible to transform the repaired area

into a pouring spout (impossible, of course, if it already has one). This is good because it is a way to "disguise" remaining imperfections, as they are less likely to be noticed.

If this would be possible, reheat the area and then remove from the flame and use a large graphite rod to form the spout (Figure 8.18). Immediately flame anneal (Figure 8.19), as this area will be certain to contain stresses not only from the repair but also from formation of the spout with the cold graphite rod.

6. Oven anneal the finished product (Figure 8.20) as soon as possible.

This procedure is also be used to repair flask rims with chips.

Figure 8.17 *Using a carbon rod (outside the flame!) to maintain the interior diameter.*

Figure 8.18 *Once totally fused, the area is reheated and (if possible) made into a spout.*

Figure 8.19 *Flame annealing the repaired area and newly formed spout.*

Figure 8.20 *The repaired beaker, which actually doesn't look too bad!*

LABORATORY EXERCISE FORTY FIVE

REPLACEMENT OF STANDARD TAPER JOINT (VOLUMETRIC FLASK REPAIR)

This exercise actually applies to a number of different types of glassware breakage. However, each of these would involve the replacement of some one part, usually the top of a flask, but it may just as well be a piece on a complex distillation apparatus. Right now, we will consider repair to a volumetric flask fitted for accepting a glass stopper.

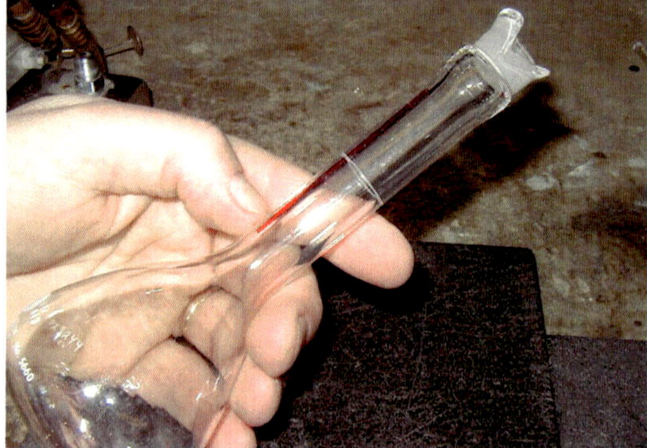

Figure 8.21 *Volumetric flask with broken top*

Earlier it was mentioned that not all damaged volumetric flasks should be repaired. Nonetheless, if as in this case, the problem is above the calibration line, it can indeed be restored to usable condition. In this exercise, the breakage involves a cracked top joint (Figure 8.21).

1. As always, make sure the whole item is clean, and carefully examine it, looking especially for hairline cracks which may emanate from the broken region. In the present case, there are no such cracks.

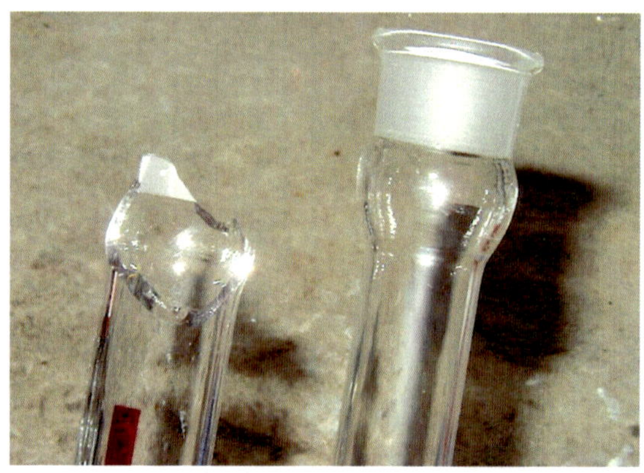

Figure 8.22 *Top of broken flask and usable top on a second unserviceable flask.*

2. Essentially, the broken top needs to be replaced with a different top. New tops, similar in size and design,

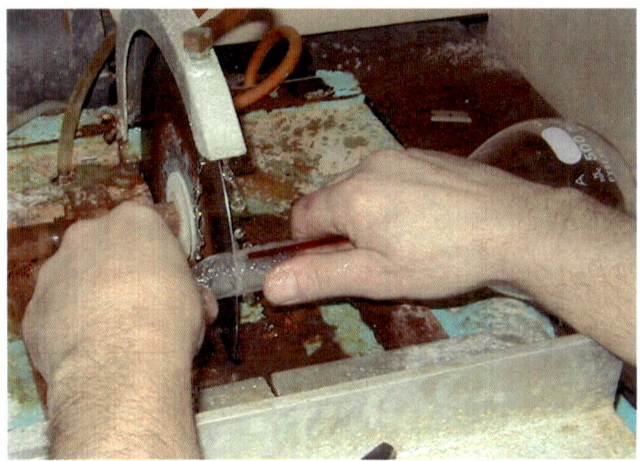

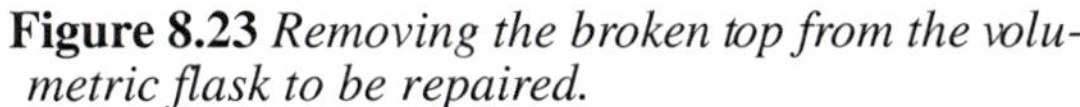

Figure 8.23 *Removing the broken top from the volumetric flask to be repaired.*

Figure 8.24 *Cutting the good top to the proper length from the second flask (or new joint).*

are commercially available, but in this particular case, we will scavenge an almost new top (Figure 8.22) from a similar flask having a badly cracked bottom. Each of these cutting operations is done best with a mechanical glass saw, as the cuts will be clean and even. But if such a saw is unavailable, normal cutting methods can be employed. Either way, clean and dry both usable parts before proceeding.

3. The broken top is sawed off the volumetric to be repaired (Figure 8.23) and a similar length is cut from the second flask (Figure 8.24). Dispose of both the broken top and the broken flask bottom, and wash and dry the new top and sawed off flask. Make the cuts in such a way so that the cut on the flask is a distance from the calibration mark and that the cut on the good top is not only the proper length, but also not too close to the tapered joint.

4. In many cases, such as in this example, the new top piece will be too short to hold and would cause any attached swivel blowpipe assembly to become too hot. Thus, if available, use an inner joint of the same size as a handle. But before inserting it into the new top, wrap the inner piece with some thin heat resistant tape. This prevents the joints from becoming stuck together. If a suitable inner joint is not available, use a piece of glass tubing with a size such that when the end is wrapped with heat resistant tape, it will fit snugly into the new top (Figure 8.25).

5. Generally, these two pieces can be held together during the repair

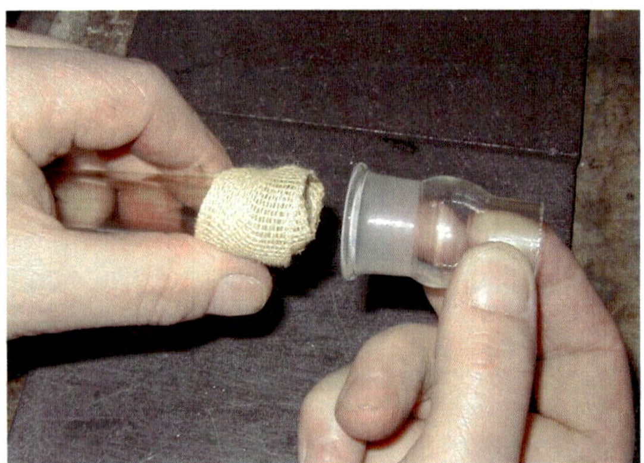

Figure 8.25 *Fitting together the new top and a piece of tubing wrapped in heat resistant tape.*

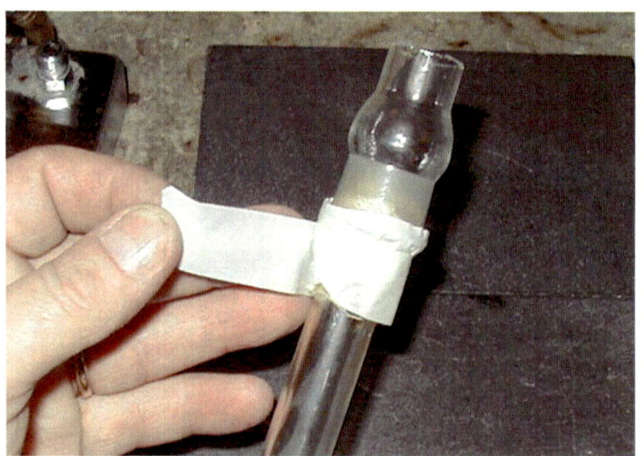

Figure 8.26 *Using making tape to hold the two piec together during the repair.*

with ordinary masking tape (Figure 8.26). However, one needs to be very careful during the following repair to keep the joint and the tape out of the flame and as far away from the heat as possible. Not only would this cause the joints to separate during the repair (not good at all), but the smell of burning masking tape is to be avoided at all costs. In situations when the joint would be too close to the heat, the pieces can be wired together.

6. Now prepare to make the seal between the top and the flask. A blowpipe needs to be added to the glass tube handle piece. Check the glass pieces to make certain that you are ready to join them (Figure 8.27). Prepare the torch with a #5 tip.

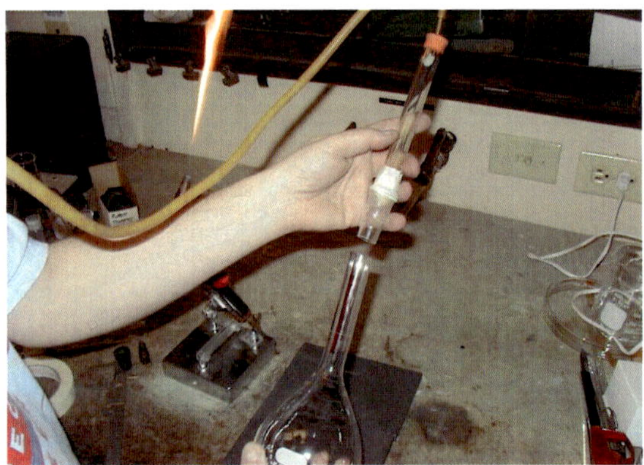

Figure 8.27 *The two glass pieces ready to be joined with a butt joint using a torch on a stand.*

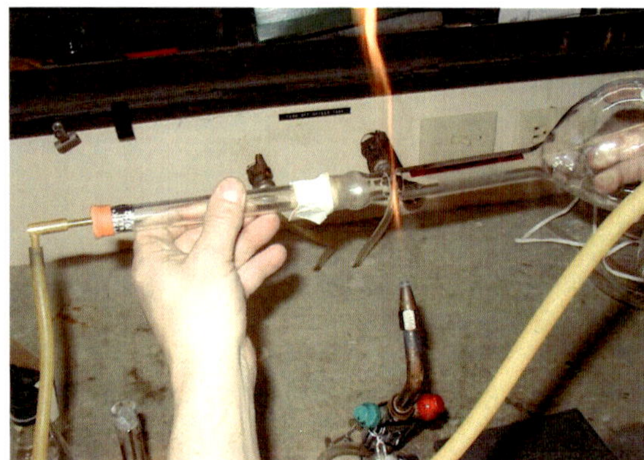

Figure 8.28 *The two pieces are preheated while being rotated at a constant rate.*

Figure 8.29 *A close-up view of the process of joining the new top to the cut off flask.*

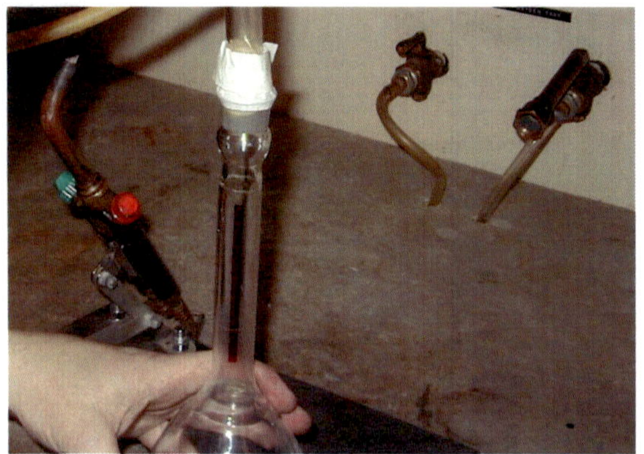

Figure 8.30 *After the joint is completed, the glass is reheated and straightened.*

7. The two pieces are first preheated with a "cool" flame (Figure 8.28). The flame is then adjusted to yield a large, hot flame, and the seal is made while maintaining constant rotation. Make this butt seal as always, blowing out when necessary to maintain the correct diameter. Once the seal is completed, the seal is reheated, and the finished product is placed on a graphite plate, allowing straightening of the joint, if necessary (Figure 8.30).

8. Once you are certain that the joint is well made and straight, remove the masking tape and the piece of glass with the blowpipe, and immediately thoroughly flame anneal the product.

9. The product (Figure 8.31) can be oven annealed, but it should be pointed out that this may lead to a very slight change in volume.

Figure 8.31 *The repaired volumetric flask.*

LABORATORY EXERCISE FORTY SIX

REPLACEMENT OF STANDARD TAPER JOINT #2 (LARGE GRADUATED CYLINDER REPAIR)

This exercise is quite similar to the previous one, but it involves repair of larger diameter pieces. Once again, it applies to numerous different types of glassware breakage.

The large diameter item that will be discussed is a graduated cylinder with a standard tapered joint on the top. Just as before, we will need to take the top off of the broken item and will again use the top from another similar graduate which happened to have a badly broken base, thus rendering it useless (Figure 8.32).

Figure 8.32 *The two tops which are to be exchanged.*

A mechanical glass saw is absolutely needed for glassware this size that requires cuts to be made so close to the ends.

Also, a glassblowing lathe is highly recommended for joining such large diameter tubing.

1. Clean and inspect the item to be repaired for hairline cracks which, as usual, may start at the broken region. Again, there are no such cracks in this piece of glassware.

2. The mechanical glass saw is now used to remove the broken end from the cylinder to be repaired and the bottom from the unneeded graduate. In making larger cuts such as these, it is wise to move the item extremely slowly into the saw blade and, once about half through, it is also wise to carefully rotate the cylinder 180° and begin to cut through from the opposite side (Figure 8.33). This reduces the chance of a chip breaking off, ruining the item to be repaired. However, as one approaches the first saw cut, move extra slowly into the saw blade. (See also endnote 2.)

3. Wash and dry both of the prepared pieces. As in the last exercise, attach the new top to a standard taper or to a piece of tubing using

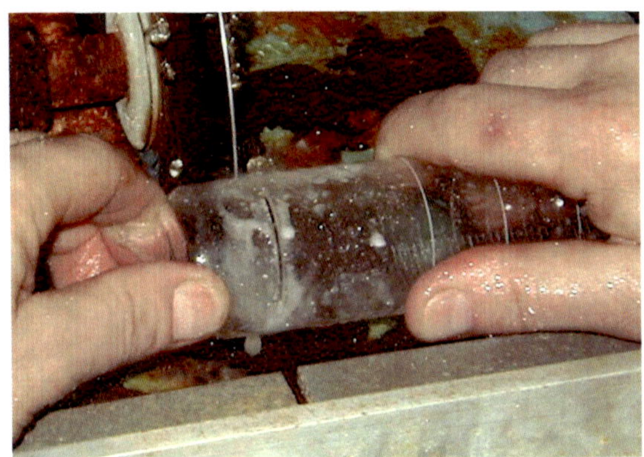

Figure 8.33 *Finishing the saw cut after rotating the graduated cylinder.*

Figure 8.34 *After cleaning the pieces, the replacement top is fitted with a blowpipe.*

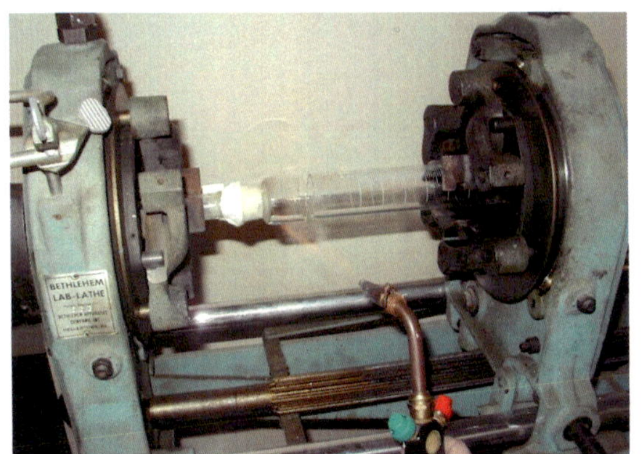

Figure 8.35 *The two pieces positioned in the lathe. While rotating pieces slowly, preheating is begun.*

Figure 8.36 *Strongly heating the glass before making the seal. Rotation is now more rapid.*

heat resistant tape between the pieces and held together by masking tape or wire, if needed (Figure 8.34).

4. Set the items up in a glass lathe as indicated in Figure 8.35 with the blowpipe assembly usually on the left. A hand held torch is used to preheat the two pieces. Use a moderate rotation speed. Initially, the two glass ends should be about one half inch apart.

5. Increase the size and intensity of the flame, maintaining separation of the glass (Figure 8.38). As the two cylinder ends become red hot and fire polished, increase the speed of rotation and then, while focusing the hottest part of a strong flame on the area between the glass.

pieces, use the lathe wheel to bring the softened ends together. Continue heating while rapid rotation is maintained (Figure 8.37).

Figure 8.37 *Strongly heating the joined pieces while rotating more rapidly.*

6. Next, slowly and carefully use the lathe wheel to pull the pieces apart (causing the diameter at the joint to decrease), and then immediately remove the flame and blow out the glass out to the original diameter. In some situations, where the glass has become too thickened at the joint, it is a good idea to blow the diameter out beyond the original diameter and then use the wheel to pull the pieces apart until the original diameter is attained again.

7. When satisfied that the joint is complete, flame anneal for several minutes. The finished repair is shown in Figure 8.38.

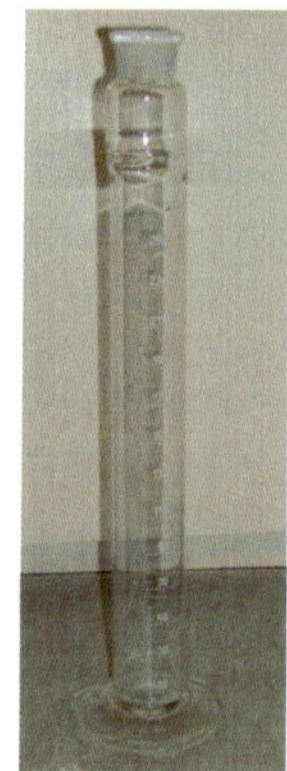

Figure 8.38 *The repaired graduated cylinder.*

LABORATORY EXERCISE FORTY SEVEN

REPAIR OF LARGE MOUTH ITEMS
REPAIR OF FUNNELS WITH BROKEN STEMS

This particular exercise is taken completely from a short note published in the ASGS Journal, Fusion.

Repair of items with large openings, such as funnels, at first seem like they would be impossible to repair, as there is no suitable place to attache a blowpipe assembly. But an ingenious way of accomplishing this is to use a funnel as an intermediate between the wide mouth item and the blowpipe hose.

In this exercise, we will address repair of funnels which often break off at the place where the narrow stem attaches to the funnel itself.

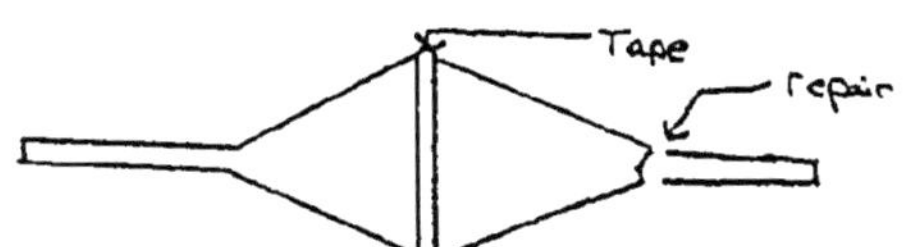

Figure 8.39 *Attaching a good funnel to the funnel with broken stem.*

1. Clean and inspect the item to be repaired.

2. Any irregular edges on the broken funnel are removed with a pair of needlenose pliers. The broken funnel is then attached to a good funnel using masking tape (Figure 8.39).

3. Tubing of the proper diameter is cut and prepared for making the seal by corking off the tubing end.

4. Attach the prepared tubing to the broken funnel with your hand torch, making the repair as quickly as possible before the tape heats up.

5. Remove the funnel with the blowpipe, and place the repaired funnel on a graphite plate to make certain that the new stem is straight. Reheat and adjust if necessary (gloves will be required).

6. Flame anneal the repair and oven anneal as soon as possible.

It is likely that this method of repair should be considered for repair of other large mouth items such as small beakers having minor cracks on the bottom region. However, since some of these items will require longer repair times, the masking tape seal may not survive the increased heat and the greater weight of the item. Use extreme care and beware of the hot glass item falling off the blowpipe funnel. As always, think safety!

LABORATORY EXERCISE FORTY SEVEN

REPAIR OF SCIENTIFIC GLASSWARE

(This exercise is designed for a classroom setting. It does not apply to those learning on your own.)

You will be given two or four pieces of broken glassware, each requiring one or more types of repair described in the preceding five exercises. Some glassware will not be repairable. This is up to you to decide. At least one repair will be straight-forward, but the others may require some more difficult (or impossible) procedures. Reconstruct each repairable piece to the best of your ability. Take your time and for those items needing multiple repairs, decide the order in which the repairs should be done. Think each of your steps and procedures out completely before proceeding. This in many ways is your "final exam" for the scientific part of the course, as these are most likely to be the type of repairs you will be doing in the future. Seek help and advice when needed.

An good overview of safe methods for handling the glass situations you are likely to experience, especially during the repair of old glassware, is presented by J. S. Korfhage. All glassworkers and laboratory personnel are encouraged to read it.[4]

ENDNOTES

1. G. Sites, *Fusion*, February, 1999, p19.
2. K. Owens, *Fusion*, May 2001, pp 18-19.
3. R. Ponton, *Fusion*, May, 1997, p 48.
4. J. S. Korfhage, "A Guide to Safe Handling and Design of Scientific Glassware", *Proceedings of the 35th Symposium on the Art of Scientific Glassblowing, American Scientific Glassblowers Society,* 1990, pp 33-38.

Appendix A
SAFETY PRECAUTIONS

Glassworking is not inherently dangerous, but it will pay to take a number of safety precautions and to know what exactly to do if an emergency arises. Below are a number of things that may help you work more safely and more enjoyably.

1. Remember that glass, especially rod, retains heat for a long time. Make a practice of always placing hot ends of glass on a certain part of your glass bench with the hot end away from you. Then you will come to expect that any glass laying in this area is probably hot.

2. Thin or superficial burns (also called first-degree burns) should be treated immediately by bathing them in a large basin of cold water for at about fifteen minutes, and this will seem like a very long time! This serves to remove some of the heat from the burn area and will keep the burn from going deeper. It will also greatly relieve the pain. If the skin is not broken, cool water (not ice cold) directly from the tap may be used, but may be more painful due to the pressure caused by the stream.[1] Running water should never be used if the skin is broken! If such cooling is done immediately, rather bad looking and feeling burns can often be turned into very minor burns if treated promptly and correctly. Never put butter, oil or ice on burns, as this could cause more damage to the skin.[2] You may apply an antibiotic cream or aloe vera lotion. **See the First Aid Summary for Superficial Burns at the end of this appendix.**

Thus, if you are working by yourself, have some cool water available–every time you work!

If you are in a larger group or class, the first person in the glass lab should always turn on the cold water faucet and let it run into a plastic pail or basin until it gets cold. The pail or basin will then be ready to be used for treating burns. There is nothing as frustrating as trying to treat a burn, but having to wait 5 minutes for any cold water to appear. Allowing the water to run awhile before you work will always prove to be a very wise procedure.

3. Keep hot glass out of the way of your oxygen and gas lines. Tygon tubing may be excellent and inert carrier of gases, but it melts very easily, producing a hole. This could be a very dangerous situation! If such a hole develops, shut off both the oxygen and the gas valves at the lab bench and do not proceed until the line has been replaced. If at all possible, it is best to run these gas lines under the lab bench. It is best to use special tubing available from most glass supply vendors.

4. Always use caution in cutting any glass rod or tubing. If you are using the scratch and break method, the glass should always break with a minimal amount of pressure. If you have to exert a lot of force, **stop**! You are doing something wrong, and you should get someone to help you.

5. Be very cautious of the razor-like edges that may be produced when the glass does not cut properly. Such protruding edges should be removed immediately after cutting by using either a pair of pliers or a wire gauze.

6. If you cut yourself, check first for glass particles. These may be best removed by holding the wound carefully under running water. Excess bleeding is stopped by applying a firm but gentle pressure on the cut with a clean cloth, tissue or piece of gauze. If blood soaks through the cloth, put more cloth on top and apply more pressure. Do not remove the first cloth until bleeding stops.[3] Most minor cuts will heal just fine without antibiotic ointment, but it can speed healing and help reduce scarring. Get medical assistance for all but the most minor cuts. **See the First Aid Summary for Minor Cuts at the end of this appendix.**

7. Always wear protective glasses while working in the glass lab. Always! The glasses will protect your eyes from the harmful infrared rays present in the yellow flame while you are working. Even when you are not glassblowing, wearing your glasses is a good idea because many times a simple act such as cleaning the lab or throwing away glass scraps can be dangerous. It is not unusual to have some glass thrown back out of the wastebasket while you are discarding some other pieces. Always keep your glasses on!

8. Know where the fire extinguisher is in the room and know how to use it. Make certain that it is in good operating condition. Replace or recharge old extinguishers.

9. If at all possible, it is best not to work alone in the glass lab. If an emergency arises, you should not have to face it alone. Working with someone else is also more enjoyable! If you do work alone, inform someone else that you will be working in your lab.

10. Never operate any equipment that you have not been officially checked out on or are not completely familiar with. This includes the annealing oven, large glassblowing torches, ribbon burners, and the glass saw. All of these things look very easy to operate, but there are a number of things that you should know

about each of them. Mistakes can be very costly, and it is not fair to have equipment broken down so that no one else can use it just because of one person's carelessness.

11. Always watch where your flame is pointed, and watch where those long pieces of tubing or rod are pointed while you are making cuts. If you are working in a group, your neighbor may not expect or appreciate your carelessness.

12. Keep your working area well organized. It is easier to find what you are looking for, and while you are working you may not have a lot of extra time to be searching for that particular tool you need which is lost in the mess. Obviously, it is also safer when things are kept neat and clean. Always clean your area with a brush and dustpan after you are done working. There is nothing like leaning on the table with your arm, only to discover that someone forgot to pick up small broken glass pieces. Clean up after every session!

13. Always wear shoes in the glass lab! The floor should always be kept clean.

14. If you are in a class, be sure to report each and every accident to your instructor. This includes burns and cuts as well as accidents with tools and equipment. Likewise, any malfunctioning equipment or broken tools should be reported. Accidents are bound to happen in any laboratory, so do not feel that you are the only one that has ever gotten burnt or cut.

15. Hydrofluoric acid should not be used in the normal glass lab. In those labs where its use is required, it should be used only by a professional glassblower or chemist, and gloves and protective eyewear must be worn.[4] Special HF kits are available, and should be kept in the lab. Nonetheless, first aid for contact with it is outlined in the **First Aid Summary at the end of this appendix.** Those requiring use of this acid should obtain and read its Material Safety Data Sheet (MSDS).[5,6,7]

16. Have a telephone handy or know where the nearest one is located. Post all important emergency telephone numbers near the phone.

A good overview of safe methods for handling the glass situations you are likely to experience is presented by Korfhage.[8] Another good discussion is given by Meyers and Gregar.[9] All glassworkers and laboratory personnel are encouraged to read these.

Three First Aid Summary Cards are printed on the next page. You may wish to make copies of this page and post at least the first two in every glass lab. These describe procedures that everyone should know.

SUPERFICIAL BURNS

Soak in cool water for 15 minutes. or If the skin is not broken, run cool water over the burn for 10-15 minutes.
Cover the burn with a non sticking sterile bandage.
If necessary take aspirin or acetaminophen to relieve any swelling or pain.
If the burn is serious, see a doctor immediately.

MINOR CUTS

Clean out wound under cool running water.
Stop bleeding by applying firm but gentle pressure using a clean cloth.
Apply a bandage if necessary.
If the cut is deep, see a doctor immediately.

HYDROFLUORIC ACID BURNS[6]

Remove any contaminated clothing.
Wash burned area with copious amount of water.
Apply calcium gluconate gel.[7]
Contact a doctor immediately. (Take MSDS sheet and gel with you.)

Endnotes

1 H. Christie, "Cold Water as a First Aid Treatment for Burns", *Fusion*, May, 1963, p. 9.

2 American Academy of Family Physicians, 2002. See specific web page for minor burns: http://familydoctor.org/handouts/638.html

3. American Academy of Family Physicians, 2002. See specific web page for minor cuts: http://familydoctor.org/health facts/041/

4. D. E. Woodyard, "Hydrofluoric Acid: HF Safety and Treatment of Injuries, *Proceedings of the 36th Symposium on the Art of Scientific Glassblowing,* American Scientific Glassblowers Society, 1991, pp 49-51.

5. MSDS searches are maintained by a number of institutions including Cornell University (http://msds.pdc.cornell.edu/msdssrch.asp) and the University of Vermont (http://siri.uvm.edu).

6. Regions Hospital (St. Paul, MN) EMS Guidelines, 2000. See specific web page for hydrofluoric acid burns: http://www.regionsems.net/2000/HAcid.htm

7. One source of calcium gluconate gel is Attard's Minerals, San Diego, CA (E-mail: attard@attminerals.com).

8. J. S. Korfhage, "A Guide to Safe Handling and Design of Scientific Glassware", *Proceedings of the 35th Symposium on the Art of Scientific Glassblowing,* American Scientific Glassblowers Society, 1990, pp. 33-38.

9. G.E,Meyers and J.S. Gregar, Health Hazards in the Glass Shop, *Proceedings of the 35th Symposium on the Art of Scientific Glassblowing,* American Scientific Glassblowers Society, 1990, pp 19-23.

Appendix B
GLOSSARY OF TERMS

The terms in this glossary are defined in the context used within this book and in other related books. If you do not find the term you are looking for here, check the index, which will refer you to specific s where the term is used.

ANNEALING The process of maintaining glass at the annealing point for a specified period of time, after which it is allowed to slowly cool. This treatment serves to remove stresses caused whenever joints are made or whenever hot glass is cooled too quickly. Annealing may be done in the flame or in a special oven.

ANNEALING OVEN An annealing oven is a piece of equipment used to remove the stress in glassware.

ANNEALING POINT The temperature at which the glass will anneal in about 15 minutes if it is then cooled very slowly.

BASE ROD The rod onto which lace or other glass is added.

BLANK An article of glass (e.g. flask bulbs, condenser parts) on which subsequent construction is made to make the desired item.

BLOWPIPE ASSEMBLY Usually a piece of latex tubing having a swivel at one end and a mouthpiece at the other. A blowpipe assembly is essential in scientific glassblowing.

BOROSILICATE GLASS A high quality, chemically resistant glass having a low coefficient of expansion. It is extremely well suited for laboratory glassware and is usually referred to by trade names such as Pyrex®, Kimax®, or Duran®. This glass contains very little soda or potash and no lime. Instead, substantial amounts of boron oxide are added as flux.

BURNER Burners are the sources of heat which can be used in the hand or for stationary use at the bench or lathe (usually stationary). The glass being worked is moved into and around the flame. Flame size is determined by valves that adjust the flow and mix of fuel gas and oxygen.

BUTT SEAL Any joint made end-to-end between two pieces of tubing or rod.

CALIPER (VERNIER CALIPER) A caliper is an instrument used to measure the diameter and thickness of glass tubing and rod. Digital versions of these are also available.

CANE Cane is another name for glass rod, usually referring to very small diameter rod (especially 2mm) used for making glass repairs or decoration.

CLOSED CIRCUIT Whenever one piece of tubing has both ends attached to another larger tube or another part of the same apparatus.

COEFFICIENT OF EXPANSION A measure of how much the particular kind of glass expands when it is heated. The lower the coefficient of expansion, the less it expands when heated. Glasses with low coefficients of expansion are highly desirable since products made from these glasses will not break as easily when heated or cooled.

COLLAPSING TEMPERATURE The same as softening point.

CONSTRICTION A reduction in the diameter of a piece of glass tubing or rod.

CORKS Stoppers used for temporarily sealing the ends of tubing during glassblowing operations.

DEVITRIFICATION Most often the term refers to a surface phenomenon which is actually a crystallization of the glass. This appears most often as a milky, white area on the glass. Most glass will devitrify if it is worked (especially bent or twisted) while the glass is at too low a temperature. This type of devitrification can be removed by reheating strongly with a small, hot flame. The term devitrification can also refer to the loss of alkali flux in the glass by weathering, aging, or chemical reactions. This type of devitrification can not be repaired, but the devitrified surface can be removed with hydrofluoric acid.

DIDYMIUM A special type of glass used for making most glassblowing goggles. The glass contains a mixture of rare earth oxides (neodymium oxide and praseodymium oxide) which effectively absorb the intense yellow color (due to traces of sodium in the glass) which would otherwise obscure the glass in the flame. In addition, this glass filters out the ultraviolet rays and most of the harmful infrared radiation produced when glass is heated.

DURAN® GLASS A registered trade name for the borosilcate glass produced by Schott Glaswerke (Mainz, W. Germany).

ETCH To attack the surface of glass with hydrofluoric acid (or similar compounds) for marking or decoration.

FIRE POLISHING The melting of sharp edges of rod or tubing so as to produce smooth, rounded, contour surfaces.

FLAMEWORKING Another name for lampworking.

FLARE A funnel-like enlarged end on a piece of tubing. Flares that are nearly 90° are often referred to as flanges.

FLINT GLASS Another name for lead glass.

FLUX Any chemical ingredient added to the glass formulation to reduce its viscosity and lower its softening point, making the glass easier to work.

FREEHAND GLASSBLOWING The same as offhand glassblowing.

FRITTED GLASS A porous form of borosilcate glass incorporated in many types of scientific equipment used for filtration. Four porosities are available: extra-coarse (EC), coarse (C), Medium (M) and fine (F). This term may also refer to any type of powdered glass.

FUSED Another word for melted.

FUSED SILICA Another name for glass which is essentially silicon dioxide (no fluxes present).

GLASS KNIFE A cutting tool which utilizes tungsten carbide or another similar alloy to make a narrow scratch on glass tubing or rod in order to break it.

GLASS A glass is any of a wide range of liquids in which the rigidity is great enough so as to permit it to be put to certain useful purposes. It is often described as a "super cooled liquid" which has no definite melting point but instead has a softening range.

GLASSBLOWING LATHE A larger piece of equipment used to aid in the constant rotation of the pieces of glass being worked.

GLASS COMPONENTS Any of a wide range of commercially available connectors, standard taper joints or stopcocks.

GLADED SEAL A special piece of glass enabling one to join two glasses having different coefficients of expansion (e.g. borosilicate to quartz).

GRAPHITE A form of carbon which is used widely in various glassblowing tools used for shaping. Plates of graphite are also extremely useful for techniques such as making marias which require a flat inert surface on the benchtop.

HARD GLASS A general term used for any brand of borosilicate or quartz glass.

HOT GLASS PROCESS Another more popular name for offhand glassblowing.

INDEX OF REFRACTION A measure of the degree to which light is bent by a particular type of glass. Each type of glass has its own characteristic index of refraction value (n_D).

INSERTION SEAL A type of through-seal made when a single piece of glass is passed through a hole in a round bottom end and is sealed to it.

INSIDE SEAL A ring seal made between an inner tube and the walls of a larger diameter outer tube.

KIMAX® GLASS A registered trade name for the borosilicate glass produced by Kimble Kontes Glass Company.

LAPPING WHEEL A larger piece of equipment with a rotating wheel used to create flat surfaces on glass.

LAMP ROOM The laboratory or studio where lampworking (flameworking or glassblowing) is done.

LAMPWORKING Glassworking using a torch to convert rod or tubing into artistic or scientific glassware.

LEAD GLASS A type of soft glass in which lead oxide is used in place of much of the soda as a flux. Lead glass bends light more strongly than most other glasses and is used extensively in making crystal glassware. It is also widely used in making neon signs because its coefficient of expansion is very close to that of the metal wires used.

LEHR Another name for annealing oven.

LIME GLASS A common name for soft glass.

LIME Another name for calcium oxide, a commonly used flux in soft glasses.

MARIA A flattened region of tubing or rod which is perpendicular to the axis of the tubing or rod. These may be end marias or intermediate marias.

MARVER In lampworking this term refers to a special paddle consisting of a handle attached to a graphite plate. In offhand glassblowing it refers to the iron table on which the molten glass is rolled into a cylindrical mass.

OFFHAND GLASSBLOWING Freehand glassblowing, starting with a mass of molten glass and without the use of molds.

POINT The drawn area on one side of a piece of tubing or rod which is often used as a handle. In this book, when a capital P is used to start the word, it will refer to the total piece consisting of a length of tubing or rod with drawn areas (points) on both sides.

POLARISCOPE Consists of a light source and two perpendicular Polaroid sheets. It is an instrument used to detect areas of stress in glassware.

POLICEMAN A short piece of tubing which is pinched shut or sealed with a cork. These are used to close off a tubing end during a glassblowing operation

POTASH A common name for potassium oxide, a commonly used flux.

PYREX® GLASS A registered trade name used for the borosilicate glass produced by the Corning Glass Company.

QUARTZ GLASS A form of silicon dioxide which may be fused to produce a very high quality, chemically inert glass, requiring very high temperatures to work.

REGULATOR A control attached to a gas or oxygen tank to reduce the pressure and to keep it constant.

RING SEAL A seal made when a piece of tubing is inserted into a larger diameter tube and sealed onto a round bottom end.

SIDE SEAL A seal made when a piece of tubing passes through a side wall rather than through a rounded end.

SIMAX® GLASS A new borosilicate glass produced by Kavalier Glassworks of the Czech Republic. It is specially designed to resist high strains in products demanding high chemical and thermal endurance.

SODA GLASS Another common name for soft glass which utilizes sodium oxide (soda) as the major flux.

SODA A common name for any of a number of sodium compounds, although it usually refers to either sodium oxide or sodium carbonate. It is a widely used flux in many types of glasses.

SOFT GLASS The most common types of glasses which utilize large amounts of lime, potash, and soda as fluxes. These glasses are more soluble and less resistant to weathering and chemical action. They usually have high coefficients of expansion.

SOFTENING POINT The temperature at which glass will change shape under its own weight. It is often called collapsing temperature.

STRAIN POINT The temperature at which the glass will anneal in 16 hours. Glass can be cooled quickly from this temperature without any damage.

STRESSES Irregularities in the structure of the glass caused by uneven or rapid cooling. These conditions of tension and compression can be detected with a polariscope and are removed by annealing.

STRIKING Heating certain colored borosilcate glasses (e.g. Northstar) to the glass annealing temperature (about 1050°F or 560°C), where it changes or "strikes" to its new color. When heated to hotter temperatures (above the working temperature), the glass returns the glass to its original un-struck color.

SURFACE TENSION A natural force which acts to reduce the total surface area of a liquid to a minimum, which is ideally a spherical shape.

T-SEAL Any joints made between the end of one piece of tubing and the side of another, usually, but not necessarily, resulting in a T shape.

TEST TUBE END A rounded end closure on a piece of glass tubing.

THERMAL STRESS A sudden cooling or heating which may produce cracks in glass.

TORCH These are sources of heat which can be used in the hand or for stationary use at the bench or lathe. The glass being worked is moved into and around the flame. Flame size is determined by valves that adjust the flow and mix of fuel gas and oxygen.

TUNGSTEN CARBIDE KNIFE A hand tool used to create a scratch on glass surfaces before making a "cut" (a break).

TUNGSTEN PICK A hand held tool used to help in the mending of small holes and cracks in glass.

VERMICULITE A form of expanded mica, often used to insulate completed pieces of hot glass, allowing slower cooling thereby preventing possible cracking of the finished piece. The cooled items are then oven annealed.

VISCOSITY A measure of fluidity or ease of flow of a substance.

VYCOR® GLASS A registered Corning trade name for a glass which is 96% silicon dioxide (silica) having a very low coefficient of expansion, extremely high softening point, and great chemical resistance. It is made by placing borosilicate glass in acid to remove all the sodium and boron oxides. The glass is then refired.

WORKING POINT The average temperature at which normal seals are made.

WORKING ROD The rod which is softened in order to furnish the glass to make up a glass lace or another shape upon the base rod.

WORKING TIME A relative measure of the amount of time that glass remains workable. This depends on the type of glass, as well as the temperature and thickness of the glass.

It should be noted that a rather interesting "Illustrated Glass Dictionary," hosted by the international organization GlassOnline, is currently available on the web.[1]

1. See http://www.glassonline.com/dictionary/index.html

Appendix C
STANDARD TAPER JOINTS

In scientific work, there is often great advantage in using ground or "standard" joints.These enable the worker to assemble glassware quickly, easily, and without the use of troublesome corks or rubber stoppers. Most ground joints are now interchangeable so that various pieces of apparatus may be substituted whenever desired. Ground glass kits are now used widely even in beginning organic chemistry laboratories. The convenience and safety afforded is more than offset by their relatively high cost.

No one is really certain as to when the first ground glass joints were used, but references are made to such joints in the literature as early as 1648. In 1929, the United States National Bureau of Standards helped to establish specifications and standards so that various pieces from different manufacturers would be compatible and interchangeable. All joints and stopcocks that are made according to these specifications are marked accordingly.

The most common type of standard ground joint is the "standard taper" joint. These joints are marked with the symbol $\overline{\mathrm{\$}}$, a combination of capital S (for standard) and capital T (for taper). These have a 1:10 taper (taper of 1 mm plus or minus 0.006 mm for each centimeter in length). These joints come in three general types of lengths: "Full length" (Figure C.1) are used widely in glassware and also in vacuum applications. "Medium length" (Figure C.2) are used in many types of glassware, especially smaller sizes. "Short length" joints are rarely used. Each type comes in a extensive range of sizes. Sizes are designated by numbers which indicate the diameter of the large

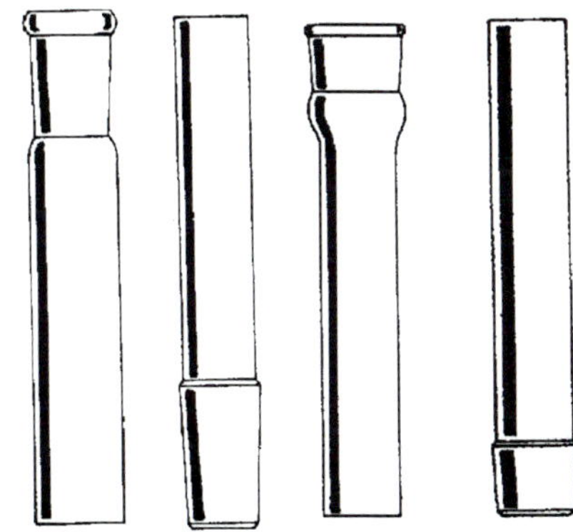

Figure C.1 *Commercial outer and inner full length standard taper joints.*

Figure C.2 *Commercial outer and inner medium length standard taper joints.*

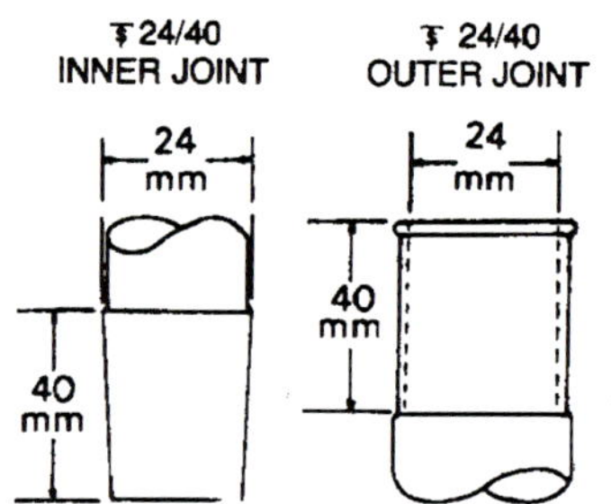

Figure C.3 (above)
Measurements of ₮ 24/40 inner (left) and outer joints (right).
Used with permission by Kimble Kontes.

Full Length ₮	Medium Length ₮
10/30	10/18
12/30	
14/35	**14/20**
19/38	**19/22**
24/40	24/25
29/42	
34/45	
45/50	

Figure C.4 (right)
Table listing important full and medium length joints. The most common sizes are shown in bold numbers.

end (in millimeters) and the length of the ground section (also in millimeters). Thus ₮ 24/40 indicates a ground section of 24 mm in diameter at the large end, and 40 mm in length. The two parts of the joints are designated inner and outer although the older terms male and female are still used by some. Standard taper joints are greased lightly with specially prepared stopcock greases. This not only insures a good seal, but also prevents the joints from freezing (sticking together). In situations where grease cannot be used, commercially produced teflon sleeves can be fitted over the inner joint. These are favored where a system needs to be absolutely inert, but care must be taken to prevent the sleeves from becoming scratched or heated too strongly. The most common sizes of standard taper joints are given in Figure C.4. Of these, the four most widely used sizes noted in bold should be memorized by all students of scientific glassblowing.

Extremely high precision, finely ground joints are also available. These are shiny in appearance and can be used without any grease or teflon sleeves. Unfortunately, they are more expensive and scratch easily.

A second important type of standard joint utilizes a semi-ball ground surface (Figure C.5). These are often called ball and socket joints and are designated by the symbol § which is a combination of capital S (for spherical) and capital J (for joint). The size of these joints is also specified. The first number indicates the diameter of the ball (in millimeters) and the second indicates the approximate inside diameter of the tubing. Thus, § 12/5 has a ball 12 mm in diameter and is made of 5 mm inside

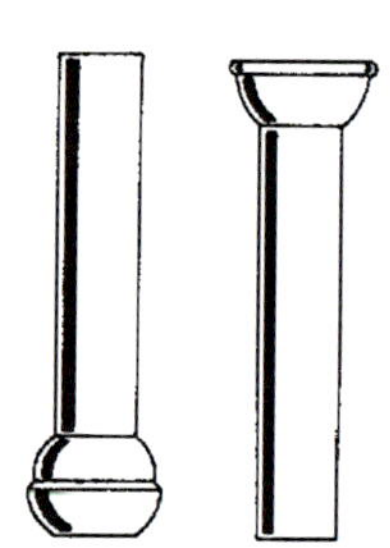

Figure C.5
Commercial outer and inner medium length standard taper joints.

diameter tubing (Figure C.6). Ball and socket joints are often used where the linear rigidity of standard taper joints is either not needed or not desired. They are used widely in the construction of glass vacuum line systems. A spring pinch clamp is usually used to secure the two parts together. The most common sizes of ball and socket joints are 12/5, 18/9, 28/15, and 35/25 with the two smaller sizes being the most common.

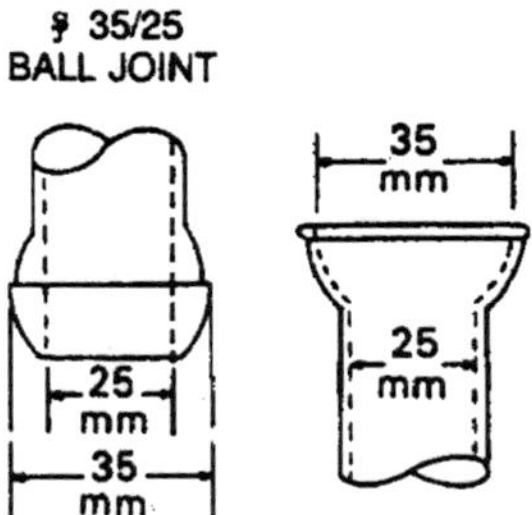

Figure C.6 *Measurements of* § *35/25 inner (left) and outer joints (right).* With permission of Kimble

A third common type of joint is the o-ring joint (Figure C-7). These are not actually ground joints, but instead precision-tooled connections which hold a rubber-type o-ring between the two pieces of glass by means of a regular ball and socket joint clamp. These give greaseless, vacuum tight connections which can be quickly assembled or dismantled. The sizes are indicated by the approximate inside diameter of the tubing. These may range anywhere from 5 to 75 mm. The "o" rings may be constructed of a number of types of rubber, the most common being Buna-N, silicone or Viton.

Another important type of joint technology is the threaded connector which provides greaseless. clampless, yet vacuum tight seals by use of a nylon or teflon bushing compressing against an "O" ring positioned on an inner tube (Figure C.8). These allow the a tube to be inserted through the joint. They can be incorporated into all types of laboratory glassware and are made by a number of different manufacturers. Some versions also incorporate a standard taper so that either type of joint can be utilized.

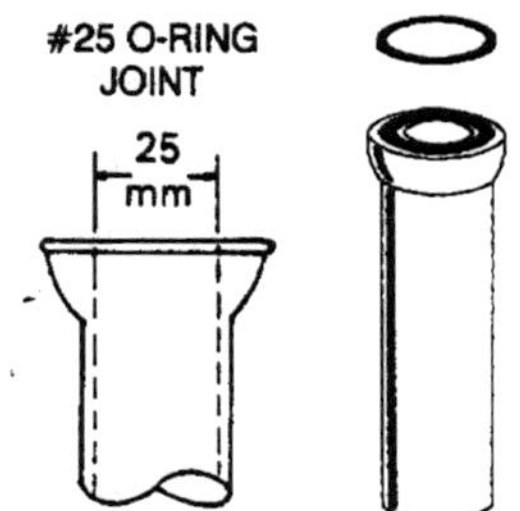

Figure C.7 *O-ring joints.*

Standard joints can be purchased from a number of different manufacturers and are extremely useful in constructing laboratory glassware. Prices of the joints depends greatly on the size, but at this time range from about $8 for the smaller sizes to $35 or more for the larger sizes. Usually the joints are constructed from heavy-walled tubing, and approximately five inches of this tubing is left attached to the joints when purchased. This piece of glass may either be cut off, or it can be incorporated into the apparatus being constructed. The usual inside and outside diameters of the tubing usually used on such joints are given in Figure C.9. Knowing these sizes will help in the planning of the construction of any scientific apparatus, as it will allow you to know what size tubing to use or what size hole needs to be made to incorporate the joint.

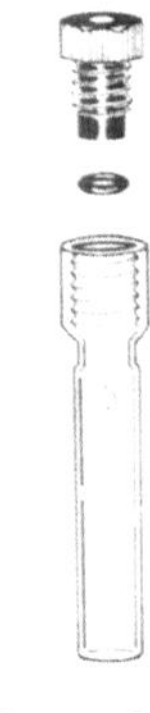

Figure C.8 *Threaded o-ring connectors*

Joint Type and Size	Tubing O.D. at Inner End	Tubing O.D. at Outer End
₮ 10/30	8 mm	14 mm
₮ 12/30	10 mm	16 mm
₮ 14/35	12 mm	18 mm
₮ 14/20	12 mm	18 mm
₮ 19/38	17 mm	22 mm
₮ 19/22	17 mm	22 mm
₮ 24/40	21.5 mm	28.7 mm
§12/55	8 mm	8 mm
§18/9	12 mm	12 mm
§28/15	19 mm	19/19

Figure C.9 *Inside and outside diameters of the tubing usually incorporated at the ends of commercial standard joints.*

It should be pointed out that the joints used on bottles and funnels are also standard taper joints, but they differ in a number of respects. First of all they are shorter. Secondly, their taper is more severe. Thus, these stoppers do not fit properly in any of the tapered joints discussed.

Although stoppers are available to fit the tapered joints described, bottles usually use a different. The size of bottle stoppers is indicated by a number on the stopper which is the same as the diameter of the largest part of the taper (Figure C.9). Bottle stoppers may be "flat head" or "penny head", and sizes may range from size 8 to size 38.

Although at the present time most scientists in most countries use the joints described above, it should be pointed out that a somewhat different international system of ground joints has been considered.[1] The new system, ISO k6, uses a consistently shorter joint for the standard. For example, 14/35 would become 14/23, 19/38 would become 19/26, and 24/40 would become 24/29. Similar shorter sizes are already in wider use outside of the United States.

Figure C.10 *A #19 (₮ 19) flat head stopper.*

The line drawing illustrations in this appendix are reproduced with the permission of the following companies:

ChemGlass Company
Kontes Kimble
Ace Glass Incorporated

1. "U.S. Industry Considering Ground Joint Standards", *Fusion*, Feb., 1978, pp 21-25.

Appendix D
COMMERCIAL STOPCOCKS

There are a number of different kinds of stopcocks commercially available. The most commonly used type is a general purpose stopcock which has a solid, interchangeable plug. Of this type, the most familiar is the all glass variety. These are recommended for the majority of laboratory applications (Figure D.1). The qualities of these are now such that they may be used even at pressures as low as 10 to 4 Torr when correctly greased. These come in a variety of sizes and in a number of different bores and shapes. Generally they have standard tapers and a single number is used to indicate the approximate diameter in millimeters of the hole or holes through the plug, not the size of the stopcock. Of course, the stopcock and tubing sizes increase proportionately as does the bore diameter. Stopcock sizes may range from #1 to #6, with #2 and #4 being the most common. Two-way stopcocks of this type normally have a straight bore and therefore linear arms. Three-way stopcocks may have the arms in a "T" shape (90° angle), or in a "Y" shape (120° angle), or such that two arms are parallel on one side and one arm opposite. Prices may range from about $30 for small two-way stopcocks to over $100 for the larger three-way sizes. Special stopcocks utilizing capillary tubing are also available.

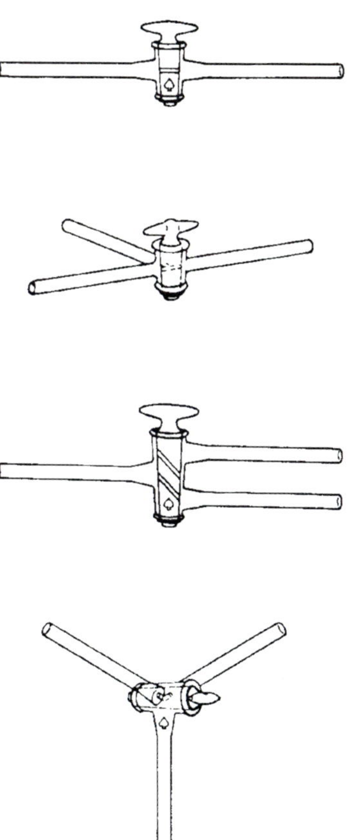

Figure D.1
Various solid plug stopcocks.

A second type of general purpose stopcock (i.e. with solid stopper) uses a glass body and a teflon plug (Figure D.2). These stopcocks are marked with a symbol which is a combination of P and S, which denotes "Product Standard". Teflon (PTFE or polytetrafluoroethylene) stoppers do not require any lubrication, thus removing a source of contamination in many scientific applications. The threads on the end of the stopcock allow easy adjustment to provide an airtight fit and to prevent leakage. Another advantage is that these do not "freeze", due to the chemical inertness of teflon. This fact is especially valuable when using alkaline solutions. These have a very different taper (1:5) than do the all-glass variety and have a smooth finish on the glass portion. The size range is the same as that for the all-glass variety, as is the selection of shapes. Prices generally are at least 50% higher than for the all-glass stopcocks. Caution should be taken to keep the teflon stopcocks away from sources of heat, and they should never be placed in drying ovens.

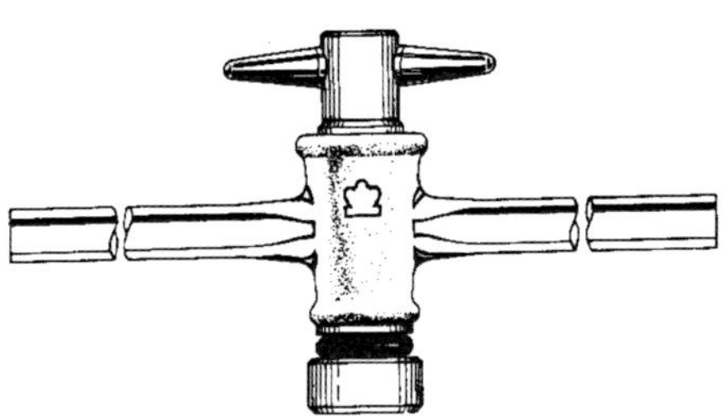

Figure D.2 *Straight teflon stopcock.*

The third kind of stopcocks generally available are the high vacuum, all glass stopcocks (Figure D.3 - D.6). These have hollow-blown, standard taper glass plugs which are individually fitted to the outer shells, thus insuring complete uniformity between the two surfaces. Both stopcock plugs and body are numbered in order to prevent inadvertent interchange of plugs. In most cases, a vacuum cup below the base of the plug allows the stopcock to be evacuated so as to insure an extremely tight fit at all times. Such stoppers are designed for all high vacuum work. The sizes of these stoppers reflect the size of the bore and are specified by a single number. Sizes may range from #2 to #15. Two-way high vacuum stopcocks may be purchased in a number of shapes. The most common are oblique bore (arms straight across from one another), offset bore (lower arm connected to vacuum source, but parallel) and 90° (lower arm connected to vacuum source, but at right angles) Prices at this time range from about $75 to over $200 each.

The fourth kind of stopcock is the o-ring high vacuum valve, sometimes referred to as needle valve type. These utilize a thread mechanism with a TFE

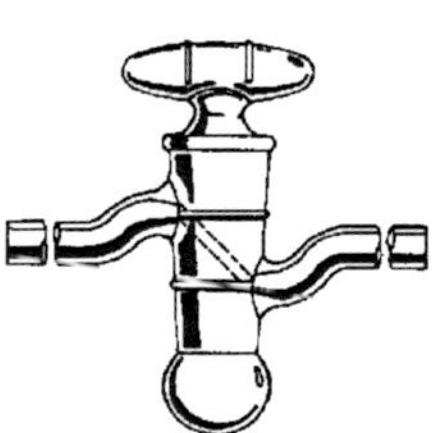

Figure D.3 *Vacuum stopcock, hollow plug, oblique.*

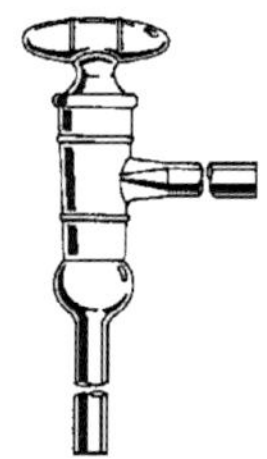

Figure D.4 *Vacuum stopcock, hollow plug, right angle.*

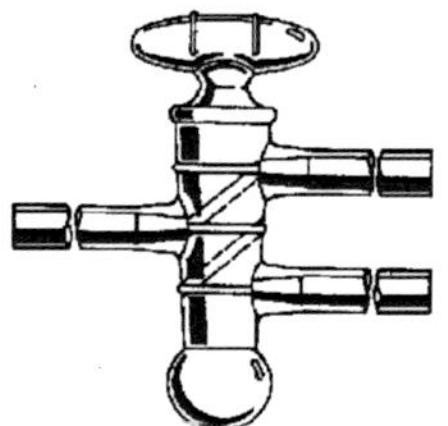

Figure D.5 *Vacuum stopcock, hollow plug, double oblique.*

(teflon®) o-ring tip (Figure D.6). The thread mechanism is also sealed with TFE o-rings. When closed, the teflon tip is firmly positioned onto a precision glass seat, making these stopcocks well suited for high vacuum or positive pressure applications. Furthermore, they can be used at elevated temperatures. Since no lubrication is needed, they are particularly useful for cases where contamination by grease is undesirable. Sizes are usually specified by the range of bore sizes (in millimeters), with 0-2 being the smallest and 0-20 the largest. Such stopcocks are available a number of configurations including in-line, right angle, low hold-up, three-way and T-type. Prices are usually about half that of the all glass high vacuum stopcocks.

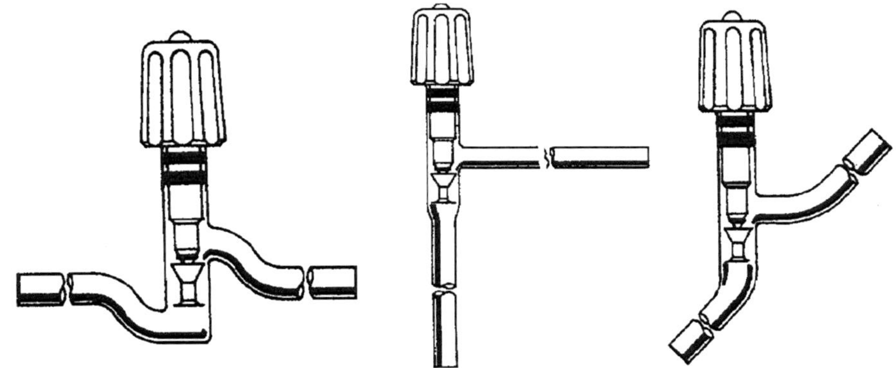

Figure D.6 *High vacuum stopcocks with TFE o-ring tip and barrel seals.* The Configurations *shown are in-line (left), right angle (middle), and low hold-up (right).*

The line drawing illustrations in this appendix are reproduced with the permission of the following companies:

ChemGlass Company
Kontes Kimble
Ace Glass Incorporated

Appendix E
SCIENTIFIC GLASSWARE 101

Scientific glassware comes in a wide range of different sizes and shapes. Some pieces are fundamental to all laboratory work while others may be so highly specialized so as to be of use to only a very few workers. In fact, the research chemist is often called upon to design and make new kinds of glass apparatus to satisfy his or her own research needs.

To some, this appendix may seem unnecessary, but it is included because many students of scientific glassblowing so far had only limited contact with the types of glassware used in an actual research lab. Thus, this is meant as a primer for these individuals. Even the seasoned student of chemistry may find a few pieces described that they had not seen before. As long as the chances are good some of the items included here may be given to the student to repair, it is wise that they also have some understanding of what the glassware is actually used for. This is not at all meant to be a comprehensive listing, but only an introduction to some of the more important types of laboratory glassware. Consult one or more of the glass catalogs provided by the manufacturers (e.g. Corning, Kimble Kontes, ChemGlass) for more complete listings. Such catalogs make great "supplementary textbooks" for any scientific glassblowing course.

In fact, hopefully this appendix may stimulate your imagination and lead you to design and make your own glassware as you need it.

Adapters, Gas Inlet (Hose Connecting) These are used whenever a rubber or plastic hose needs to be connected to a standard taper joint. Numerous varieties are possible. In some cases, stopcocks are included (Figures G.1 - G.5).

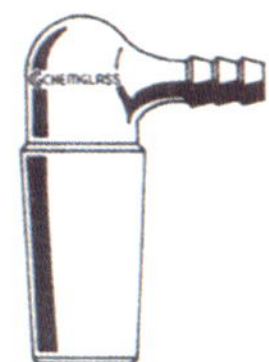

Figure G.1 *Gas inlet adapter with inner joint.*

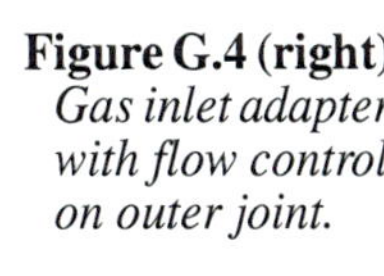

Figure G.2 (*left*) *Gas inlet adapter with inner joint.*
Figure G.3 (rt) *Same with outer joint.*

Figure G.4 (right) *Gas inlet adapter with flow control on outer joint.*

Figure G.5 (far right) *Gas inlet adapter with flow control on outer joint.*

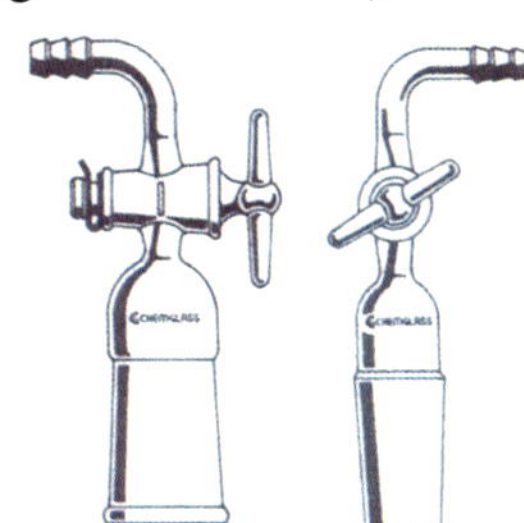

Adapters (Reducing or Enlarging) Adapters are used to change a given ground glass joint to a larger size or a smaller size or a different type of ground joint. Various types of adapters permit a wide variety of all glass assemblies for distillation, refluxing, and other processes utilizing the standard flasks and condensers usually available. Such adapters may vary greatly in length, and in some cases these are bent in order to permit special applications. Just a few representative examples are shown in Figures G.6 - G-11).

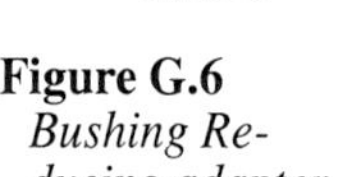

Figure G.6 *Bushing Reducing adapter.*

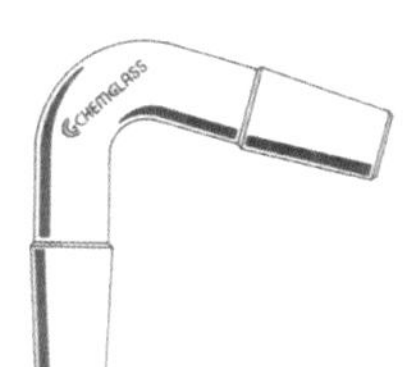

Figure G.7 *Bent adapter (inner - inner).*

Figure G.8 *Straight adapter (outer).*

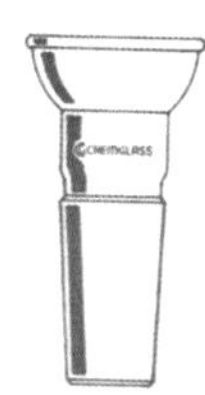

Figure G.9 *Outer ball joint (inner $\$$ joint).*

Figure G.10 *Offset reducing (outer - inner).*

Figure G.11 *Offset adapter (outer - inner).*

Addition Funnel (Pressure Equalizing) This funnel is especially useful for addition of material to a reactive mixture in a system where an inert atmosphere is provided (Figure G.12).

Chromatography Columns These are filled with solid packing material (e.g. alumina, silica, or various ion exchange resins) and used in column chromatography separations. Some columns include a stopcock (Figure G.13) while others may also have a fritted disk and standard taper joints (Figure G.14).

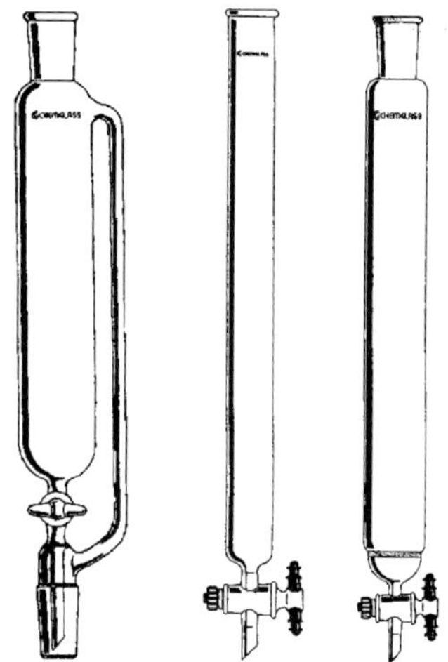

Figure G.12 *Pressure equalized addition funnel.*
Figure G.13 *Simple chromatography column.*
Figure G.14 *Chromatography column with glass frit.*

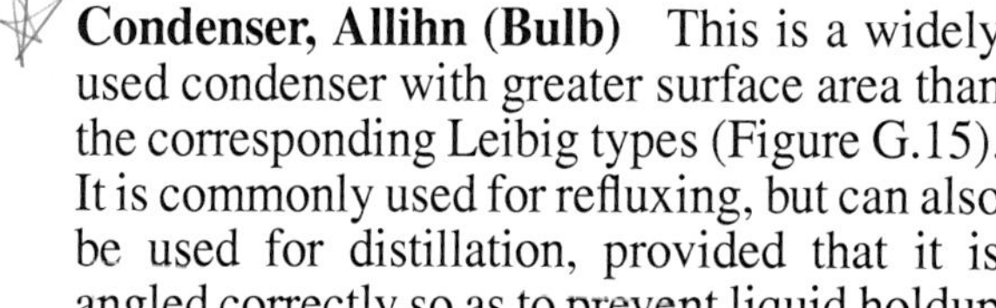

Condenser, Allihn (Bulb) This is a widely used condenser with greater surface area than the corresponding Leibig types (Figure G.15). It is commonly used for refluxing, but can also be used for distillation, provided that it is angled correctly so as to prevent liquid holdup in the bulbs.

Condenser, Coil (Reflux) A highly efficient condenser which at first appears to be similar to the Graham Condenser, but in the coil condenser, the coolant passes through the coil and the distillate goes through the jacket (Figure G-16).

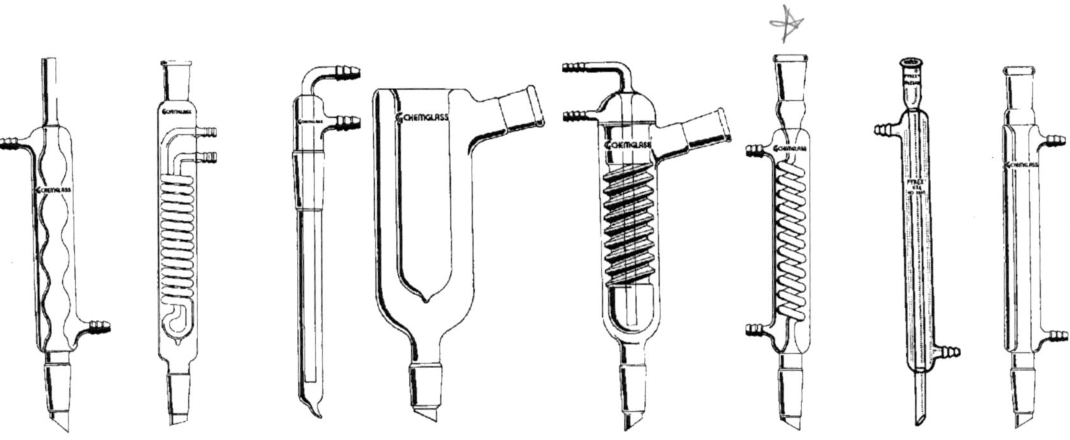

Figure G. 15 (left) *Allihn condenser.*
Figure G. 16 (right) *Coil condenser,*

Figure G. 17 (left) *Coldfinger Condenser.*
Figure G. 18 (right) *Dewar condenser.*

Figure G. 19 (left) *Friedrichs condenser.*
Figure G. 20 (right) *Graham condenser.*

Figure G. 21(left) *Liebig Condenser.*
Figure G. 22 (right) *West condenser.*

Condenser, Coldfinger A simple condenser of relatively low efficiency, often used to regulate refluxing by adjusting the flow of air or water through it (Figure G.17). It is often incorporated into larger distillation heads because of its great simplicity.

Condenser, Dewar These condensers have a large center opening at the top for solid coolants such as ice or dry ice (Figure G.18). These are used whenever very low temperatures are necessary to condensate liquids.

Condenser, Friedrichs This is a very efficient and widely used condenser in which the helical inner tube fits closely within the jacket (Figure G.19). The vapor tube is sealed to the jacket at an angle of about 75°.

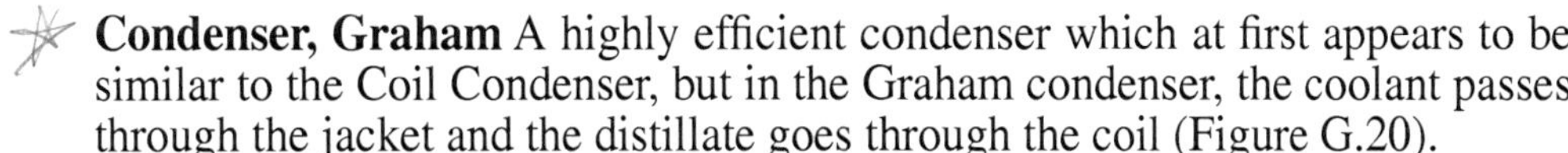

Condenser, Graham A highly efficient condenser which at first appears to be similar to the Coil Condenser, but in the Graham condenser, the coolant passes through the jacket and the distillate goes through the coil (Figure G.20).

Condenser, Liebig This is a general purpose condenser which can be used for distillation and extraction (Figure G.21). Although the condensing area per unit length of a jacket is low, the large capacity water jacket gives sufficient cooling. The ends may or may not contain standard ground joints.

Condenser, West This condenser appears to be very much like the Liebig Condenser, except that the water jacket is smaller in diameter (Figure G.22). Commercially purchased condensers usually have a heavy-walled outer jacket to provide sturdiness, but the inner tube is made out of a thinner walled tubing for more efficient heat transfer.

Distillation Column, This is a plain distillation column which is used in fractional distillations. It has indentions at the bottom which support any added packing such as glass beads, glass helices, or stainless steel (Figure G.23). Packing is used to increase the efficiency of the column by increasing the number of "theoretical plates".

Distillation Column, Vacuum Jacketed This is similar to the distillation column described above, but it also has a vacuum jacket which serves to insulate the packing, keeping the distillate from condensing before reaching the condenser (Figure G.24).

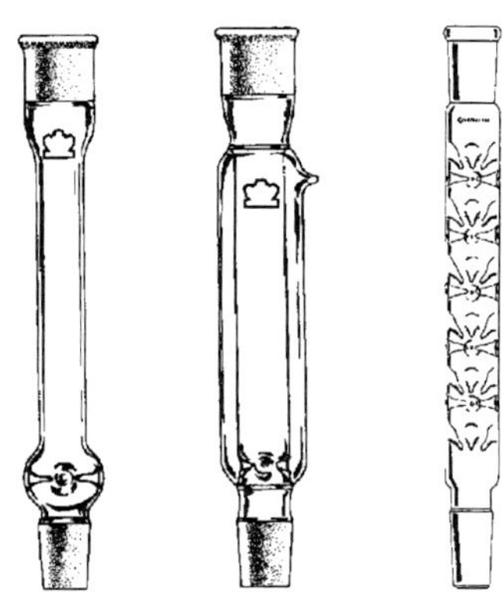

Figure G.23 (left)
Distillation column.
Figure G.24 (middle)
Vacuum jacket distillation column.
Figure G.25 (right)
Vigreaux distillation column.

Distillation Column, Vigreaux This column is probably the most widely used in fractional distillations. It incorporates a number of indentations into the column which serve as built-in packing (Figure G.25). The horizontal indentations insure close contact between the vapor and liquid, while the slanting indentations promote the redistribution of the liquid from the walls to the center of the column.

Distillation Heads There are many different types of distillation heads. These usually involve a standard taper joint for a thermometer (to measure the temperature of the vapor) and a condenser (Figures G.26 and G.27).

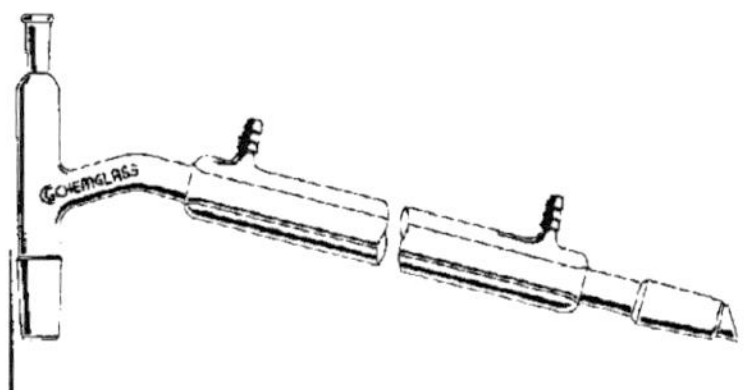

Figure G.26
Simple distillation head.

Distillation Head (Variable Reflux) One of the more important types of distillation heads includes a coldfinger condenser which can be rotated to permit regulation of the reflux-product ratio. Manipulation of the stopcock withdraws the condensate as product or returns it to the column as reflux. A joint is provided directly above the flask for a standard taper thermometer. The apparatus shown in Figure G.28 is equipped with two additional stopcocks, allowing the product

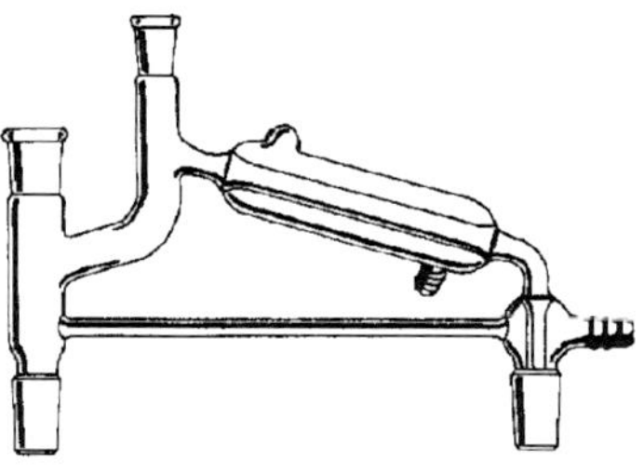

Figure G.27
Distillation head with standard taper joint above the flask joint, allowing liquids to be added.

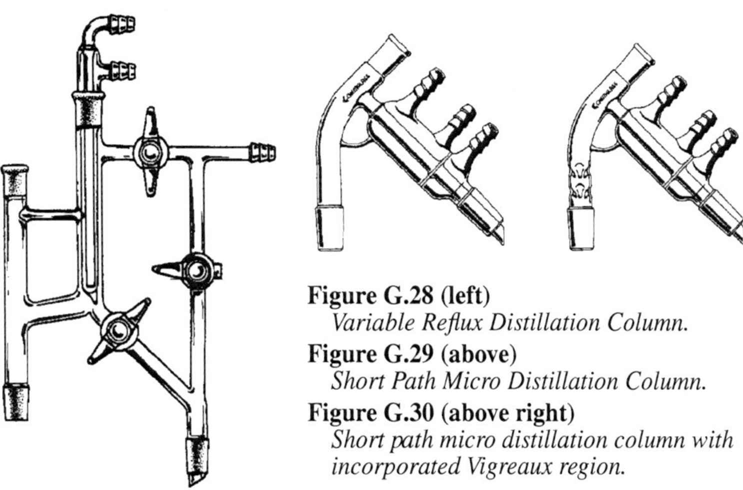

Figure G.28 (left)
Variable Reflux Distillation Column.
Figure G.29 (above)
Short Path Micro Distillation Column.
Figure G.30 (above right)
Short path micro distillation column with incorporated Vigreaux region.

to be removed in vacuum distillations without interrupting the distillation. Heads of this design may vary greatly in size and capacity.

Distillation Head, Short Path This head is designed for the distillation of very small amounts of liquid (Figure G.29). When a standard taper thermometer is inserted in the top of this apparatus, the bulb and stem serve as column packing. Closely coupled condenser inlet, outlet and vacuum connections offer an extremely short condensate travel path. Some variations include additional theoretical plates by including a small Vigreaux region (Figure G-30). The side and bottom joints are usually no larger than $\mathrm{\$}$14/20.

Drying Apparatus, Abderhalden Solid materials can be conveniently dried in this apparatus at a constant temperature and under reduced pressure (Figure G.31). Desiccating material is placed behind the indentation of the desiccant chamber, which is designed to make it easy to add or remove this material. The temperature of the heating chamber is kept constant at the boiling point of the liquid which is refluxed in the flask. A wide range of temperatures is possible by using liquids of different boiling points. The upper tapered joint is offset so that condensing liquid does not drip over the tube. The opening to the inside chamber is an inner taper joint. This arrangement protects samples, boats, or tubes from coming in contact with the lubricant used on the joints. A stopcock is supplied on the vacuum connection tube.

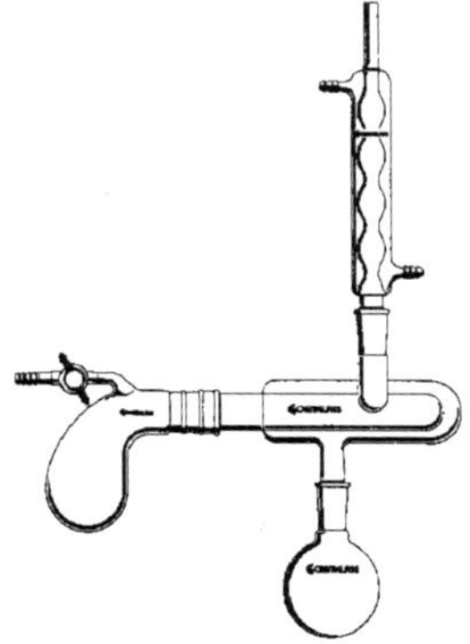

Figure G.31
Abderhalden drying apparatus (for solids).

Drying Tube (Calcium Chloride) A special tube which has a single bulb desiccant chamber. These may be straight or bent and may be fitted with a standard taper joint.

Evaporative Concentrator (Kuderna-Danish) This apparatus is used for the concentration of materials dissolved in volatile solvents (Figure G.32). It has found wide applications in the field of pesticide analysis. The flask is charged with material to be concentrated (to about 50% of the flask capacity). The assembly is set over a vigorously boiling water bath, allowing the volatiles to evolve and escape while the heavier fractions reflux until the final concentrate is collected in the lower tube. The Snyder Fractionalizing column utilizes floating ball valves for improved vapor-liquid contact and prevents the less volatile components from escaping.

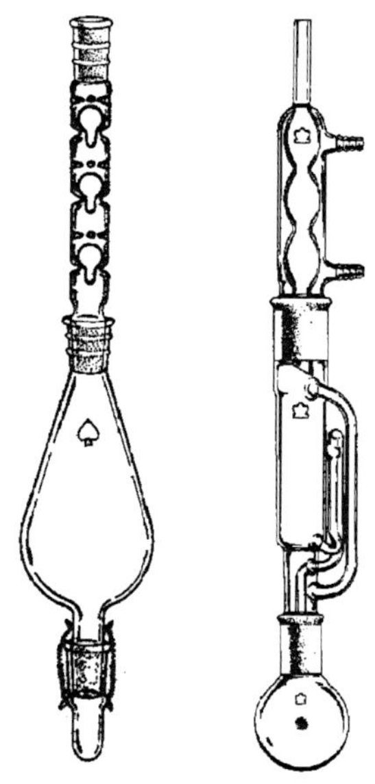

Figure G.32 (left) *Kuderna-Danish concentrator.*
Figure G.33 (right) *Soxhlet extraction apparatus.*

Extraction Apparatus (Soxhlet) This an apparatus used for the extraction of soluble components or impurities from solids by a continuous process of soaking the solid with a solvent and then siphoning (Figure G.33). The solid to be extracted is held in a paper extraction thimble. Various sizes are available to meet the scale of work being carried out.

Figure G.34 *Boiling (round bottom) flask.*

Flasks, Boiling These are single necked, round bottom flasks which usually have an "outer" standard taper joint which allows for quick and easy connection to condensers and other apparatus. In some cases the flasks may utilize a socket joint which makes the flask particularly useful wherever added flexibility is required. These flasks come in sizes which range from the extremely large (7 liters or more) to the very small (5 mL or less). Of course, the standard taper size is proportional to the size of the flask, with the smaller ones having ₸14/20 and the larger ones usually ₸55/50 joints. Sometimes, side tubulation is added to allow a thermometer to be inserted into the flask using a rubber thermometer holder.

Flasks, Distilling These older style flasks are suitable for most simple distillations. The necks may terminate in standard taper joints or in straight tubing to accept rubber stoppers or corks. The side arm is normally about 77mm below the top of the neck at an angle of 75°. The side arm is usually attached to a condenser. A double neck type flask (Claisen head) may be used whenever additional attachments are necessary.

Flasks, Multiple Neck Multiple neck flasks are used for general laboratory work and especially for many organic reactions. Standard taper joints or ground socket joints again allow quick and easy connection to condensers, stirring devices, and other apparatus. Anywhere from two to four necks are possible (Figures G.35 - G.37). These may be vertical (i.e. parallel to one another) or may be at an angle to one another. The angled necks are particularly suited for situations where bulky items need to be attached. The center neck of the flask is usually the one of greatest diameter. Although most of these flasks are round bottom, some are pear shaped (Figures G.38 - G.39). These are useful for reactions requiring only small volumes. The size of all these flasks ranges from the extremely large (7 liters or more) to the very small (5 mL or less). Of course, the standard taper size is proportional to the size of the flask, with the middle (or top) joint usually being larger than the side joints.

Figure G.35
Two neck round bottom reaction flask.

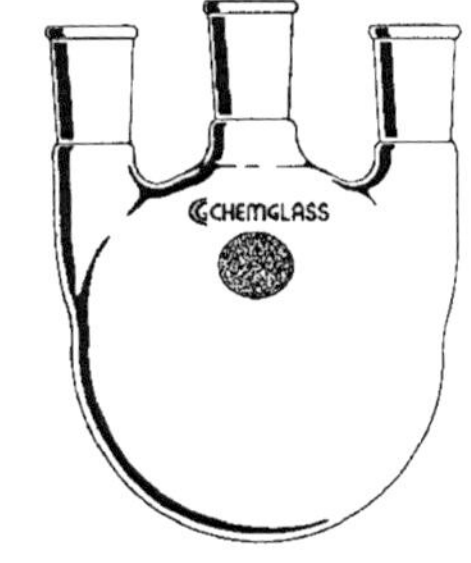

Figure G.36
Three neck round bottom reaction flask (vertical).

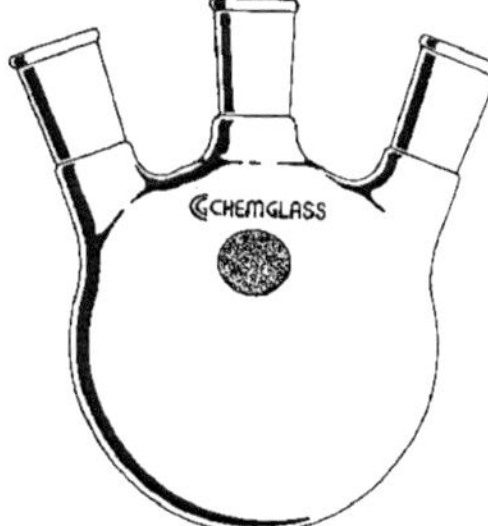

Figure G.37
Three neck round bottom reaction flask (angled).

Figure G.38
Two neck pear shaped reaction flask.

Figure G.39
Three neck pear shaped reaction flask.

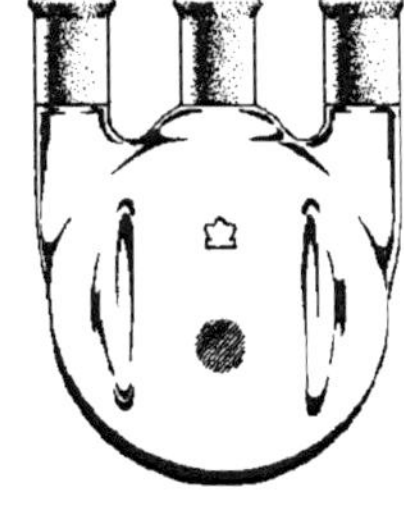

Figure G.40
Three neck morton reaction flask (with indentions).

Flasks, Morton This is a regular round bottom boiling flask with a number of indentations. The indentations serve to increase agitation when stirring. Normally these are three necked flasks (Figure G.40).

Gas Washing Bottle This type of apparatus provides an effective method of washing and drying gases. The gas enters the bottle through the center vertical tube, the lower end of which is below the surface of the washing medium. After passing through the medium, the gas rises and is removed via the side arm of the bottle stopper. Various types of distributors may be used to disperse the gas bubbles for efficient absorption. In many cases a fritted disk or cylinder is used for this purpose.

Glassblowing Blanks These "blanks" usually include apparatus parts which would be difficult or expensive to produce in a normal glassblowing lab. They are then used by the glassblower to construct more complex or unusual glassware which is not normally commercially available. These include fritted tubes (Figure G.41), flask bottoms (Figures G.42 - G.43), or condenser parts (Figure G.44 - G.46).

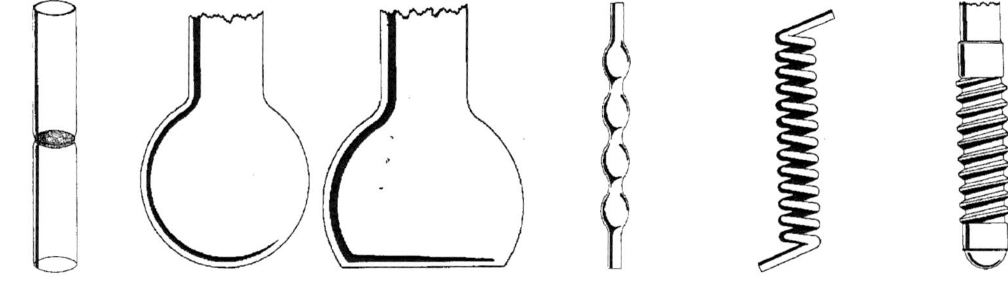

Figure G.41 *Fritted tube.*

Figure G.42 *Boiling flask blank.*

Figure G.43 *Flat bottom flask blank.*

Figure G.44 *Allihn condenser blank*

Figure G.45 *Coil condenser blank*

Figure G.46 *Friedrich condenser blank.*

Lyophilizing Drying Apparatus This is a freeze drying apparatus with three sample flasks attached to a central condensing chamber which has a vacuum connection at the top and a center well for dry ice. A central flask is located at the bottom to collect the distillate.

Sublimation Apparatus This apparatus can be used for atmospheric or reduced pressure sublimation purifications of volatile solids. The substance to be purified is placed into the flask and heated under vacuum. The sublimate is collected on a colder upper region of the apparatus (Figures G.47 - G.49). In most cases this is a flat bottom, cold finger type condenser. Some designs collect the purified crystals on a large cylindrical condenser surface of this apparatus.

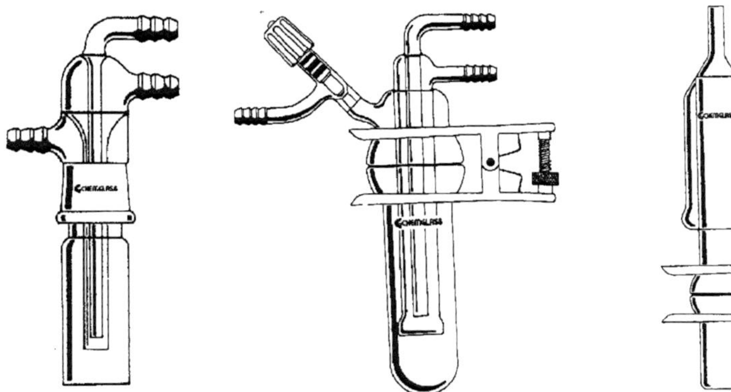

Figure G.47
Micro sublimation apparatus.

Figure G.48
High vacuum o-ring sublimation apparatus.

Figure G.49
Micro o-ring sublimation apparatus.

In these, a lubricant-free o-ring connector enables the two glass parts to be gently separated for maximum product recovery. When inverted, the vacuum connector at the condenser top serves as a convenient funnel for product removal (Figure G.49).

.

Trap, Dean Stark (Barrett Receiver) A Dean Stark Trap is a special type of distillation receiver used to remove water from a refluxing reaction system while the lighter organic solvent is either returned to the reaction or removed in a separate flask. These are normally used in organic reactions where water is produced as one of the products. Removal of the water makes the reaction more complete and also allows one to determine the extent of the reaction at any time

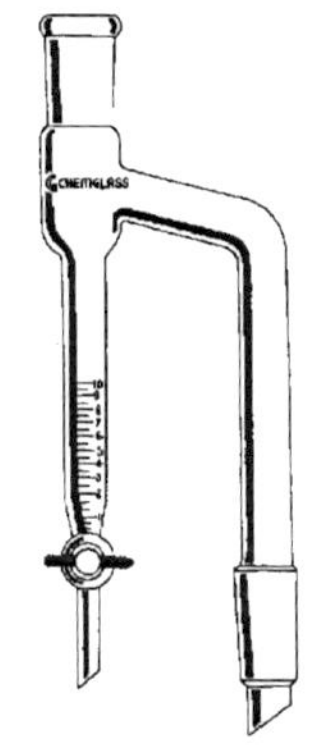

Figure G.50
Dean Stark trap.

Vacuum Traps When immersed in a cold bath, these are used to trap out condensable liquids from a flow of gas. These traps may be either one piece in construction or separable for easy removal of the condensed liquid from the trap.

The line drawing illustrations in this appendix are reproduced with the permission of the following companies:

ChemGlass Company
Kontes Kimble
Ace Glass Incorporated

Appendix F
GLASSBLOWING REFERENCES

FLAMEWORKING REFERENCES

BOOKS

1. B. S. Dunham, *Contemporary Lampworking Vol. I & II*, Third Edition, Salusa Glassworks, 2002.
2. R. Barbour, *Glassblowing for Laboratory Technicians*, Second Edition, Pergamon Press, London, 1978.
3. J. Burton, *Glass: Philosophy and Method*, Bonanza Books New York, 1967.
4. M. Hart, *Manual of Scientific Glassblowing, British Society of Scientific Glassblowers*, St. Helens, Merseyside, England, 1992.
5. L. M. Garr & C.A. Hendley, *Laboratory Glassblowing*, Chemical Publishing Co., New York, 1957.
6. J. E. Hammesfahr & C.L. Stong, *Creative Glassblowing*, W.H. Freeman & Co., San Francisco, 1968.
7. P. N. Hasluck, *Traditional Glassblowing Techniques*, Dover Publishing, New York, 1988.
8. H. L. Hoyt, *Glassblowing: An Introduction to Solid and Blown Glass Sculpturing*, Crafts & Arts Publishing, Golden, CO, 1989.
9. E. Mears, *Flameworking: Creating Glass Beads, Sculptures and Functional Objects*, Lark Books, Asheville, NC, 2003.
10. A. J. B. Robertson, *Laboratory Glass-working for Scientists*, Academic Press, New York, 1957.
11. F. Schuler, *Flameworking: Glassmaking for the Craftsman*, Chilton Book Co., Philadelphia, 1968.

12. E. L. Wheeler, *Scientific Glassblowing*, Interscience Publishers, New York, 1958.

13. R. E. Wright, *Manual of Laboratory Glass-blowing*, Chemical Publishing Co., New York, 1943.

PAMPHLETS

1. *Glassblowing on the Glass Lathe: A Manual of Basic Techniques*, Bethlehem Apparatus Co., Hellertown, PA, 1956.

2. *Laboratory Glass Blowing With Corning's Glasses*, Corning Glass Works, Bulletin B-72, 1967.

3. *Manual of Simplified Glassblowing*, Bethlehem Apparatus Co., Hellertown, PA.

PORTIONS FROM BOOKS

1. G. J. Shugar & L. Bauman, "Techniques of Glassblowing" *Chemical Technicians' Ready Reference Handbook*, Second Edition, McGraw-Hill, New York, 1983, pp.823-852.

JOURNALS

1. *Fusion*, Journal of the American Scientific Glassblowers' Society, P. O. Box 778, Madison, NC 27025. (Web page: http://www.asgs-glass.org)

SELECTED JOURNAL ARTICLES

1. D. Briening, "Artistic Glassblowing at Salem Community College", *Proceedings of the 33rd Symposium on the Art of Scientific Glassblowing, American Scientific Glassblowers Society,* 1988, pp. 48-50.

2. F. Birkhill, "Ancient to Modern Bead Making Techniques," *proceedings of the 37th Symposium on the Art of Scientific Glassblowing, American Scientific Glassblowers Society,* 1992, pp. 8-11.

3. E. Carberry, "The Introductory Scientific Glassblowing Course At Southwest State University", *Proceedings of the 34th Symposium on the Art of Scientific Glassblowing, American Scientific Glassblowers Society,* 1989, pp. 36-43.

4. R. Keller et al., "Lampworking with Glass", *Fusion*, February, 1977, pp. 9-16.

5. J. S. Korfhage, "A Guide to Safe Handling and Design of Scientific Glassware", *Proceedings of the 35th Symposium on the Art of Scientific Glassblowing, American Scientific Glassblowers Society,* 1990, pp. 33-38.

6. G. E. Myers, "Optical Hazards in Glassblowing", *Fusion*, August, 1976, pp. 9-19.

7. G. E. Meyers and J.S. Gregar, Health Hazards in the Glass Shop, *Proceedings of the 35th Symposium on the Art of Scientific Glassblowing, American Scientific Glassblowers Society,* 1990, pp. 19-23.

8. R. J. Ponton, "A Glassblower's View of the Soviet Union", *Proceedings of the 36th Symposium on the Art of Scientific Glassblowing, American Scientific Glassblowers Society,* 1991 pp. 1-2.

9. R. C. Smith, "An Interim Scientific Glassblowing for Chemistry Students", *Proceedings of the 38th Symposium on the Art of Scientific Glassblowing, American Scientific Glassblowers Society,* 1993, pp. 72-79.

10. J. Tassin, "Effectiveness of Eye Glass to Remove Damaging Radiation From Gas Flames", *Proceedings of the 26th Symposium on the Art of Scientific Glassblowing, American Scientific Glassblowers Society,* 1991, pp. 36-43.

11. L. Williams, "The History and Technology of Novelty Lampworking-Part I", *Fusion*, August, 1969, pp. 37-38.

12. L. Williams, "The History and Technology of Novelty Lampworking Part II", *Fusion*, November, 1969, pp. 25-26.

13. L. Williams, "The History and Technology of Novelty Lampworking: Part III", *Fusion*, February, 1970, pp. 23-24.

14. L. Williams, "The History and Technology of Novelty Lampworking: Part IV", *Fusion*, May, 1970, pp. 18-19.

REFERENCES TO OTHER RELATED AREAS

BOOKS

1. R. J. Charleston, *Masterpieces of Glass: A World History From the Corning Museum of Glass*, H. N. Abrams, Inc., 1980. (Picture history of glass)

2. B. S. Dunham, *Contemporary Lampworking Vol. I & II*, Third Edition, Salusa Glassworks, 2002. (Good introduction to all facets of flameworking)

3. H. K. Littleton, *Glassblowing- A Search for Form, Van* Nostrand Reinhold Co., New York, 1972. (Off-hand method)

4. P. N. Haasluck, *Traditional Glassworking Techniques*, Dover Publishing, New York, 1988. (Off-hand method)

5. F A. Macfarland and G. Martin, *Glass: A World History*, University of Chicago Press, Chicago, 2002. (History of glass and glassblowing)

6. T. Rothenberg, *The Complete Book of Creative Glass Art*, Crown Publishers, New York, 1974. (Off-hand method)

7. F. Schuler & L. Schuler, *Glassforming: Glassmaking for the Craftsman*, Chilton Book Co., Philadelphia,1970. (Glass-forming methods: sagging, laminating, enameling, fusing, and casting)

8. C. Zerwick, *A Short History of Glass*, The Corning Museum of Glass, Corning, New York, 1990.

SELECTED JOURNAL ARTICLES

1. R. H. Charles, "The Nature of Glasses", *Scientific American*, September, 1967, pp. 69-84.

2. R. F. Jones, "The Prince Rupert Drop", *Chemistry*, December, 1976, pp. 21-22.

3. T.A. Michalske and B.C. Bunker, "The Fracturing of Glass", *Scientific American*, December, 1987, pp. 122-129.

Appendix G
LIST OF SUPPLIERS

This appendix catalogs the names of a number of retail companies which sell the various tools, equipment, and glass needed by flameworkers. This listing is not meant to be complete, but it should enable the interested worker to get started on his own. It has always been rather frustrating for the beginner to try to track down companies which handle the items that are needed. This section of the book was designed to cut down on these frustrations, at least to some degree.

The major glass manufacturers usually do not sell directly to individuals. In fact, even some retail dealers do not allow purchases from individuals not associated with a recognized company. The dealers listed below, however, do accept small orders from the beginning glassblower. But keep in mind that in many cases when ordering glass, the minimum order may be one case (25 to 30 pounds) of a given size of glass rod or tubing. On the other hand, a few companies do allow purchases of the various sizes by the pound, but they may still require a minimum order of about twenty-five pounds. Be sure to ask! Some have cases of assorted rod (usually a mixture of 3 mm to 11 mm) and/or tubing. When calling or writing, ask for the order desk and identify yourself as an individual glassblower. This may allow you to get a significant discount on your order.

Although some of the companies below handle only a few special items of interest to the glassblower, many also handle a wide range of glassblowing supplies, tools and equipment. You will probably find that most will be extremely helpful to you. Remember, they are anxious to see the number of glassblowers increase.

If you write or call any of these suppliers, you may wish to indicate to them that you found their name and number in this book. Be sure to ask for a current catalog and price list.

Many of the firms listed now accept Visa or Mastercharge cards, and most accept orders online. However, with some companies you should be prepared to prepay your order or have it sent C.O.D. This usually will not be necessary after your first order or once your credit rating has been established.

GLASSBLOWING SUPPLIES, TOOLS, EQUIPMENT AND GLASS

Ace Glass Inc.

Products: borosilicate glass, glass components, glass products
Address: P.O. Box 688, Vineland NJ 08362-0688
Phone: (800) 223-4524
Webpage: http://www. aceglass.com
E-mail: sales@aceglass.com

Andrews Glass Co.

Products:
Address: 3740 Northwest Boulevard, Vineland, NJ 08360
Phone: (856) 692-4435
Webpage: http://www.andrews-glass.com
E-mail: mail@andrews-glass.com

Attard's Minerals

Products: calcium gluconate gel for hydrofluoric acid burns
Address: P.O. Box 17263, San Diego, CA 92177
Phone: (619) 275-2016
Webpage: http://attminerals.com/other_items.htm
E-mail: attard@attminerals.com

Aura Lens

Products: glassblowing eyewear
Address: P.O. Box 763, St. Cloud, MN 56302-0763
Phone:800/281-2872
Webpage: http://www.auralens.com
E-mail: admin@auralens.com

Bethlehem Apparatus Company

Products: supplies, equipment
Address: P.O. Box Y, 890 Front St., Hellertown, PA 18055
Phone: (610) 838-7034
Webpage: http://www.bethlehemburners.com
E-mail: info@bethlehemapparatus.com

Carlisle Machine Works

Products: wide range of torches
Address: P.O. Box 746, Millville, NJ 08332
Phone: (800) 922-1167 or (609) 696-0014
Webpage: http://www.carlislemachine.com
E-mail: carlisle@carlislemachine.com

Chemglass

Products: borosilicate glass, glass components, glass products
Address: 3861 North Mill Road, Vineland, NJ 08360
Phone: (800) 843-1794 or (609) 696-0014
Webpage: http://www.chemglass.com
E-mail: customer-service@chemglass.com

Contemporary Kiln Inc.

Products: annealing ovens
Address: 24C Galli Drive, Novato, CA 94949
Phone: (4d15) 883-8921

Ed Hoy's International

Products: (wholesale only) borosilicate glass, glass components
Address: 27625 Diehl Rd., Warrenville, IL 60555
Phone: (800) 323-5668 or (312) 420-0890
Webpage: http://www.edhoy.com

Edmund Scientific Company

Products: polarized plastic sheets and disks
Address: 60 Pearce Ave., Tonawanda, NY 14150-6711
Phone: (800) 728-6999
Webpage: http://www.scientificsonline.com
E-mail: scientifics@edsci.com

Friedrich & Dimmock, Inc.,

Products: borosilicate glass (including Simax®), soft glass, glass products
Address: P.O. Box 230, 2127 Wheaton Ave., Millville, NJ 08332
Phone: (800) 524-1131 or (609) 825-0305
Webpage: http://www.fdglass.com
E-mail: sales@fdglass.com

Glass Warehouse

Products: borosilicate glass and glass components
Address: P.O. Box 1039, 800 Orange St., Millville, NJ 08332-8039
Phone: (800) 833-0410 or (856) 327-5228
Webpage: http://www.thomasregister.com/olc/glasswarehouse/home.htm
E-mail: glass.warehouse@wheaton.com

Houde Glass Company

Products: borosilicate glass and glass components
Address: 1177 McCarter Highway, Newark, NJ 07104
Phone: (800) 526-1275 or (201) 485-1761

Kimble Kontes

Products: borosilicate glass and glass components
Address: Drawer F, Crystal Ave., Vineland, NJ 08360
Phone: (800) 331-2706
Webpage: http://www.kimble-kontes.com/html/Home.html
E-mail: cs@kimkon.com

Macalster Bicknell of NJ

Products: borosilicate glass
Address: P.O. Box 109, Millville, NJ 08332-0109
Phone: (800) 257-8405
Webpage: www.macbicnj.com
E-mail: macbincn@eticomm.net

Mancine Optical

Products: glassblowing eyewear
Address: P.O. Box 109, Millville, NJ 08332-0109
Phone: (800) 887-3937
Webpage: http://www.macbicnj.com/index.htm
E-mail: info@macbicnj.com

NorthStar Glassworks Inc.

Products: colored borosilicate rods, frits, powders
Address: P.O. Box 230488, 9450 SW Tigard St. Tigard OR 97281
Phone: (866) 684-6986 or (503) 684-6986
Webpage: http://www.northstarglass.com/
E-mail: customerservice@northstarglass.com

Litton Engineering Laboratories

Products: Colrex colored borosilcate glass, supplies, equipment
Address: P.O. Box 950, 1300 East Main Street, Grass Valley CA 95945
Phone:(800) 821-8866 or (530) 273-6176
Webpage: http://www.littonengr.com
E-mail: sales@littonengr.com

Pegasus Glass

Products: borosilicate glass
Address: 15 Lawrence Bell Drive, Amherst, NY 14221
Phone:(800) 315-0387
Web: http://www.pegasus-glass.com
E-mail: info@pegasus-glass.com

Phillips Safety Products

Products: glassblowing eyewear
Address: 700 Cedar Avenue, Middlesex, NJ 08846
Phone:(888) 440-9797
Web: http://www.phillips-safety.com/asp/prodtype.asp?prodtype=1
E-mail: info@Phillips-Safety.com

Pistorius Machine Co., Inc.

Products: glass saws
Address: 1785 Express Drive North, Hauppauge, NY 11788-5395
Phone:(631) 582-6000
Web: http://www.pistorius.com
E-mail: sales@pistorius.com

Pope Scientific, Inc.

Products: borosilicate glass and glass components
Address: P.O. Box 495, Menomonee Falls, WI 53051
Phone:(414) 251-9300
Web: http://www.popeinc.com; http://www.glassonline.com/popescientific
E-mail: sales@popeinc.com

Sundance Art Glass Center

Products: borosilicate glass, supplies, equipment
Address: 178 Stierlin Rd., Mountain View, CA 94043.
Phone:(888) 446-8452 and (800) 946-8452
Webpage: http://www.artglass1.com/glass-bead.htm
E-mail: sundance@artglass1.com

TecnoLux, Inc.

Products: borosilicate glass, colored glass, glass components
Address: 103 14th St., Brooklyn, NY 11215
Phone: (800) 333-6366
Webpage: http://www.signweb.com/tecnolux
E-mail: info@tecnolux.com

US Precision Glass Company
Products: borosilicate glass
Address: 1900 Holmes Rd., Elgin, IL 60123
Phone: (847) 931-1200

Wale Apparatus Company
Products: borosilicate glass, supplies, equipment
Address: P.O. Box D, Hellertown, PA 18055
Phone: (215) 838-7047 or (800) 344-9253
Webpage: http://www.waleapparatus.com
E-mail: wale@main.gv.net or mdemasi@waleapparatus.com

Will Process Equipment (borosilicate glass)
Products: borosilicate glass
Address: P.O. Box 308, Jonesboro, GA 30237
Phone: (800) 433-7254 or (770) 478-6665
E-mail: wiilprcess@aol.com

Wilt Industries Inc.,
Products: annealing ovens and glassblowing equipment
Address: Route 8, Lake Pleasant, NY 12108
Phone: (800) 232-9458
Webpage: http://www.wiltindustries.com
E-mail: dan@wiltindustries.com

Witeg Scientific
Products: borosilicate glass, equipment
Address: 14235 Commerce Drive, Garden Grove, CA 92643
Phone: (714) 265-1855
Webpage: http://www.witeg.com
E-mail: http://www.witeg.com

OXYGEN GAS SERVICE AND RENTALS

Contact any of your local welder's supply companies. These are usually listed in the Yellow Pages of your phone book under "Welding Equipment & Supplies". Normally these tanks can be rented by the month or leased for a five or ten year period of time.

Those who use large amounts of oxygen or those unable to obtain tanks of oxygen should consider commercial oxygen generators, some of which are designed for medical purposes. Some representative companies are given.

UltraNebs

Products: large and small oxygen generating equipment
Address: 160 Pvt. Rd. 7869, Big Sandy, TX 75755
Phone: (888) 255-2509
Webpage: http://www.portablenebs.com/concentrator.htm
E-mail: sales@portablenebs.com

Oxygen Generating Systems Inc.

Products: large and small oxygen generating equipment
Address: 2221 Niagara Falls Blvd., PO Box 196, Niagara Falls, NY 14304
Phone: (716) 215-1060
Webpage: http://www.ogsi.com

Wale Apparatus Company

Products: oxygen generating equipment for individuals
Address: P.O. Box D, Hellertown, PA 18055
Phone: (215) 838-7047 or (800) 344-9253
Webpage: http://www.waleapparatus.com
E-mail: wale@main.gv.net or mdemasi@waleapparatus.com

PROPANE GAS SERVICE AND TANKS

Contact your local L. P. Gas dealer. Normally these are listed in the Yellow Pages of your phone book under "Gas-Liquefied Petroleum-Bottled & Bulk". Twenty pound tanks can normally be purchased and filled for under fifty dollars.

An option to natural gas or propane gas for those who use large amounts or those unable to obtain tanks is a commercial system such as that available from the source below.

G-Tec

Products: natural gas generating equipment
Address:
Phone: (800) 451-8294
Webpage: http://www.portablenebs.com/concentrator.htm
E-mail: info@gas-tech.com

Appendix H
NOTES TO INSTRUCTORS

The following notes refer to the glassblowing courses which were taught at Southwest State University in Marshall, Minnesota over a period of more than twenty years.[1] Today, similar courses are being taught at many other institutions, usually by the university glassblower or by an interested chemistry professor.[2,3,4] Although most art departments or independent companies prefer to offer hot glass (offhand) courses, more and more are starting to add a flameworking component as well. Bead making is one of the most popular areas of emphasis. It is hopeful that notes presented in this appendix may be of some help to all those who wish to set up some sort of flameworking courses within their institutions and companies.

BOOK Everyone in the class is required to purchase their own copy of the text, usually from the bookstore. Students are expected to do the assigned readings and are asked to bring their book to each and every class meeting.

FEES Because glassblowing is a rather expensive course and is not a chemistry course in the usual sense, a lab fee is charged to cover some of the costs of the supplies used. In addition, a breakage deposit is held until after the final class period. Any breakage or damage to the tools or to the laboratory is then deducted. In rare cases, additional damages may be charged if warranted. All money transactions are handled by the business office of the university.

GLASSWORKING TOOLS Each student is furnished with their own locker, a wooden box containing the necessary glassworking tools, and a similar wooden box for handing in completed pieces. Obviously, it may be more economical initially to have only a few sets of tools which can be used by a number of people, but over the years, we have found it to be better in the long run to furnish each student with their own set. Shared tools seem to get damaged more easily and more often, and usually no one seems to be the guilty one. Since moving to individual sets of tools, we have had little or no loss or damage! The items listed in Figure H.1 are included in each student's set of tools. Items prefaced with an "A" are included in sets for "artistic" glassblowing classes and those with an "S" are included in sets for scientific sections.

Figure H.1 Tools and supplies provided for each student		
		Description of Item
A	S	Glass knife (expensive, but best)
A		Triangular file (used to impart patterns, not to cut)
A	S	Forceps (seven inch)
A		Carbon rod (1/4 inch diameter, six inches long)
A	S	Needle nose pliers (five inch size, insulated handles)
A		Blue borosilicate glass (small two inch piece)
	S	Blow-pipe assemblies with swivel (two furnished)
	S	Rubber septa with hole (for blow-pipe insertion)
A	S	Protective glasses (either regular or clip-on)
A	S	Matches, flint tip or pietzieo torch lighter

In addition, each glassworking station is provided with a National hand torch, one 5 tip and one 3 tip (for artistic work) or one 2 tip and one 3 tip (for scientific work), a torch holder, a graphite plate, and a small aluminum pan for waste glass and used matches. A number of graphite paddles (marvers) and other cutting tools are also made available for class use. At least one good set of rollers is needed for the scientific sections.

LARGE EQUIPMENT An annealing oven is absolutely necessary. A polariscope, a glass saw, and a small glass lathe are recommended but not mandatory.

CLASS MEETINGS Each section meets formally for two consecutive hours each week. Sections may have anywhere from eight to eighteen students. (The glassblowing lab at Southwest State has eighteen stations.) The first hour involves a review of previous work, comments on assignments handed in, and demonstrations of new techniques. During the second hour, students are allowed to practice the new techniques and to begin work on the assignment. The instructor should spend some time with each student during this hour. In addition to these two hours of formal class, each student is required to work at least two additional hours on his own during the week. During these additional labs, students must sign in and sign out, and the instructor should be available in a nearby office. The hours the lab will be open are posted for all to see. No student is allowed to work alone in the lab, so at least one other student must be present before a person may begin work. Most students complete their assignments during these two hours.

GLASS STOCK Obviously, it is most advantageous to purchase glass by the case, but if economics demand, smaller amounts can be obtained from some suppliers. Glass of the sizes indicated in Figure H.2 sizes are recommended for each type of glassblowing class. Of course, it is better to have a wider range of sizes available. In the artistic classes, 5 mm rod is used most often, primarily because of cost concerns. If cost or availability permits, instructors may wish to substitute 6 mm rod (a much more "usual" size of rod) in the exercises and projects. In this table and in all my class notes or assignments written on the blackboard, I have used "4 R" to represent 4 mm rod, whereas 15 T is to represent 15 mm tubing. All glass is assumed to be borosilicate! Never allow soft glass to be brought into the glass lab.

Figure H.2 Recommended sizes and types of glass for glassblowing classes

Glass Recommended for Artistic Sections		Glass Recommended for Scientific Sections	
Type	**Comments**	**Type**	**Comments**
4 R		2 R	Used as "cane" for repairs.
5 R	An economical substitute for the more desirable but more expensive 6 R.	6 R	Only for beginning exercises.
6 R	The most widely used size.	8 T	Widely used.
8 R		10 T	Widely used.
12 T	Only for Chapter 6.	12 T	Widely used.
15 T	Only for Chapter 6.	15 T	Widely used.
		20 T	Used only in later Projects.

As mentioned before, it is a good idea to have additional sizes of rod and tubing available for repairs or projects not listed in the text. Likewise, it is also useful to have a supply of various sizes of standard taper joints and stopcocks for scientific repairs or construction.

CHECKING OUT GLASS STOCK Glass stock is cut into 24 inch lengths before being handed out to students. Glass used in the week's work is distributed at the beginning of each period. Students store their unused glass stock in their lockers (which are 25 inches deep). The extra stock is kept in a locked glass cabinet, otherwise a few enthusiastic students would go through their semester's worth of glass in only a few weeks!

OXYGEN TANKS Oxygen is purchased from our local Welder's Supply in 244 cubic foot tanks which are leased on a monthly basis. On the average, one tank will usually supply enough oxygen for about forty person-hours of glassworking.

ASSIGNMENTS AND GRADES As will be seen in the lesson plans outlined below, on most days, a reading as well as an exercise and/or project is assigned for the next class meeting. Students are required to familiarize themselves thoroughly with each exercise or project before attempting it in class. Practice pieces from the exercises or products from the projects are handed in when completed. At Southwest State, each student is given a small wooden box in which the completed pieces are placed, along with an evaluation card. The instructor then evaluates and grades the work, noting the grade on the card along with constructive comments on the work. Exercises are normally graded "check-plus", "check" or "check-minus". Projects are graded "A - F". Final class grades are also "A - F". At our university, students are permitted to keep any completed item as long as it has been checked for safety by the instructor. However, it is required that each student leave at least one completed item, hopefully their best work, for our display case of recent student work.

SUGGESTED SYLLABUS FOR ARTISTIC CLASS

Class 1 Introduction to course, tour of glass lab, operation of torch (Exercise 1), and check out of tools. **Assignments**: Read Appendix A, Chapter 1, Chapter 2, and Chapter 3 (up to Annealing).

Class 2 Cutting (Exercise 2), fire polishing (Exercise 3), and rotation. **Assignments:** Do Exercise 4 (Rotation) and read Chapter 4 (up to Project Two.

Class 3 Joining rod (Exercise 11 and Exercise 12), flame cuts (Exercise 7), shaping with tools, drawing out (Exercise 9), and demonstration of Project Artistic One (Flower). **Assignments:** Do Project Artistic One and read Project Artistic Two.

Class 4 Review Flower construction. Scroll shapes (Exercise 9), demonstration of Project Artistic 2 (Bird), discuss flame annealing, polariscope and oven annealing. **Assignments:** Do Project Artistic Two, read Project Artistic Three.

Class 5 Review Bird construction. Major review of all previous techniques and demonstrate Project Artistic Three (Dog). Short quiz on properties of borosilicate glass and the glassblowing terms used in class. **Assignments:** Do Project Artistic Three, read Project Artistic Four.

Class 6 Review Dog construction. Marias (Exercise 5 and Exercise 6), demonstrate Project Artistic Four (Pumps, except handle construction). **Assignments:** Do Project Artistic Four (without handles).

Class 7 Review intermediate marias, go through pump construction again but include handle construction (Project Artistic Four, pump handles). **Assignments:** Do Project Artistic Four (all steps), read Project Artistic Six.

Class 8 Review Pump construction. Demonstrate Project Artistic Six (Snowflakes) and show variations on previous projects (e.g. make seagull). **Assignments:** Do Project Artistic Six.

Class 9 Review Snowflake construction. Demonstrate Project Artistic Five (Tree Branches). **Assignments:** Do Project Artistic Five and some item of student's original design.

Class 10 Review problem techniques, demonstrate some advanced techniques (lace or blowing), view slides of other items, discuss additional items shown at the ends of Chapters 4 and 5.

Class 11 Final Examination which includes simple questions about borosilicate glass, the construction any one item of student's choice, and making a copy of the displayed item (usually an abstract object including marias, drawn out glass and scrolls). Check in tools.

SUGGESTED SYLLABUS FOR SCIENTIFIC CLASS

Class 1 Introduction to course, tour of glass lab, operation of torch (Exercise 1), and check out of tools. **Assignments:** Read Appendix A, Chapter 1, Chapter 2, Chapter 3 (up to Annealing Section), and Chapter 7 (up to Exercise 22).

Class 2 Cutting (Exercise 2), fire polishing (Exercise 3), rotation, joining rod (Exercise 11 and Exercise 12), flame cuts (Exercise 7), and demonstrate joining tubing (Exercise 21). **Assignments:** Redo Exercises 11 and 12, and read section on T-tube construction.

Class 3 Review tubing butt seals (spot welding method), demonstrate hot seal technique (Exercise 22), demonstrate T-seals (Exercise 27), discuss repairing cracks, and introduce polariscope and annealing oven. **Assignments:** Redo Exercise 27.

Class 4 Review T-seals and demonstrate round-bottoms (Exercise 25). **Assignments:** Redo Exercise 25 and Exercise 27, and read section on through-seals.

Class 5 Review round-bottoms and demonstrate through-seals (Exercise 30). Short quiz on borosilicate glass and glassblowing terms used in class. **Assignments:** Redo Exercise 30, and read Project Scientific One.

Class 6 Review through-seals and demonstrate Project Scientific One (Vacuum Trap). **Assignments:** Do Project Scientific One, and read Project Scientific Three.

Class 7 Review Project Scientific One and demonstrate Project Scientific Three (Condenser). **Assignments:** Do Project Scientific Three and read sections on constrictions, flares, & hose connector tubes.

Class 8 Demonstrate constrictions (Exercise 23), rims, hose connectors (Exercise 36), flares (Exercise 29), and use of mechanical saw. **Assignments:** Redo Project Scientific 3 including rim & hose connectors, and read Appendix C, D and E.

Class 9 Analysis of complex scientific glassware (discuss Exercise 40), Chapter 8 (Repairs), and making bends (Exercise 33). **Assignments:** Exercise 40 and Exercise 41.

Class 10 Review difficult techniques, analyze other glass pieces, and analyze glassware in need of repairs. **Assignment:** Exercise 43.

Class 11 Final Examination which includes simple questions about borosilicate glass, the construction of a vacuum trap, and the analysis of a piece of scientific glassware listing likely steps in its construction. Check in tools.

ENDNOTES

1. E. Carberry, "The Introductory Scientific Glassblowing Course At Southwest State University", *Proceedings of the 34th Symposium on the Art of Scientific Glassblowing, American Scientific Glassblowers Society*, pp. 36-43, 1989.

2. R. C. Smith, "An Interim Scientific Glassblowing Course for Chemistry Students", *Proceedings of the 38th Symposium on the Art of Scientific Glassblowing, American Scientific Glassblowers Society*, pp. 72-79, 1993.

3. L. Williams, "Teaching Glassblowing to the Non-Glassblower", *Proceedings of the 33rd Symposium on the Art of Scientific Glassblowing, American Scientific Glassblowers Society*, pp. 8-9, 1988.

4. D. Briening, "Artistic Glassblowing at Salem Community College", *Proceedings of the 33rd Symposium on the Art of Scientific Glassblowing, American Scientific Glassblowers Society*, pp. 48-53, 1988.

Appendix I
SCHOOLS AND ORGANIZATIONS

Over the years, many individuals interested in flameworking have asked where they may obtain formal classroom instruction. If you are interested in artistic flameworking, in bead making or in hot glass (offhand glassblowing), you will find many studios, schools and organizations available to you across the country. If you are interested only in borosilicate flameworking, your choices will be considerably fewer. For those wanting to study scientific flameworking, there is only one significant school. Nonetheless, there are a number of universities and community colleges that offer such courses, perhaps once a year.

The following is an attempt to list at least some of the more well known schools which offer at least some flameworking. Schools offering only lessons in hot glass are not included. You will find that some of those listed below offer full classes, some only workshops and others offer both. Again, be aware that this list is not complete, but the references should provide good places to start.

ARTISTIC FLAMEWORKING SCHOOLS AND CLASSES

Corning Museum of Glass

Instruction: wide range of glassblowing and flameworking classes
Address: One Museum Way, Corning, NY 14830-2253
Phone: (800) 732-6845 or (607) 974-6467
Web: http://www.artglass1.com/glass-bead.htm
E-mail: studio@cmog.org

Ed Hoy's International

Instruction: short workshops in flameworking
Address: 27625 Diehl Rd., Warrenville, IL 60555
Phone: (800) 732-6845 or (607) 974-6467
Web: http://www.edhoy.com

Eugene Glass School

Instruction: wide range of glassblowing and flameworking classes
Address: 575 Wilson St., Eugene, OR 97402
Phone: (541) 342-2959
Web: http://www.eugeneglassschool.org/classes.cfm
E-mail: info@eugeneglassschool.org

Gossamer Glass

Instruction: wide range of flameworking workshops
Address: 19 E. Laurel Rd. Bellingham, WA 98226
Phone: (866) 813-9706 or (360) 398-7061
Web: http://www.inspirationfarm.com/
E-mail:gossamer@inspirationfarm.com

More Fire Glass Studio

Instruction: wide range of glassblowing and flameworking classes
Address: 80 Rockwood Place, Rochester, NY 14610
Phone:(716) 242-0450
Web: http://www.morefireglass.com/index.html
E-mail: info@morefireglass.com

Penland School of Crafts

Instruction: wide range of glassblowing and flameworking classes
P.O. Box 37, Penland NC 28765
Phone 704-765-2359
http://www.penland.org/
office@penland.org

Phat Katz Glass Design

Instruction: classes in borosilicate/Northstar glasses
Address: 10215 SE Foster Rd., Portland, OR 97266
Phone: (503) 771-0799
Web: http://wwwhandblownglass.htm

Pilchuck Glass School

Instruction: wide range of glassblowing and flameworking classes
430 Yale Ave N., Seattle, WA 98109
Phone 206-621-8422
http://www.pilchuck.com
PWatkinson@Pilchuck.com

Pittsburgh Glass Center

Instruction: wide range of glassblowing and flameworking classes
Address: 5472 Penn Ave., Pittsburgh, PA 15206
Phone: (412) 365-2145
Web: http://www.pittsburghglasscenter.org/

Sundance Art Glass Center

Instruction: wide range of glassblowing and flameworking classes
Address: 178 Stierlin Rd., Mountain View, CA 94043
Phone:(888) 446-8452 and (800) 946-8452
Web: http://www.artglass1.com/glass-bead.htm
E-mail: sundance@artglass1.com

Urban Glass

Instruction: wide range of glassblowing and flameworking classes
Address: 647 Fulton Street, Brooklyn, NY 11217-1112
Phone: 718-625-3685
Web: http://www.urbanglass.org
E-mail: director@urbanglass.org

SCIENTIFIC FLAMEWORKING SCHOOLS AND CLASSES

As mentioned previously, there is only one institution offering a complete course of study in scientific flameworking. However, you are encouraged to check with universities and community colleges in your area, as they may offer introductory classes from time to time.

Salem Community College

Instruction: This is the only major institution which offers instruction in scientific glassblowing. They offer either a one year program which leads to a Certificate in Scientific Glass Technology or a two year program which leads to an Associate in Applied Science - Scientific Glass Technology degree. Artistic Glass Classes are also offered, and in the fall of 2001, an Associate Degree in Glass Art was added.

Address: 460 Hollywood Ave, Carneys Point, NJ 08069-2799
Phone: (856) 299-2100
Webpage: http://www.salemcc.org/glass
E-mail: dcsmith@salemcc.edu

PROFESSIONAL ORGANIZATIONS

There are numerous regional, national and international organizations serving those interested in artistic flameworking (lampworking). Many of these focus on beadmaking, but nearly every other form of the art is represented as well. In addition, some also cover hot glass (off-hand) arts. The best way to obtain up-to-date information on these societies is to search the web. Many sites provide addtitional links to other organizations. Two representative examples are listed below:

International Society of Glass Beadmakers

Address: 1120 Chester Avenue #470
Cleveland, OH 44114 USA
Phone: (888) 742-0242
Webpage:http://www.isgb.org/index.shtml
Email: membership@isgb.org

Glass Art Society

Address: 1305 Fourth Avenue, Suite 711
Seattle Washington 98101 USA
Phone: (206) 382-1305
Webpage: http://www.glassart.org/
Email: info@glassart.org

In the case of scientific glassblowing, there are fewer organizations, usually one per country, and these seem to be more focused in purpose. In the United States, the professional group is the American Scientific Glassblowers Society (ASGS). National meetings are held each summer. Twelve regional sections are set up across the country (and Canada). These sections meet on a regular basis throughout the year. A journal, entitled *Fusion*, is published quarterly covering a wide range of subjects including technical articles, lamp shop hints, abstracts of current literature and classified ads.

American Scientific Glassblowers Society

Address: P.O. Box 778, Madison, NC 27025
Phone: (336) 427-2406
Fax: (336) 427-2496
Webpage: http://www.asgs-glass.org/index.htm
E-mail: natl-office@asgs-glass.org

British Society of Scientific Glassblowers

Address: "Glendale", Sinclair St, Thurso, Caithness, Scotland. KW14 7AQ
Phone: 01847 802629
E-mail: ian.pearson@ukaea.org.uk
Webpage: http://www.bssg.co.uk/

Appendix J
ANTIQUE SCIENTIFIC GLASSWARE

This last appendix is was added "just for fun". It is not meant to be a catalog nor an informative source about these old glass items. Instead, it is simply a gallery of some of the author's collection of vintage scientific glass-

Figure J.1 *A three-necked Woulfe bottle which was widely used as a wash bottle. The flask was hand blown (pontil mark on bottom; see figure J.4) and the joints were hand crafted.*

Figure J.2 *Some different Woulfe bottles, all hand blown with handcrafted joints. These bottles, named after English Chemist Peter Woulfe, had either two or three necks and were used to wash or absorb various gases.*

Figure J.3 *A hand blown desiccator (a special glass container used to keep substances dry by use of a chemical desiccant which is placed in the bottom portion. Again, this piece shows a pontil mark on the bottom (Figure J.4). The top opening was ground to be flat, as is the glass cover.*

Figure J.4 *The bottoms of two pieces of the previous glassware, clearly showing the characteristic ground down region where the pontil rod had been attached during the item's construction. The three-necked Woulfe bottle shown in Figure J.1 is on the left and the desiccator shown in Figure J.3 is on the right.*

ware. Although some comments are made about the photographs within this Appendix, more in-depth information concerning these items, their use and their construction, is sought by the author. Any additional knowledge offered concerning these items will be considered for use in later editions of this book. Please share your information and stories.

Those interested in antique glassware are encouraged to read the informative article on old glassware and glass shop equipment recently published by Leslie.[1]

Figure J.5 *Three early round bottom flasks (boiling flasks) produced by Corning. All top joints hand crafted. The sandblasted logos on the first two flasks are enlarged below in Figures J.7 and J.8.*

Figure J.6 *Six graduates, ranging in size from 10 cc to 500 cc. All calibrations are etched by hand, and some show elaborate calligraphy.*

Figure J.7 *An early Corning sandblasted logo reading "PYREX, PAT:5-27-19, 1L".*

Figure J.8 *Sand-blasted logo reading "PYREX, T.M. REG. U.S. PAT. OFF., MADE IN U.S.A., 500." Sources indicate that Corning used this logo between 1915 and 1925.*[2]

Figure J.9 *A large, one liter retort used many years ago in the USSR. A small red seal marking reads "SIAL, CZECHOSLOVAKIA". Retorts of this type were used extensively until the early 1900's to distill corrosive liquids. These were manufactured in a wide range of sizes.*

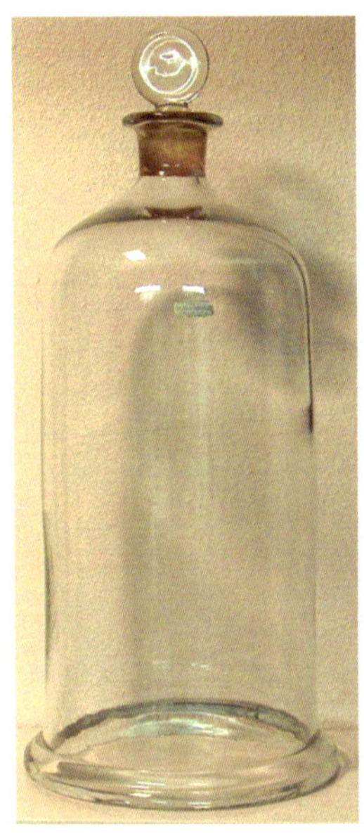

Figure J.10 *A large bell jar with label reading:*

"SOLD BY
CHICAGO APPARATUS CO.
CHICAGO U.S.A."

Figure J.11 *Kipp gas generator, marked with Kimble's sand blasted logo "K". The apparatus was commonly used to prepare gases such as hydrogen.*

Figure J.12 *A vacuum filter flask and stoppered Erlenmeyer flask, both marked with Kimble's sand blasted logo "K"*

Figure J.13 *Wash bottle assembly with cork hand grip and rubber top.*

ENDNOTES

1. F. Leslie, "A Glass Shop and its Equipment from the Past", *Fusion*, November, 2002, pp. 39-44.

2. F. Leslie, p. 40.

About The Author

Photo courtesy of Jeffrey Grosscup.

The author, Edward Carberry, is Professor of Chemistry at Southwest State University in Marshall, Minnesota, where he has taught since 1968. In addition to teaching inorganic chemistry, he was able to develop and set up a rather elaborate glassblowing program which included both artistic (general) and scientific glassblowing. Over a period of twenty five years, close to four hundred students enrolled in these classes. Dr. Carberry has always been an enthusiastic professor and has been recognized twice at the state level for excellence in teaching. In 1990, Carberry lead a delegation of chemists and scientific glass-blowers to the Soviet Union. He has returned to Russia a number of times as an invited lecturer and during these trips was able to see a number of Russian glassblowing labs across the vast country. The second edition of this glassblowing book has been translated into Russian.

For nearly thirty years, the author has maintained a part time glassblowing business in his home, where he has produced and repaired glass products for a number of commercial laboratories, but has really specialized in making Christmas items. The annual Carberry angel has been awaited by a surprisingly large number of individuals across the country for the past twenty six years.

Thanks in part to this enjoyable and successful business, he and his wife, Linda, own a two hundred acre farm, complete with its own twenty six acre lake, in beautiful northern Minnesota. Here they manage the land for wildlife, raise both pheasants and Christmas trees, and enjoy a wide range of outdoor activities. They have two adult children, Daniel and Cristin, and two very spoiled dogs.

Any portrayal of the author would not be complete without mentioning that he is an addicted collector. His brewerianna collection is one of the largest in the country, and his mineral collection one of the largest in the state. In addition, he collects Russian paper money, old Soviet banners, other Soviet items, antique scientific glassware, historical chemistry books, antique logging tools and owns three vintage automobiles and trucks (1930 Model A, 1950 and 1951 F-1 Ford trucks). Life has been good and certainly has never been dull!

He operates a small desktop publishing company and has published a number of books in chemistry and glassblowing, including this present book. One of his next projects, a history of life in the early 1900's in northern Minnesota, will be based on the unusual diaries of a boy growing up and becoming a young man, each day faithfully recording the joys, the challenges and hardships of life in the wilderness. Like mine, his life was never dull either.

Please contact the author, through the publisher, with your comments, corrections, and suggestions concerning this book. Hopefully, it has been of some use and interest to you.

Index

A

B

C

D

E

F

G

H

I

P

Q

R

S

T